Women of the Iberian Atlantic

Women of the
Iberian Atlantic

EDITED BY SARAH E. OWENS AND JANE E. MANGAN

Louisiana State University Press

Baton Rouge

Published by Louisiana State University Press
Copyright © 2012 by Louisiana State University Press
All rights reserved
Manufactured in the United States of America
LSU Press Paperback Original
First printing

Designer: Laura Roubique Gleason
Typeface: Ingeborg
Printer: IBT Global

LIBRARY OF CONGRESS CATALOGING-IN-PUBLICATION DATA

Women of the Iberian Atlantic / edited by Sarah E. Owens and Jane E. Mangan.
   p. cm.
  "LSU Press Paperback Original."
  Includes bibliographical references and index.
  ISBN 978-0-8071-4772-6 (pbk. : alk. paper) — ISBN 978-0-8071-4773-3 (pdf) — ISBN 978-0-8071-4774-0 (epub) — ISBN 978-0-8071-4775-7 (mobi) 1. Women—Atlantic Ocean Region—History. 2. Women—Atlantic Ocean Region—Social conditions. 3. Women—Iberian Peninsula—History. 4. Women—Iberian Peninsula—Social conditions. 5. Iberian Peninsula I. Owens, Sarah E., 1969- II. Mangan, Jane E., 1969-
  HQ1818.85.W66 2012
  305.420946—dc23

2012011756

The paper in this book meets the guidelines for permanence and durability of the Committee on Production Guidelines for Book Longevity of the Council on Library Resources. ∞

Contents

Acknowledgments   vii

Introduction
Women of the Iberian Atlantic: Gendered Dimensions of Empire   1
SARAH E. OWENS AND JANE E. MANGAN

1
Navigating the Atlantic Divide: Women, Education, and Literacy in Iberia and the Americas   18
LISA VOLLENDORF

2
An Ocean Apart: Reframing Gender in the Spanish Empire   37
ALLYSON M. POSKA

3
Spanish Women in the Caribbean, 1493–1540   57
IDA ALTMAN

4
Indigenous Women as Mothers in Conquest-Era Peru   82
JANE E. MANGAN

5
Women and Kinship in Spanish East Texas at the End of the Eighteenth Century   101
CARLA GERONA

6
Cloistered Women in Health Care: The Convent of Jesús María, Mexico City   128
NURIA SALAZAR SIMARRO AND SARAH E. OWENS

7
The Role and Practices of the Female Folk Healer
in the Early Modern Portuguese Atlantic World   148

TIMOTHY D. WALKER

8
The Botany of Colonial Medicine: Gender, Authority, and
Natural History in the Empires of Spain and Portugal   174

HUGH GLENN CAGLE

9
Mother Nganga: Women Experts in the Bantu-Atlantic
Spiritual Cultures of the Iberian Atlantic World   196

RAS MICHAEL BROWN

10
Gendering the African Diaspora in the Iberian Atlantic:
Religious Brotherhoods and the *Cabildos de Nación*   230

MATT D. CHILDS

Contributors   263

Index   267

Acknowledgments

This volume would not exist without the support of the College of Charleston and the Carolina Lowcountry Atlantic World Program, who sponsored the initial conference, "Women in the Ibero-American Atlantic (1500–1800)," in February of 2010. Indeed, it was the intellectual spark from that conference that prompted us to pursue the present volume. We are also grateful for additional critical funding for the conference from the Program for Cultural Cooperation between Spain's Ministry of Culture and United States Universities, the Grupo de estudios sobre la mujer en España y las Américas, and different entities at the College of Charleston, including the Department of Hispanic Studies, the Women and Gender Studies Program, the Program in Latin American and Caribbean Studies, and the School of Languages, Cultures, and World Affairs. In addition to economic support, we would like to acknowledge the contributors themselves, who researched the insightful and innovative essays that have made this project possible. In particular, Ida Altman offered a careful reading of the introductory chapter. The incisive feedback from two anonymous readers for the press helped shape both individual chapters and the volume as a whole. We owe a debt of gratitude to Alisa Plant for her expression of interest in the project at the beginning and for guiding us through the editorial process. Finally, we are thankful to have experienced the value of collaboration through editing this volume. Together, these essays provide a view of women in the Iberian Atlantic that no one scholar could achieve.

Women of the Iberian Atlantic

Introduction

Women of the Iberian Atlantic

Gendered Dimensions of Empire

SARAH E. OWENS AND JANE E. MANGAN

To read *Women of the Iberian Atlantic* is to watch a picture emerge, a collage of women participating in the creation of the Iberian Atlantic. The ten essays in this volume resist stereotypes of early modern women as one-dimensional, subservient, or secondary to their male counterparts, revealing the complex interplay of gender as related to race, class, and religious practices in the early modern Iberian Atlantic (1500–1800).[1] While women of this era shared certain experiences, the essays as a whole point to the diversity of women's influences in the shaping of empire in the Atlantic. Women's activities in the fields of healing, ritual, literacy, and family shared intimate links with the politics and economics of the empire. While these complex ties prompted Ann Stoler's influential work on the nineteenth-century empire, they have remained less explored for the first age of Iberian empire in the Atlantic.[2] In these pages poignant stories of women, such as that of Josefa, who journeyed from Galicia, Spain, to Rio de la Plata in the Americas, or the mother *ngangas,* who were uprooted from their native West African villages and enslaved on the other side of the Atlantic in Brazil and Cuba, help to decipher links among early modern women. To date, much has been written on the women of the Spanish elite (especially queens and nobility),[3] but here we have decided to shift the focus more to the interactions and mutual influences in the lives of marginalized and peripheral women. This collection offers a fuller perspective of the broad scope of the Atlantic basin, including not only women of Spanish descent but also of Portuguese descent, and not only indigenous women but also enslaved and free African women.

Empire and gender are the unifying factors for the historical subjects of this volume, as all were women who lived in some part of the Iberian world. What do the experiences of women on the Texas frontier have in common with those of a female servant in Portuguese Goa, or illiterate Portuguese folk healers with women of the African diaspora in the Caribbean? The shared history, culture, and experiences of the metropole shaped the colonial system in which women of the Iberian Atlantic functioned. The first wave of Atlantic expansion set the precedent in locations like Santo Domingo and Mexico. As empire expanded to far-off destinations such as Peru or Goa, both represented here, the imperial institutions forged in the first wave of empire carried over into these new regions. The Atlantic experiences of empire building, then, informed colonial societies in the Pacific and the Indian oceans as well. Though the locations might be as far apart as Lisbon and Mexico City, these areas had a unified set of laws and customs based on Iberian legal practices shaped in part by the medieval Spanish book of laws, the *Siete Partidas*. As Carla Gerona shows in her essay on the Texas frontier, even in the outermost borderlands of the Iberian empire we see remnants of the Iberian statutory code. The links between Iberian monarchy and Catholicism also signified religious models and prerogatives (while not implying religious hegemony). Many women who traveled from Iberia to their new environs carried with them elements of restrictive European gender ideology. Inevitably, gender practices were exported along with language, food, and material culture. Migrating women, such as female communities of nuns, bespeak empire in action. As empire expanded into new areas, so did hierarchies of gender and of racial discrimination. These chapters purposefully offer a gendered view of the early modern Atlantic world. In their sum, they highlight women as actors, no matter how peripheral or marginalized, in the creation of the Atlantic.

 The essays here are grouped thematically, rather than according to chronology or geography. Pieces by Vollendorf and Poska open the book with an overview of the current state of women's and Atlantic studies. The following three essays by Altman, Mangan, and Gerona focus on law, marriage, and family. Women in this era found both restrictions and opportunities within Iberian legal codes. These essays allow us to understand how particulars of time and place as well as racial identity created different possibilities of social, political, and economic influence for wives, mothers, and lovers in colonial societies. The thematic emphasis of the volume shifts next to health and healing in the chapters by Salazar Simarro and Owens, Walker, and Cagle. Their essays make patent the wide range of women (African, indigenous, and servant classes) who participated as healers. Moreover, women's legal and marital status as well as racial identity marked their work as healers. In the final section, the essays by Brown and Childs focus on African women in the diaspora and use gender to analyze economic influences, social organizations, and spiritual beliefs within the Iberian-American context.

DEFINING THE IBERIAN ATLANTIC

How is the Iberian Atlantic defined? And what does the study of women in this Iberian Atlantic add to our knowledge of the peoples touched by the Spanish and Portuguese empires? Scholarship during the past two decades has increased our understanding of the Atlantic world, and in particular the slave trade, the Middle Passage, and the African diaspora.[4] Many works, though, offer a decidedly British and male picture of the Atlantic world.

The Iberian-centric focus of this volume highlights the expansion of Portugal and Spain into the Atlantic world prior to English exploration. Given this difference in time frame, historian Jorge Cañizares-Esguerra argues that the English model of colonization was (and its history continues to be) constructed both on and against the Spanish model.[5] This is what J. H. Elliott refers to as "time-lag" when he argues that any comparison of the British and the Spanish in the Atlantic is "not between two self-contained cultural worlds, but between cultural worlds that were well aware of each other's presence, and were not above borrowing each other's ideas when this suited their needs."[6] Altman's essay offers an in-depth look at colonial society in the Caribbean in the early 1500s, with heightened attention to the role of Spanish women. It is this experience that prompts the first royal decrees on family and marriage in the colonies. For example, the Spanish Crown tried to link the privileges of *encomenderos* (holders of land grants of indigenous labor) to their marital status. Further, the Crown supported "abandoned" wives in their efforts to track down spouses in the Americas. The earliest pronouncement on the separation of husbands and wives in the Indies came from King Ferdinand to Royal Governor Nicolás de Ovando in 1505. He ordered Spaniards who had married in Spain to return and collect their wives. As Mangan's essay highlights, New World families began through the sexual relationships of indigenous women and Spanish men at the same time that the Crown stipulated general doctrine on the issue: married men were to return to

Spain or bring their wives to them in the New World. Through legal discourse and royal decrees, the Crown showed it would not favor single Spanish men who roamed the Indies after conquest endeavors turned to long-term settlement plans. In time, sixteenth-century Iberian models served as comparison for seventeenth-century English settlement patterns. The complex family situations that arose in the Spanish context in areas of particularly high indigenous settlement served as markers of women's experience that were more common to the Iberian context than the Anglo Atlantic one.

For some scholars, the Atlantic forms a neat geographical unit that would exclude, for instance, any country or area that does not have direct access to the currents of the Atlantic Ocean.[7] Such definitions omit vast parts of the world that *did* experience the effects of Iberian empire and expansion. Instead of narrowing our definition of the Atlantic, this volume seeks to probe the complexities of gender and their interchanges that transcended specific geographical areas, such as Portuguese Goa in India and the Andean area of South America's Pacific coast. Did not the Portuguese repeatedly crisscross the Atlantic and the Pacific to maintain their colony in India? Did not the Spaniards and Africans who crossed the Atlantic make the Andes a de facto part of the Atlantic world? Moreover, sites like colonial Peru were within relatively easy reach of Spain's Atlantic empire and shared with Mexico and the Caribbean numerous economic, political, cultural, and demographic similarities. As Atlantic history has matured, historians have acknowledged this by "globalizing" their approaches. Alison Games rightly contends that "the story of Indian [indigenous] migration in the Atlantic world has often been obscured by an emphasis on transatlantic migration . . . [yet] these two narratives are actually intertwined."[8] We see this, for instance, in the case of Andean *mita* (forced labor draft), which helped transform the silver mining town of Potosí into one of the most important urban centers of the colonial Western Hemisphere.[9]

Given the interconnectedness of Latin America and Iberia, scholars of these regions have long viewed their subjects in a transatlantic fashion.[10] Like the example of Potosí *mita,* which must be connected to labor demands and migration, the transatlantic movement of peoples in this era demands that analysis of historical themes be integrated on local and global terms. Yet women as subject and gender as mode of analysis have been underexplored in the transatlantic realm.[11] These essays highlight how women in the Iberian Atlantic moved about frequently and acted as important conduits of knowledge and central points of family and domestic life. The study of the Atlantic is not only about place, but about the people, the products, and the paths that connect those places. The ten distinct Iberian Atlantic contexts examined here provoke further discussion about how Iberian empire shaped gender and how these female subjects shaped empire. The book offers the basis for important comparisons *within* the empire (rather than, say, English-Spanish or French-Spanish). As a whole, these essays embrace the notion of "entangled histories" and find them not between Spanish or English-controlled regions, but rather in the engagements of native lives, cultures, and political institutions.[12]

WOMEN AS SUBJECT: GENDER AS METHOD OF ANALYSIS

Writing on women as a subject has shifted in important ways since the rise of gender analysis.[13] The task at hand for many of the first historians of women and of women's writing in the 1970s was to increase our understanding of females' actions in historical context. By the early 1990s, in the wake of calls to place the analysis of gender in the forefront, scholars began to study women and men through a lens of gender. For example (and pertinent to three essays in this volume), when we study how women acted as healers in society, our findings enrich our understanding of early modern life. If we can compare women's actions as healers to the actions of men in society who have cultural significance and measures of economic or social power, this tells us much more. Scholarship still has much to offer by focusing our view on women's roles as the contours of empire emerged in the Atlantic world. (As for where women were in this world, we can assume safely that they were everywhere, though ratios favored males among slave populations and in certain locales, such as ships.) After depicting women's roles in this historical context, these essays reveal the significance of their activities through detailed and systematic studies, as opposed to operating solely in the realm of caricature or as shadowy figures (the nun, the folk healer, the trader's wife). The study of women further demands critical analysis of the actions relative to other elements of analysis (class or race or sexuality) *and* especially in relative terms to men's actions in the same historical context. Thus, gender analysis integrates the female subjects of these essays into the male-dominated project of expansion. By focusing on what one might consider traditional women's roles, yet doing so through the critical analysis of actions and language, these essays reveal how women's wealth of knowledge in realms of family, ritual, and health created colonial systems of knowledge in the ever expanding empire of the Atlantic world.

A parallel trend to the emergence of women's and gender history is the increased study of texts written by women religious. As we enter the second decade of the twenty-first century, more scholars are finding and publishing women's manuscripts buried in a wide variety of archives, including Church, public, and private holdings. The unearthing of these heretofore overlooked texts reveals the relatively prolific nature of early modern women writers. Actually, this fact is not groundbreaking. The first edition of *Apuntes para una biblioteca de autoras españolas* (1903) referred to eleven hundred women writers (many who resided in monastic communities) between the years of 1401 and 1833.[14] For many years, however, the literary canon has largely ignored these works, devaluing them as trivial and frivolous. Fortunately, recent literary criticism has started to reclaim texts such as *vidas* (spiritual autobiographies), convent chronicles, and letters previously rejected by the literary canon.[15]

The intersection of gender history and women's writing (particularly religious writing)[16] has created the foundation for a more comparative analysis through which to study women on both sides of the Atlantic. Part of the goal of this book, then, is to include the peninsula more directly (see the essays by Vollendorf, Walker, and Poska) because these comparative examples help us to analyze the impact of colonialism on women's experiences. Furthermore, Childs's and Brown's essays bring to the table topics on African women who exerted African cultural influences within the structure of Iberian slavery. The works' close-up focus on multiple locales, taken together, enrich our understanding of the complex milieu that made up the early modern world. Only with this panorama in place can we understand when and how women's experiences across the oceans were shaped directly by the forces of Iberian law and culture.

INTERCONNECTIVITY OF ATLANTIC WOMEN: RELIGIOUS WOMEN AND MOBILITY

The interconnectivity of women throughout the Atlantic basin is remarkable. The reasons for the mobility between communities are varied. Slave routes and the forced migration of thousands of African women from their homes in West and Central Africa throughout the Caribbean and Latin America provide an obvious example. Spanish women, as in the case of Altman's essay, followed in the footsteps of the conquistadors and traveled across the ocean alongside men as the first colonists of the Caribbean. On all levels, these women brought with them preconceived notions on many issues, such as health care, family, and shared governance, as adeptly articulated in Childs's essay on the African confraternities in Cuba.

Furthermore, the mobility of religious women, albeit small in number, speaks to a larger dynamic of the interconnectivity of religious communities. Cloistered nuns could break their walls of seclusion to set up new nunneries, importing Church doctrine to their new environs. In most instances these women only needed to cover short distances, as in the case of the Convent of Jesús María, when the seed group of women came from another community in Mexico City. However, there were examples of small groups of nuns who traveled from the Iberian Peninsula, crossed oceans, traversed jungles, and trekked across mountains to establish their religious orders in far-off places, such as Mexico, Peru, and beyond. These female missionary pursuits were a key component in the Crown's desire to spread Iberian culture throughout its empire. Once established throughout the Iberian Atlantic, these women spread their values, not only on religious themes, but also on questions of class, race, and gender hierarchies. Many of these religious women who ventured beyond the gates of their home communities could read and write because literacy within convents was much higher than for the average early modern woman outside the cloister. In the majority of cases, in order to profess as a black-veiled nun (upperclass women who held offices and governed a convent), a novice was required to be able to at least read. In the words of Asunción Lavrin, "Religious orders demanded literacy from its members for a practical reason: convents had to be run by women capable of institutional management."[17] Furthermore, much of our knowledge about these women comes from their own writings, including diaries, letters, biographies, and foundation accounts.

Across the Iberian Atlantic the majority of these writers were either of noble lineage or of spiritual vocation. While some lived in palaces or noble residences, many lived in religious centers. Nuns were not, as a rule, from the lower strata of early modern society, but we include them here because their lives as marginalized women, living apart from society, offer a multi-colored prism through which to view class, race, and gender within convents. The chapter by Salazar Simarro and Owens touches on the diversity within convents and helps illuminate why, in many instances, upperclass women chose a life behind cloistered walls. In the capital of New Spain and elsewhere, as in the viceroyalty of Peru, these women could live lavish lifestyles attended to by servants and slaves. Even outside the capitals, in a city like Arequipa, Peru, the Convent of Santa Catalina housed over five hundred women, the majority belonging to the servant class. They tell the story of the social milieu that made up these large religious communities. In Mexico, for example, Sor Juana Inés de la Cruz penned her magnum opus, *The Answer,* defending a woman's right to an education in a society dominated by misogynous ideas—contradicting Saint Paul's edict that women should keep silent. Sor Juana's writings remind us that, although many black-veiled nuns came from elite families, patriarchal society still viewed them as marginalized and on the periphery. Nonetheless, her writings show that women engaged patriarchal authority and that the nuances of that authority were fluid.

A century earlier in Spain, Saint Teresa of Avila began to pave a path for future female writers and religious women. Unlike Sor Juana Inés de la Cruz or the Conceptionist nuns of Jesús María, the Spanish saint dedicated her life to reforming the Carmelite order, adhering to the strict rules of a discalced lifestyle. After witnessing the excesses and lavish standard of living in Spanish convents, she trekked across Spain founding seventeen new nunneries. Meanwhile, she followed her intellectual and spiritual vocation, writing four seminal works: *The Book of Her Life, The Interior Castle, The Way of Perfection,* and *The Book of Foundations.* According to Arenal and Schlau, "Saint Teresa of Avila's impact on the lives and writing of Hispanic nuns can scarcely be overestimated."[18] We know that even before their publication, manuscripts of her works circulated in convents across Spanish America. Due to their subsequent publication and Saint Teresa's canonization in 1622 (only forty years after her death), nuns and *beatas* (lay religious women) felt bolstered by her success. They saw her as a role model, one who dodged the trappings of the Inquisition, and they too began to take up the pen.

Saint Teresa was also well known and an inspiration for women religious in early modern Portugal and Brazil. For example, in 1753 the Brazilian woman Jacinta de São José traveled all the way from Rio de Janeiro to Lisbon and back in her efforts to found the first Carmelite convent in Brazil. Convents came relatively late to Brazil[19]—there was only one foundation in the 1600s (Convento do Desterro, 1667, in Bahia), and the second was the Carmelite convent that Jacinta founded in 1781, although she died before she saw her dream come to fruition. In brief, the Portuguese Crown discouraged female religious centers because they did not want white women becoming nuns when there were so few of them available for marriage. Before her death, Jacinta de São José had amassed a small collection of spiritual books for the future convent, many of them in Portuguese and Spanish.[20]

Examples such as Jacinta de São José show the interconnectivity of religious communities throughout the Iberian world, including the ability of some to communicate in both Spanish and Portuguese. Vollendorf's essay in this volume speaks to the need to explore these commonalities between Portugal and Spain and their far-reaching effects, even beyond the Atlantic basin.[21] Current scholarship provides vivid examples of Portuguese women who embraced the Spanish language, producing their own works in Castilian instead of Portuguese.[22] Sarah E. Owens's recent edition, *Journey of Five Capuchin Nuns,* helps to paint a vibrant picture of this polyglot atmosphere. The five nuns who traveled all the way from Madrid to Lima in the early seventeen hundreds were waylaid by Dutch corsairs and subsequently left off as "prisoners" in two convents in Lisbon, Portugal. The Portuguese nuns practically smothered the newly arrived sisters with gifts, parties, and attention. The common nexus of their religious affiliation trumped any political affiliations. In the words of the Spanish abbess Madre María Rosa, "These affable nuns are so fond of the Castilian nation that they never left us alone, not even to pray the Divine Office."[23]

A small cohort of women religious journeyed to the outermost boundaries of the Spanish and Portuguese empires. The most remarkable case involves the Spanish nun Madre Jerónima de la Asunción (1555–1630). At the age of sixty-five she traveled with several other nuns all the way to Manila to establish the first nunnery in the Spanish Philippines. Although Sor Jerónima did write a spiritual autobiography and kept notes concerning the foundation in Manila, her original texts have long been lost. Much of what we know about the nun from Toledo comes from her close friend and traveling companion, Sor Ana de Cristo, who wrote the first biography of the abbess. Fortunately, she had access to the original manuscripts, often quoting directly from Sor Jerónima, a practice very common during the early modern period.[24] During the first part of the epic journey, Sor Jerónima stopped in Seville, where she posed for two portraits by the budding young artist Diego de Velázquez (one now hangs in the Prado and the other in a private collection).[25] Sor Jerónima and her Franciscan sisters traveled to Asia by way of Mexico, where one of the women succumbed to a deadly fever, and her body had to be thrown overboard shortly after departing from the port of Acapulco. Finally the small party of nuns arrived in Manila on August 5, 1621, a year and a half after departing the Iberian Peninsula. Sor Jerónima's missionary zeal did not end in Manila. Before her death she inspired a seed group of six Spanish nuns and one novice to found the new Convent of Saint Clare on the Portuguese colony of Macau. That novice became the first native Filipino to take the habit. She was, however, a lay nun, belonging more to the servant class than to the privileged status of black-veiled nuns.[26] Sor Martha, referred to as "La Morenita," embodies the race and gender hierarchies of imperial ideology propagated by these Iberian nuns. Moreover, these structures of difference speak to the complex landscape that made up the Spanish and Portuguese empires and shaped these early modern religious women. Scholars Andrew Fisher and Matthew O'Hara have aptly described the foundational ideology of Iberian imperialism: "the Iberian project in the Americas rested on the presumption of a long-term, discernible boundary between the colonizers and the colonized that reflected a sliding scale of inferiority among subsets of the Crown's vassals."[27] In this case, Spanish nuns brought with them a class system that prioritized whiteness as racially superior, thus relegating indigenous, African, and mixed-race women to positions of servitude behind the walls of their religious centers. Whether they knew it or not, they actively participated in imposing these hierarchical and class-based structures on their new convents in the Americas and beyond.[28]

CONCLUSION

The figure of traveling nuns serves as a symbol to the promise of this volume. A nun evokes the quintessential virtues of the Iberian female, enclosed and devout. Yet the aforementioned nuns who traveled across Iberia and into the reaches of the empire represent an altogether different side of female religiosity in this era. As such, the traveling nuns readily represent the actions of women in an era of imperial expansion. The impression of women's lives in the early modern era was never as simplistic as the first glance of a habit or the perusal of a legal code or a religious treatise. Like the nuns, young Spanish brides, female Afro-Cuban leaders, and knowledgeable healers as well as practices, symbols, and texts all moved along Atlantic pathways in the early modern Iberian world. These chapters reshape traditional male images of empire by highlighting women's lives in the Atlantic world, but they also acknowledge that women operated within the same apparatus of Iberian law, culture, restriction, and oppression as their male counterparts. Women traveled for religious vocation, out of economic necessity, to be with spouses in the New World, and due to forced migration because of the African slave trade as well as indigenous slavery. These examples dispute the basic formula that men were on the move and women stayed home in the historical context of the Iberian Atlantic. In addition to reshaping our ideas of mobility, other essays in the volume highlight how Iberian expansion shaped the world of women who stayed put and how those women challenged the Iberian legal code, as in the cases of East Texas and the indigenous women of the Andes.

Women of the Iberian Atlantic provides a more inclusive framework to study Iberian women. Most of the studies to date focus on only one side of the Atlantic: either Spain or Latin America.[29] The contributors seek to challenge conventional boundaries in a collective effort to expand our definition of the Atlantic basin. This book addresses race and class issues by probing how these women—even though many of them were marginalized—accepted and even spread some aspects of imperial ideology while rejecting others. Breaking away from the typical dichotomy of Spain/Latin America or Portugal/Brazil, our contributors have included women from the fringes, proving that our traditional classifications of the "Atlantic" are too limiting. Our work confirms that these discussions on gender and empire can grow as further studies become even more integrative, finding other examples from the Pacific and Far East. By pinpointing the inherently gendered nature of the Iberian empire as well as upending conventional frameworks, narratives, and theories that have traditionally defined Atlantic research, these essays reveal the widespread impact of women on the emergence of the Iberian Atlantic world.

NOTES

1. Recent works which embrace gender as a locus of analysis include Daniella Kostroun and Lisa Vollendorf, eds., *Women, Religion, and the Atlantic World (1600–1800)* (Toronto: Univ. of Toronto Press, 2009), and Nora E. Jaffary, ed., *Gender, Race and Religion in the Colonization of the Americas* (Burlington, Vt.: Ashgate, 2007).

2. Ann Laura Stoler, *Carnal Knowledge and Imperial Power: Race and the Intimate in Colonial Rule* (Berkeley: Univ. of California Press, 2002).

3. Select examples from a varied field include Theresa Earenfight, ed., *Queenship and Political Power in Medieval and Early Modern Spain* (Burlington, Vt.: Ashgate, 2005); Bar-

bara F. Weissberger, *Queen Isabel I of Castile: Power, Patronage, Persona* (Rochester, N.Y.: Tamesis, 2008); and David A. Boruchoff, ed., *Isabel la Católica, Queen of Castile: Critical Essays* (New York: Palgrave Macmillan, 2003).

4. For some key examples, see Stephanie Smallwood, *Saltwater Slavery: A Middle Passage from Africa to the American Diaspora* (Cambridge: Harvard Univ. Press, 2007); David Armitage and Michael J. Braddick, eds., *The British Atlantic World, 1500–1800*, 2nd ed. (New York: Palgrave Macmillan, 2009); and Nicholas Canny and Philip Morgan, eds., *The Oxford Handbook of the Atlantic World, 1450–1850* (Oxford: Oxford Univ. Press, 2011). For debate on the field of Atlantic history, see the forum "Entangled Empires in the Atlantic World," in *American Historical Review* 112, no. 3 (June 2007): 710–799.

5. Jorge Cañizares-Esguerra, *Puritan Conquistadores: Iberianizing the Atlantic, 1550–1700* (Stanford: Stanford Univ. Press, 2006).

6. J. H. Elliott, *Empires of the Atlantic World: Britain and Spain in America 1492–1830* (New Haven: Yale University Press, 2006), xvii.

7. For instance, Nicholas Canny, "Writing Atlantic History, or Reconfiguring the History of British Colonial America," *Journal of American History* 86 (1999): 1104.

8. Alison Games, "Migrations and Frontiers," in *The Atlantic World, 1450–2000*, ed. Toyin Falola and Kevin D. Roberts, 61 (Bloomington: Indiana Univ. Press, 2008).

9. See Jane E. Mangan, *Trading Roles: Gender, Ethnicity, and the Urban Economy in Colonial Potosí* (Durham: Duke Univ. Press, 2005).

10. The work of Ida Altman stands as an excellent model of this transatlantic Iberian work that emerged prior to the rise of Atlantic history as a field in its own right. See Altman, *Emigrants and Society: Extremadura and Spanish America in the Sixteenth Century* (Berkeley: Univ. of California Press, 1989).

11. See Karen Graubart's recent call for frameworks that integrate gender more fully into the study of the Atlantic world in "Toward Connectedness and Place," *William and Mary Quarterly* 68, no. 2 (April 2011): 235.

12. Eliga H. Gould, "Entangled Histories, Entangled Worlds: The English-Speaking Atlantic as a Spanish Periphery," *American Historical Review* 112, no. 3 (June 2007): 764–786. See Poska's essay in this volume for more on the concept of "entangled histories" and how it can be applied to a gendered interpretation of the Iberian Atlantic.

13. The seminal work on gender history is Joan Scott, *Gender and the Politics of History* (New York: Columbia Univ. Press, 1988). A more recent scholarly debate on gender history is the AHR Forum "Revisiting 'Gender: A Useful Category of Historical Analysis,'" *American Historical Review* 113, no. 5 (December 2008): 1344–1429. An insightful early piece on gender history in the context of the early Americas is Kathleen Brown, "Brave New Worlds: Women's and Gender History," *William and Mary Quarterly* 1, no. 2 (1993): 311–328. For gender and women's texts see Marta V. Vicente and Luis R. Corteguera, eds., *Women, Texts and Authority in the Early Modern Spanish World* (Burlington, Vt.: Ashgate, 2003).

14. Manuel Serrano y Sanz, ed., *Apuntes para una biblioteca de escritoras españolas* (Madrid: Rivadeynera, 1903–1905; reprint, Madrid: Atlas, 1975).

15. As a result of the last three decades of solid research, a variety of anthologies have been written about early modern women and their scholarly vocations—almost all of which include religious writers. In her introduction to *Women Writers of Early Modern Spain* (New Haven: Yale Univ. Press, 2004), xxiii–xxx, Bárbara Mujica does an excellent job of summarizing works dedicated to Spanish writers. Other examples are editions by Teresa Soufas,

Women's Acts: Plays by Women Dramatists of Spain's Golden Age (Lexington: Univ. Press of Kentucky, 1997); Judith A. Whitenack and Gwyn E. Campbell, *Zayas and Her Sisters: An Anthology of Novelas by 17th-Century Spanish Women* (Asheville: Pegasus Press and University of North Carolina, Asheville, 2000); Amy Katz Kaminsky, ed., *Water Lilies: Flores de Agua* (Minneapolis: Univ. of Minnesota Press, 1996); and for convent literature, Electa Arenal and Stacey Schlau's landmark study *Untold Sisters: Hispanic Nuns in Their Own Works* (Albuquerque: Univ. of New Mexico Press, 1989) covers religious writers from Spain and Hispanic America.

16. Kathleen Myers, "Recent Trends in the Study of Women and Religion in Colonial Mexico," *Latin American Research Review* 43, no. 2 (2008): 291. This article builds on her earlier reflections in "Crossing Boundaries: Defining the Field of Female Religious Writing in Colonial Latin America," *Colonial Latin American Review* 9 (2000): 151–165. For an overview of gender and convent literature, see Sherry M. Velasco, "Visualizing Gender on the Page in Convent Literature," in *Women, Texts and Authority in the Early Modern Spanish World*, ed. Marta V. Vicente and Luis R. Corteguera, 127–148 (Burlington, Vt.: Ashgate, 2003).

17. Asunción Lavrin, *Brides of Christ: Conventual Life in Colonial Mexico* (Stanford: Stanford Univ. Press, 2008), 310. On literacy for religious and secular women in Spain and the New World, see Anne J. Cruz and Rosilie Hernández, eds., *Women's Literacy in Early Modern Spain and the New World* (Burlington, Vt.: Ashgate, 2011).

18. Arenal and Schlau, eds., *Untold Sisters*, 9.

19. Convents were not the only institutions to come late to Brazil. Ralph Bauer and José Antonio Mazzotti write: "Unlike the Spanish who transplanted many of their cultural institutions in the New World, the Portuguese did not establish a single university or printing press in their American territories until the nineteenth century" ("Introduction: Creole Subject in the Colonial Americas," in *Creole Subjects in the Colonial Americas: Empires, Texts, Identities*, ed. Ralph Bauer and José Antonio Mazzotti, 27–28 [Chapel Hill: Univ. of North Carolina Press, 2009]).

20. See Célia Maia Borges, "Las hijas de Teresa de Ávila: Espiritualidad mística entre mujeres de la península ibérica y del Brasil colonial," in *Historias compartidas. Religiosidad y reclusión femenina en España, Portugal y América. Siglos XV–XIX*, ed. María Isabel Viforcos Marinas and Rosalva Loreto López, 177–193 (León: Universidad de León, 2007); for a list of the works that Jacinta de São José brought back with her from Portugal, see Leila Mezan Algranti, "Biografías y autobiografías de mujeres ejemplares: los escritos de conciencia de la madre Jacinta de São José y las prácticas religiosas femeninas en el Brasil Colonial," in *Historias compartidas*, 132–137.

21. For a good starting point to learn more about women in the Portuguese colonial empire in English, see Clara Sarmento, ed., *Women in the Portuguese Colonial Empire* (Newcastle: Cambridge Scholars Publishing, 2008). This recent volume sets out to give a voice to marginalized women from the sixteenth century until as recent at 1974 (although it is heavy on the nineteenth century). In her introduction Sarmento writes: "Notably absent from history are the voices of women who have, by and large, been silenced by historiography in general and by Portuguese historiography in general," xi.

22. See Vanda Anastácio, "Challenging Borders, Nations and Identities: Portuguese Women Writers of the Modern Period" (paper presented at the biannual meeting of Grupo de estudios sobre la mujer en España y las Américas, Mt. Holyoke, Mass., September 23–25, 2010). For the interconnectivity between Spanish and Portuguese noble women, see María

Isabel Barbeito Carneiro, "Mujeres peninsulares entre Portugal y España," *Revista de Estudios Ibéricos* no. 0 (2003): 209–224.

23. Madre María Rosa, *Journey of Five Capuchin Nuns,* ed. and trans. Sarah E. Owens, The Other Voice in Early Modern Europe Series (Toronto: Iter and Centre for Reformation and Renaissance Studies, 2009), 114.

24. For excerpts from Sor Ana's biography and Sor Jerónima's original writing, see María Victoria Triviño, ed., *Escritoras clarisas españolas* (Madrid: Biblioteca de autores cristianos, 1992), 46–59. Sor Ana's complete manuscript is held by the nuns of Santa Isabel in Toledo, Spain.

25. There is also a third portrait of Sor Jerónima that is attributed to Velázquez. See Tanya J. Tiffany's chapter "Portraiture and the 'Virile Woman': Madre Jerónima de la Fuente," in *Diego Velázquez's Early Paintings and the Culture of Seventeenth-Century Seville* (University Park: Pennsylvania State Univ. Press, 2012).

26. For more on Sor Jerónima and women religious in Manila, see Pedro Ruano, *Jerónima de la Asunción* (Quezon City, Philippines: Monasterio de Santa Clara, 1992). See also Luciano Santiago, *To Love and to Suffer: The Development of the Religious Congregations for Women in the Spanish Philippines, 1565–1898* (Quezon City, Philippines: Ateneo de Manila Univ. Press, 2005), 49–72; and Marya Svetlana Camacho, "Los beaterios y recogimientos en Manila en el siglo xviii. Acomodación religiosa y aportación social," in *Historias compartidas. Religiosidad y reclusión femenina en España, Portugal y América. Siglos XV–XIX,* ed. María Isabel Viforcos Marinas and Rosalva Loreto López, 367–390 (León: Universidad de León, 2007).

27. Andrew B. Fisher and Matthew D. O'Hara, "Introduction: Racial Identities and Their Interpreters in Colonial Latin America," in *Imperial Subjects: Race and Identity in Colonial Latin America,* ed. Andrew B. Fisher and Matthew D. O'Hara, 2 (Durham: Duke Univ. Press, 2009).

28. For astute insight on race and convents in the Americas, see Mónica Díaz, *Indigenous Writings from the Convent. Negotiating Ethnic Autonomy in Colonial Mexico* (Tucson: Univ. of Arizona Press, 2010). See also Nancy E. van Deusen, "Circuits of Knowledge among Women in Early Seventeenth-Century Lima," in *Gender, Race and Religion in the Colonization of the Americas,* ed. Nora E. Jaffary, 137–150 (Burlington, Vt.: Ashgate, 2007).

29. In explaining her selection of only peninsular Spanish writers for her anthology, *Water Lilies,* Amy Katz Kaminsky writes: "They include no Latin Americans, even from the colonial period, since it seems to me that those writers belong to quite another tradition" (preface, xviii).

WORKS CITED

Altman, Ida. *Emigrants and Society: Extremadura and Spanish America in the Sixteenth Century.* Berkeley: Univ. of California Press, 1989.

Anastácio, Vanda. "Challenging Borders, Nations and Identities: Portuguese-Women Writers of the Modern Period." Paper presented at the biannual meeting of Grupo de estudios sobre la mujer en España y las Américas, Mt. Holyoke, Mass., September 23–25, 2010.

Arenal, Electa, and Stacey Schlau, eds. *Untold Sisters: Hispanic Nuns in Their Own Works.* Albuquerque: Univ. of New Mexico Press, 1989.

Armitage, David, and Michael J. Braddick, eds. *The British Atlantic World, 1500–1800*, 2nd ed. New York: Palgrave Macmillan, 2009.
Barbeito Carneiro, María Isabel. "Mujeres peninsulares entre Portugal y España." *Revista de Estudios Ibéricos* no. 0 (2003): 209–224.
Bauer, Ralph, and José Antonio Mazzotti. "Introduction: Creole Subject in the Colonial Americas." In *Creole Subjects in the Colonial Americas: Empires, Texts, Identities*, edited by Ralph Bauer and José Antonio Mazzotti, 27–28. Chapel Hill: Univ. of North Carolina Press, 2009.
Borges, Célia Maia. "Las hijas de Teresa de Ávila: Espiritualidad mística entre mujeres de la península ibérica y del Brasil colonial." In *Historias compartidas. Religiosidad y reclusión femenina en España, Portugal y América. Siglos XV–XIX*, edited by María Isabel Viforcos Marinas and Rosalva Loreto López, 177–193. León: Universidad de León, 2007.
Boruchoff, David A., ed. *Isabel la Católica, Queen of Castile: Critical Essays*. New York: Palgrave Macmillan, 2003.
Brown, Kathleen. "Brave New Worlds: Women's and Gender History." *William and Mary Quarterly* 1, no. 2 (1993): 311–328.
Camacho, Marya Svetlana. "Los beaterios y recogimientos en Manila en el siglo xviii. Acomodación religiosa y aportación social." In *Historias compartidas. Religiosidad y reclusión femenina en España, Portugal y América. Siglos XV–XIX*, edited by María Isabel Viforcos Marinas and Rosalva Loreto López, 367–390. León: Universidad de León, 2007.
Cañizares-Esguerra, Jorge. *Puritan Conquistadors: Iberianizing the Atlantic, 1550–1700*. Stanford: Stanford Univ. Press, 2006.
Canny, Nicholas. "Writing Atlantic History, or Reconfiguring the History of British Colonial America." *Journal of American History* 86 (1999): 1093–1114.
Canny, Nicholas, and Philip Morgan, eds. *The Oxford Handbook of the Atlantic World, 1450–1850*. Oxford: Oxford Univ. Press, 2011.
Cruz, Anne J., and Rosilie Hernández, eds. *Women's Literacy in Early Modern Spain and the New World*. Burlington, Vt.: Ashgate, 2011.
Díaz, Mónica. *Indigenous Writings from the Convent: Negotiating Ethnic Autonomy in Colonial Mexico*. Tucson: Univ. of Arizona Press, 2010.
Earenfight, Theresa, ed. *Queenship and Political Power in Medieval and Early Modern Spain*. Burlington, Vt.: Ashgate, 2005.
Elliott, J. H. *Empires of the Atlantic World: Britain and Spain in America 1492–1830*. New Haven: Yale Univ. Press, 2006.
Fisher, Andrew B., and Matthew D. O'Hara. Introduction to *Imperial Subjects. Race and Identity in Colonial Latin America*. Edited by Andrew B. Fisher and Matthew D. O'Hara, 1–38. Durham: Duke Univ. Press, 2009.
Games, Alison. "Migrations and Frontiers." In *The Atlantic World, 1450–2000*, edited by Toyin Falola and Kevin D. Roberts, 48–66. Bloomington: Indiana Univ. Press, 2008.

Gould, Eliga H. "Entangled Histories, Entangled Worlds: The English-Speaking Atlantic as a Spanish Periphery." *American Historical Review* 112, no. 3 (June 2007): 764–786.

Graubart, Karen. "Toward Connectedness and Place." *William and Mary Quarterly* 68, no.2 (April 2011): 233–235.

Jaffary, Nora E., ed. *Gender, Race and Religion in the Colonization of the Americas*. Burlington, Vt.: Ashgate, 2007.

Kaminsky, Amy Katz, ed. *Water Lilies. Flores de Agua*. Minneapolis: Univ. of Minnesota Press, 1996.

Kostroun, Daniella, and Lisa Vollendorf, eds. *Women, Religion, and the Atlantic World (1600–1800)*. Toronto: Univ. of Toronto Press, 2009.

Lavrin, Asunción. *Brides of Christ. Conventual Life in Colonial Mexico*. Stanford: Stanford Univ. Press, 2008.

Mangan, Jane E. *Trading Roles: Gender, Ethnicity, and the Urban Economy in Colonial Potosí*. Durham: Duke Univ. Press, 2005.

María Rosa, Madre. *Journey of Five Capuchin Nuns*. Edited and translated by Sarah E. Owens. The Other Voice in Early Modern Europe Series. Toronto: Iter and Centre for Reformation and Renaissance Studies, 2009.

Mezan Algranti, Leila. "Biografías y autobiografías de mujeres ejemplares: los escritos de conciencia de la madre Jacinta de São José y las prácticas religiosas femeninas en el Brasil Colonial." In *Historias compartidas. Religiosidad y reclusión femenina en España, Portugal y América. Siglos XV–XIX*, edited by María Isabel Viforcos Marinas and Rosalva Loreto López, 132–137. León: Universidad de León, 2007.

Mujica, Bárbara. Introduction to *Women Writers of Early Modern Spain*. Edited by Bárbara Mujica, xxiii–xxx. New Haven: Yale Univ. Press, 2004.

Myers, Kathleen Ann. "Crossing Boundaries: Defining the Field of Female Religious Writing in Colonial Latin America." *Colonial Latin American Review* 9 (2000): 151–165.

———. "Recent Trends in the Study of Women and Religion in Colonial Mexico." *Latin American Research Review* 43, no. 2 (2008): 290–301.

Ruano, Pedro. *Jerónima de la Asunción*. Quezon City, Philippines: Monasterio de Santa Clara, 1992.

Santiago, Luciano. *To Love and to Suffer: The Development of the Religious Congregations for Women in the Spanish Philippines, 1565–1898*. Quezon City, Philippines: Ateneo de Manila Univ. Press, 2005.

Sarmento, Clara, ed. *Women in the Portuguese Colonial Empire*. Newcastle: Cambridge Scholars Publishing, 2008.

Scott, Joan. *Gender and the Politics of History*. New York: Columbia Univ. Press, 1988.

Serrano y Sanz, Manuel, ed. *Apuntes para una biblioteca de escritoras españolas*. Madrid: Rivadeynera, 1903–1905. Reprint, Madrid: Atlas, 1975.

Smallwood, Stephanie. *Saltwater Slavery: A Middle Passage from Africa to the American Diaspora.* Cambridge: Harvard Univ. Press, 2007.

Soufas, Teresa, ed. *Women's Acts: Plays by Women Dramatists of Spain's Golden Age.* Lexington: Univ. Press of Kentucky, 1997.

Stoler, Ann Laura. *Carnal Knowledge and Imperial Power: Race and the Intimate in Colonial Rule.* Berkeley: Univ. of California Press, 2002.

Tiffany, Tanya J. *Diego Velázquez's Early Paintings and the Culture of Seventeenth-Century Seville.* University Park: Pennsylvania State Univ. Press, 2012.

Triviño, María Victoria, ed. *Escritoras clarisas españolas.* Madrid: Biblioteca de autores cristianos, 1992.

Velasco, Sherry M. "Visualizing Gender on the Page in Convent Literature." In *Women, Texts and Authority in the Early Modern Spanish World,* edited by Marta V. Vicente and Luis R. Corteguera, 127–148. Burlington, Vt.: Ashgate, 2003.

Van Deusen, Nancy E. "Circuits of Knowledge among Women in Early Seventeenth-Century Lima." In *Gender, Race and Religion in the Colonization of the Americas,* edited by Nora E. Jaffary, 137–150. Burlington, Vt.: Ashgate, 2007.

Vicente, Marta V., and Luis R. Corteguera, eds. *Women, Texts and Authority in the Early Modern Spanish World.* Burlington, Vt.: Ashgate, 2003.

Weissberger, Barbara F. *Queen Isabel I of Castile: Power, Patronage, Persona.* Rochester, N.Y.: Tamesis, 2008.

Whitenack, Judith A., and Gwyn E. Campbell, eds. *Zayas and Her Sisters: An Anthology of Novelas by 17th-Century Spanish Women.* Asheville: Pegasus Press and University of North Carolina, Asheville, 2000.

1

Navigating the Atlantic Divide

Women, Education, and Literacy in Iberia and the Americas

LISA VOLLENDORF

The study of Iberia and the Americas traditionally has occurred in two parallel worlds, and the study of women in those spaces is no exception.[1] Iberianists and Latin Americanists have made significant advances in understanding women's economic, cultural, and political engagement in early modern Iberia and the Iberian Atlantic in the past thirty years, yet most of the work has involved women on one continent or the other and has not attended to the to and fro of people, objects, and ideas that defined the age of transatlantic contact. More recently, as suggested by the present volume, a transatlantic focus on women's cultural history has emerged. Not coincidentally, the new scholarly focus coincides with a cultural turn in the field of Atlantic studies.[2] John Elliott has captured that turn by defining the approach as the study of "the creation, destruction, and re-creation of communities as a result of the movement, across and around the Atlantic basin, of people, commodities, cultural practices, and ideas."[3] Studies of women and gender in the Iberian Atlantic have built on initial research that focused discretely on women in Europe and, separately, in the Americas, to bring broader, more integrative perspectives to bear. One such example is my volume, coedited with Daniella Kostroun, *Women, Religion, and the Atlantic World (1600–1800),* which looks at the Atlantic space vis-à-vis gender, religion, and spirituality.

Recently, more attention has been given to questions of community, diaspora, and networks that formed part of the broader Iberian Atlantic space. The vast and diverse nature of that space and its communities presents a challenge that requires delimitation of one sort or another. Therefore, the present essay operates with the definition of the early modern Iberian Atlantic as the geographical space affected by contact between Iberian Europeans and non-Europeans and centered primarily on areas that bordered the Atlantic Ocean. From a cultural perspective, the movement of people, ideas, and objects during the early modern period offers an opportunity for decentered examination of individual lives, group networks, and both commonalities and differences from a transatlantic perspective. The approach reminds scholars that the exchange of ideas, people, and objects can and should be examined for synergies and mutual influences, and not just from a one-dimensional perspective.

One case that exemplifies the benefits of expanding approaches to early modern women's studies to encompass a transatlantic framework can be found in studies on Sor Juana Inés de la Cruz (1648–1695). Sor Juana now is understood as a writer who forged a uniquely American baroque aesthetic that both drew and expanded on European philosophy and style.[4] As one of the few Ibero-American women who has been studied in terms of her Atlantic presence, Sor Juana provides direct evidence for the impact of the movement of people, books, and ideas in the seventeenth century. Her political connections with the viceroys of New Spain gave her access to colonial high society. When she ran into controversy with the Church, it was due to her critique of a sermon by Portuguese Jesuit Antonio Vieira. Her resulting controversial piece, *La respuesta* (*The Answer*), was published posthumously across the Atlantic in Spain in 1700.[5] *La respuesta* constitutes a defense of women's right to both secular and religious education and to this day stands among the most important examples of women's literature from the baroque period. Significant for its brilliant structure and all-encompassing defense of multidisciplinary knowledge as the bedrock of a solid Catholic education, *La respuesta* also gives us insight into Sor Juana's participation in a transatlantic writing community of women, as she mentions the writing of four Spanish nuns and draws on many ideas and writing strategies found in European texts. Sor Juana wrote another explicitly transatlantic piece: her *Enigmas ofrecidos a la Casa del Placer,* a compilation of riddles written for nuns in a Lisbon convent and likely transported to Europe by the Countess of Paredes.[6] This collection written for Atlantic sisters was not rediscovered until the 1960s, thus reminding us of the thousands of texts that remain buried in archives throughout the Atlantic sphere.

Sor Juana's explicit engagement with transatlantic women in these texts provides concrete evidence of a widespread community of female readers and writers who built on each others' self-authorizing strategies.[7]

Thanks to Sor Juana's premier status as one of the finest and most studied authors of the baroque, we have a firm understanding of the ways in which she placed herself within a transatlantic sphere of readership and exchange. These two texts speak to the ways in which Sor Juana provides us with an initial foray into understanding the deep and complex intellectual and cultural exchanges that occurred throughout the Atlantic and provides one path for us to follow to better understand women's place in the Atlantic sphere. As recent movement in the field of early modern and colonial women's studies attests, scholars now can use knowledge of Sor Juana's and other women's engagement with a transatlantic world to uncover more connections among those whose life stories and texts are less readily accessible and less easily studied.

The case of Sor Juana serves as one example of what scholars stand to learn by expanding conceptualizations of women's history to include the broader Atlantic basin as a point of reference. For instance, the role played by the Countess of Paredes in the transport of Sor Juana's *Enigmas* serves as a reminder that women's travel between Europe and the Americas has yet to be sufficiently analyzed.[8] Jacqueline Holler has probed this field in her study of the *beatas* (lay religious women) who traveled from Spain to model Christianity in New Spain. Throughout the early modern period, select groups of nuns were called on by their orders to found convents in Peru, Mexico City, and Guatemala.[9] Like other religious men and women who would follow, they undertook rigorous journeys for which no monastic training or personal experience had prepared them. Like men, they were called to duty by the Church. Unlike men, they broke with religious and gender codes that dictated enclosure when they ventured out of the cloister onto the high seas. For Sarah E. Owens's group of intrepid Spanish Capuchin nuns who traveled to Peru in the early eighteenth century to found a convent, the notion of a navigable space that both bridged and separated Europe from other continents likely would have resonated on a very personal level.[10] These women endured two years of travel delays, including a stint as prisoners of Dutch corsairs, before docking in the New World. The Capuchins' example also highlights one of the challenges of viewing the early modern world through an Atlantic lens: a space colonized by the Spanish yet bordering the Pacific, Peru is one of the many locales that can be considered from the lens of both Atlantic and Pacific studies. As the Jesuits who traveled to Asia knew, the impulse to expansion encompassed a broad global territory in the period.[11] In all of these cases, the Atlantic framework serves as a space of connections and communities, offering a lens through which scholars might reconsider their understandings of the early modern Ibero-American world and the possible gender differentiation of individual and group experiences.

Not all who set forth for the Americas or traveled to Europe had religious missions. Many women who came to the Americas did so to accompany husbands and other male relatives who had sought better opportunities in the uncharted territory of the Americas. Indeed, Allyson Poska's essay in the present volume opens the understudied arena of women's migration to the Americas and pushes historians to question the extent to which the separation of Iberian and colonial history has resulted in a lack of understanding of gender relations throughout the empire. Like some male travelers, a few of those women wrote letters to loved ones in Iberia in which they detailed material and emotional hardship.[12] Similarly, many travelers stayed closer to home, such that the conceptualization of movement of people also should include a focus on migrations on the same continent. Catholicism's most famous nun of the period, Saint Teresa of Avila, traveled extensively within her home country and interacted with those who had gone abroad. Madre Teresa's tireless travels and labor led to the foundation of Carmelite convents across Spain. She wrote of her own travels to her brother in the Americas, emphasizing that she traveled to "so many places" and "so many people speak" to her.[13]

The question of travel provides a point of entry into broader considerations of women's lives in the Iberian Atlantic and to the ways in which scholars can further deepen understanding of women in that space. First and foremost, as suggested by the examples mentioned above, much of the nuance brought to the understanding of women and gender in recent years is based on texts written by and about women in the Iberian Atlantic. Literacy and education have been very difficult to trace except insofar that, for certain individuals and groups, we have access to texts produced by or about women, thus providing suggestive evidence about women's relationship to the written word. Of fundamental importance is the reality that reading and writing were taught as separate skills in the early modern period, a fact that will continue to help scholars interpret emerging evidence of engagement with the written word. Stories of literate merchant-class women who owned books, took legal action, wrote their own wills, and ran businesses increasingly reveal that girls across class lines were educated in both skills more than previously imagined.[14] Private and communal reading was an important part of the early modern experience, as only those who could read had access to private reading experiences.[15]

Fundamentally, reading must be understood to be both private and public, since the aural consumption of texts was by far the most common means by which people accessed the written word. Indeed, recent statistics for sixteenth-century Spain suggest that female reading literacy rates ranged dramatically, with some rural areas at 0 percent female literacy and most urban areas reaching as high as 40 percent.[16] Women's book inventories from the sixteenth century show chivalric novels, such as *Amadís de Gaula,* recipe books, and devotional books among those that women from the merchant and aristocratic classes most frequently owned, thus suggesting commonalities among women's reading experiences and suggesting lines of inquiry about women readers that remain unexplored.

Women's access to education adds yet another point of differentiation among women's lives, which varied depending on time frame, place, class, and ethnic identity. Women's relationship to the written word intimately relates to the broader question of how scholars approach women's history for the Iberian Atlantic. Better deciphering who had access to education promises to move the field to a more nuanced understanding of how local and community variations manifest themselves and how women and the disenfranchised in general accessed authority and power throughout the Atlantic basin. Many scholars—including many whose work appears in the current volume—have articulated an urgent need for us to pay attention to the local particularities found in different communities and places. Some standouts in this large field include studies on Iberian women's influence in the political and cultural realms; cultural minorities; rural women; widows; and women's writing.[17] For the Americas, an even larger body of work has focused on authority, race, economics, and gender.[18] The religious sphere has received significant attention for Ibero-America and Iberia alike. This attention is well represented in this volume's essays by Ras Michael Brown, Matt D. Childs, Nuria Salazar Simarro, and Sarah E. Owens.[19]

Alison Weber has summarized the ways in which historians of women and gender have struggled to find appropriate frameworks to understand women's history, relying in the early years on "Terms such as 'gendered domains,' 'separate spheres,' and 'the public/private dichotomy.'"[20] In calling for a methodology that would "account for how power and agency sometimes elide spatial categorization and migrate between spaces and subjectivities," Weber addresses the need for early modern studies to assess current methodologies and to develop new critical questions that will help us move forward in our efforts to develop more nuanced understandings of women in different times and places as well as of individuals and groups in the early modern world.[21]

The call for more attention to local culture also must be considered in light of the great ethnic and racial variation of the Atlantic population. One cannot possibly assume great commonalities among the experiences of the women featured in the present volume. Sor Juana's life was different from the experiences of women settlers in the early Caribbean, as explored by Ida Altman's essay; those experiences differed from the lives of the indigenous mothers in conquest-era Peru discussed by Jane E. Mangan; and the ritual experts in Bantu spiritual cultures analyzed by Ras Michael Brown certainly had different lives from those of Timothy D. Walker's folk healers in the Luso-Brazilian world or the women of the East Texas Borderlands discussed by Carla Gerona, for example. As all essays in this volume attest, scholars can develop a better understanding of women's position vis-à-vis the broader Iberian and Ibero-American cultures by examining the ways in which women navigated belief, religion, laws, and economic systems. Within this context, scholars can and should seek ways to further decipher how women and other groups engaged, upheld, subverted, and circumvented mechanisms aimed at social control. While scholars still have direct textual or material evidence about only a small minority of individuals who inhabited the Iberian Atlantic space, with each passing year that knowledge expands to include more individuals and groups. Only a small portion of the population had access to any kind of education, but recent scholarship has focused on the significant shift in roles played by women in the New Christian (Judeo-converso and Hispano-Arab Morisco) communities of Iberia.[22] Even among the marginalized New Christian groups of the Conversos and the Moriscos, information now suggests women's increasingly important roles as protectors of Judaic and Islamic customs and culture. With the public practice of Judaism and Islam banned in the early modern period, those religions increasingly were driven into the home, where women's roles gained new importance. Evidence is mounting that within the home women ensured the maintenance of traditions and beliefs related to food, clothing, and ritual.

For the Hispano-Arabs, the mid-sixteenth-century violence between

Morsicos and Christians led to a reduction in the male population. The rebellion of the Alpujarras (1568–1570) led to the enslavement of some twenty-five thousand Moriscos and the forced relocations of another fifty thousand individuals from Granada. Although 25 percent of the relocated Moriscos died en route, this still left some thirty-eight thousand Moriscos dispersed throughout Spain working in the silk trade, mines, and other industries. The 1589 census revealed a ratio of 35 women to 31 men in the Morisco community and also showed women to be living together in all-female compounds. This is merely some of the data that suggest the ways in which women formed communities and took on new roles within marginalized groups to ensure the survival of families and their cultural traditions in Inquisitional times.[23]

On the other side of the Atlantic, evidence suggests myriad ways in which people mobilized complex strategies for survival. One important example of this complexity can be found in indigenous and mestizo girls' and women's participation in suits related to paternity and ecclesiastical separation, as detailed by Bianca Premo in *Children of the Father King: Youth, Authority, and Legal Minority in Colonial Lima*.[24] Similarly, as Kathryn Burns has detailed in *Colonial Habits: Convents and the Spiritual Economy of Cuzco, Peru,* the positioning of convents as the economic and cultural centers of entire communities provides another way of deciphering women's roles in colonial settings.[25] Finally, studies of Inquisition documents, confessors and their penitents, and the history of science continue to uncover complex interactions between native, African, and European cultures both in the colonial setting and in their impact on the Americas. In particular, substantial evidence shows women of different classes, religions, and ethnicities using Catholic codes of femininity for personal gain or protection.[26] These works confirm that the Atlantic did indeed serve as a bridge, but it also served as a space of contention and negotiation, and as a space in which local particularities held as much or more sway than imperial politics in defining opportunities, relationships, and actions.

In light of what we know about the individuals and groups that traveled through the Atlantic space, we must conceive of people's movement in that space both in terms of obligation and opportunity. And, as the example of Sor Juana's *Enigmas* attests, we have the ability to reconstruct the flow of ideas and objects as a means of deciphering connections among communities and individuals in the broader Iberian Atlantic world. Spanish-Portuguese relations represent one area in which we have failed to trace cultural connections and to do justice to the Iberian aspect of the Atlantic. Until very recently, we primarily have seen discrete studies on Spain, the Spanish empire, and the Luso-Brazilian world.[27] I agree here with Lisa Voigt, who has drawn attention to the possibility of deciphering "the global networks that were not just created by, but that also shaped" the Atlantic world and has called for the incorporation of the inter-imperial, inter-religious, and inter-cultural aspects of that world.[28] When we consider the wide geographical range of the Portuguese empire, it becomes clear just how much of the world we exclude when failing to consider the Portuguese and the entire Lusophone world. It also highlights what many scholars only come to realize after graduate training: that the persistent demarcation between Spain or the Spanish empire as separate from the Lusophone world and the entire Iberian Atlantic make very little intellectual, cultural, or historical sense for the early modern period.

Women's history provides an example of how we also must Iberianize our approaches to understand global networks and intercultural influences on women's lives. For example, women's engagement with empire, nation-building, and Catholic hegemony provides one general understudied arena for our consideration. In a recent bilingual edition of aristocratic writer María de Guevara's *Warnings to the Kings and Advice on Restoring Spain,* Nieves Romero-Díaz positions Guevara (d. 1683) within the political maneuvering of the Spanish courts of the day. Guevara dispenses advice to nobles and the king, including her claims that the ongoing seventeenth-century war against Portugal constituted a crusade against foreigners and "Jews that King Ferdinand expelled from Castile and that Portugal welcomed. But since they are rich and that kingdom is so poor, they mixed with the common people. The consequence is obvious: the war is not against Christians."[29] The overlap of anti-Semitism, xenophobia, classism, and nationalism in Guevara's writing points to the need for more studies on women's engagement with imperial policies and the ways in which women of different classes sought authority.

A complement to Guevara's appropriation of imperialist discourse can be found in a short autobiographical statement written by Bernarda Manuel, a Portuguese merchant-class woman accused of Judaizing by the Spanish Inquisition in 1650. Manuel (c. 1616–?) wrote a twelve-folio memorial in which she detailed her life story and defended her Catholic beliefs and behavior. Like many other Conversos in the seventeenth century, Manuel's family emigrated from the Algarve to southern Spain around 1630. They may have been motivated to take advantage of job opportunities for New Christians that were part of the reforms of Philip IV and his favorite, the Conde-Duque de Olivares, in the 1620s. Alternatively, they may have faced the Inquisition in Portugal and thus sought a safe haven in Spain. The trial record does not provide evidence of Manuel's true religious identity, but numerous details do point to converso lineage and possible religious identification as a Jew. For example, details about her male family members' occupations (her father was a physician and her husband was a cloth trader), their social circumstances as a Portuguese immigrant family in southern Spain, and a planned escape to Italy (where presumably they would have freely practiced Judaism) provide hints of a Crypto-Jewish identity.

Manuel's discourse deploys Catholic ideologies of femininity, including devotion to her husband and family, her compliance with Catholic rituals, and her denunciation of her husband as a failed Christian husband. Drawing on the emphasis on female enclosure and domesticity, for instance, she asserts that she "only left her house to go to mass and to my father's house" and she always attended to her family, even in the face of adversity: "No matter how many problems I had in my household, I always sat at the table to calm my husband and children."[30] The engagement with Catholic hegemony did not prevent Manuel from being sentenced as a Judaizer. She received *cárcel perpetua* (a life sentence), which may have resulted in anything from a few months to a few years of incarceration. For a mother of five children under the age of eleven—including a breast-feeding baby—that may well have been a death sentence.

Guevara and Manuel represent two distinct Iberian perspectives, yet their textual legacies point to a multiplicity of ideological, cultural, and political connections that linked Spain to Portugal in the era. Other women's texts also highlight the links between the two nations. Portuguese-born novella author Leonor de Meneses (1620–1664) wrote in Spanish, as did poet and chronicler Bernarda Ferreira de Lacerda (c. 1595–1644), who was a Discalced Carmelite in Lisbon's San Alberto convent. Lisbon-born playwright Angela de Azevedo (1600–?) served in Philip IV's court and wrote her plays in Spanish, while Dominican nun Violante do Ceo (d.1693) of Lisbon's Monasterio de la Rosa wrote in both Spanish and Portuguese. The linguistic and cultural journeys made by these women across the borders of Spain and Portugal provide strong evidence for Iberian women's literary and cultural communities.

Connections among Luso-Portuguese and Spanish or Spanish American women in the Iberian Atlantic have yet to be explored in a systematic way. Vanda Anastácio's call for a more concerted effort to study the circulation of unpublished materials in Portuguese studies represents a welcome step forward for an Iberian Atlantic literary history, and in particular, the attention to letters, legal documents, and prohibited books that nonetheless crossed the seas promises to add much to our understanding of this little-known arena.[31] Work by Anastácio and other scholars on late eighteenth-century literary academies in Portugal and on women's transatlantic connections in the Luso-Brazilian diaspora also have begun to support the Atlantic nature of the Lusophone literary and cultural world.[32]

Like all of the early modern authors mentioned thus far—including Saint Teresa, Sor Juana, María de Guevara, Bernarda Manuel, and the bilingual and bicultural Portuguese writers—many Portuguese women from within and outside the convent deployed strategies of self-denigration, using tropes that attempted to downplay their deft skill and instead emphasized their status as female authors. In one famous example, the future Marquesa d'Alorna, Leonor de Almeida (1750–1839), wrote in 1806 that she never had any intention of publishing her poems, which she claimed to have written only to soothe her personal pain. As Anastácio has suggested, Almeida only felt authorized to publish work that she deemed to have political and didactic value.[33] This example of self-censorship by the most famous Portuguese female author of the time points to yet another common strategy enacted by women throughout the long early modern period and into modern times. Constrained by dominant ideologies that exhorted women to contain their pride, vanquish their vanity, and limit their interaction with the public sphere, women developed strategies to simultaneously assert authority while also embodying chaste, obedient, self-controlled Catholic femininity.

The examples here point to the reality that women's self-authorization strategies shared commonalities but that they also varied tremendously based on time, place, and personal position. María de Guevara and Leonor de Almeida were privileged aristocrats who used their class status to authorize their incursions into politics and culture. Bernarda Manuel speaks to us only from the Inquisition archives, revealing the strategies that a merchant-class Conversa thought might be useful against the mighty force of the Inquisition. These examples provide a glimpse into the research that remains to be done to forge more connections among women's lives, ideas, and ideologies throughout the early modern Iberian Atlantic.

The field has begun to probe the ways in which gender, class, race, ethnicity, marital status, and other influencing factors on personal and group identity played out in different locales. More work remains to be done. To date, we have a limited understanding of which characteristics of the early modern Atlantic held strong across time and space. The diversity of religious beliefs and ethnic backgrounds of the citizens of the Iberian Atlantic highlights the importance of framing any discussion of the shared Atlantic space in terms of the wide range of experiences people had of Inquisitional culture and the emerging mercantilist economic order. Simultaneously, we must recognize that our access to different women's lives and stories is defined to a large extent by the available sources.

Having built upon the singular example of Sor Juana, whose brilliant work clearly grew out of an intimate engagement with American and European ideas, and upon our understanding of the ever influential Teresa of Avila, we now have knowledge of multilingual female writers and of women who forged literary and cultural spaces for expression of their concerns. We also have begun to learn more about nuns and others who crossed the seas in the name of religious expansion or personal opportunity. We are developing better tools to examine women's engagement with dominant gender codes and the manipulation of those codes to their own advantage. Furthermore, a promising area of research relates to women's interaction with empire, at times upholding patriarchal culture, and at others, undermining it.

Moving forward in the twenty-first century, scholars must resist the urge to see women travelers, writers, and rebels as exceptions. Similarly, women who worked to expand imperial policies and who expressed what today we read as classist, elitist, or even racist ideologies must be understood within their particular cultural contexts. Instead, the field would benefit from rigorous comparative analyses of women's strategies of self-authorization, their interactions with patriarchal culture, and the clues they provide in local contexts about an Atlantic diaspora in which the circulation of ideas, objects, and people altered and perhaps sometimes forged commonalities among otherwise disparate lives. We also must learn from our colleagues in early American and British studies—as seen in Heidi Brayman Hackel and Catherine E. Kelly's *Reading Women: Liter-*

acy, Authorship, and Culture in the Atlantic World, 1500–1800—who have looked to samplers and other items from women's material culture for evidence of women's education and literacy in the absence of traditional written texts.[34]

By expanding the discrete fields of Iberian and Latin American studies to encompass the exchange and mutual impact of people, objects, and ideas throughout the Iberian Atlantic, scholars can decipher the ways in which gender codes, patriarchal norms, and multicultural identities informed each other to create the fabric of what today we recognize as a richly diverse and complex Atlantic diaspora. This shift will continue to allow scholars to focus on deciphering specificity and simultaneously identify commonalities among and between women and men, Europeans and Americans, slave and free, New Christians and Old, and the Lusophone and Hispanophone worlds. The ways in which gender norms on one continent or in one community shaped people across the Atlantic remain to be traced and promise to open a new field of inquiry for those interested in sexual, religious, and cultural practices, to name just a few ways in which the Atlantic framework will enrich the historiography. With this framework, we will be able to deepen our knowledge of women's history in the early modern period and lay the groundwork for a more nuanced understanding of the individuals, networks, and communities that comprised the Iberian Atlantic sphere.

NOTES

1. The bibliography on women in Spain, Portugal, and Latin America is too vast to detail here. Electa Arenal and Stacey Schlau's *Untold Sisters: Hispanic Nuns in Their Own Works*, with translations by Amanda Powell (Albuquerque: Univ. of New Mexico Press, 1989), was one of the first publications to bring Iberian and Ibero-American women together for consideration.

2. Daniella Kostroun and I situate women's history within Atlantic studies in the introduction to *Women, Religion, and the Atlantic World (1600–1800)* (Toronto: Univ. of Toronto Press, 2009), 3–27. For an overview of Atlantic studies today, see Bernard Bailyn, *Atlantic History: Concepts and Contours* (Cambridge: Harvard Univ. Press, 2005); Jorge Cañizares-Esguerra and Erik Seeman, eds., *The Atlantic in Global History* (New York: Prentice Hall, 2006); Donna Gabbacia, "A Long Atlantic in a Wider World," *Atlantic Studies: Literary, Cultural, and Historical Perspectives* 1, no. 1 (2004): 1–27; Jack P. Greene and Philip D. Morgan, *Atlantic History: A Critical Appraisal* (Oxford: Oxford Univ. Press, 2009); William O'Reilly, "Genealogies of Atlantic History," *Atlantic Studies* 1, no. 1 (2004): 66–84; and Carla Rahn Philips, "Twenty Million People United by an Ocean: Spain and the Atlantic World Beyond the Renaissance," *Renaissance Quarterly* 62, no. 1 (2009): 27–40.

3. J. H. Elliott, "Afterword: Atlantic History: A Circumnavigation," in *The British Atlantic*

World, 1500–1800, ed. David Armitage and Michael J. Braddick, 233–249, 239 (New York: Palgrave Macmillan, 2002).

4. Among the important studies that form part of the evolution of Sor Juana studies toward a broader transatlantic context are: Arenal and Schlau, *Untold Sisters*; Elías Trabulse, "El universo científico de Sor Juana Inés de la Cruz," *Colonial Latin American Review* 4, no. 2 (1995): 41–50; and Stephanie Merrim, *Early Modern Women's Writing and Sor Juana Inés de la Cruz* (Nashville: Vanderbilt Univ. Press, 1999).

5. Juana Inés de la Cruz (Sor), *La respuesta / The Answer,* ed. and trans. Electa Arenal and Amanda Powell (New York: The Feminist Press, City University of New York, 1994).

6. For a discussion of the *Enigmas* and their relationship to a broader female literary academy, see Stephanie L. Kirk, chapter five of *Convent Life in Colonial Mexico: A Tale of Two Communities* (Gainesville: Univ. Press of Florida, 2007). For the text itself, see Juana Inés de la Cruz (Sor), *Enigmas ofrecidos a la Casa del Placer,* ed. Antonio Alatorre (Mexico City: Colegio de Mexico, 1995).

7. The most probing work on Sor Juana's transnational connections is Merrim's *Early Modern Women's Writing and Sor Juana Inés de la Cruz*. For more about Sor Juana with respect to women's writing communities, see Lisa Vollendorf, "Across the Atlantic: Sor Juana, *La respuesta,* and the Hispanic Women's Canon," in *Approaches to Teaching Sor Juana Inés de la Cruz,* ed. Emilie Bergmann and Stacey Schlau, 95–102 (New York: Publications of the Modern Language Association, 2007).

8. Peter Boyd-Bowman's *Indice geobiográfico de cuarenta mil pobladores Españoles de América en el siglo XVI* (Bogotá: Instituto Caro y Cuervo, 1964) and *Patterns of Spanish Emigration to the New World (1493–1580)* (Buffalo: Council on International Studies, State University of New York at Buffalo, 1973) have a wealth of information about immigrants, as does Pilar Gonzalbo Aizpuru and Berta Ares Queija's *Las mujeres en la construcción de las sociedades iberoamericanas* (Seville: Consejo Superior de Investigaciones Científicas, Escuela de Estudios Hispano-Americanos; México: Colegio de México, Centro de Estudios Históricos, 2004).

9. Sarah E. Owens notes that at least five groups of cloistered nuns were sent to the New World to found convents between 1600–1800 (Sarah E. Owens, ed. and trans., *Journey of Five Capuchin Nuns,* by Madre María Rosa, The Other Voice in Early Modern Europe Series [Toronto: Iter and Centre for Reformation and Renaissance Studies, 2009], 1–20). Jacqueline Holler examines the complex response to the *beatas* who were sent to New Spain in *Escogidas Plantas: Nuns and Beatas in Mexico City, 1531–1601* (New York: Columbia Univ. Press, 2002).

10. Owens, ed., *Journey of Five Capuchin Nuns.*

11. For a gender analysis of Jesuit travel in the Atlantic and the Pacific, see J. Michelle Molina and Ulrike Strasser, "Missionary Men and the Global Currency of Female Sanctity," in Kostroun and Vollendorf, eds., *Women, Religion, and the Atlantic World,* 233–267.

12. María de Lourdes Aguilar Salas, "Imagen de las Indias en cartas escritas por mujeres en el siglo XVI," in *La voz del silencio. Tomo I, Fuentes directas para la historia de las mujeres (siglos VII–XVIII),* ed. Cristina Segura Graíño, 157–169 (Granada: Asociación Al-Mudayna, 1992).

13. Teresa de Jesús (Santa), *Correspondencia de Santa Teresa de Jesús,* Biblioteca Nacional de España, Manuscript 12764, siglo XVII, fol. 52. The translation is mine.

14. Pedro M. Cátedra and Anastasio Rojo, *Bibliotecas y lecturas de mujeres. Siglo XVI* (Salamanca: Instituto de Historia del Libro y de la Lectura, 2004), 39–44, 59–63. For economic and legal activity, see Mary Elizabeth Perry, *Gender and Disorder in Early Modern Seville*

(Princeton: Princeton Univ. Press, 1990), 14–32. For literacy, see Anne J. Cruz and Rosilie Hernández, eds., *Women's Literacy in Early Modern Spain and the New World* (Burlington, Vt.: Ashgate, 2011), and Nieves Baranda Leturio, *Cortejo a lo prohibido. Lectoras y escritoras en la Edad Moderna* (Madrid: Arco Libros, 2006), 17–33. For girls' schooling, see Elizabeth Howe, *Education and Women in the Early Modern Hispanic World* (Aldershot, England: Ashgate, 2008), 91–127.

15. Fernando J. Bouza Alvarez provides a fine overview of issues related to literacy and communication in *Communication, Knowledge, and Memory in Early Modern Spain* (Philadelphia: Univ. of Pennsylvania Press, 2004).

16. Cátedra and Rojo, *Bibliotecas y lecturas de mujeres. Siglo XVI*, 39–44. Also see Baranda Leturio, *Cortejo a lo prohibido*, 17–33.

17. See, for example, Howe, *Education and Women in the Early Modern Hispanic World*; Perry, *Gender and Disorder in Early Modern Seville*; Allyson Poska, *Regulating the People: The Catholic Reformation in Seventeenth-Century Spain* (Boston: Brill, 1998), and Allyson Poska, *Women and Authority in Early Modern Spain: The Peasants of Galicia* (Oxford: Oxford Univ. Press, 2005); Magdalena Sánchez, *The Empress, the Queen, and the Nun: Women and Power at the Court of Philip III of Spain* (Baltimore: Johns Hopkins Univ. Press, 1998); Lisa Vollendorf, *The Lives of Women: A New History of Inquisitional Spain* (Nashville: Vanderbilt Univ. Press, 2005); and Alison P. Weber, *Teresa of Avila and the Rhetoric of Femininity* (Princeton: Princeton Univ. Press, 1990). A bibliography on women in Converso and Hispano-Arab communities appears in note 22.

18. See, for example, Kathryn Burns, *Colonial Habits: Convents and the Spiritual Economy of Cuzco, Peru* (Durham: Duke Univ. Press, 1999); Kimberly Gauderman, *Women's Lives in Colonial Quito: Gender, Law, and Economy in Spanish America* (Austin: Univ. of Texas Press, 2003); Nora E. Jaffary, ed., *Gender, Race, and Religion in the Colonization of the Americas* (Aldershot, England: Ashgate, 2007); Asunción Lavrin, ed., *Sexuality and Marriage in Colonial Latin America* (Lincoln: Univ. of Nebraska Press, 1989); Jane Mangan, *Trading Roles: Gender, Ethnicity, and the Urban Economy, Potosí, 1545–1700* (Durham: Duke Univ. Press, 2005); and María Elena Martínez, *Genealogical Fictions: Limpieza de Sangre, Religion, and Gender in Colonial Mexico* (Stanford: Stanford Univ. Press, 2008).

19. See, for example, Margaret Chowning, *Rebellious Nuns: A Troubled History of a Mexican Convent (1752–1863)* (New York: Oxford Univ. Press, 2006); Holler, *Escogidas Plantas*; Kristine Ibsen, *Women's Spiritual Autobiography in Colonial Spanish America* (Gainesville: Univ. Press of Florida, 1999); Stephanie Kirk, *Convent Life in Colonial Mexico*; Stephanie Kirk and Sarah Rivett, "Religious Transformations in the Early Modern Americas," *Early American Literature* 45, no. 1 (2010): 61–91; Asunción Lavrin, *Brides of Christ: Conventual Life in Colonial Mexico* (Stanford: Stanford Univ. Press, 2008); Asunción Lavrin and Rosalva Loreto López, *Monjas y beatas: la escritura femenina en la espiritualidad barroca novohispana: siglos XVII y XVIII* (Mexico City: Archivo General de la Nación / Universidad de las Américas, 2002); Elizabeth A. Lehfeldt, *Religious Women in Golden Age Spain: The Permeable Cloister* (Aldershot, Hants, England: Ashgate, 2005).

20. Alison Weber, "Locating Holiness in Early Modern Spain: Convents, Caves, and Houses," in *Structures and Subjectivities: Attending to Early Modern Women*, ed. Joan E. Harman and Adele Seeff, 50 (Newark: Univ. of Delaware Press, 2007).

21. Ibid., 51.

22. For women in converso culture, see Renée Levine Melammed, *A Question of Identity: Iberian Conversos in Historical Perspective* (Oxford: Oxford Univ. Press, 2004), 40, 142–144; Gretchen Starr-LeBeau, *In the Shadow of the Virgin: Inquisitors, Friars, and Conversos in*

Guadalupe, Spain (Princeton: Princeton Univ. Press, 2003); and Stacey Schlau, "A Judaizing 'Old Christian' Woman and the Mexican Inquisition: The 'Unusual' Case of María de Zárate," in Kostroun and Vollendorf, *Women, Religion, and the Atlantic World*, 223–251; and Richard L. Kagan and Phillip D. Morgan, eds., *Atlantic Diasporas: Jews, Conversos, and Crypto-Jews in the Age of Mercantilism, 1500–1800* (Baltimore: Johns Hopkins Univ. Press, 2009). On women in Morisco culture, see Mary Elizabeth Perry, *The Handless Maiden: Moriscos and the Politics of Religion in Early Modern Spain* (Princeton: Princeton Univ. Press, 2005).

23. Information on women in Morisco culture taken from Perry, *The Handless Maiden*, 93–107, 122–126.

24. Bianca Premo, *Children of the Father King: Youth, Authority, and Legal Minority in Colonial Lima* (Chapel Hill: Univ. of North Carolina Press, 2005).

25. See Burns, *Colonial Habits*. For similar research on Spain, see Lehfeldt, *Religious Women in Golden Age Spain*.

26. Some examples include: Jodi Bilinkoff, *Related Lives: Confessors and Their Female Penitents, 1450–1750* (Ithaca: Cornell Univ. Press, 2005); Jorge Cañizares-Esguerra, *How to Write the History of the New World* (Stanford: Stanford Univ. Press, 2002); Mary E. Giles, ed., *Women in the Inquisition: Spain and the New World* (Baltimore: Johns Hopkins Univ. Press, 1999), and Hugh Glenn Cagle's essay in the present volume.

27. Cañizares-Esguerra has been among the most vocal proponents of Iberianizing Atlantic studies. See his *Puritan Conquistadors: Iberianizing the Atlantic, 1550–1700* (Stanford: Stanford Univ. Press, 2006), 114.

28. Lisa Voigt, "Hispanism and the Cultural Geography of the Early Modern Atlantic," *Renaissance Quarterly* 62, no. 1 (2009): 40–49. For a model of how to better integrate European and "New World" women's history, see Susan E. Dinan and Debra Meyers, eds., *Women and Religion in Old and New Worlds* (New York: Routledge, 2001).

29. María de Guevara, quoted in *Warnings to the Kings and Advice on Restoring Spain: A Bilingual Edition*, ed. and trans. Nieves Romero-Díaz (Chicago: Univ. of Chicago Press, 2007), 27.

30. Manuel citation from Vollendorf, *The Lives of Women*, 42–43.

31. Vanda Anastácio, "'Mulheres varonis e interesses domésticos': Reflexões acerca do discurso produzido pela História Literária acerca das mulheres escritoras da viragem do século XVIII para o século XIX," *Cartographies: Mélanges offerts à Maria Alzira Seixo* (Lisbon: Universidade Aberta, 2005). Citation is from page 5 of online version: www.vanda-anastacio.at/articles/1_Mulheres%20varonis_locked.pdf. Also see Maria de Deus Manso, "The 'Other Woman' in the Overseas Space: The Case of Portuguese India," in *Eastwards / Westwards: Which Direction for Gender Studies in the Twenty-First Century?* ed. Clara Sarmento, 131–142 (Newcastle: Cambridge Scholars, 2007).

32. See, for example, Vanda Anastácio, "The Eighteenth Century," in *A Companion to Portuguese Literature*, ed. Stephen Parkinson, Cláudia Pazos Alonso, and T. F. Earle, 103–108 (London: Tamesis, 2009).

33. Vanda Anastácio, "Cherchez la femme: À propos d'une forme de sociabilité litteraire a Lisbonne a la fim du XVIIeme siècle," in *Arquivos do Centro Cultural Português*, vol. 49 (Paris: Centre Culturel C. Gulbenkian, 2005), 93–101, 93–94.

34. Heidi Brayman Hackel and Catherine E. Kelly, eds., *Reading Women: Literacy, Authorship, and Culture in the Atlantic World, 1500–1800* (Philadelphia: Univ. of Pennsylvania Press, 2008).

WORKS CITED

Aguilar Salas, María de Lourdes. "Imagen de las Indias en cartas escritas por mujeres en el siglo XVI." In *La voz del silencio. Tomo I. Fuentes directas para la historia de las mujeres (siglos VII–XVIII)*, edited by Cristina Segura Graiño, 157–169. Granada: Asociación Al-Mudayna, 1992.

Anastácio, Vanda. "Cherchez la femme: À propos d'une forme de sociabilité litteraire a Lisbonne a la fim du XVIIeme siècle." In *Arquivos do Centro Cultural Português*, special issue on *Sociabilités intellectuelles XVI–XX siècles*. Vol. 49, 93–101. Paris: Centre Culturel C. Gulbenkian, 2005.

———. "The Eighteenth Century." In *A Companion to Portuguese Literature*, edited by Stephen Parkinson, Cláudia Pazos Alonso, and T. F. Earle, 103–108. London: Tamesis, 2009.

———. "'Mulheres varonis e interesses domésticos': Reflexões acerca do discurso produzido pela História Literária acerca das mulheres escritoras da viragem do século XVIII para o século XIX." In *Cartographies: Mélanges offerts à Maria Alzira Seixo*. Lisbon: Universidade Aberta, 2005. www.vanda-anastacio.at/articles/1_Mulheres%20varonis_locked.pdf. Accessed 1 November 2011.

Arenal, Electa, and Stacey Schlau. *Untold Sisters: Hispanic Nuns in Their Own Works,* 2nd ed. Translated by Amanda Powell. Albuquerque: Univ. of New Mexico Press, 2009.

Bailyn, Bernard. *Atlantic History: Concepts and Contours.* Cambridge: Harvard Univ. Press, 2005.

Baranda Leturio, Nieves. *Cortejo a lo prohibido. Lectoras y escritoras en la Edad Moderna.* Madrid: Arco Libros, 2006.

Bilinkoff, Jodi. *Related Lives: Confessors and Their Female Penitents, 1450–1750.* Ithaca: Cornell Univ. Press, 2005.

Bouza Alvarez, Fernando J. *Communication, Knowledge, and Memory in Early Modern Spain.* Philadelphia: Univ. of Pennsylvania Press, 2004.

Boyd-Bowman, Peter. *Indice geobiográfico de cuarenta mil pobladores Españoles de América en el siglo XVI.* Bogotá: Instituto Caro y Cuervo, 1964.

———. *Patterns of Spanish Emigration to the New World (1493–1580).* Buffalo: Council on International Studies, State University of New York at Buffalo, 1973.

Brayman Hackel, Heidi, and Catherine E. Kelly, eds. *Reading Women: Literacy, Authorship, and Culture in the Atlantic World, 1500–1800.* Philadelphia: Univ. of Pennsylvania Press, 2008.

Burns, Kathryn. *Colonial Habits: Convents and the Spiritual Economy of Cuzco, Peru.* Durham: Duke Univ. Press, 1999.

Cañizares-Esguerra, Jorge. *How to Write the History of the New World.* Stanford: Stanford Univ. Press, 2002.

———. *Puritan Conquistadors: Iberianizing the Atlantic, 1550–1700.* Stanford: Stanford Univ. Press, 2006.
Cañizares-Esguerra, Jorge, and Erik Seeman, eds. *The Atlantic in Global History.* New York: Prentice Hall, 2006.
Cátedra, Pedro M., and Anastasio Rojo. *Bibliotecas y lecturas de mujeres. Siglo XVI.* Salamanca: Instituto de Historia del Libro y de la Lectura, 2004.
Chowning, Margaret. *Rebellious Nuns: A Troubled History of a Mexican Convent (1752–1863).* New York: Oxford Univ. Press, 2006.
Cruz, Anne J., and Rosilie Hernández, eds. *Women's Literacy in Early Modern Spain and the New World.* Burlington, Vt.: Ashgate, 2011.
Deus Manso, Maria de. "The 'Other Woman' in the Overseas Space: The Case of Portuguese India." In *Eastwards / Westwards: Which Direction for Gender Studies in the Twenty-First Century?* edited by Clara Sarmento, 131–142. Newcastle: Cambridge Scholars, 2007.
Dinan, Susan E., and Debra Meyers, eds. *Women and Religion in Old and New Worlds.* New York: Routledge, 2001.
Elliott, J. H. "Afterword: Atlantic History: A Circumnavigation." In *The British Atlantic World, 1500–1800,* edited by David Armitage and Michael J. Braddick, 233–249. New York: Palgrave Macmillan, 2002.
Gabbacia, Donna. "A Long Atlantic in a Wider World." *Atlantic Studies: Literary, Cultural, and Historical Perspectives* 1, no. 1 (2004): 1–27.
Gauderman, Kimberly. *Women's Lives in Colonial Quito: Gender, Law, and Economy in Spanish America.* Austin: Univ. of Texas Press, 2003.
Giles, Mary E., ed. *Women in the Inquisition: Spain and the New World.* Baltimore: Johns Hopkins Univ. Press, 1999.
Gonzalbo Aizpuru, Pilar, and Berta Ares Queija, coordinators. *Las mujeres en la construcción de las sociedades iberoamericanas.* Seville: Consejo Superior de Investigaciones Científicas, Escuela de Estudios Hispano-Americanos; México: Colegio de México, Centro de Estudios Históricos, 2004.
Greene, Jack P., and Philip D. Morgan, eds. *Atlantic History: A Critical Appraisal.* Oxford: Oxford Univ. Press, 2009.
Guevara, María de. *Warnings to the Kings and Advice on Restoring Spain: A Bilingual Edition.* Edited and translated by Nieves Romero-Díaz. Chicago: Univ. of Chicago Press, 2007.
Holler, Jacqueline. *Escogidas Plantas: Nuns and Beatas in Mexico City, 1531–1601.* New York: Columbia Univ. Press, 2002.
Howe, Elizabeth. *Education and Women in the Early Modern Hispanic World.* Aldershot, England: Ashgate, 2008.
Ibsen, Kristine. *Women's Spiritual Autobiography in Colonial Spanish America.* Gainesville: Univ. Press of Florida, 1999.
Jaffary, Nora E., ed. *Gender, Race, and Religion in the Colonization of the Americas.* Aldershot, England: Ashgate, 2007.

Juana Inés de la Cruz (Sor). *Enigmas ofrecidos a la Casa del Placer*. Edited by Antonio Alatorre. Mexico City: Colegio de Mexico, 1995.

———. *La respuesta / The Answer*. Edited and translated by Electa Arenal and Amanda Powell. New York: The Feminist Press, City University of New York, 1994.

Kagan, Richard L., and Phillip D. Morgan, eds. *Atlantic Diasporas: Jews, Conversos, and Crypto-Jews in the Age of Mercantilism, 1500–1800*. Baltimore: Johns Hopkins Univ. Press, 2009.

Kirk, Stephanie. *Convent Life in Colonial Mexico: A Tale of Two Communities*. Gainesville: Univ. Press of Florida, 2007.

Kirk, Stephanie, and Sarah Rivett. "Religious Transformations in the Early Modern Americas," *Early American Literature* 45, no. 1 (2010): 61–91.

Kostroun, Daniella, and Lisa Vollendorf, eds. Introduction to *Women, Religion, and the Atlantic World (1600–1800)*, 3–27. Toronto: Univ. of Toronto Press, 2009.

Lavrin, Asunción. *Brides of Christ. Conventual Life in Colonial Mexico*. Stanford: Stanford Univ. Press, 2008.

———, ed. *Sexuality and Marriage in Colonial Latin America*. Lincoln: Univ. of Nebraska Press, 1989.

Lavrin, Asunción, and Rosalva Loreto López. *Monjas y beatas: la escritura femenina en la espiritualidad barroca novohispana: siglos XVII y XVIII*. Mexico City: Archivo General de la Nación / Universidad de las Américas, 2002.

Lehfeldt, Elizabeth A. *Religious Women in Golden Age Spain: The Permeable Cloister*. Women and Gender in the Early Modern World. Aldershot, Hants, England: Ashgate, 2005.

Mangan, Jane. *Trading Roles: Gender, Ethnicity, and the Urban Economy, Potosí, 1545–1700*. Durham: Duke Univ. Press, 2005.

Martínez, María Elena. *Genealogical Fictions: Limpieza de Sangre, Religion, and Gender in Colonial Mexico*. Stanford: Stanford Univ. Press, 2008.

Melammed, Renée Levine. *A Question of Identity: Iberian Conversos in Historical Perspective*. Oxford: Oxford Univ. Press, 2004.

Merrim, Stephanie. *Early Modern Women's Writing and Sor Juana Inés de la Cruz*. Nashville: Vanderbilt Univ. Press, 1999.

Molina, J. Michelle, and Ulrike Strasser. "Missionary Men and the Global Currency of Female Sanctity." In *Women, Religion, and the Atlantic World (1600–1800)*, edited by Daniela Kostroun and Lisa Vollendorf, 233–267. Toronto: Univ. of Toronto Press, 2009.

O'Reilly, William. "Genealogies of Atlantic History." *Atlantic Studies* 1, no. 1 (2004): 66–84.

Owens, Sarah E., ed. and trans. *Journey of Five Capuchin Nuns*, by Madre María Rosa. The Other Voice in Early Modern Europe Series. Toronto: Iter and Centre for Reformation and Renaissance Studies, 2009.

Perry, Mary Elizabeth. *Gender and Disorder in Early Modern Seville*. Princeton: Princeton Univ. Press. 1990.

———. *The Handless Maiden: Moriscos and the Politics of Religion in Early Modern Spain*. Princeton: Princeton Univ. Press, 2005.

Philips, Carla Rahn. "Twenty Million People United by an Ocean: Spain and the Atlantic World Beyond the Renaissance." *Renaissance Quarterly* 62, no. 1 (2009): 27–40.

Poska, Allyson. *Regulating the People: The Catholic Reformation in Seventeenth-Century Spain*. Boston: Brill, 1998.

———. *Women and Authority in Early Modern Spain: The Peasants of Galicia*. Oxford: Oxford Univ. Press, 2005.

Premo, Bianca. *Children of the Father King: Youth, Authority, and Legal Minority in Colonial Lima*. Chapel Hill: Univ. of North Carolina Press, 2005.

Sánchez, Magdalena. *The Empress, the Queen, and the Nun: Women and Power at the Court of Philip III of Spain*. Baltimore: Johns Hopkins Univ. Press, 1998.

Schlau, Stacey. "A Judaizing 'Old Christian' Woman and the Mexican Inquisition: The 'Unusual' Case of María de Zárate." In *Women, Religion, and the Atlantic World (1600–1800)*, edited by Daniela Kostroun and Lisa Vollendorf, 223–251. Toronto: Univ. of Toronto Press, 2009.

Starr-LeBeau, Gretchen. *In the Shadow of the Virgin: Inquisitors, Friars, and Conversos in Guadalupe, Spain*. Princeton: Princeton Univ. Press, 2003.

Teresa de Jesús (Santa). *Correspondencia de Santa Teresa de Jesús*. No date. Biblioteca Nacional de España, Manuscript 12764, siglo XVII.

Trabulse, Elías. "El universo científico de Sor Juana Inés de la Cruz." *Colonial Latin American Review* 4, no. 2 (1995): 41–50.

Voigt, Lisa. "Hispanism and the Cultural Geography of the Early Modern Atlantic." *Renaissance Quarterly* 62, no. 1 (2009): 40–49.

Vollendorf, Lisa "Across the Atlantic: Sor Juana, *La respuesta*, and the Hispanic Women's Canon." In *Approaches to Teaching Sor Juana Inés de la Cruz*, edited by Emilie Bergmann and Stacey Schlau, 95–102. New York: Publications of the Modern Language Association, 2007.

———. *The Lives of Women: A New History of Inquisitional Spain*. Nashville: Vanderbilt Univ. Press, 2005.

Weber, Alison. "Locating Holiness in Early Modern Spain: Convents, Caves, and Houses." In *Structures and Subjectivities: Attending to Early Modern Women*, edited by Joan E. Harman and Adele Seeff, 50–74. Newark: Univ. of Delaware Press, 2007.

———. *Teresa of Avila and the Rhetoric of Femininity*. Princeton: Princeton Univ. Press, 1990.

2

An Ocean Apart

Reframing Gender in the Spanish Empire

ALLYSON M. POSKA

During the early modern period, the evolution of the Atlantic Ocean from the perceived end of the known world to the opening to a new global empire transformed the lives of women. Thousands of peninsular women felt the Atlantic's presence as their husbands migrated, never to return; indigenous women experienced the impact of the Atlantic through the trauma of conquest; women on the African coast watched in agony as their loved ones were captured, enslaved, and shipped to ports on the other side of the ocean. Finally, although many women in the Spanish empire never left their native villages and had little or no direct connection to Spain's far flung possessions, for others, the Spanish empire was not a hypothetical construct but an entity that they experienced firsthand—whether it was by crossing the Atlantic from Seville to Cartagena or by moving from Havana to Buenos Aires. However, we know very little about the Atlantic's impact on women's experience and gender norms in the empire. From a gendered perspective, it is unclear whether the Atlantic Ocean linked Spain to its American colonies or if it acted as a cultural divide, separating two worlds that had only tenuous connections to one another.

The life of one young woman provides some insight into how women may have experienced gender expectations differently as they moved from place to place around the Iberian Atlantic. In 1778, thirteen-year-old Josefa left her tiny native village of Santa Eulalia Chamin near the Atlantic coast in Galicia.[1] Chamin was more or less like other rural farming villages in northern Spain, where men and women worked side by side growing mostly wheat, corn, and an array of vegetables.[2] Josefa began her travels in response to an edict issued by the Crown calling for volunteers to come to the port at La Coruña and journey at the monarchy's expense to the Rio de la Plata as part of an imperial project to colonize Patagonia.[3] She (or her family on her behalf) made the decision to emigrate very quickly. The royal decree went out on September 19, and within two months she left Chamin in the company of her uncle and his wife, their two young girls, Joaquina and Josefa, and her uncle's mother-in-law. Although Galicia traditionally had high rates of migration, it is impossible to know exactly why the family decided to leave. The edict called for only the poorest of Galicia's population, so maybe the family had faced some hardship that left them in financial or personal distress, or maybe the region's emphasis on partible inheritance left Josefa's uncle with a plot too small to feed his growing family.[4] Presumably, Josefa accompanied them to care for her young cousins, who were only two and a half and five years old.

After making the relatively short (seventeen kilometer) journey up the coast, the family arrived in the bustling city of La Coruña, where Josefa spent a month or two waiting for the ship to depart. If Josefa had not seen the city before, it would have been quite a revelation and very different than the sleepy village of her childhood. She would have been surprised by the size and the busy, cosmopolitan nature of the port.[5] From a gendered perspective, as she and her relatives wandered around the city, she would have found that the possibilities for women were greater than those she would have known at home. Unlike Chamin, where the sex ratio was relatively balanced, the city had a substantial excess of women (1.15 women for every man) and 16 percent of its households were headed by women.[6] In fact, as she walked the streets, she probably would have noticed that the city was teeming with young women who had journeyed from their tiny villages in search of work as domestic servants.[7] Women ran boarding houses, owned their own shops, sold fruit and fish in the public market, and worked in a variety of professions, including bakers and cloth makers.[8] Although hardworking women were the norm in farming villages, the extent of women's engagement in the port city's economy may have been eye opening for this rural child.

In late December 1778, Josefa's adventure began in earnest, as the family set sail for the Americas on the *Nuestra Señora de los Dolores* along with 140 other colonists. During the crossing, two adults and three children died, including her uncle's mother-in-law. Yet, all in all, it was a relatively easy crossing and after approximately four months at sea, in early April, they all arrived safely at the port of Montevideo.[9]

Shortly after arriving in the Rio de la Plata, authorities decided to terminate their plans to colonize Patagonia. The problem was that the outposts in Patagonia had not yet been completed, as an outbreak of scurvy and mutinous soldiers held up construction.[10] Unable to decide what to do with the colonizers, authorities held the family and the rest of the passengers in Montevideo for the next year and a half. Although the monarchy provided the family with housing, food, and one *real* a day, the family was not allowed to leave the city and other colonizers complained regularly about the living conditions. Indeed, Josefa and her relations suffered greatly during those months, as the little girls died within two weeks of one another in January of 1780.[11]

From a gendered perspective, Montevideo must have also been a new experience for Josefa. Unlike La Coruña, with its excess of women, the relatively new town was quite the frontier outpost, with 946 single men to only 175 single women.[12] Young women were highly sought after, but Josefa chose not to take that route and marry upon arrival (as some of her colonizer peers had done) despite the fact that she was, according to American standards, of marriageable age.[13]

Eventually, royal officials moved Josefa, her uncle, and her aunt to the military outpost at Luján, outside of Buenos Aires, hoping that the settlers would help secure the contested territories against Portuguese incursions and bands of unconquered natives. She remained in Luján for a while, during which time her aunt bore two more children.[14] She lived among other colonizers from northern Spain, a few Spaniards who had married into colonizing families, some indigenous residents, some African slaves, and some soldiers. At this point, she was living in the multiracial Americas, exposed to an entirely new array of gendered hierarchies and expectations.

Josefa then traveled to Buenos Aires, where in 1786 (at the age of twenty-one) she married a man named Antonio Gómez.[15] Buenos Aires had much in common with La Coruña.[16] Both were port cities at the peak of late colonial trade, and closely connected, as La Coruña had been opened up to direct trade with the Rio de la Plata in 1767. Buenos Aires also had an excess of women,[17] and about 15 percent of its households were headed by women.[18] But, certainly, her life was not going to be the same in Buenos Aires as it would have been had she remained in Galicia. When she married at the age of twenty-one, she was older than most brides in Buenos Aires, but about six years younger than she likely would have married had she remained in Chamin.[19] Maybe she was pregnant. She was just about as likely to bear a child out of wedlock in the Rio de la Plata as she would have been at home in Galicia, but much less so than she would have been in other parts of Latin America where illegitimacy rates were particularly high.[20] In Galicia, she would have worked the land alongside her siblings. In Buenos Aires, she may have purchased a slave to help her in her work or taken in an indigenous girl to help her with her chores. Josefa then disappears from the historical record.

From a demographic perspective, it is clear that much changed for Josefa over the course of her travels. Expectations about marriage and female sexuality differed significantly at each stage of her adventures. However, it is less evident how she experienced those changes in expectations. As she moved from place to place, was she struck by the differences or comforted by the similarities? Did she struggle to maintain the traditional ways of her home village or did she easily adapt to new social norms?

Traditionally, historiography has formulated the Spanish empire as a cohesive entity in terms of gender norms. It has argued that "Spanish" gender norms centered on female chastity transcended the cultural, class, and racial divisions that marked the places that Josefa lived on both sides of the Atlantic.[21] As articulated in the prescriptive literature of the period, women derived their honor from their chastity and men derived theirs from maintaining the chastity of the women in their care. Loss of honor led to family shame and ostracism.[22]

However, recent scholarship indicates that few Spanish women acquiesced to these rigid social and sexual expectations. Rather than some ideal of female chastity that constrained all women's behavior, the research indicates that regional and class differences among Spaniards were critical in establishing expectations for women's activity. Women in central and southern Spain were more likely to conform to the constrained sexual expectations of the honor code than their counterparts in the north, where illegitimacy rates were high, women married late, if at all, and inheritance patterns often favored women.[23] While aristocratic women were expected to remain chaste (although they regularly did not), lower-class women could maintain their honor through hard work, honesty, and self-reliance, their chastity notwithstanding. In fact, peninsular scholars have worked hard to refine their understandings of female honor. Rather than a defining set of behaviors for women, scholars have moved toward a conceptualization of honor as a rhetorical strategy with multiple meanings.[24] So, from an Iberian perspective, there is nothing that scholars any longer refer to as early modern "Spanish" gender norms.

The emphasis on constrained female sexuality does not accurately describe the gendered context on the other side of the Atlantic either. Demographic data indicate that most colonial women, like their peninsular counterparts, demonstrated less concern for their chastity than is typically presumed. Across the Americas, illegitimacy rates were considerably higher than on the peninsula, even among Spanish women, and concubinage was common.[25] The other essays in this collection reveal how female chastity was not necessarily privileged above other factors in many women's experiences. In Ida Altman's essay, the earliest Spanish settlements on Hispaniola included Spanish women who were prostitutes and mistresses of prominent men. Carla Gerona reveals how, three centuries later, women on the Texas frontier engaged in a variety of relationships outside of marriage despite the threat of punishment from local officials. As was true of their peninsular counterparts, colonial women may have understood and strategically employed the rhetoric of honor, but their lives did not conform to its ideals. Thus, there is little evidence to indicate that any type of "Spanish" gender norms focused on the control of female sexuality completely dominated women's lives in either Spain or in colonial Spanish America.

So, if control of female sexuality was not the critical factor in determining Josefa's gendered experience as she moved from town to city and metropole to colony, it is important to consider other possible factors that may have defined women's experience and whether any common gender norms even existed in the Spanish empire. However, in order to do that research, scholars must work to transcend the historiographic divide between peninsular and Latin American historians. Eliga Gould has recently argued that "it is difficult if not impossible to separate the entangled (and entangling) histories of colonial peripheries from the metropolitan histories of which they are an integral part."[26] However, until recently, the histories of Spain and its empire were anything but "entangled." In fact, the historiographies of Spain and its colonies have followed completely different trajectories. On one side of the Atlantic, since at least the 1970s, colonial Latin Americanists have formulated their work around a paradigm that privileges the distinctiveness of the colonial setting over the connections between colony and metropole.[27] As few Latin Americanists have the opportunity to do graduate fields in Spanish history, they often have little knowledge of the peoples, institutions, or society on the other side of the Atlantic. Thus, to many colonialists, early modern Spain has remained the monolith of nineteenth- and mid-twentieth-century textbooks—an absolutist national monarchy unified in purpose and identity governing a forcibly homogenized population. The complications of peninsular politics and the rich linguistic and cultural diversity of the peninsula have yet to make their way into colonial conceptualizations of the mother country. In fact, in monographs about colonial Latin America, Spain is mentioned rarely, if at all.

Peninsular analyses of the Spanish empire have suffered from other blinders. For the most part, Spanish scholarship has been defined by contemporary politics. By the time that Spanish history was freed from the constraints of Francoism, colonial power was no longer fashionable and historians of early modern Spain preferred to focus inward, mining the nation's rich, largely untouched local and national archives to create new histories of peninsular law, religion, and society. In the past couple of decades, the changing political context in Europe has turned the subject matter in a different direction. As Spanish exceptionalism waned and the European Union took shape, peninsular historians migrated toward issues of interest to other continental historians rather than to the ideas and issues that have intrigued their colonial peers.

Fortunately, the relationship between Spanish history and colonial Latin American history has begun to change. Recently, interest in transatlantic studies has provided a new forum for historiographic interchange.[28] Scholars have begun to examine issues such as citizenship, state building, and scientific endeavors as the product of transatlantic interactions.[29] Latin Americanists have expressed renewed interest in the relationship between colonial ideas about race and identity and those on the peninsula.[30]

All of this interaction is very exciting and intellectually promising; however, in terms of gender analysis, the gulf between the two groups of scholars has only slightly diminished. Although both colonial and peninsular women's history had their roots in religious history, especially female monasticism, from early on, colonial and peninsular scholars studying women and gender were influenced by different intellectual trends and have continued to follow very different historiographic paths.[31] While religion still dominates the scholarship on peninsular women, the early influence of anthropology took the colonial scholarship in a decidedly different direction as Latin Americanists moved toward an emphasis on indigenous women and on contacts between indigenous women and Europeans. The two scholarly trajectories separated in the 1970s, and they have yet to regain that sense of entanglement which would allow us to understand how Josefa experienced gender in different parts of the empire.

One step toward reentangling the two historiographies would be to use gender as a means to reconceptualize Spain and its colonies as two parts of a single empire. Although Atlantic history often appears as merely a substitute for traditional imperial histories, gendered analysis offers a particularly fruitful framework for transatlantic research. If we begin to see the Atlantic as a site of contestation and negotiation over gender expectations, whose dynamic goes both east to west and west to east (as well as north to south and vice versa), Spain and its colonial territories might begin to look more like an empire. Moreover, if we use gender as the central framework for that transatlantic analysis, we have a strong basis for understanding the conjunctions and disjunctions in the lives of the diverse inhabitants of that empire.

A gendered perspective on imperial governance may be a useful place to begin that analysis. Monarchical policies and priorities affected women on both sides of the Atlantic, sometimes in their enforcement and at other times in the lack thereof. Yet, in general, there is a dearth of research on the enforcement and impact of royal decrees in the context of imperial authority, let alone on their gendered implications. Take the Royal Pragmatic on Marriage (1776), for example. Latin Americanists have done exceptional work on the impact of the decree on marriage and family relations, but we know almost nothing about the way the Pragmatic influenced life on the peninsula and even less about how it influenced gender relations across the empire.[32]

The legal system also provides an interesting opportunity for transatlantic gender analysis. If we piece together the works of peninsular scholars and colonialists, white women on both sides of the Atlantic seem to have had similar encounters with the law, but as yet, we have no sense of what circumstances might have led to differential engagement of and treatment by the legal system according to class. Moreover, despite its remarkable accessibility to women of color, the Spanish legal system was neither gender-neutral nor color-blind, but it has been difficult to come to broad conclusions about the relationship between class, race, and gender in either access to or success with judicial institutions.[33]

Economic activity may also be a good focus for transatlantic gender analysis. A major problem with the historiography as it stands is that we know so little about women's economic lives on the peninsula and more and more about their lives in the Americas.[34] The experience of market women, farming women, and female artisans and their place in familial, municipal, and regional economies provokes an array of research problems that might be answered with a transatlantic analysis. We need to know the degree to which women across the empire were linked by notions of work, authority, and desires for economic stability or even social mobility. We need to figure out the degree to which the place of origin or the race or the marital status of the woman altered those expectations or if class was really the overriding factor in the way that a woman functioned as an economic entity in the empire. To what degree did the economic expansion that accompanied the creation of the Spanish empire affect women's economic lives beyond the local setting? It is hard to imagine that over the course of the colonial period there were no changes in women's work lives as a result of the evolving economic relationship between the colonies and the metropole; however, at this point, there is no evidence either way.

Just as important as understanding the links between peninsular and colonial women is a focus on what made their lives substantially different and what facets of the peninsular or colonial setting altered gender expectations. Scholars have painstakingly teased out the distinguishing gendered features of Spain's diverse communities. Their work has revealed the complex interplay of family structures, land tenure, and labor systems that governed the gendered experiences of people in the Spanish empire. Imperial policy, economic conditions, and ethnicity also had roles in determining gender norms. In some places, society tolerated couples who engaged in nonmarital sex and bore children out of wedlock. In others, inheritance practices, economic conditions, and the presence of strong ecclesiastical structures made such activity taboo. While some women actively participated in public life, others were excluded (or secluded) from public interactions. Class hierarchies and regional cultures differentiated women on the peninsula. A Basque woman spoke a different language, wore different clothing, and inherited different property than her counterpart in Extremadura. The wife of an artisan in Madrid may have had little in common with an aristocratic woman in Seville. Yet, in colonial historiography, much of this rich regional and class diversity is lost. All peninsular immigrants and their descendants suddenly become "Spaniards," an identity that would have had little resonance for them before they crossed the ocean.

In the colonies, race and servitude created an even more complicated gender hierarchy. Presumably, an indigenous woman in Guatemala did not experience the same gender constraints as either a wealthy white woman in Quito or a *mestiza* shopkeeper in Mexico City. Certainly, the experience of slavery altered the gendered lives of African women and their descendants. However, scholars have been hesitant to explicitly compare the lives of these seemingly different women and their gendered experiences, so we do not really know the degree to which gender norms bound these women together or whether servitude or class left them unalterably disconnected.

Indeed, teasing out the similarities and differences in the experiences of African and indigenous women may be key to deepening our understanding of gender in the Spanish empire. Before the Spanish conquest, indigenous groups held a wide variety of gender expectations, from patriarchal and patrilineal to more complex combinations that involved matrilineal and bilineal descent. In some native groups, women exercised substantial political authority, while in others their authority was limited to the economic and/or domestic sphere. Despite their demographic decline and Spanish attempts to transform native cultures, indigenous women maintained critical aspects of their traditions throughout the colonial period. The same was true of African women, whose rich cultural diversity persisted despite the homogenization that accompanied enslavement.[35] Yet, the scholarship on women has been predicated on the assumption that both indigenous and African women rapidly acculturated to "Spanish" gender expectations. Without a doubt, they learned the rhetoric of honor that was commonplace in colonial culture.[36] However, thus far, the notion of a "gender frontier" that has had such resonance in colonial North American studies has attracted little interest in Spanish America.[37] As indigenous populations were the majority in many regions, it seems unlikely that no aspect of either African or indigenous gender expectations persisted in any way or influenced the evolution of gender norms in the parts of Spanish America where they had a strong cultural presence. (Ras Michael Brown's essay in this volume fills a much needed gap on this issue.) Recent scholarship indicates that in border areas, indigenous gender norms were remarkably resilient, but we have no knowledge of the process of assimilation or the depth of gender syncretism.[38] Even more provocatively, considering the significant differences across the colonies, women of color (both free and enslaved) may have experienced gender differently as they moved to other parts of the empire.

Finally, a transatlantic gender analysis will help us understand how being a part of an empire affected gender norms on the peninsula. It is hard to imagine that Spain could be an empire upon which the sun never set, yet the lives of men and women in the metropole remained unaffected by that empire. The key issue here is the historiographic blinders of peninsular and colonial scholars mentioned above. Peninsular scholars still too often see early modern Spain as impervious to outside influence, while colonialists see the peninsula as too distant and too different to be affected by colonial society.

Although the need for broad-based, comparative research is clear, the challenge for gender scholars is to deal with the tensions inherent in emphasizing difference versus emphasizing similarity. It is difficult in both the colonial and the peninsular historiography to accurately assess what was different across the empire and the reasons for differences, including illegitimacy rates, numbers of female-headed households, and inheritance practices (as distinct from inheritance law). Without a doubt, living in Quito was in some ways different than living in the tropical regions of Central America, but it is not clear how to understand those differences in terms of gender. The same is true for a woman in a tiny village in Andalucía and her counterpart in the Caribbean. We need to consider how local cultures influenced gender expectations and what were the primary or secondary factors behind those differences. A transatlantic perspective may provide the framework to zoom the scholarly eye out far enough that researchers can more clearly ascertain which similarities and differences are the most important and which ones wash out in the context of the broader Spanish empire.

Such work will be challenging and require some intellectual bravery, as demonstrated in this volume. Comparative work requires a certain comfort level with an unequal level of expertise, as few scholars will become equally knowledgeable about both sides of the comparison. Yet, the movement toward a more imperial perspective will allow scholars to see gender norms as the ever changing and complex result of a variety of different circumstances. Such a multicausal/multifaceted approach will make our work more difficult, but inevitably much richer, as it will help formulate an understanding of gender in the Iberian world that articulates both the diversity and the cultural bonds of the empire.

With those ideas in mind, we can return to young Josefa. She epitomizes the imperial subject. During her formative years she emigrated from a small village in northwestern Spain to a major port city. She then crossed the Atlantic. In the Americas, she lived in a frontier town, a newly established outpost, and a major port. She lived what, at this point in the historiography, we have a difficult time articulating: the complex experience of gender in the Spanish empire. Yet, seeing Spain and its colonies as parts of a single empire has the potential to change our understanding of gender in the empire. In order to understand Josefa's life, we have to understand how the Spanish empire was connected *and* separated by the Atlantic Ocean.

NOTES

1. Chamin had only 360 inhabitants in 1829 (Sebastián de Miñano, *Suplemento al Diccionario geográfico-estadístico de España y Portugal dedicado al Rey Nuestro Señor,* tomo 9 [Madrid: Imprenta de Moreno, 1829], 215).

2. Ibid.

3. On the project to colonize Patagonia, see Juan Alejandro Apolant, *Operativo Patagonia: Historia de la mayor aportación demográfica masiva a la Banda Oriental* (Montevideo: Ediciones El Galeón, 1970), and Miguel Longo Formoso, *Expedición militar a las Californias, Sonoras y Cinaloa (1768-1771), expediciones de familias al Río de la Plata (1778-1784) y a la Costa de Mosquitos (1787)* (M. Longo: A Coruña, 2002).

4. On Galician migration, see a number of the essays in Antonio Eiras Roel and Ofelia Rey Castelao, eds., *Migraciones internas y medium-distance en la península Ibérica, 1500-1900,* 2 vols. (Santiago de Compostela: Xunta de Galicia, 1994); Antonio Eiras Roel, "La emigración gallega a América. Panorama general," in *La emigración española a Ultramar, 1492-1914,* ed. Antonio Eiras Roel, 17-40 (Madrid: Ediciones Tabacalera, 1991); Allyson M. Poska, *Women and Authority in Early Modern Spain: The Peasants of Galicia* (Oxford: Oxford Univ. Press, 2005), chapter 1. On female migration from Galicia, see Pilar Cagiao Vila, *Muller e emigración* (Santiago de Compostela: Xunta de Galicia, 1991), and Hortensio Sobrado Correa, "Movimientos migratorios en la Galicia oriental: el interior Lucense, 1700-1899," in *Migraciones internas y medium-distance en la península Ibérica, 1500-1900,* ed. Antonio Eiras Roel and Ofelia Rey Castelao, 2:535 (Santiago de Compostela: Xunta de Galicia, 1994).

5. La Coruña had a population of about fourteen thousand (Alfredo Vigo Trasancos, *A Coruña y el siglo de las luces: La construcción de una ciudad de comercio [1700-1808]* [A Coruña: Universidade de A Coruña, 2007], 265).

6. Alfredo Martín García, "El impacto de la actividad portuaria en el mundo urbano de Galicia: A Coruña, Ferrol, y Vigo en el siglo XVIII," in *La ciudad portuaria atlántica en la historia, siglos XVI-XIX,* ed. José Ignacio Fortea Pérez and Juan E. Gelabert González, 206 (Santander: Universidad de Cantabria, 2006).

7. On women and domestic service in Galicia, see Poska, *Women and Authority,* 59-66, and Isidro Dubert, "Domestic Service and Social Modernization in Urban Galicia, 1752-1920," *Continuity and Change* 14, no. 2 (1999): 207-226.

8. Baudilio Barreiro Mallón, *La Coruña 1752. Según las respuestas generales del Catastro De Ensenada* (Madrid: Tabapress, Colección Alcábala del Viento, 1990).

9. For information on the *Nuestra Señora de los Dolores,* see Apolant, *Operativo Patagonia,* 230–243.

10. Much of the archival documentation on the problems in Patagonia is found in Archivo General de Indias, Buenos Aires, 328. For a discussion of the decision, see Apolant, *Operativo Patagonia,* chapter 14.

11. Apolant, *Operativo Patagonia,* 231.

12. Padrón of 1780 in *Territorio y Población,* vol. 12, *Documentos para la Historia Argentina* (Buenos Aires: Compañía Sud-Americana de Billetes de Banco, 1919), 389.

13. Average age at first marriage for young women in the region was about seventeen, but some of the other colonizer girls who married soon after disembarking were as young as thirteen. For average age of marriage in the Rio de la Plata, see José Luis Moreno, *Historia de la familia en el Río de la Plata* (Buenos Aires: Editorial Sudamericana, 2004), 109, and Susan Socolow, "Acceptable Partners: Marriage Choice in Colonial Argentina, 1778–1810," in *Sexuality and Marriage in Colonial Latin America,* ed. Asunción Lavrin, 212 (Lincoln: Univ. of Nebraska Press, 1989). Age at marriage declined further during the nineteenth century to just below seventeen years old (Mark D. Szuchman, *Order, Family, and Community in Buenos Aires, 1810–1860* [Stanford: Stanford Univ. Press, 1988], 199). The mean age at first marriage in Mexico City in 1811 was 22.7 (Sylvia Marina Arrom, *The Women of Mexico City, 1790–1857* [Stanford: Stanford Univ. Press, 1985], 116–117). In Parral, Mexico, Spanish women married at approximately twenty-one years old (Robert McCaa, "Calidad, Clase, and Marriage in Colonial Mexico: The Case of Parral, 1788–90," *Hispanic American Historical Review* 64, no. 3 [August 1984]: 484). On the rising age at marriage, see Robert McCaa, "Marriageways in Mexico and Spain, 1500–1900," *Continuity and Change* 9, no. 1 (May 1994): 27.

14. Archivo General de Indias, Buenos Aires, 330, nf.

15. Ibid.

16. Buenos Aires had a population of about twenty-four thousand in 1787 (Lyman L. Johnson and Susan Migden Socolow, "Población y espacio en Buenos Aires del siglo XVIII," *Desarrollo económico* 20, no. 79 [1980], 331).

17. There were 1.15 women for every man in La Coruña (Antonio Eiras Roel, *La población de Galicia, 1700–1860: Crecimiento, distribución especial y estructura de la población en los siglos XVIII y XIX* [Santiago de Compostela: Fundación Caixa Galicia, 1996], 508). There were 1.04 women for every man in Buenos Aires (Johnson and Socolow, "Población y espacio," 332).

18. Women headed 15.2 percent of households in Buenos Aires (Szuchman, *Order, Family, and Community,* 202). The average age at first marriage was 23.5 years for women and 23.2 for men in La Coruña (Eiras Roel, *La población de Galicia,* 197). In 1810, the average at age marriage for women in Buenos Aires was 17.4 years (Szuchman, *Order, Family, and Community,* 199).

19. See data for nearby Herboedo and Cayon in Eiras Roel, *La población de Galicia,* 532.

20. There is no published data for Buenos Aires itself, but surrounding areas had illegitimacy rates of approximately 13 percent (José Luis Moreno, "Sexo, matrimonio y familia: la ilegitimidad en la frontera pampeana del Río de la Plata, 1780–1850," *Boletín del Instituto de Historia Argentina y Americana Dr. Emilio Ravignani* 16–17 [1997–1998]: 68). Illegitimacy rates in Galicia ranged between 5 and 15 percent. In seventeenth-century Guadalajara, up-

ward of one-third of Spanish children were illegitimate (Thomas Calvo, "Concubinato y mestizaje en el medio urbano: el caso de Guadalajara en el siglo XVII," *Revista de Indias* 44, no. 173 [1984]: 211). For eighteenth-century Bogotá, see Guiomar Dueñas-Vargas, *Los hijos del pecado: ilegitimidad y vida familiar en la Santa Fe de Bogotá colonial* (Bogotá: Universidad Nacional de Colombia, 1997), chapter 7.

21. See, for instance, some of the essays in Lyman L. Johnson and Sonya Lipsett-Rivera eds., *The Faces of Honor: Sex, Shame, and Violence in Colonial Latin America* (Albuquerque: Univ. of New Mexico Press, 1998); Susan Migden Socolow, *The Women of Colonial Latin America* (Cambridge: Cambridge Univ. Press, 2000), 78–79; Susan Kellogg, *Weaving the Past: A History of Latin America's Indigenous Women from the Prehispanic Period to the Present* (Oxford: Oxford Univ. Press, 2005), chapter 3, note 1; Karen Vieira Powers, *Women in the Crucible of Conquest: The Gendered Genesis of Spanish-American Society, 1500–1600* (Albuquerque: Univ. of New Mexico Press, 2005); Mary Elizabeth Perry, *Gender and Disorder in Early Modern Seville* (Princeton: Princeton Univ. Press, 1990), chapter 1.

22. The two most famous examples of prescriptive literature that articulated the demand for female chastity in early modern Spain are Juan Luis Vives, *The Education of a Christian Woman: A Sixteenth-Century Manual*, ed. and trans. Charles Fantazzi (Chicago: Univ. of Chicago Press, 2000), and Fray Luis de León, *A Bilingual Edition of Fray Luis de León's La Perfecta Casada: The Role of Married Women in Sixteenth-Century Spain*, ed. and trans. John A. Jones and Javier San José Lera (Lewiston: Edwin Mellon Press, 1999). The original studies of the Mediterranean honor code were produced by anthropologists, including, most famously, Julian Pitt-Rivers, *The Fate of Shechem or the Politics of Sex: Essays in the Anthropology of the Mediterranean* (Cambridge: Cambridge Univ. Press, 1977), and the essays by Stanley Brandes, J. Caro Baroja, and others in *Honour and Shame: The Values of Mediterranean Society*, ed. J. G. Peristiany (London: Weidenfeld and Nicolson, 1965).

23. For an extended discussion of this issue, see Poska, *Women and Authority*, chapter 7.

24. Poska, *Women and Authority*, 106–109; Renato Barahona, *Sex Crimes, Honour, and the Law in Early Modern Spain: Vizcaya, 1528–1735* (Toronto: Univ. of Toronto Press, 2003), chapter 5; Scott K. Taylor, *Honor and Violence in Golden Age Spain* (New Haven: Yale Univ. Press, 2008), chapter 5. On noblewomen and extramarital sex, see Grace Coolidge, "'A Vile and Abject Woman': Noble Mistresses, Legal Power, and the Family in Early Modern Spain," *Journal of Family History* 32, no. 3 (2007): 195–214. On nonelite women and sexuality, see Poska, *Women and Authority*, chapter 3.

25. The table on page 12 in Ann Twinam, *Public Lives, Private Secrets: Gender, Honor, Sexuality, and Illegitimacy in Colonial Spanish America* (Stanford: Stanford Univ. Press, 1999), vividly demonstrates the extent of nonmarital sexuality in Latin America. On illegitimacy rates in Spain, see Allyson M. Poska, "Elusive Virtue: Rethinking the Role of Female Chastity in Early Modern Spain," *Journal of Early Modern History* 8, no. 1–2 (June 2004): 135–146.

26. Eliga H. Gould, "Entangled Histories, Entangled Worlds: The English-Speaking Atlantic as a Spanish Periphery," *American Historical Review* 112, no. 3 (June 2007): 764–786.

27. For a notable exception, see Ida Altman, *Emigrants and Society: Extremadura and Spanish America in the Sixteenth Century* (Berkeley: Univ. of California Press, 1989).

28. The literature on the Atlantic world is extensive, although more extensive for the British Atlantic than for the Iberian Atlantic. Among the many recent discussions in the *American Historical Review*, see "Entangled Empires in the Atlantic World," *American*

Historical Review 112, no. 3 (June 2007) and 112, no. 5 (December 2007). For the most recent survey, which includes an extensive bibliography, see Jack P. Greene and Philip D. Morgan, *Atlantic History: A Critical Appraisal* (Oxford: Oxford Univ. Press, 2009). On the Iberian Atlantic, see Harold E. Braun and Lisa Vollendorf, eds., *Theorising the Ibero-American Atlantic*, The Medieval and Early Modern Iberian World Series (Leiden: Brill, forthcoming [2012]); J. H. Elliot, *Empires of the Atlantic World: Britain and Spain in America 1492–1830* (New Haven: Yale Univ. Press, 2006); John Thornton, *Africa and Africans in the Creation of the Atlantic World, 1400–1800* (Cambridge: Cambridge Univ. Press, 1992); Stuart B. Schwartz, *All Can Be Saved: Religious Tolerance and Salvation in the Iberian Atlantic World* (New Haven: Yale Univ. Press, 2009).

29. A few examples include Tamar Herzog, *Defining Nations: Immigrants and Citizens in Early Modern Spain and Spanish America* (New Haven: Yale Univ. Press, 2003); Gabriel Paquette, *Enlightenment, Governance and Reform in Spain and Its Empire, 1759–1808* (Basingstoke: Palgrave McMillan, 2008); the works of Jorge Cañizares-Esguerra, including *How to Write the History of the New World: Histories, Epistemologies, and Identities in the Eighteenth-Century Atlantic World* (Stanford: Stanford Univ. Press, 2001); Antonio Barrera-Osorio, *Experiencing Nature: The Spanish American Empire and the Early Scientific Revolution* (Austin: Univ. of Texas Press, 2006); Marcy Norton, *Sacred Gifts, Profane Pleasures: A History of Tobacco and Chocolate in the Atlantic World* (Ithaca: Cornell Univ. Press, 2008).

30. María-Elena Martínez, *Genealogical Fictions: Limpieza de Sangre, Religion, and Gender in Colonial Mexico* (Stanford: Stanford Univ. Press, 2008).

31. For an excellent overview of the historiography of colonial Latin America, see Ann Twinam, "Women and Gender in Colonial Latin America," in *Women's History in Global Perspective* vol. 2, ed. Bonnie G. Smith, 187–237 (Urbana: Univ. of Illinois Press, 2005). For an overview of Spanish women's history, see Allyson M. Poska, "How Women's History has Transformed the Study of Early Modern Spain," *Bulletin of the Association for Spanish and Portuguese Historical Studies* 33, no. 1 (2008), available at www.ucmo.edu/asphs/2008/women.html.

32. On the Royal Pragmatic on Marriage, see Twinam, *Public Lives, Private Secrets*, esp. 301–313; Steinar A. Saether, "Bourbon Absolutism and Marriage Reform in Late Colonial Spanish America," *Americas* 59 (2003): 475–509; Patricia Seed, *To Love, Honor, and Obey in Colonial Mexico: Conflicts over Marriage Choice, 1574–1821* (Stanford: Stanford Univ. Press, 1988), chapter 13.

33. Some useful works on women and the legal system in Spain include Grace Coolidge, "'Neither Dumb, Deaf, nor Destitute of Understanding:' Women as Guardians in Early Modern Spain," *Sixteenth Century Journal* 36 no. 3 (fall 2005): 673–693; Dana Wessell Lightfoot, "Family Interests? Women's Power: The Role of the Family in Dowry Restitution Cases in Fifteenth-Century Valencia," *Women's History Review* 15, no. 4 (September 2006): 511–520; Barahona, *Sex Crimes, Honour, and the Law*; Margarita Ortega López, "Protestas de las mujeres castellanas contra el orden patriarcal privado durante el siglo XVIII," *Cuadernos de Historia Moderna* 19 (1997): 65–89. On women and the legal system in Latin America, see Kimberly Gauderman, *Women's Lives in Colonial Quito: Gender, Law, and Economy in Spanish America* (Austin: Univ. of Texas Press, 2003); Karen B. Graubart, *With Our Labor and Sweat: Indigenous Women and the Formation of Colonial Society in Peru* (Stanford: Stanford Univ. Press, 2007), and many of the essays in Susan Schroeder, Stephanie Wood, and Robert Haskett, eds., *Indian Women of Early Mexico* (Norman: Univ. of Oklahoma Press, 1997).

34. Some useful works on women and the economy in Latin America include Jane E. Mangan, *Trading Roles: Gender, Ethnicity, and the Urban Economy in Colonial Potosí* (Durham: Duke Univ. Press, 2005); Graubart, *With Our Labor and Sweat*; Marcela Aguirrezabala, "Mujeres casadas en los negocios y el comercio ultramarino entre el Río de la Plata y la Península a fines del siglo XVIII," *Anuario de estudios americanos* 58, no. 1 (2001): 111–133; Pablo Lacoste, "Wine and Women: Grape Growers and Pulperas in Mendoza, 1561–1852," *Hispanic American Historical Review* 88, no. 3 (2008): 361–391. On women and the economy in Spain, see Serrana M. Rial García, *Las mujeres en la economía urbana del antiguo régimen: Santiago durante el siglo XVIII* (Santiago de Compostela: Ediciós do Castro, 1995); Carmen Sarasúa, *Criados, nodrizas, y amos: El servicio doméstico en la formación del mercado del trabajo madrileño, 1758–1868* (Madrid: Siglo veintiuno, 1994); Marta Vicente, "Textual Uncertainties: The Legacy of Women Entrepreneurs in Eighteenth-Century Barcelona," in *Women, Texts and Authority in the Early Modern Spanish World*, ed. Marta V. Vicente and Luis R. Corteguera, 185–198 (Aldershot, England: Ashgate, 2003).

35. On this issue, see James H. Sweet, *Recreating Africa: Culture, Kinship, and Religion in the Afro-Portuguese World, 1441–1770* (Chapel Hill: Univ. of North Carolina Press, 2003); Joan Cameron Bristol, *Christians, Blasphemers, and Witches: Afro-Mexican Ritual Practice in the Seventeenth Century* (Albuquerque: Univ. of New Mexico Press, 2007).

36. See the essays in Johnson and Lipsett-Rivera, *Faces of Honor*.

37. Kathleen M. Brown, "The Anglo-Algonquin Gender Frontier," in *Negotiators of Change: Historical Perspectives on Native American Women*, ed. Nancy Shoemaker, 27 (New York: Routledge, 1995).

38. For examples of the persistence of indigenous gender expectations, see Kathleen Deagan, "Reconsidering Taíno Social Dynamics after Spanish Conquest: Gender and Class in Culture Contact Studies," *American Antiquity* 69, no. 4 (October 2004): 597–626; Juliana Barr notes, "Native gender patterns predominated whether the Spaniards fought them or encouraged them," in *Peace Came in the Form of a Woman: Indians and Spaniards in the Texas Borderlands* (Chapel Hill: Univ. of North Carolina Press, 2007), 142, 138–139.

WORKS CITED

Primary Sources

ARCHIVO GENERAL DE INDIAS

Buenos Aires

Secondary Sources

Aguirrezabala, Marcela. "Mujeres casadas en los negocios y el comercio ultramarino entre el Río de la Plata y la Península a fines del siglo XVIII." *Anuario de estudios americanos* 58, no. 1 (2001): 111–133.

Altman, Ida. *Emigrants and Society: Extremadura and Spanish America in the Sixteenth Century.* Berkeley: Univ. of California Press, 1989.

Apolant, Juan Alejandro. *Operativo Patagonia: Historia de la mayor aportación demográfica masiva a la Banda Oriental.* Montevideo: Ediciones El Galeón, 1970.

Arrom, Sylvia Marina. *The Women of Mexico City, 1790–1857*. Stanford: Stanford Univ. Press, 1985.

Barahona, Renato. *Sex Crimes, Honour, and the Law in Early Modern Spain: Vizcaya, 1528–1735*. Toronto: Univ. of Toronto Press, 2003.

Barr, Juliana. *Peace Came in the Form of a Woman: Indians and Spaniards in the Texas Borderlands*. Chapel Hill: Univ. of North Carolina Press, 2007.

Barreiro Mallón, Baudilio. *La Coruña 1752. Según las respuestas generales del Catastro de Ensenada*. Madrid: Tabapress, Colección Alcábala del Viento, 1990.

Barrera-Osorio, Antonio. *Experiencing Nature: The Spanish American Empire and the Early Scientific Revolution*. Austin: Univ. of Texas Press, 2006.

Braun, Harold E., and Lisa Vollendorf, eds. *Theorising the Ibero-American Atlantic*. The Medieval and Early Modern Iberian World Series. Leiden: Brill, forthcoming (2012).

Bristol, Joan Cameron. *Christians, Blasphemers, and Witches: Afro-Mexican Ritual Practice in the Seventeenth Century*. Albuquerque: Univ. of New Mexico Press, 2007.

Brown, Kathleen M. "The Anglo-Algonquin Gender Frontier." In *Negotiators of Change: Historical Perspectives on Native American Women,* edited by Nancy Shoemaker, 26–48. New York: Routledge, 1995.

Calvo, Thomas. "Concubinato y mestizaje en el medio urbano: el caso de Guadalajara en el siglo XVII." *Revista de Indias* 44, no. 173 (1984): 203–212.

Cañizares-Esguerra, Jorge. *How to Write the History of the New World: Histories, Epistemologies, and Identities in the Eighteenth-Century Atlantic World*. Stanford: Stanford Univ. Press, 2001.

Coolidge, Grace. "'Neither Dumb, Deaf, nor Destitute of Understanding': Women as Guardians in Early Modern Spain." *Sixteenth Century Journal* 36, no. 3 (fall 2005): 673–693.

———."'A Vile and Abject Woman': Noble Mistresses, Legal Power, and the Family in Early Modern Spain." *Journal of Family History* 32, no. 3 (2007): 195–214.

Deagan, Kathleen. "Reconsidering Taíno Social Dynamics after Spanish Conquest: Gender and Class in Culture Contact Studies." *American Antiquity* 69, no. 4 (October 2004): 597–626.

Dubert, Isidro. "Domestic Service and Social Modernization in Urban Galicia, 1752–1920." *Continuity and Change* 14, no. 2 (1999): 207–226.

Dueñas-Vargas, Guiomar. *Los hijos del pecado: ilegitimidad y vida familiar en la Santa Fe de Bogotá colonial*. Bogotá: Universidad Nacional de Colombia, 1997.

Eiras Roel, Antonio. "La emigración gallega a América. Panorama general." In *La emigración española a Ultramar, 1492–1914,* edited by Antonio Eiras Roel, 17–39. Madrid: Ediciones Tabacalera, 1991.

———. *La población de Galicia, 1700–1860: Crecimiento, distribución especial y es-*

tructura de la población en los siglos XVIII y XIX. Santiago de Compostela: Fundación Caixa Galicia, 1996.

Eiras Roel, Antonio, and Ofelia Rey Castelao, eds., *Migraciones internas y medium-distance en la peninsula Ibérica, 1500–1900,* 2 vols. Santiago de Compostela: Xunta de Galicia, 1994.

Elliott, J. H. *Empires of the Atlantic World: Britain and Spain in America 1492–1830.* New Haven: Yale Univ. Press, 2006.

"Entangled Empires in the Atlantic World." *American Historical Review* 112, no. 3 (June 2007), and 112, no. 5 (December 2007).

Formoso, Miguel Longo. *Expedición militar a las Californias, Sonoras y Cinaloa (1768–1771), expediciones de familias al Río de la Plata (1778–1784) y a la Costa de Mosquitos (1787).* M. Longo: A Coruña, 2002.

García, Alfredo Martín. "El impacto de la actividad portuaria en el mundo urbano de Galicia: A Coruña, Ferrol, y Vigo en el siglo XVIII." In *La ciudad portuaria atlántica en la historia, siglos XVI–XIX,* edited by José Ignacio Fortea Pérez and Juan E. Gelabert González, 195–220. Santander: Universidad de Cantabria, 2006.

Gauderman, Kimberly. *Women's Lives in Colonial Quito: Gender, Law, and Economy in Spanish America.* Austin: Univ. of Texas Press, 2003.

Gould, Eliga H. "Entangled Histories, Entangled Worlds: The English-Speaking Atlantic as a Spanish Periphery." *American Historical Review* 112, no. 3 (June 2007): 764–786.

Graubart, Karen B. *With Our Labor and Sweat: Indigenous Women and the Formation of Colonial Society in Peru.* Stanford: Stanford Univ. Press, 2007.

Greene, Jack P., and Philip D. Morgan, eds. *Atlantic History: A Critical Appraisal.* Oxford: Oxford Univ. Press, 2009.

Herzog, Tamar. *Defining Nations: Immigrants and Citizens in Early Modern Spain and Spanish America.* New Haven: Yale Univ. Press, 2003.

Johnson, Lyman L., and Sonya Lipsett-Rivera, eds. *The Faces of Honor: Sex, Shame, and Violence in Colonial Latin America.* Albuquerque: Univ. of New Mexico Press, 1998.

Johnson, Lyman L., and Susan Migden Socolow, "Población y espacio en Buenos Aires del siglo XVIII." *Desarrollo económico* 20, no. 79 (1980): 329–349.

Kellogg, Susan. *Weaving the Past: A History of Latin America's Indigenous Women from the Prehispanic Period to the Present.* Oxford: Oxford Univ. Press, 2005.

Lacoste, Pablo. "Wine and Women: Grape Growers and Pulperas in Mendoza, 1561–1852." *Hispanic American Historical Review* 88, no. 3 (2008): 361–391.

León, Fray Luis de. *A Bilingual Edition of Fray Luis de León's La Perfecta Casada: The Role of Married Women in Sixteenth-Century Spain.* Edited and translated by John A. Jones and Javier San José Lera. Lewiston: Edwin Mellon Press, 1999.

Lightfoot, Dana Wessel. "Family Interests? Women's Power: The Role of the Family in Dowry Restitution Cases in Fifteenth-Century Valencia." *Women's History Review* 15, no. 4 (September 2006): 511–520.

Mangan, Jane E. *Trading Roles: Gender, Ethnicity, and the Urban Economy in Colonial Potosí.* Durham: Duke Univ. Press, 2005.

Martínez, María-Elena. *Genealogical Fictions: Limpieza de Sangre, Religion, and Gender in Colonial Mexico.* Stanford: Stanford Univ. Press, 2008.

McCaa, Robert. "Calidad, Clase, and Marriage in Colonial Mexico: The Case of Parral, 1788-90." *Hispanic American Historical Review* 64, no. 3 (August 1984): 477–502.

———. "Marriageways in Mexico and Spain, 1500–1900." *Continuity and Change* 9, no. 1 (May 1994): 11–43.

Miñano, Sebastián de. *Suplemento al Diccionario geográfico-estadístico de España y Portugal dedicado al Rey Nuestro Señor,* tomo 9. Madrid: Imprenta de Moreno, 1829.

Moreno, José Luis. *Historia de la familia en el Río de la Plata.* Buenos Aires: Editorial Sudamericana, 2004.

———. "Sexo, matrimonio y familia: la ilegitimidad en la frontera pampeana del Río de la Plata, 1780–1850." *Boletín del Instituto de Historia Argentina y Americana Dr. Emilio Ravignani* 16–17 (1997–1998): 61–84.

Norton, Marcy. *Sacred Gifts, Profane Pleasures: A History of Tobacco and Chocolate in the Atlantic World.* Ithaca: Cornell Univ. Press, 2008.

Ortega López, Margarita. "Protestas de las mujeres castellanas contra el orden patriarcal privado durante el siglo XVIII." *Cuadernos de Historia Moderna* 19 (1997): 65–89.

Paquette, Gabriel. *Enlightenment, Governance and Reform in Spain and Its Empire, 1759–1808.* Basingstoke: Palgrave McMillan, 2008.

Peristany, J. G. ed. *Honour and Shame: The Values of Mediterranean Society.* London: Weidenfeld and Nicolson, 1965.

Perry, Mary Elizabeth. *Gender and Disorder in Early Modern Seville.* Princeton: Princeton Univ. Press, 1990.

Pitt-Rivers, Julian. *The Fate of Shechem or the Politics of Sex: Essays in the Anthropology of the Mediterranean.* Cambridge: Cambridge Univ. Press, 1977.

Poska, Allyson M. "Elusive Virtue: Rethinking the Role of Female Chastity in Early Modern Spain." *Journal of Early Modern History* 8, no. 1–2 (June 2004): 135–146.

———. "How Women's History has Transformed the Study of Early Modern Spain." *Bulletin of the Association for Spanish and Portuguese Historical Studies* 33, no. 1 (2008), available at www.ucmo.edu/asphs/2008/women.html.

———. *Women and Authority in Early Modern Spain: The Peasants of Galicia.* Oxford: Oxford Univ. Press, 2005.

Powers, Karen Vieira. *Women in the Crucible of Conquest: The Gendered Genesis of Spanish-American Society, 1500–1600*. Albuquerque: Univ. of New Mexico Press, 2005.

Rial García, Serrana M. *Las mujeres en la economía urbana del antiguo régimen: Santiago durante el siglo XVIII*. Santiago de Compostela: Ediciós do Castro, 1995.

Saether, Steinar A. "Bourbon Absolutism and Marriage Reform in Late Colonial Spanish America." *Americas* 59 (2003): 475–509.

Sarasúa, Carmen. *Criados, nodrizas, y amos: El servicio doméstico en la formación del mercado del trabajo madrileño, 1758–1868*. Madrid: Siglo veintiuno, 1994.

Schroeder, Susan, Stephanie Wood, and Robert Haskett, eds. *Indian Women of Early Mexico*. Norman: Univ. of Oklahoma Press, 1997.

Schwartz, Stuart B. *All Can Be Saved: Religious Tolerance and Salvation in the Iberian Atlantic World*. New Haven: Yale Univ. Press, 2009.

Seed, Patricia. *To Love, Honor, and Obey in Colonial Mexico: Conflicts over Marriage Choice, 1574–1821*. Stanford: Stanford Univ. Press, 1988.

Sobrado Correa, Hortensio. "Movimientos migratorios en la Galicia oriental: el interior Lucense, 1700–1899." In *Migraciones internas y medium-distance en la peninsula Ibérica, 1500–1900*, edited by Antonio Eiras Roel and Ofelia Rey Castelao, 2:533–553. Santiago de Compostela: Xunta de Galicia, 1994.

Socolow, Susan M. "Acceptable Partners: Marriage Choice in Colonial Argentina, 1778–1810." In *Sexuality and Marriage in Colonial Latin America*, edited by Asunción Lavrin, 209–251. Lincoln: Univ. of Nebraska Press, 1989.

———. *The Women of Colonial Latin America*. Cambridge: Cambridge Univ. Press, 2000.

Sweet, James H. *Recreating Africa: Culture, Kinship, and Religion in the Afro-Portuguese World, 1441–1770*. Chapel Hill: Univ. of North Carolina Press, 2003.

Szuchman, Mark D. *Order, Family, and Community in Buenos Aires, 1810–1860*. Stanford: Stanford Univ. Press, 1988.

Taylor, Scott K. *Honor and Violence in Golden Age Spain*. New Haven: Yale Univ. Press, 2008.

Territorio y Población, vol. 12, *Documentos para la Historia Argentina*. Buenos Aires: Compañía Sud-Americana de Billetes de Banco, 1919.

Thornton, John. *Africa and Africans in the Creation of the Atlantic World, 1400–1800*. Cambridge: Cambridge Univ. Press, 1992.

Trasancos, Alfredo Vigo. *A Coruña y el siglo de las luces: La construcción de una ciudad de comercio (1700–1808)*. A Coruña: Universidade de A Coruña, 2007.

Twinam, Ann. *Public Lives, Private Secrets: Gender, Honor, Sexuality, and Illegitimacy in Colonial Spanish America*. Stanford: Stanford Univ. Press, 1999.

———."Women and Gender in Colonial Latin America." In *Women's History in Global Perspective,* vol. 2, edited by Bonnie G. Smith, 187–237. Urbana: Univ. of Illinois Press, 2005.

Vicente, Marta. "Textual Uncertainties: The Legacy of Women Entrepreneurs in Eighteenth-Century Barcelona." In *Women, Texts and Authority in the Early Modern Spanish World,* edited by Marta V. Vicente and Luis R. Corteguera, 185–198. Aldershot, England: Ashgate, 2003.

Vila, Pilar Cagiao. *Muller e emigración.* Santiago de Compostela: Xunta de Galicia, 1991.

Vives, Juan Luis. *The Education of a Christian Woman: A Sixteenth-Century Manual.* Edited and translated by Charles Fantazzi. Chicago: Univ. of Chicago Press, 2000.

3

Spanish Women in the Caribbean, 1493–1540

IDA ALTMAN

The timing, nature, and geography of contacts among the representatives of distinctive peoples and places are fundamental to the study of the late medieval and early modern Atlantic world (or worlds). The appropriation and settlement of island groups (the Canaries, Azores, Madeiras, and Cabo Verde Islands) lying well to the west and south of the Iberian Peninsula marked the first phase of European expansion into the Atlantic. The second phase—in some respects coinciding with the first in its latter stages, both chronologically and to an extent in terms of personnel, ambitions, and organization—began with Columbus's initial voyages to the Caribbean and the establishment of the first European settlements in the Americas on the island that Spaniards called Isla Española (modern Hispaniola, home to Haiti and the Dominican Republic). Even as Columbus continued his reconnaissance of the islands and parts of the circum-Caribbean mainland, the European newcomers on Hispaniola searched for ways to turn a profit. Finding few items to sustain trade besides dyewoods in the early years, Europeans soon became directly involved in gold mining. In doing so, they exploited the labor and productivity of the indigenous peoples of the islands, who for the most part were agriculturalists. The early movement of people from Europe to Hispaniola was largely, but not exclusively, a migration of men.

The rapid transition from reconnaissance to gold mining using the forced labor of the indigenous inhabitants of the Caribbean, later supplemented by that of African slaves, brought Hispaniola and the other large islands of the Greater Antilles into a complex transatlantic milieu. The arrival from across the Atlantic of hundreds of men intent on participating in the mining economy and later in the immensely profitable pearl fisheries profoundly altered the lives of the native peoples of the Caribbean and forged the first transatlantic economy. Profits from gold and later pearls flowed back to Spain, and commercial activity burgeoned as Italian, Castilian, Flemish, and Basque merchants extended their trade networks to include the islands. From the time of Columbus onward, European men who arrived there were quick to take advantage of indigenous women who, willingly or not, became their concubines, domestic servants, mothers of their *mestizo* (person of mixed European and indigenous parentage or descent) children, and sometimes their wives. The heavy preponderance of male participation in mining and mercantile activity, however, has obscured the presence and influence of European women in this milieu.

As a result, Spanish women barely have figured in our understanding of the history and society of the Caribbean after contact. Yet they were present nearly from the outset, in small but growing numbers, arriving in the islands as wives, daughters, or servants or on their own after a journey that entailed undeniable risks. Here I mainly consider Spanish women to around 1540, focusing on Hispaniola and Puerto Rico, with some attention to the influence and importance of women who belonged to other ethnic or racial groups. The main focus is on the dimensions of European women's presence in the islands, official policies that promoted the emigration of married couples, and the ways official and ecclesiastical views of acceptable marriages changed. Analysis of Spanish women suggests that from an early time they contributed to the creation of a stable Hispanic society in the islands, although detailed study of individual experiences is seldom possible, given the nature of the existing records.

SPANISH WOMEN, MARRIAGE, AND SETTLEMENT

While the Caribbean in the early sixteenth century afforded Spanish women some of the trappings of European society, these were mixed with elements of the exotic frontier context of the islands. Indigenous women worked in their households, preparing the foods of the islands in their accustomed manner and using the vessels they fashioned; everyone—Spanish men as well as women—learned to eat the cassava bread of the Tainos as their main dietary staple. Native women were not just domestic servants; they lived with, married, and had children with Spanish men. In the early years of settlement, probably most Spanish women on the islands lived in close contact not only with indigenous women but, virtually from the outset, with their *mestizo* children as well. African women also joined Spanish households very early, adding their domestic and culinary knowledge and practices to the mix. Archaeological study of the material culture of early towns reveals that Spanish Caribbean households were sites of cultural and social interaction where women played major roles. Archaeological work is crucial to our understanding of the organization of households and conduct of daily life in this period because little of the mundane documentation in which women might be expected to figure (dowries, wills, economic transactions) exists.[1]

Official interest in promoting the migration of married couples that would form the basis for a civil society in the new territories of the islands and beyond surfaced fairly early. Efforts to encourage people to move into unoccupied or newly acquired territories in medieval Spain during the Reconquista—the centuries-long southward expansion of the Christian kingdoms—often included special incentives for men who were willing to settle with their wives and families; not surprisingly, similar incentives were offered for the colonization effort in the islands.[2] In his instructions to don Diego Colón regarding assignment of indigenous labor in 1509, for example, the king stipulated that royal officials should receive one hundred workers; *caballeros* (nobles) with their wives, eighty; *escuderos* (gentlemen) with their wives, sixty; and *labradores* (farmers) with their wives, thirty.[3]

Such inducements were matched by official efforts to compel men who migrated without their wives to return or send for them. On February 8, 1505, for example, King Ferdinand wrote to governor Fray Nicolás de Ovando in Santo Domingo that "it is well done . . . that you've made the married men return for their wives. We will order that in the future they bring them with them." Four years later the king wrote that "the married men who go there should be obligated to bring their wives within three years."[4] Despite the reiteration of this order, then and subsequently, it never was particularly effective, even when married men faced fines or loss of grants as a consequence of failing to produce their wives. When don Francisco de Monroy received a fairly substantial grant of Indian workers as part of the *repartimiento* of 1514, for example, he was told that retaining the grant was contingent on his bringing his wife to Hispaniola within one year.[5] In 1529 or 1530 the bishop of Santo Domingo wrote to the king explaining the difficulty of determining if men had mistresses, because if they lived with women, "it is with their Indian servants, and it cannot be verified. It would be better that if a married man is here for five or six years without going to see his wife, he should be ordered to go without any further inquiry."[6]

Royal policy to promote emigration of women and married couples and to encourage men to bring or send for their wives developed during the first ten or fifteen years following Columbus's early voyages. Apparently at least a few European women sailed with the very large expedition of around 1500 people recruited for Columbus's second voyage of 1493 that represented the real beginnings of European settlement of the island. Ships transported livestock and seeds for planting as well as men representing a variety of trades and occupations.[7] One of the women on board, María Fernández, served as Columbus's *criada* (servant or retainer), but how long she remained in Hispaniola is not known.[8] The organizers of the 1497 voyage stipulated that thirty women should be included in the projected total of 330 passengers—not, it should be noted, married men with their wives.

It seems unlikely that anywhere close to thirty women crossed the Atlantic to Hispaniola in 1497; but in 1500, when the Spanish monarchs sent the *comendador* (commander of a military order) Francisco de Bobadilla to investigate Columbus's conduct in office, there were at least a few European women living in Isabela, the first town founded by Columbus on the island's north coast. Several women arrived to the island of Hispaniola in the spring of 1498 when two ships mistakenly landed at the town of Xaraguá. Although the composition of the ships' crew and passengers (which included forty-seven crossbowmen) suggests that the main purpose of that group was to strengthen the Spaniards' military presence on the island, four women figured among them, including one who accompanied her husband, Pedro de Salamanca, one of the crossbowmen, and two who probably were gypsies.[9]

Recruitment of married couples was more extensive in the organization of the large expedition that accompanied royal governor Fray Nicolás de Ovando, also a *comendador* of the Order of Alcántara, who arrived in Hispaniola in 1502. Luis de Arriaga, a *vecino* (citizen) of Seville, agreed to undertake an ambitious project of recruiting two hundred men with their wives. He experienced difficulties and delays in finding willing emigrants, and the ships on which they were to travel departed late as a result. In the end he sent to the island only seventy-three married men, who with their wives and families accounted for what was still a fairly substantial group of some two hundred potential settlers.[10]

The perceived importance of marriage as a stabilizing influence in society meant that official efforts were not always confined to ensuring that Spanish men brought or sent for their wives, although initially that was a major focus. Columbus discouraged the men under his authority from marrying native women.[11] For some years the desirability of such marriages was debated, especially given the complications that could arise if marital and kinship relations (and thus potential claims to indigenous labor and possibly to land) conflicted with the official assignment of *repartimientos* or *encomiendas* (grants of rights to indigenous labor).[12] The king even went so far as to make the following proposal to officials in Seville in 1512, reflecting a mingling of social and fiscal concerns typical of royal policy on governance of the islands:

> It seems convenient that [female] white slaves and Christians should go [to the islands], because there being such a need for women there, one must think that since some marry Indian women, they would also marry them, because they would serve better than Indians, and because there would be a benefit in [selling] licenses, charging more than ten ducats per license. See if some can be sent on our account, and do it without delay, especially as in San Juan there is a greater necessity of women and workers.[13]

The bias against Spanish-indigenous marriages did not last, and in 1514 the king instructed the bishop of Concepción, Governor don Diego Colón, and other officials that any Spaniard wishing to marry a native woman should be permitted to do so.[14] Fifteen years later the bishop of Santo Domingo recommended that if a man in Puerto Rico wished to marry an Indian woman, she should be taken away from her *encomendero* (the grantee entitled to her labor) and allowed to wed.[15] Indeed, intermarriage (at least with high-ranking native women) began to be seen as a potentially advantageous political strategy, as suggested by instructions in 1516 to the three Jeronymites who were sent to Hispaniola to implement reforms in the organization of indigenous communities and *repartimientos*. Their official orders stated:

> If a Spanish settler with the agreement of the priest and administrator [of the community] marries a *cacica* (female native ruler), or the daughter and heir of a *cacique,* he will become cacique and will be regarded and obeyed as such. In this way all the caciques will come to be Spaniards and it will avoid many expenses.[16]

Ironically, this policy echoes the actions of early settlers in Hispaniola who sought advantage (or in the earliest years, perhaps basic survival) by choosing to live in indigenous communities and establishing ties with native peoples through marriage or name exchange (*guatiao*), which created a kind of fictive kinship or alliance. As a result of the military conflicts of the Columbus period and Ovando's campaign to eliminate much of the cacique group that remained in Hispaniola during the early years of his governorship, by the second decade of the sixteenth century much of the native leadership had passed into the hands of women.[17] Perhaps officials thought it would be possible to achieve a relatively easy transition from rule by native women to rule by their Spanish husbands. In any case, these policies would have had relatively little impact due to the ongoing—and irreversible—decline of the native population and the indigenous chiefdoms.

The earliest fairly complete record of the Spanish population of Hispaniola is the so-called *repartimiento* of 1514. The Spanish Crown designated two officials to assign (or reassign) what remained of the fast-decreasing indigenous labor force to the Spaniards living on the island.[18] The *repartimiento* was not a complete census, either of Europeans or indigenous. Given that many people received only a very small number of *naborías* (servants), in some cases only one or two, it is reasonable to assume that most Spaniards residing on the island appeared on the list. Transients, of course, would not have been included. Absolute numbers in any case are of less interest here than what the document reveals about the presence of Spanish women some twenty years after Columbus's first voyages.

There were Spanish women living in all but one of Hispaniola's fourteen towns (the western town of Salvatierra de la Sabana), with the largest numbers in Santo Domingo (forty), Salvaleón de Higüey (nineteen), and Concepción (eleven). Most of these women were not listed by name—rather, their presence is inferred by the notation that a man was "married to a woman from Castile." A total of twenty-three women, however, appeared on their own, usually receiving assignments of one or two *naborías*.[19] Some were widows or received grants in the absence of their husbands; in other cases their marital status was not indicated. Nearly half (ten) of these women, most listed by their own names, lived in Santo Domingo.

These numbers probably are low. The marital status of royal officials, for example, seldom was noted, although in many cases their wives accompanied them. As wives of high-ranking men, these women would have been key figures in whatever existed in the way of a Spanish women's world, forming the core of an early island elite. In addition, of course, many men married indigenous women, regardless of whether official policy favored this choice.[20] With the exception of Santo Domingo (where only four men were listed as being "married to a woman from this island") and Salvaleón de Higüey, where the number of indigenous wives was only slightly over half the number of Spanish wives, in most places the numbers were close to even. A fair assumption can be made, however, that very few men, especially in the smaller towns, lived by themselves. For a number of married men there is no information on their spouses; but probably most of those whose wives were not specified, as well as most of the men not listed as being married, lived with indigenous women.[21] When the presence of domestic servants (*naborías de casa*) in Spanish-headed households also is taken into account, there is little doubt that, at least outside of Santo Domingo, many or most Spanish women in Hispaniola lived in a context that was strongly indigenous. In San Juan de la Maguana, for example, only two out of twenty-seven *vecinos* were recorded as having Spanish wives, although the actual number could have been somewhat higher.

Despite the drastic decline in the indigenous population that already had occurred by the time of the *repartimiento* of 1514, gold production was robust and the island's Spanish population might have been increasing. By the late 1520s, however, many of the towns in Hispaniola's mining zones had shrunk considerably, and other destinations in the Indies, especially New Spain, were attracting growing numbers of emigrants. A report of 1528 from Licenciados Espinosa and Zuazo, *oidores* (judges) of the *audiencia* (high court) in Santo Domingo, to the Crown detailed the notable losses of population in many of the once-thriving towns:

> The city of Concepción was the leading one of this island, for which reason it was made the head of the bishopric. It's in the middle of the island and there is a fort and stone church and a Franciscan monastery of stone and a city hall and another 25 or 30 very good stone buildings. There used to be 200 *vecinos,* of whom 100 were horsemen, hidalgos and prominent persons. Now there barely are 20 *vecinos* . . . old and unmarried and lacking sons from whom one could anticipate permanence. The town of Santiago used to have 100 *vecinos,* also prominent people. It had 80 horsemen but now has only 8 *vecinos* of that standing . . . and they are [living] on their properties and not in the manner of a town. . . . The town of Salvaleón de Higuey once

was inhabited by more than 100 married men, most of them with women from Castile; at present it barely has 15 *vecinos*.[22]

The *oidores* made similar observations about Puerto Real, Lares de Guahaba, San Juan de la Maguana, Santa María del Puerto, and Salvatierra de la Sabana. Although some of the inhabitants of Hispaniola's smaller (and shrinking) towns might have taken up residence in Santo Domingo, strengthening the Spanish presence there, others probably left the island for more promising destinations or returned to Spain. Notably, with regard to the significance of Spanish women in this era, the *oidores* emphasized the absence of wives and families as indicative of the failure to establish a basis for permanence and continuity in these towns.[23]

Increasingly desperate officials turned to colonization schemes that, as ever, emphasized attracting married couples. There was, of course, precedent for recruiting married couples and families—although, as seen, they never emigrated in the numbers desired. In July 1520 *oidor* Licenciado Figueroa reported the arrival of "thirty-seven households of *labradores*" bringing their wives, children, and servants. They were from the town of Antequera, near Málaga in southern Spain. Apparently their ship first stopped in Puerto Rico, where officials noted their "poverty."[24] Although some of the emigrants wanted to stay in Puerto Rico, where the officials suggested they would be better off (they too hoped to attract more married settlers), the emigrants went on to Hispaniola. On arrival there the entire group fell ill. Figueroa wrote that some were recovering and that they planned to find a place where they could all settle together.[25]

In 1528 Licenciados Zuazo and Espinosa proposed a similar colonization scheme. They wrote to the king that they had discussed their plan with "certain men" on the island who were willing to underwrite the founding of new settlements, each to consist of "at least fifty married *vecinos* with their wives, provided that half be Spaniards and the other half blacks and that all should be brought from Spain" (or Portugal). Each of the new pueblos would have a church and priest. The settlers would receive land and livestock and other forms of assistance. The *oidores* apparently did not intend for these to be modest farming communities, however; each of the new settlers would be permitted to bring as many as one hundred African slaves to the island free of any duty, suggesting that the planners might have envisioned these new settlements as a means to expand sugar production. The founders and sponsors of the new pueblos should be prominent hidalgos who would receive in perpetuity a portion of the royal revenues generated.[26]

A royal *cédul*a (decree) issued the following year confirms that the king at least endorsed the proposal. Whether anyone undertook a colonization project under this plan is uncertain, but a petition of 1538 from Diego Caballero, the long-time and well-connected secretary of the *audiencia,* asking for the concession of hereditary rights and a league of land in the area where he had constructed a sugar mill suggests that this model of colonization persisted. Witnesses in the deposition that he presented to the *audiencia* supported his claim to have established a community with more than sixty houses, built of both stone and straw, in which lived a diverse population of fifteen or twenty Spaniards, some of them married, and 150 Indians and Africans. Caballero maintained a large vineyard and was experimenting with cultivating wheat and raising goats. He also had built a church where a priest performed the sacraments for the people of the sugar mill and others in the region.[27]

A census conducted in Puerto Rico in 1530 suggests that Spaniards continued to settle in those parts of the Caribbean that still appeared to offer attractive economic opportunities.[28] Spanish settlement and exploitation of Puerto Rico began after 1506,[29] and in 1530 its economy based on gold mining still was flourishing, although as in Hispaniola the indigenous population was fast disappearing. More accurately described as a survey of the number of Indian workers and Indian and African slaves held by individuals living on the island than as a census, the report made in 1530 by Lieutenant Governor Francisco Manuel de Lando probably included most of the island's European residents.[30] At that time there were two main towns, San Germán and San Juan. The marital status of most residents of both towns is indicated, but only for San Juan are the wives' origins noted. There, more than half of the eighty-nine married men were listed as wed to a "woman from Castile" (twenty-five) or an *"española"* (Spanish woman; twenty-seven). Nine men were married to indigenous women, two were married to women described as "woman of color" (probably both of these men were themselves of African or mixed origins), and the wives of seven other men were not specified. The wives of nineteen men were in Castile. Six women in San Juan and two women in San Germán were listed by name.

The notation "married to a Spanish woman" is curious. Although Lando might have been making a deliberate distinction between women from Castile and *"españolas,"* there is no way to know for certain what his intention was in doing so. He might have used the term *española* primarily for women born in the islands, including *mestiza* girls who grew up in Spanish society. Certainly by 1530 there would have been a number of women born and raised in Spanish households in Hispaniola if not in Puerto Rico, and there was a substantial movement of people from one island to the other as the economy of Puerto Rico opened up. Blas Hernández, the lieutenant chief constable of San Juan, was listed as "married to a Spanish woman," but his wife, Mari Nuñez, who was listed separately under her own name, was called *portuguesa*. That suggests that she was not born in the Caribbean, although there were a number of Portuguese settlers, including married couples, living on the islands from an early time.[31] Possibly *española* was Lando's catch-all category for women whose background was unclear, or the term was interchangeable with "woman from Castile."

This census, like the *repartimiento* of 1514, tells us little about the lives of Spanish women on the islands. It does, however, clearly establish their presence and conveys some notion of its dimensions. In San Juan alone there were more than fifty households in which Spanish or at least culturally Hispanic women presided. One important development very likely affected the cultural mix of those households. By 1530, African slaves (a total of 2,071 for the two towns) were nearly twice as numerous in Puerto Rico as indigenous slaves and servants (who totaled 1,026). Although presumably most African slaves worked in mines or on rural estates, many of the 356 women among them likely were employed in domestic work. Given the apparently fairly small number of men married to native women, the strength of the African element might have meant that African influence was relatively stronger there earlier than in Hispaniola and left a greater imprint on Spanish households, at least in San Juan, than did indigenous culture.[32] In terms of the strength of Spanish women's presence in households, the town of San Juan may have resembled Santo Domingo more than it did the towns of Hispaniola, where Spanish-indigenous marriages and unions were more common. Indigenous influence may have been stronger in San Germán than in San Juan, but it is impossible to judge from the census.

WOMEN AND THE FORMATION OF SPANISH SOCIETY

Within twenty years or so of the beginnings of Spanish settlement in Hispaniola and Puerto Rico, and probably in other parts of the Caribbean as well, the presence of Spanish women had become substantial enough that at least in the largest towns—Santo Domingo and San Juan—the core of a Hispanic society came into existence. Most likely this occurred not so much as a result of official efforts to encourage the migration of married couples but rather because the early prosperity from gold and pearls made the islands attractive destinations for couples seeking to improve their economic circumstances or even for single women in need of employment.[33] The number of single men (including married men unaccompanied by their spouses) lured by the gold mines or pearl fisheries dwarfed those of the single and married women who arrived in the islands from Spain or Portugal. Yet many—perhaps the majority—of those single men were transient, their presence ephemeral, as the difficulties and disappointments of small-scale mining, and later the appeal of new opportunities on the mainland, forced or persuaded many to move on to other destinations.[34] Despite their much smaller numbers, women were more likely to remain in one place and contribute to the growth of civil society, although certainly this was not always the case. Life for women in the Caribbean in the years following first contact was by no means easy.

Among the first women to live on the islands, Inés de Malaver and Teresa de Baeza, who apparently arrived in 1495, suffered brutal punishment at the hands of Columbus's brother Bartolomé Colón. The former was flogged and the latter's tongue was cut out. Several witnesses in Bobadilla's investigation in 1500 offered conflicting and confusing testimony about the ostensible offenses and punishments. The women were accused of casting aspersions on the Colón family and its origins, and Teresa possibly used her house to arrange extramarital trysts.[35] Teresa was married to a Spaniard, Pedro Daza. Much of the testimony in Bobadilla's inquiry centered on the harsh punishments and executions that had taken place at the orders of Columbus or his brother, in some cases for seemingly trivial offenses. Obviously the Spanish women present in Hispaniola during the very early years, some of whom probably were prostitutes or the mistresses of the leading men on the island, enjoyed no special protection because of their sex.[36]

The arrival of more married couples and especially the formation of a small aristocratic elite in Hispaniola centered on the *virreina,* don Diego Colón's high-born wife, doña María de Toledo,[37] and the wives of the *oidores* and other high-ranking officials might have helped to underscore the importance of women in establishing a stable Hispanic society in Hispaniola. Some of these women and their families forged long-term ties with island societies and with multiple locales in the Indies. One member of the *virreina*'s entourage was Diego Suárez Pacheco, who traveled to Hispaniola with his wife, doña María de Marcaida, and family. The Suárez family at some point moved to Cuba, where Diego Suárez's son, Juan, held an *encomienda* jointly with Hernando Cortés, future conqueror of Mexico. Cortés seduced and then under pressure married Juan's sister, Catalina, who after the conquest traveled to Mexico to join her husband and died there under mysterious circumstances.[38]

Daughters of merchants, officials, or other prominent men either born in the Caribbean or taken there at a young age figured in marital alliances that strengthened or consolidated ties of economic or political interest or common origin. Lucas Vázquez de Ayllón was *oidor* of the first *audiencia* of Santo Domingo and served as Ovando's *alcalde mayor* (district magistrate or governor) in northern Hispaniola. During his first sojourn on the island, Vázquez de Ayllón was a *vecino* and *encomendero* of Concepción involved in mining and agriculture. He became a partner of a leading merchant of Santo Domingo, Lope Bardecí, but continued to be involved in the economy of the north, receiving a grant of two hundred Indians as a *vecino* of Santiago in the *repartimiento* of 1514. He married Ana Becerra, the daughter of the *regidor* (town councilman) Licenciado Francisco Becerra, the town's leading entrepreneur.[39] Lucas Vázquez, along with his father-in-law and other associates—including the other judges of the *audiencia*—became very active in organizing raids in the Bahamas and elsewhere to capture Indians for sale as slaves.[40]

Lucas Vázquez de Ayllón was connected to the large Manzorro-Becerra clan through his marriage.[41] Rodrigo Manzorro, one of his partners in the slave-hunting business, lived in Hispaniola from an early time.[42] Forty years of age in 1512, in 1514 he was a *vecino* and *regidor* of Santiago and received a *repartimiento* of one hundred Indians; he was recorded as married to a woman from Castile.[43] In 1518 his daughter doña Elvira Manzorro, most likely a *mestiza,* married Francisco de Barrionuevo, the wealthy and powerful *encomendero* of the island of Mona, near Puerto Rico. In these years Mona was the largest producer of cassava bread, supplying some three thousand *cargas* (a *carga* was the equivalent of several bushels) a year, primarily to the mines of Puerto Rico and pearl fisheries of Cubagua.[44] Appointed governor of Tierra Firme after several years' absence from the Caribbean, Barrionuevo also was responsible for the negotiations that brought the lengthy rebellion of Enriquillo on Hispaniola to a conclusion in 1533.

Around 1518, doña Elvira accompanied her father to Castile so that he could "instruct her in the matters of our Holy Faith." He died there and she married Barrionuevo. The marriage was controversial, as the Jeronymite governors of Hispaniola apparently had another marriage partner in mind for her. Probably at issue was the disposition of her father's *repartimiento,* which the king decided should pass to doña Elvira. In Seville she owned "five black and white slaves," which Barrionuevo petitioned to take with them when they returned to the islands.[45] Barrionuevo, like his father-in-law, was an active investor in slave raiding expeditions and a very successful entrepreneur in the pearl trade, working in partnership with his nephew, Pedro de Barrionuevo, who established himself in Cubagua. In 1527 he took his wife to Spain to recuperate from an illness and went to live in his hometown of Soria, but she died soon after they arrived there.[46] If doña Elvira's mother was an Indian, her marriage to the powerful Barrionuevo suggests that her wealth and connections more than compensated for her mixed parentage.[47] Born in Hispaniola, during her brief lifetime she traveled twice to Spain and died there far from home.

The advantages to be gained from strategic marriages might have outweighed the personal preferences of daughters, especially ones as young and wealthy as doña Elvira Manzorro. Doña Luisa de Aux, daughter of Miguel Díaz de Aux and Isabel de Cáceres, wealthy and high-ranking *vecinos* of San Germán, married Francisco de Alvarado, also a leading *vecino* of the island whose property at his death in slaves, gold, and other possessions was worth more than 20,000 *ducados* (a unit of currency worth 350 *maravedís*).[48] Blas de Villasante, a longtime treasurer of Puerto Rico who was active in mining and sugar production, married the daughter of Tomás de Castellón, a merchant and sugar entrepreneur of Genoese origins.[49] She inherited her father's sugar mill, San Juan de las Palmas, when he died in 1526. In addition to the mill, Castellón's estate included one hundred Indian and African slaves, one hundred Indians in *repartimiento,* fifty mares and horses, and two estates that probably produced yucca, all valued at around 20,000 pesos.[50]

These marriages point to the concentration of wealth in the hands of a relatively small number of men and families and the importance of marriageable (and often inheriting) daughters in forging and maintaining partnerships and associations in the multifaceted early Caribbean and transatlantic economy. They also underscore the extensive involvement of royal and local officials in the most lucrative aspects of that economy: gold mining, pearls, slave raiding, trade, and sugar production. Surely many officials realized that the most efficient route to a profitable sojourn in the islands was to make useful business connections, and the right marriage partner could promote or enhance the formation of such relations. In June 1520, officials in San Juan complained that the recently arrived royal justice, Licenciado Antonio de la Gama, had married a daughter of governor Juan Ponce de León, seemingly without permission from the king. "It has seemed an impetuous thing and the island is somewhat scandalized," they wrote.[51]

The wealthiest entrepreneurs of the early Caribbean became involved, as seen, in multiple sectors of the economy and maintained important connections with Genoese, Burgalés, or Andalusian merchants and financiers in Spain; many royal officials did the same. Men who lacked or failed to forge such connections did not necessarily share the profits of the early boom years. One such example was Marcelo Villalobos, an *oidor* of the first *audiencia,* whose large entourage that accompanied him to Santo Domingo in 1512 was matched by the social pretensions (and entourage) of his noble wife, doña Isabel de Manrique. Villalobos arrived in Hispaniola in debt, a state that he never overcame. Doña Isabel clearly expected to live in aristocratic style, as suggested by her efforts to provide a suitable dowry for her favorite *criada,* Isabel Serpa, who wed Jerónimo Colón in doña Isabel's home in February 1524. She had raised Isabel Serpa from an early age and brought her to Hispaniola. Given the couple's limited financial means, she could provide her favorite servant with little more than sumptuous furnishings for her bedroom and several items of elegant clothing, probably chosen from among her own possessions, along with an indigenous slave or servant. Villalobos became ill and died in 1526, leaving considerable debts and naming his young daughters, doña Aldonza de Villalobos and doña María Manrique, his heirs. Considering his financial difficulties, it is surprising that the year before he died the Crown granted Villalobos the contract to establish a colony on the island of Margarita (near the coast of Venezuela). Not surprisingly, he made little progress toward settling the island before his death, but in 1527 the Crown confirmed the seven-year-old doña Aldonza de Villalobos as governor of Margarita; her mother would exercise authority until doña Aldonza reached the age of majority or married.[52] In the mid-1550s, doña Aldonza was governor of the island, although it is unlikely she ever lived or even visited there.[53]

In the 1530s the pearl islands of Cubagua and Margarita figured as something of an open frontier on the southern fringe of the Spanish Caribbean, where women as well as men seem to have found a good measure of social freedom as well as economic opportunity.[54] In contrast, life for women in Hispaniola, or at least in Santo Domingo, probably had begun to resemble more closely the Spanish society that they (or their parents) left behind. In 1545, members of Santo Domingo's city council wrote to the king that they planned to establish a convent for women, which they felt "compelled" to do, given the "multitude of women and orphans." The archdeacon Alvaro de Castro died that year, leaving his stone house and urban property for that purpose. The council said they had sent (presumably to Spain) for four nuns of Santa Clara.[55] The convent came into existence under the Franciscan order, and by the mid-1550s the Dominicans were hoping to establish a second convent for women.[56]

Women were expected to play a role in the colony's religious life well before any formal institution was established for them. A report of 1513 mentioned that Ovando had sent two *cacicas* to be instructed in Christianity by the wife of an unnamed *vecino*.[57] In the *repartimiento* of 1514 an Indian woman named Luisa, whose Spanish husband, Alonso de Cazares, had died, was "deposited" with Gaspar de Astudillo "so that his wife will have her with her in their house, and teach her to embroider and about the things of the faith, and she should not serve in any other respect."[58] The assumption that Spanish women would act as models of Christian life and belief reflected an idealized understanding of their social and religious role that did not always dovetail with reality. Not only did some Spanish women flout sexual and marital norms, especially in the early years of settlement, but they also might share with men the callous disregard for the welfare of the indigenous population so characteristic of the early years of European settlement in the Caribbean. Officials in Cuba in the 1540s, for example, investigated charges that doña Guiomar de Guzmán, a *vecina* of Santiago and widow of the *contador* (accountant) Pedro de Paz, did not bother to provide her Christianized slaves or servants with Christian burials.[59]

In contrast to life in Spain, outside the largest centers of Spanish society in the Caribbean such as Santo Domingo or Puerto Rico, Spanish women faced dangers peculiar to the islands—pirates, hurricanes, and raids by natives or fugitive Africans. Two women and sixteen *vecinos* of Puerto Rico died when the town was burned during the indigenous rebellion of 1513.[60] The *audiencia* reported in February 1520 that a Spanish woman, along with two of her children and fourteen slaves, had been killed in a raid near Puerto Real in Hispaniola, possibly by followers of the indigenous rebel Enrique.[61] In 1537 a ship carrying gold back to Spain from San Juan stopped at the island of Mona because it was Ash

Wednesday. When most of the Spaniards went ashore to hear mass, a small number of non-Spaniards who stayed on board took control of the ship, threw ten or twelve Africans into the sea, and sailed off with more than 4,000 pesos in gold and two married Spanish women who happened to have remained on board.[62] In 1553, officials in la Yaguana reported to the *audiencia* that French corsairs had occupied the town for a month, sacking and burning it and causing many residents to flee to the mountains with their wives and children. They seized some men and women and "held on their ships for sixteen days the wife of captain Pedro Martín with an Indian woman of hers and two *criados*." They demanded an outrageous ransom of 10,000 pesos for the hostages but apparently settled for the more modest sum of 1,500 pesos, which was all that could be found after the town was looted.[63]

Other dangers specifically affected women, especially those entailed in travel. María García brought criminal charges against Francisco García, a ship captain and *vecino* of Triana in Seville, accusing him of attempting to rape her one night in the spring of 1527 as she traveled on his ship from Santo Domingo to Spain. María described herself as a "virtuous widow and very honorable woman" who had worked for many years for Licenciado Lebrón, an *oidor* of the *audiencia,* under whose protection she ostensibly traveled. She alleged that Francisco García entered her cabin one night and tried to force himself on her, choking her when she resisted his advances and threatening to kill her if she did not comply. She was able to escape, however, and as she fled sobbing some men intervened and prevented García from carrying out "his evil intent."[64]

If on the whole less mobile than men, nonetheless it probably was fairly common for women, especially widows, to return to Spain from the islands in the early years. In June 1513 the widow Beatriz García was trying to recover from a man named Antonio de Angulo the 40 pesos that she had given him when she left Santo Domingo to pay off a debt that her deceased husband had owed; presumably Angulo had kept the money and failed to repay the debt.[65] In 1533 Isabel de Avila, who had lived in San Juan with her by-then deceased husband, Diego Guilarte, asked for permission to sell her property and go to live in Spain with her three children.[66] Many Spanish men were leaving Hispaniola and Puerto Rico in these years for other destinations, and widows could have found themselves isolated and facing an uncertain economic future, in which case a return to Spain might have promised greater security. Women, like men, also left the islands for other destinations in the Indies. A list of licenses conceded by the *audiencia* to individuals wishing to leave Hispaniola (mainly for New Spain, Santa Marta, or Nicaragua) in 1528–1529 includes a number of women. While the majority planned to travel with husbands or other relatives, or to join men who already had relocated, several women are listed individually.[67]

The *oidores*' report of a "multitude" of widows and orphans and the desirability of providing for at least some of them by founding a convent suggests the limited means and choices available to some women. Ana Márquez was the widow of longtime *audiencia portero* (doorman) Pedro de Vidaguren. Vidaguren had earned a very modest annual salary of 20,000 *maravedís*. Shortly before his death he petitioned for a salary increase of 10,000 *maravedís* and a guarantee that one of his sons would succeed him in the office. After Vidaguren died, his wife and sons faced not only the loss of his income but of their home as well, as they always had lived in lodgings in the *audiencia* building itself. In 1544 she requested that they be allowed to continue to live there and that the office of porter be reserved for one of her sons until he came of age, with someone serving in a temporary capacity until that time, because she was "poor and a widow and her sons little and there remained for them, after God, no other remedy than this office."[68]

CONCLUSION

By the 1530s, Spanish society in the Caribbean had undergone rapid development and change. The numerous and mainly male immigrants who responded to the potential of gold mining or pearl fishing for the most part did not remain in the islands. In the same years, however, a perhaps surprising number of European women also arrived and participated in the settlement of the Caribbean. There they found a society strikingly different in composition, nature, and appearance from what they had left behind. Forty years—two full generations—after Columbus's first voyages, the majority of houses in even the largest urban centers still would have been constructed of wood and thatch. Indeed, some residents of Santiago de Cuba complained that stone houses—cherished Spanish symbols of permanence, wealth, and power—were inappropriate, as they retained humidity and created unhealthful living conditions; they argued that houses built of planks with tile roofs were more practical.[69] The social and cultural milieu was as distinctive as the physical one; Spanish women were surrounded by indigenous and African slaves and servants and interacted with the *mestiza* daughters of longtime residents who to a great degree were accepted as Spanish. Spanish women also faced considerable uncertainties, ranging from the deaths of husbands, who often married late and therefore were a good deal older, to the impact of economic shifts and the attractions offered by other destinations as Spanish settlement expanded to the mainland. The enormous and rapid demographic changes occasioned by the arrival of Europeans—the drastic reduction and relocation of indigenous populations, the introduction of growing numbers of African slaves—guaranteed the profound and permanent transformation of Caribbean societies before the middle of the sixteenth century. The presence of substantial numbers of women who presided over Spanish-type households helped to shape the direction of that change. Spanish women were important participants in the formation of the first transatlantic society.

NOTES

1. For a good introduction to and discussion of the importance of historical archaeology in studying early post-contact society in the Caribbean, particularly with regard to gender distinctions and the role of women, see Kathleen Deagan, "Colonial Transformation: Euro-American Cultural Genesis in the Early Spanish American Colonies," *Journal of Anthropological Research* 52, no. 2 (summer 1996): 135-160.

2. In 1502, for example, when Vélez de Mendoza of Moguer agreed to transport fifty emigrants to Hispaniola, the Crown stipulated that at least ten should be married men with their households. It further instructed Governor Nicolás de Ovando that in the division of lands or Indians married men should receive grants one-third larger than those of single men. (Roberto Marte, ed., *Santo Domingo en los Manuscritos de Juan Bautista Muñoz* [Santo Domingo: Ediciones Fundación García Arévalo, 1981], 39.) Married men who brought their wives with them received other concessions in the form of tax exemptions and permission to bring larger entourages. Despite instructions to favor married men in the distribution of grants, the *repartimiento* of 1514, discussed below, does not reflect any systematic privileging of men married to Spanish women in the assignments.

3. Ibid., 73. Don Diego Colón succeeded Nicolás de Ovando as governor in 1509.

4. Ibid., 57, 64. All translations from the Spanish are mine unless otherwise noted.

5. *Repartimiento* means a distribution or division, in this case of native labor. Monroy was assigned the cacique Porras de la Sierra with fourteen *"personas de servicio"* (workers) and the cacique Argüello with another nineteen; see Emilio Rodríguez Demorizi, *Los dominicos y las encomiendas de indios de la Isla Española* (Santo Domingo: Editora del Caribe, 1971), 112. His was not a unique case.

6. Marte, *Santo Domingo,* 345. Such inquiries, however, did take place in the 1520s; see the *audiencia* case involving Benito de Astorga's efforts to convince his wife Isabel de Mayorga to join him in Santo Domingo in Archivo General de Indias (AGI) Santo Domingo 9, ramo 2, no. 18. Astorga's deposition dates to 1527-1528.

7. See Varela's introduction to the transcription of the *pesquisa* (inquiry) in Consuelo

Varela, *La caída de Cristóbal Colón. El juicio de Bobadilla.* Edición y transcripción de Isabel Aguirre (Madrid: Marcial Pons Historia, 2006), 20.

8. Ibid., 156.

9. Ibid., 40.

10. Marte, *Santo Domingo*, 150. At least one of the original thirty ships in Ovando's expedition was lost near the Canaries, apparently with some of these couples or families on board.

11. Columbus's reluctance to sanction marriages between his men and Indian women seems to have hinged mainly on the question of conversion to Christianity; women who were not baptized could not participate in the Christian sacrament of marriage. On this question see Varela, *La caída*, 104–107. Both Bobadilla and Ovando continued Columbus's policy of restricting mixed marriages. In 1504, for example, Ovando exiled the interpreter Cristóbal Rodríguez, who helped arrange the marriage of a Spaniard to an Indian woman without official license (see Varela, *La caída*, 105).

12. In 1509 the king wrote to don Diego Colón that he had been informed by Ovando that "many men married to Indian women believe that their wives and children should be the heirs of their parents, and even after being corrected they will not abandon this way of thinking; for which reason it is said that the Indians they first had should be taken from them and they should be ordered to move away from the lands of their parents-in-law and relatives to deflect them from this notion" (Marte, *Santo Domingo*, 68). According to Varela, *La caída*, 106, in 1508 King Ferdinand issued a *cédula* prohibiting Spaniards from inheriting property from their Indian wives.

13. In Marte, *Santo Domingo*, 103. The term "white slaves" most likely referred to Muslim women or Moriscas.

14. Ibid., 121–122.

15. Ibid., 344.

16. Ibid., 191.

17. While the existence of women among the cacique group probably predated the arrival of Spaniards in the island, the growth in the numbers of women rulers most likely reflected the circumstances and results of warfare and the imposition of Spanish rule.

18. For a transcription, see Rodríguez Demorizi, *Los dominicos*, 74–248. The volume includes extensive annotations on a number of the Spaniards listed in the *repartimiento* as well as a transcription of the "*Interrogatorio Jeronimiano*" of 1517, another important source of information for Hispaniola in those years (273–354).

19. The situation of the *virreina,* doña María de Toledo, wife of don Diego Colón, was unlike that of most other married Spanish women in Hispaniola, as she held an *encomienda* in her own right. She was not, however, the only woman who held an *encomienda* in this period. In August 1515, for example, the king ordered that the *encomienda* of Francisco de Herrera should be restored to his widow, Beatriz Sánchez; see AGI Indiferente 419, leg. 5, fol. 448v. When the Pero Núñez de Guzmán, the treasurer of Cuba, died in 1527, his widow inherited his estate and was assigned what remained of his *encomienda* since the couple had no children. The widow, doña Catalina de Agüero, subsequently married the governor of Cuba, Gonzalo de Guzmán, who had ensured that she would receive the grant. See Irene Wright, *The Early History of Cuba* (New York: Macmillan, 1916), 118–119, and AGI Santo Domingo 1121, leg. 1. The grant subsequently was disputed, both in Cuba and by Nuñez's mother in Castile; see Leví Marrero, *Cuba: Economía y sociedad,* vol. 2 (Madrid: Editorial Playor, 1974), 10.

20. Despite earlier hedging on the issue of marriage to indigenous women, by 1514 the Crown was promoting it; see Marte, *Santo Domingo*, 121–122.

21. Ibid., 153, includes this excerpt from an anonymous report of 1512, probably written by a member of one of the orders: "of all the Christians who raise Indian girls [in their households], some take them for housekeepers, and these are the nobles and priests; others take them for cooks, and these are the cattle raisers and workers, of whom many are married in Castile, and there they are with Indian women; even worse, others take them to instruct them to learn to serve and dress [properly?] and even to make a living in a very bad fashion; and after they are so instructed they sell them to cowboys and miners for bad purposes."

22. Ibid., 277–278.

23. Officials seem to have been concerned about the need to retain women in Hispaniola even earlier than this. Leví Marrero, *Cuba: Economía y sociedad,* vol. 1 (Rio Piedras, Puerto Rico: Editorial San Juan, 1972), 130, quotes from a royal *cédula* that prohibited any constraints on the relocation of women who wished to join husbands who had taken up residence in Cuba.

24. In this period the island that later became known as Puerto Rico was known as San Juan and the main town and port was Puerto Rico; the usage later reversed. For clarity I use the modern names for the island and the port city.

25. Marte, *Santo Domingo,* 324. For the reaction of officials in Puerto Rico, see AGI Patronato 176, ramo 5. They noted that "ordinarily we see that those who are newly arrived in the first year they experience much illness and many die." Luis de Berrio received a royal commission to recruit fifty new *vecinos* for this project, but in this instance, as in other efforts at recruitment, the total fell far short of the objective. The prospective emigrants were to have their own settlement organized with the standard officials of a municipality. A man named Alonso de Torres was promised a *regimiento* (seat on the town council) and the position of notary for one of his sons if he were qualified; see AGI Indiferente General 420, lib. 8, fols. 149v–151r (October 1519).

26. Marte, *Santo Domingo,* 284–286, 290. See also José Luis Saez, S.J., *La iglesia y el negro esclavo en Santo Domingo. Una historia de tres siglos* (Santo Domingo: Patronato de la Ciudad Colonial de Santo Domingo, Colección Quinto Centenario, 1994), 251, Document 37, taken from AGI Patronato, leg. 18, ramo 5 (Toledo, January 15, 1529). The consistent use in both these documents (the *oidores*' proposal and the royal *cédula*) of the term *vecinos* to refer to both free settlers and slaves as well as the emphasis on recruiting married men for both groups suggests that the Crown possibly viewed the Africans more as potential settlers than as slaves. See Marrero, *Cuba,* 1:217, on a royal *cédula* of 1526 sent to Cuba that seemed to endorse the possibility of a transition to free status for slaves and their families.

27. AGI Santo Domingo 118.

28. Enrique Otte's superb study *Las perlas del Caribe: Nueva Cádiz de Cubagua* (Caracas: Fundación John Boulton, 1977) documents the growth of the pearl trade during the 1520s and 1530s and Spanish settlement of the so-called pearl islands. On the impact on the environment and local indigenous groups of pearl fishing, see Michael Perri, "Ruined and Lost: The Destruction of the Pearl Coast," *Environment and History* 15, no. 2 (2009): 129–161. The important scholarly work of Jalil Sued Badillo, *El Dorado borincano. La economía de la conquista, 1510–1550* (San Juan: Ediciones Puerto, 2001), definitively establishes the early profitability of gold mining in San Juan.

29. Usually the beginning of the Spanish occupation of Puerto Rico is dated to 1508 or 1509, but the first organized foray to the island led by Juan Ponce de León took place in 1506,

at which time Spaniards found gold on the island. See the deposition of Juan González Ponce de León, who played a key role in that first episode, done in Mexico City in 1532 (AGI Mexico 203), transcribed with annotations in Aurelio Tió, *Nuevas fuentes para la historia de Puerto Rico* (San German: Ediciones de la Universidad Interamericana de Puerto Rico and Barcelona: Ediciones Rumbos, 1961), documento 1.

30. AGI Justicia 106, no. 3. See Sued Badillo, *El Dorado borincano,* 51–53, for a discussion of this census and population figures in the early Caribbean; Cuadro I (53) offers a comparison of numbers of *vecinos* living in towns throughout the region in the first half of the sixteenth century.

31. A report to the Council of the Indies in 1535 discussing the presence of Portuguese on Hispaniola stated that "there are some who are married and have become *vecinos,* and more than 200 single men, skilled workers in the sugar estates, farmers, carpenters, masons, ironsmiths and all other trades in all the settlements, and they are very useful. . . . To remove them would cause great damage to the land, because of the lack of people" (Marte, *Santo Domingo,* 369). Portuguese emigrants also played a prominent role in the settlement of the Canary Islands, so their presence in the Spanish Caribbean had ample precedent.

32. For comparison, see Deagan, "Colonial Transformation," 147, who notes that "by 1550 Taino wares were almost nonexistent at Puerto Real, and the new, possibly African-influenced pottery was extremely abundant." I do not wish to imply that the African presence was any less strong in Hispaniola than in Puerto Rico in the 1530s, only that the indigenous element might have been weaker in the latter. A 1533 description of sugar estates in Hispaniola and a detailed inventory of one estate clearly indicate the presence of considerable numbers of African slaves, both men and women, in the countryside; see Saez, *La iglesia,* 267–272, document 46, and 278–282, document 52. See also Lynne A. Guitar, "Cultural Genesis: Relationships among Indians, Africans, and Spaniards in Rural Hispaniola, First Half of the Sixteenth Century" (Ph.D. diss., Vanderbilt University, 1998).

33. On the role of women in couples' decisions regarding emigration in the sixteenth century, see Ida Altman, "Spanish Women and the Indies: Transatlantic Migration in the Early Modern Period," in PLAS *Cuadernos,* no. 4, 21–46 (Princeton: Program in Latin American Studies, 2001).

34. On this phenomenon, see Sued Badillo, *El Dorado borincano,* 320.

35. See Varela, *La caída,* 137.

36. Ibid., 157.

37. Doña María de Toledo was the niece of the Duke of Alba. As patriarch of one of Spain's most powerful noble families, the Duke of Alba exercised considerable influence over King Ferdinand. Doña María and don Diego Colón married in 1508 and departed for Hispaniola in June 1509. Initially they took up residence in Santo Domingo's *fortaleza* (fortress), as there was no appropriate house available. On doña María's background and the arrangement of the marriage, see Luis Arranz Márquez, *Don Diego Colón, Almirante, Virrey y Gobernador de las Indias* (Madrid: Consejo Superior de Investigaciones Científicas, 1982), tomo 1, chapter 4. For the couple's departure and arrival in Hispaniola, see page 108. It has been suggested that Colón's marriage to doña María and the pressure brought to bear by her powerful relatives had a great deal to do with the king's decision to send don Diego Colón to replace Ovando as governor of Hispaniola.

38. See Camilla Townsend, *Malintzin's Choices* (Albuquerque: Univ. of New Mexico Press, 2006), 136.

39. See Otte, *Las perlas del Caribe,* 111–112.

40. Ibid., 113–115.

41. Rodrigo Manzorro was joined in Hispaniola by his brother, Licenciado Hernando Becerra, and another relative, Bachiller Juan Becerra; another cousin, Bartolomé Becerra, lived in Sabana de Salvatierra; see Troy S. Floyd, *The Columbus Dynasty in the Caribbean, 1492–1526* (Albuquerque: Univ. of New Mexico Press, 1973), 79–80. Floyd names Juan Becerra as the father-in-law of Lucas Vázquez, differing from Otte (see Otte's note 52). Possibly the names have been confused. It seems clear that Lucas Vázquez made a marital alliance with this extended family, but he probably was not Manzorro's brother-in-law.

42. He testified in Bobadilla's inquiry; see Varela, *La caída*, 211ff.

43. Marte, *Santo Domingo*, 110.

44. See Sued Badillo, *El Dorado borincano*, 177, 178, 201–202.

45. AGI Indiferente General 419, leg. 7, fol. 830r–831r and legajo 420, fol. 40r. Varela, *La caída*, 74, refers to doña Elvira as a *mestiza*, as do other scholars. In 1518 doña Elvira claimed she was of "young age." Her mother's name never appears, and the phrasing—that her father wanted to "instruct her in the matters of our Holy Faith"—suggests that her mother probably was indigenous to the Caribbean. On Christianization as a justification for sending *mestizo* children to Castile, see Juan Gil, "Los primeros mestizos indios en España: Una voz ausente," in *Entre dos mundos. Fronteras culturales y agentes mediadores,* coordinadores Berta Ares Queija and Serge Gruzinski, 15–36 (Seville: Escuela de Estudios Hispano-Americanos, 1997). On the removal of *mestizo* children from their indigenous mothers in the Andean region and sending *mestizo* children to Spain, see Jane Mangan's chapter, "Indigenous Women as Mothers in Conquest-Era Peru," in this volume.

46. Otte, *Las perlas del Caribe*, 202–203.

47. Manzorro's having married a woman from Castile certainly did not preclude the possibility that he fathered a child with an Indian woman; see Mangan's chapter in this volume. Esteban Mira Caballos, *Las Antillas Mayores: 1492–1550* (Madrid: Iberoamericana, 2000), 286, notes that the first *mestizo* born in Hispaniola known to have survived to adulthood was the son of Miguel Díaz de Aux and a *cacica* known as "Catalina." On August 26, 1533, Francisco de Barrionuevo wrote a report from Hispaniola to the Crown (AGI Santo Domingo 77, ramo 4, no. 69) in which he complained about the *mestizos* of the island, but apparently his negative feelings did not extend to *mestizas* since, as noted, he probably married one.

48. Sued Badillo, *El Dorado borincano*, 210. Doña Luisa de Aux was born in early April 1517, and her father Miguel Díaz apparently died shortly thereafter. Doña Luisa and her mother (who probably accompanied Díaz to the islands, where he had long been active, when he returned from Spain in 1511 or 1512) were living in San Germán in 1525 (see AGI Santo Domingo 77, ramo 2, no. 36).

49. According to Sued Badillo, *El Dorado borincano*, 113, Villasante was a *converso* (convert from Judaism or descendant of converts), as was Andrés de Haro, a member of a *converso* family from Burgos who partnered with Castellón in the establishment of the first sugar mill in the western part of San Juan, near San German, in 1522. Castellón was from a Genoese family and with his brother, Jácome, became a *vecino* of Española; he "complemented his mercantile activities with the traffic in Indian slaves and mineral extraction on both islands" (278). Felipe Fernández-Armesto, *The Canary Islands after the Conquest* (Oxford: Clarendon Press, 1982) writes of the Genoese involvement in the settlement of the Canaries and other Atlantic island groups that "there is no clearer instance of how the early exploitation of the Atlantic was a 'Mediterranean' enterprise which not only opened up a new economic system, but also extended an old one" (32). The observation applies to the early

Caribbean as well; see Ruth Pike, *Enterprise and Adventure: The Genoese in Seville and the Opening of the New World* (Ithaca: Cornell Univ. Press, 1966).

50. Sued Badillo, *El Dorado borincano,* 298.

51. AGI Patronato 176, ramo 5. The letter was signed by Antonio Sedeño, Hernando Mogollón, Pedro Moreno, and Baltasar de Castro. An anonymous report (possibly from Bartolomé de Las Casas) called into question the marriage of Juan Ponce de León himself, stating that he had arrived in the Indies with Columbus and in Hispaniola married *"una moza de un mesonero"* (a tavern girl) before going to Puerto Rico (Marte, *Santo Domingo,* 239). The uncertain status of Juan Ponce de León's wife is suggested by her apparently having taken her husband's name—she consistently appears as Leonor Ponce de León in documents relating to the family. Juan Ponce himself is thought to have been of illegitimate birth but related to a noble family. On the marriage of his daughter, Isabel, to Antonio de la Gama, see Tió, *Nuevas fuentes,* 304, note 21.

52. Otte, *Las perlas del Caribe,* 264–266, 269–271. It is not clear if Jerónimo Colón was related to Columbus's family.

53. See the letter of April 12, 1554, from Gonzalo Fernández de Oviedo written in Santo Domingo referring to doña Aldonza Manrique as governor of the island in Marte, *Santo Domingo,* 433.

54. See the interesting discussion of women in Cubagua and Margarita in Otte, *Las perlas del Caribe,* 350–354.

55. Marte, *Santo Domingo,* 407. In her study of Santa Clara convent in Cuzco, founded in the 1550s, Kathryn Burns, *Colonial Habits: Convents and the Spiritual Economy of Cuzco, Peru* (Durham: Duke Univ. Press, 1999), writes, "For a cabildo to sponsor a convent was . . . a striking departure from the norm. Most foundations in the Americas, as in Spain and throughout Catholic Europe, were initiated by individuals or families" (24). The establishment of this convent by Santo Domingo's city council suggests that such a foundation by a municipality possibly was not as unusual as Burns supposes. Perhaps in Santo Domingo, as in Cuzco, making adequate provision for *mestiza* girls was among the motivations for founding the convent.

56. The idea of establishing a convent in Santo Domingo apparently had been conceived some time earlier, as a royal *cédula* directed to Rodrigo de Bastidas in 1538 referred to funds that Bastidas had designated for the purpose (AGI Caracas 1, leg. 1, fols. 54v–57r). A *cédula* of 1547 referred to the establishment of the convent of Santa Clara and sending "some elderly religious women of good conduct and living" from Spain (AGI Santo Domingo 868, leg. 2, fol. 352). Another *cédula* in the following year referred to providing passage to Hispaniola for ten nuns of the order of Santa Clara and two Franciscan friars to establish a monastery for "the daughters of the *vecinos* of that island" (AGI Indiferente General 1964, leg. 11, fols. 84–84v). In 1556, it was noted that sixteen daughters of *vecinos principales* (leading citizens) had entered the convent and that upwards of 10,000 pesos had been spent on the church, sleeping quarters, and other construction. In the same year a *vecina* of Santo Domingo who was traveling to Spain left a house in the city with six African slaves to establish a Dominican convent. The Crown asked the *audiencia* officials if a city of five hundred *vecinos* which already had a cathedral, three monasteries, a convent, and two hospitals really needed a second convent (AGI Santo Domingo 899 leg. 1, fols. 17v–18).

57. Marte, *Santo Domingo,* 307.

58. Rodríguez Demorizi, *Los dominicos,* 148.

59. Mira Caballos, *Las Antillas Mayores,* 264. The case is in AGI Justicia 73, no. 3. Doña

Guiomar might not have arrived in the islands until the mid-1530s, possibly after her husband's death (see AGI Justicia 726, no. 5).

60. Sued Badillo, *El Dorado borincano*, 59.
61. Marte, *Santo Domingo*, 357.
62. Sued Badillo, *El Dorado borincano*, 397.
63. Marte, *Santo Domingo*, 430.
64. AGI Justicia 698, no. 7.
65. AGI Justicia 697, no. 3.
66. Sued Badillo, *El Dorado borincano*, 210.
67. AGI Santo Domingo 77, ramo 3, no. 52. The documents in this *legajo* (bundle) appear to have been renumbered recently according to chronological order, thus the information on *ramo* (section) and number may no longer be current. Ninety-five licenses were conceded for the period from March 1528 to November 1529; sixteen of those included women. The actual numbers of women involved were higher, however, as licenses could include more than one person and thus in some instances more than one woman. One such case was that of Cecelia Lucero. She was the wife of Diego de Jaramillo, a *vecino* of New Spain who had sent for her to join him. She was to travel with her daughter and a nephew (May 1528). Pedro de Aldaña received a license to go to New Spain, taking with him his wife, Marina Ruiz de Monjaraz, as well as two nieces and an African slave woman (December 1528). Inés García, the wife of Diego Martín, obtained a license to take her daughters, Marina and Isabel, to San Juan in April 1529, although there was no mention of whether her husband was there.
68. AGI Santo Domingo 133.
69. For a brief discussion of domestic construction in the early Caribbean, see Mira Caballos, *Las Antillas Mayores*, 310–311. On differing ideas regarding construction in Cuba around 1540, see Marrero, *Cuba*, 2:372–373.

WORKS CITED

Primary Sources

ARCHIVO GENERAL DE INDIAS, SEVILLE, SPAIN

Caracas
Indiferente General
Justicia
Patronato
Santo Domingo

Secondary Sources

Altman, Ida. "Spanish Women and the Indies: Transatlantic Migration in the Early Modern Period." In *PLAS Cuadernos*, no. 4. 21–46. Princeton: Program in Latin American Studies, 2001.

Arranz Márquez, Luis. *Don Diego Colón, Almirante, Virrey y Gobernador de las Indias.* Madrid: Consejo Superior de Investigaciones Científicas, 1982.

Burns, Kathryn. *Colonial Habits: Convents and the Spiritual Economy of Cuzco, Peru.* Durham: Duke Univ. Press, 1999.

Deagan, Kathleen. "Colonial Transformation: Euro-American Cultural Genesis in the Early Spanish American Colonies," *Journal of Anthropological Research* 52, no. 2 (summer 1996): 135–160.
Fernández-Armesto, Felipe. *The Canary Islands after the Conquest.* Oxford: Clarendon Press, 1982.
Floyd, Troy S. *The Columbus Dynasty in the Caribbean, 1492–1526.* Albuquerque: Univ. of New Mexico Press, 1973.
Gil, Juan. "Los primeros mestizos indios en España: Una voz ausente." In *Entre dos mundos. Fronteras culturales y agentes mediadores,* coordinadores Berta Ares Queija and Serge Gruzinski, 15–36. Seville: Escuela de Estudios Hispano-Americanos, 1997.
Guitar, Lynne A. "Cultural Genesis: Relationships among Indians, Africans, and Spaniards in Rural Hispaniola, First Half of the Sixteenth Century." Ph.D. diss., Vanderbilt University, 1998.
Marrero, Leví. *Cuba: Economía y sociedad,* vol. 1. Rio Piedras, Puerto Rico: Editorial San Juan, 1972.
———. *Cuba: Economía y sociedad,* vol. 2. Madrid: Editorial Playor, 1974.
Marte, Roberto, ed., *Santo Domingo en los Manuscritos de Juan Bautista Muñoz.* Santo Domingo: Ediciones Fundación García Arévalo, 1981.
Mira Caballos, Esteban. *Las Antillas Mayores: 1492–1550.* Madrid: Iberoamericana, 2000.
Otte, Enrique. *Las perlas del Caribe: Nueva Cádiz de Cubagua.* Caracas: Fundación John Boulton, 1977.
Perri, Michael. "Ruined and Lost: The Destruction of the Pearl Coast." *Environment and History* 15, no. 2 (2009): 129–161.
Pike, Ruth. *Enterprise and Adventure: The Genoese in Seville and the Opening of the New World.* Ithaca: Cornell Univ. Press, 1966.
Rodríguez Demorizi, Emilio. *Los dominicos y las encomiendas de indios de la Isla Española.* Santo Domingo: Editora del Caribe, 1971.
Saez, José Luis, S.J. *La iglesia y el negro esclavo en Santo Domingo. Una historia de tres siglos.* Santo Domingo: Patronato de la Ciudad Colonial de Santo Domingo, Colección Quinto Centenario, 1994.
Sued Badillo, Jalil. *El Dorado borincano. La economía de la conquista, 1510–1550.* San Juan: Ediciones Puerto, 2001.
Tió, Aurelio. *Nuevas fuentes para la historia de Puerto Rico.* San German: Ediciones de la Universidad Interamericana de Puerto Rico and Barcelona: Ediciones Rumbos, 1961.
Townsend, Camilla. *Malintzin's Choices.* Albuquerque: Univ. of New Mexico Press, 2006.
Varela, Consuelo. *La caída de Cristóbal Colón. El juicio de Bobadilla.* Edición y transcripción de Isabel Aguirre. Madrid: Marcial Pons Historia, 2006.
Wright, Irene. *The Early History of Cuba.* New York: Macmillan, 1916.

4

Indigenous Women as Mothers in Conquest-Era Peru

JANE E. MANGAN

The lives of indigenous women in the Andes changed immeasurably when Spanish conquistadores stirred a battle that would cripple the Inca empire and enmesh Andean systems of rule with Spanish ones. The indigenous Leonor, a native of Cuzco, lived in Peru during this hectic time that saw the gradual emergence of colonial society with the increased arrival of men and women from Spain and Africa.[1] In 1561, she gave birth to a daughter, María de Herrera, from a relationship with a Spaniard named Luis Villareal. Her union with Villareal may have taken her from her native Cuzco to the city of Guamanga some 150 miles away. After María's birth, Leonor, assisted by a dowry from Villareal, married the tailor Francisco de Aguilera. The dowry consisted of a plot of land with a house in the city of Guamanga as well as a bar of silver. Leonor and her new husband relocated to Lima, where Leonor was a member of the *cofradía* (lay religious organization) of Nuestra Señora de Candelaria at the Monasterio of San Francisco. Her daughter, María, lived in the home and care of Juan de Hinojosa, an arrangement likely made by Villareal at the time Leonor married, as Spanish fathers (living in urban households) often took over the care of their *mestiza* daughters in the sixteenth-century Andes. At some point in the interim, Villareal died in Guamanga.

In 1579, when Leonor was ill in the Hospital of Santa Ana, she made a last will and testament in which she named her daughter, María, by then an eighteen-year-old, as her sole heir with the specific hope that her estate could be used as the young woman's dowry. The sketch of Leonor's life that stands in relief through her will and testament highlights two elements of sixteenth-century life that are the focus of this chapter: the relationship of indigenous mothers to *mestizo* children and the economic status of indigenous women who bore the children of Spaniards in the early colonial period.

Historians have shown that indigenous women were active agents who shaped colonial Andean society in the 1500s.[2] In this chapter, I emphasize indigenous women *as mothers* and look in particular at those who bore children to Spanish men. Andean history establishes mothers as historical actors in many treatments of colonial society. Yet, if we study in more detail about these indigenous women's experiences with their sons and daughters as well as their social and economic partnerships after bearing children to Spaniards, we begin to build a basis to analyze women as mothers in a comparative framework across the Iberian Atlantic. Admittedly, the historical record yields less on these women than it does, say, on elite families with coats of arms. Many indigenous women bore children and raised them without ever appearing in the historical record. Yet cases do emerge in detail, largely in notarial records, and I have analyzed those for the cities of Potosí, Lima, and Arequipa, all major urban centers of the Viceroyalty of Peru. This focus reveals very specific ways in which the expansion of Spanish rule and culture into the Andes (that is, the Iberian elements that crossed the Atlantic) affected indigenous women as mothers. Iberian legal codes shaped the processes by which indigenous mothers made bequests that influenced their children's lives. The laws required women to name their children as heirs. The emerging markets of colonial cities created opportunities whereby these women could earn property or other goods for their children. Further, Spanish men's financial or material donations to mothers and *mestizo* children constituted an economic advantage that created something of a colonial family economy. This subject adds to the overall volume an emphasis on indigenous women, economy, and family roles. Leonor of Cuzco is representative of the many indigenous women who gave birth to a child of the first colonial generation in Peru, and whose lives as mothers emerged as colonial society expanded and solidified. Instead of assuming a universality of mothers' experiences, I argue here that as women lived in a world that simultaneously included traditional Andean family structures, a declining Inca empire, and an emerging Spanish colonial system, they found their role as mothers challenged. Women who bore children to Spaniards, especially elite women, might lose physical control of their children. At the same time, women's connections to Spanish men in the colonial system could bring them enhanced economic status.

The precedents for the sexual relationships between Spanish conquistadors and native women came from both sides of the Atlantic. On the Andean side, the exchange of women to cement political alliances was well established among the Incas as well as nonelite Andean society.³ From the Spanish side, men's cohabitation with native women "replicated the patriarchal pattern between the masculine head of family and the network of servants, where powerful men took sexual favors from servants."⁴ The particulars of most of these relationships remain inaccessible to historians, and one must imagine a range of possibilities as described by historian Karen Powers: "Though rape and betrayal probably represented opposite poles of the spectrum, in its interstices we are likely to find mutual consent, economic opportunism, physical attraction, political alliances, social mobility, genuine love."⁵

The use of native women as sexual companions occurred from the top of the Spanish hierarchy to the bottom. Francisco Pizarro, conqueror of Peru, acquired Quispe Sisa, later baptized as doña Inés Huaylas Yupanqui, as his lover at the behest of her brother, Atahualpa. She bore him two children, only to have Pizarro marry her to his page, a man named Francisco de Ampuero.⁶ In such instances, Emma Mannarelli argues, "lovers behaved like fathers," as they played matchmaker and even provided dowries so that their former lovers (also the mothers of their children) could be married to Spaniards of lesser social status.⁷

What of the role of these women as mothers, however? A painful reality for some indigenous mothers in this era was that they lost their sons or daughters to the legal, imperial power of Spanish fathers. To be clear, many indigenous women bore children to Spaniards as a result of violent sexual encounter or brief, coercive relationships. These children likely did not know their fathers and lived among their indigenous relatives. Yet those Spanish men who made claims on children they fathered with indigenous women typically took the children from their mothers.⁸ The earliest such examples come from the Caribbean, where Ida Altman's essay reveals that the *mestizo* children were accepted as Spanish. Extant historical records for the first decades after conquest in the Andes reveal that Spanish fathers considered the upbringing of their *mestizo* children, both its material and cultural aspects, as part of their fatherly obligation.⁹ The most famous example of this arrangement is El Inca Garcilaso de la Vega. Born to a Spanish conquistador father and an Inca noble mother,

Garcilaso lived in Cuzco as a boy. His father eventually took him to Spain, where he would die without ever returning to Peru. Generally speaking, Spanish fathers gave little value to the mother's role in the upbringing of these children and in many cases opposed it over concerns of providing a proper Christian education.[10] Thus, for many of these mothers the degree of involvement in their children's lives could be circumscribed.

To ensure that a *mestizo* child of illegitimate status had a chance for cultural and social salvation, fathers took legal steps to remove them from their mothers' care. The practice is evident in the legal power-of-attorneys assigned in the city of Lima between the 1540s and 1560s. With these powers in hand, third parties claimed natural *mestizo* children from the locations on the route of Spanish conquest in the New World: first Mexico, then Central America, and finally parts of the Andes.

Spanish father Mateo Veneciano clarified why taking the *mestizo* boys and girls from indigenous mothers was an imperative. According to Veneciano, a Spaniard needed to "raise and indoctrinate and impress good habits upon" his son. In Lima, in February 1552, Veneciano put into action a plan to move and provide proper care for his young son, Alejandro. He enacted a legal power that gave his uncle Pedro Tomas Griego the right to claim Alejandro from the town priest of Huarochirí.[11] Alejandro was still a baby—only fourteen or fifteen months old in his father's estimation, and in the company of his indigenous mother, Isabel, a natural of Huarochirí. Veneciano had left the town at the beginning of February, but ordered a messenger, Griego, to return to Huarochirí to claim Alejandro and his mother. In contrast to other cases of children being taken from mothers, Veneciano may have wanted Isabel removed from the house of the priest as much as he hoped to recover his son. Still, his specific instructions to Griego suggest he wanted the boy's upbringing in Griego's hands and not in those of his indigenous mother. Veneciano did not specify that the child be taken from his mother at this juncture, perhaps because of his very young age. Yet his appointment of Griego as caretaker highlights the perception that the boy's mother could not raise the child properly, as only a Spaniard could fill that role.

The idea of moving the child from the mother's care to another household was not a completely new idea for *mestizo* children in mid-sixteenth-century Peru, as apprenticeships in early modern Spain had the same end. Moreover, even before the arrival of the Spanish, the movement of peoples within the Inca empire was common, and children had been used to fulfill important roles for the Inca state. The *aclla*, an institution where young women learned weaving and *chicha* (fermented corn beer) production in enclosed female-only communities, was empire-wide. Inca rulers chose specific girls to leave their families and their *ayllus,* or kin-groups, in order to fill the *aclla*.[12] That said, the power dynamics of the colonial context—pitting Veneciano against the indigenous mother—were quite different.

Some men used different legal approaches, such as donations or bequests in wills, to orchestrate moving children from the care of their mothers. Antonio de Medina pledged a 1,000-peso dowry to his *mestiza* daughter María in return for a promise from the girl's mother that she would allow him to raise her.[13] Medina made the legal transaction in June of 1577. He had come to Peru from Ronda, Spain, and fathered the girl, María, with Isabel Yanaguar of Cuzco. Isabel lived on the land of the Spaniard Miguel Sanchez (and, in theory, also under his control). While Medina never married Isabel, he acknowledged his natural daughter and claimed he loved her. Thus he felt compelled to rescue her from being raised by her mother and among her mother's relatives. "In her mother's power," he stated, "she cannot be well-schooled and raised with polish and good breeding like I, as her father, would want to raise her and marry her off."[14] In the same document, Isabel declared that eight years prior, while working for Antonio de Medina in Charcas, she had physical relations with him, became pregnant, and gave birth to his child, María. She acknowledged that it was she who had raised the girl to the age of eight. Isabel then agreed (though she had little legal say in the matter) to give her daughter to Medina. Medina reiterated his plea for the girl, claiming that she would be raised better in the power of her father and her Spanish relatives than among Indians and with her mother. His petition shows how Spanish fathers in Peru used legal power to gain control of their sons and daughters. If we consider the process of travel within Peru and then from Peru to Spain, we can imagine a high level of instability for the children who moved between families and households of different cultures and locales. Some indigenous women were separated from their children within Peru or even across the Atlantic.

At the same time Spanish fathers claimed their children, they typically gave indigenous mothers some form of material or financial donation. These men might give money prior to testating, specifically in order to dower indigenous women who had served in both productive and reproductive roles. It was perhaps more common *not* to offer notarized dowries or arrange marriages, as many informally acknowledged their indigenous lovers. No legal requirement compelled a man to make a donation to his child's mother. Yet by the 1540s, Spaniards routinely used a donation to offer some material provision for the women who satisfied physical desire and, as a result, frequently bore them children. These acts also represented a spiritual obligation, as men cleared their consciences of adultery or cohabitation with gifts of money, land, or goods. The following examples show the range of gifts mothers received. We do well to acknowledge that many of the women who bore sons and daughters to Spaniards in the early decades after conquest also worked as their servants.[15]

Women commonly received a lump sum of silver pesos. In 1553, Diego Maldonado bequeathed 50 pesos to the indigenous Ana, mother of his daughter, "for the good service she gives me and for raising my said daughter."[16] One year later, Juan Flores, native of Merida, Spain, donated 25 pesos each to the two indigenous women with whom he had four children.[17] In 1560, Gonzalo Gutierrez, also known as Juan Gutierrez, left a bequest of 20 pesos to Isabel, the mother of his natural son, Juan, along with a strict order to "take care to look after my son."[18] Gutierrez also provided for one year of sustenance for Isabel, provided she live in the house of and under the supervision of Pedro de Lupiana, a tutor of his son. Unlike many indigenous mothers, Isabel was ordered to stay close by the boy, perhaps still an infant, for at least one year.[19] Indigenous women laboring as servants received a maximum of 10 pesos a year salary for much of the sixteenth century, thus these sums represented more than a typical annual wage.

Some indigenous mothers received property bequests. Arequipa *vecino* Francisco Ramirez ordered that 300 pesos from his estate be used to purchase a plot of land in the city for the indigenous Ana, mother of his natural son, Juan Rafael.[20] Ramirez acknowledged Ana's services to him and said that the bequest was made to relieve his conscience. The donation of an urban property was valuable, especially since people could rent them for income.

Other women found themselves recipients of goods, primarily cloth or animals. Francisco Martinez's will left bequests of cloth to the indigenous mothers of his two children.[21] In Arequipa, Francisco de Quiroz had two daughters with the indigenous Isabel, a native of Arequipa.[22] He left her clothing in the form of a *cumbi* dress and two cotton dresses (dresses would have included both the dress [*lliclla*] and shawl [*anaca*]), thirty pregnant goats, and a *fanega* of corn per month for fifteen months. Isabel's portion of his estate came her way "for services she has made me."

At the same time, he bequeathed clothing or goats to his other servants, though none received as many as Isabel and none received the added bequest of corn. In that sense, Isabel's treatment was special, relative to other servants (a stratum of which he clearly considered her a part).

Thus, indigenous mothers of *mestizos* frequently gained some economic means from their former Spanish partners. Formal documents from the 1540s through the 1590s reveal hundreds of these cases, and the practice likely existed informally as well. At the same time, women might be separated from their sons and daughters. If indigenous women did not raise their children in close proximity, what did this mean for their role as mothers? In this historical context, the connection between mothering and the donations from Spanish fathers is critical because indigenous mothers of *mestizos* might enact an economic role in their children's lives even when they did not raise them in their households. The opening example of this essay, Leonor of Cuzco, is a clear case in point.

Indigenous women's gifts from Spanish men had consequences for these women's other family members as well. Catalina Anpo had two sons, Francisco and Juan Pastor, with the Spaniard Lucas Pastor.[23] Then she married an indigenous man, Lázaro Quispe. The ties to Pastor, however, were not severed completely because at his death he bequeathed 800 pesos to her. Catalina's own will showed she would give part of that sum to her husband if possible. "I don't know if any of those 800 pesos pertains to my husband," she said, showing her doubt on the legality of passing the money to Quispe. If allowed, however, she indicated that one half of that sum should go to her indigenous husband and the other half to her two sons with Pastor.

Women acquired money or material goods through relationships with Spanish men, but they also accumulated wealth through family connections (inheritance) and activities in the urban economy. Primarily, women used what they accumulated in two important ways: as a dowry to marry for themselves and as inheritance for their children. Indigenous women might come to marriage with means from indigenous family networks. For instance, the indigenous Ana Velazquez had a dowry of clothing and a slave when she married Simón Ginoves.[24] Her husband immediately employed the clothing (not described in the document) for a colonial trade venture. He sent the clothing to Chile with a compatriot, Antonio Ginoves. The use of the clothing as merchandise suggests she had kin connections to textile production. Here indigenous women's goods, likely obtained through an indigenous family network, helped an enterprising Genoese merchant increase his exports of clothing to the province of Chile.

Indigenous mothers who had the means to do so enacted legal and economic modes of care for their children and frequently used the Iberian legal customs of wills to do so. Costança, a single woman who was originally from Cuzco, bore two children to different Spanish men.[25] In her will she named the two children as her sole heirs and indicated her estate contained goods as well as close to 500 pesos. This sum was enough to provide an investment for her children in a small property or the purchase of goods to trade.

Mothers provided for their children through inheritance in part because it was required. Spanish law required that legitimate children inherit an estate, unless they had committed some unforgiveable act.[26] If a testator had no legitimate children, parents were the next in line to inherit an estate. If a man or woman had children born outside of wedlock, these children had a right to inherit the estate, but certain conditions had to be in place. First, the child had to have been born when both parents were unmarried. Second, a father had to publicly acknowledge the natural child in order to name him or her as an heir. For a woman, the case was slightly different: a mother's natural child was automatically considered an heir if named in the will.[27] The following example illustrates such a case.

Elvira, an indigenous woman from Jauja, named her daughter, Lorenza Romana, as her sole heir.[28] Elvira had given birth to Lorenza as an unmarried woman and later in life Elvira married Juan de Popayán. The father of Lorenza, a man named Rafael Durán, acknowledged the girl. Notably, Elvira named Juan Martín Durán as one of the executors in the will; given his last name, it is conceivable that he was a brother or son of Rafael. Elvira's choice of Martín Durán as an executor suggests a trust that the blood connection to this out-of-wedlock *mestiza* would ensure that her daughter received what was due her from the inheritance. Even before she made her will, Elvira had already given away some of her possessions. She wanted her daughter, Lorenza, to inherit her *llicllas*. To her husband, Juan de Popayán, Elvira gave two pairs of silver *cocos* (typical Andean drinking vessels).[29] Elvira's will noted that she sold goods in the market. The link between economic activity and the ability of an indigenous woman to provide a dowry (of any level) to a daughter born out of wedlock was a fundamental one. In addition, the continued connection of Elvira to her daughter and her daughter to her Spanish relatives reveals the false dichotomy through which we have often viewed the experiences of these indigenous mothers and their *mestizo* children.

Some *mestiza* women's lives followed the same pattern of having a child with a Spanish man outside of marriage and managing to amass some estate to leave behind. María de Carvajal was born to an indigenous mother and a Spanish father in sixteenth-century Lima.[30] She maintained a close relationship with her sister, Juana, who lived nearby. Carvajal had one child, a daughter, Teresa, with Cristóbal Maldonado, a Spanish man she never married, sometime after 1560. In Lima, Carvajal engaged in petty economic interactions especially with indigenous and black women. She collected clothing and jewelry, mainly earrings and necklaces. In 1572, she fell ill, dictated a will, and left her estate to her daughter, Teresa. Carvajal named a Señor Francisco de Carvajal (relationship unspecified) as the legal guardian for her child and asked her friend María de Santiago to care for Teresa until such time as her father came for her. In this family's case, the expectation that Maldonado might provide for Teresa suggests the lifelong connection of mother and father through obligations to a child, even in the absence of marriage.

The maternal roles of indigenous women in this complex era emerge in skeletal view from the notarial records. A sixteenth-century lawsuit, a lengthier and more detailed archival record, reveals the history of Isabel Tocto, an indigenous mother whose life highlights the extreme possibilities of motherhood in the sixteenth-century Iberian Atlantic. Tocto's two daughters, María and Francisca Ortíz, traveled from Potosí to the village of Lepe, Spain, as young girls.[31] Their father, the Spaniard Baltazar Ortíz, accompanied them on the crossing and then left them in the house of his sister, doña Ana de Beneventes. Baltazar Ortíz returned to the Indies, where he would later die. It was Ana's husband, Pedro Ramirez Cavala, who became the girls' paternal figure, at least from a legal standpoint. An indigenous woman from the Cuzco region, Tocto named the girls as her universal heirs in her last will and testament dictated from her sickbed in October of 1569. Married to the indigenous don Juan Marachai, Tocto seems to have had the girls with Baltazar Ortíz prior to her marriage with Marachai. She tallied up her debts owed and debts owed her in the course of her testament. Then she ordered her belongings to be sold. After paying for masses and funeral costs, any remaining proceeds were to be sent to "my daughters María Ortíz and Francisca Ortíz who are in the Kingdoms of Spain."

The girls had not seen their mother in at least twelve years, but her testament affirmed maternal ties. The record, however, is short on many points. What relationship did Tocto have with her daughters' father? Did she work for him in his house as a servant? Did she want to accompany him to Spain? Did she agree to have the girls leave Potosí? Finally, did she want to leave her estate to the girls, or did Spanish officials or Baltazar's relatives prompt her to do so? These questions remain for us to ponder. The lives of mother and daughters played out in locales thousands of miles apart, in different cultural contexts.

Tocto's testament provides details of her Potosí life that allow for informed imaginings of what the Ortíz sisters would have experienced if they had remained in the high Andes. Isabel Tocto knew Spaniards intimately, and she, like many other indigenous women of her generation, recognized and incorporated elements of Spanish culture as part of their urban colonial life in Potosí. Tocto opened her will with a request that masses be said for her at both the church in the San Francisco parish and the church of Our Lady of Mercy. The will began in the formulaic legal culture of colonial Peru (an influence of Spanish practice).[32] She closed the testaments with an additional request for masses on the high altar of Santo Domingo.[33] That these requests are evidence of her devotion to Spanish culture is unknowable at this vantage point, but we can see its influence in her life. Moreover, she chose the Spanish witness Juan de Montenegro to attest to the legitimacy of her will.

These reflections of Spanish culture in Tocto's life were spiritual and official. The many people who came and went in her life, as seen through her witnesses to the testament, those with her when she died, and those who were her debtors, show a markedly indigenous foundation to her life. Five of seven witnesses to the will were indigenous men. Those who nursed her in her final illness included the indigenous Ana Tocto Ollo, Isabel Tocto Coca, Isabel Taquima, and Alonso Ocuro. She loaned money to a group of exclusively indigenous men and women. In this listing, several appear with indigenous names only (no baptismal Spanish first name), such as Uricarba and Tomay.[34] Tocto is referred to by some as a *palla,* a reference to Inca nobility that had, by the late sixteenth century, taken on a more general meaning of ties to indigenous elite. Tocto's sister, Ana Tocto Ollo was a *palla* from Cuzco, an indication that the whole family had its roots in the Cuzco region. They probably came to Potosí because of the dynamic coca trade between those two cities in the sixteenth century. The neighborhood in which Isabel Tocto lived bolsters the proof that these indigenous networks were dominant in her life. She resided in what the scribe referred to as a *buhío,* the classic indigenous (and most modest) form of housing in Potosí made of clay and straw. Tocto's home sat in the *ranchería* of San Francisco, an old parish located at the foot of the Cerro Rico. It had been the first area used for housing indigenous migrants to Potosí, and as such it was somewhat removed from the city center. Tocto's home, friends, work, and worship suggest that had the Ortíz girls remained in Potosí, they would have known Spanish Catholic religion and related cultural practices, but they would have lived and moved in primarily indigenous circles.

The material goods that surrounded Tocto in her *buhío* and in her neighborhood suggest a similar blend of indigenous and Spanish cultures. She kept six llamas at her house. It was not unheard of to keep animals in the *ranchería,* but it was unusual to find such a listing in the will of an urban indigenous woman in Potosí. The animals suggest a rural element to urban colonial life as well as possible ties to ancestral homelands. The majority of her possessions were clothes. Tocto dressed in the garb of an indigenous woman, with an *acsu, lliclla,* and *chumbe.* She possessed many of these outfits and in different colors, like purple, green, and black; some old and some new; some made of coarse cloth, *abasca,* for everyday wear and others made from the finely woven wool, *cumbi,* for more special occasions. Tocto also owned five pairs of silver *topos,* the archetypal Andean dress pins used to hold together the *lliclla.* Her household items were few: bed linens (a blanket, sheet, and three pillows); an image of the Virgin Mary; three pairs of silver *cocos,* one silver spoon, and scissors. If her daughters María and Francisca had been living nearby, practice in other wills suggests that Tocto would have bequeathed her most precious items to them (probably the *cumbi*-cloth items, silver *topos,* or silver *cocos*). As young girls, María and Francisca would have worn indigenous-style clothing. They would have known important symbolic native Andean objects as part of their world (like the *cocos*) along with some of Spanish society (such as the Virgin Mary). Despite their Spanish blood, the Ortíz sisters would have lived as colonial urban Indian women.

What do we know about the girls' life in Spain? They had left the relatively new mining city at thirteen thousand feet for an ancient village located within ten miles of the coast of southern Spain. The proximity to Seville and to the coast more generally suggests many people in this town had ties to the expansion of empire. The makeup of their village would not have had the diversity of indigenous, Spanish, and African peoples that they had experienced as girls in Potosí, though they may have noticed some Africans or Muslims in the community.

María and Francisca traveled to Spain with a *mestiza* cousin, Juana Ortíz. After several years in Spain, cousins Juana and Francisca took their vows and became professed nuns. As Juana would testify, this signified that Francisca renounced all her worldly belongings to Pedro Ramirez. Ramirez sponsored both girls' entry into the convent, Juana into Santo Domingo and Francisca into Santa Clara.[35] In the Andes, and occasionally in Spain, Spanish fathers looked to convents to house, sometimes temporarily, young *mestizo* women even if those women did not always take vows. If Juana and Francisca had remained in the Andes in the care of a Spanish household, they might also have spent time in a convent. In their mothers' care, they might well have done what many *mestiza* women did in Potosí: entered Potosí's then-thriving economy as traders.

Isabel Tocto's bequest to her girls was a transatlantic act of mothering. Likewise, children in Spain might carry out transatlantic family obligations with mothers to whom they bid goodbye at an early age. *Mestizo* children from Peru who grew to adulthood in Spain carried with them knowledge or memories of family that compelled acts of devotion, even if they never returned to Peru to see their mothers. In another example, Alonso de Nava and his sisters, María and Catalina, went to Spain under the tutelage of their father, Alonso de Nava, and lived in Seville, in the San Isidro neighborhood. When their father passed away, the children (and their inheritances) were under the control of Juan de Rojas. Alonso de Nava, the son, admitted that Rojas fed, dressed them, and tended to him while he was ill. His sister María died after their father did. The mother of all three children was Catalina de Taquena from the village of Taquena in Arequipa, Peru. When Alonso dictated his will, he did not know if his mother was still alive, but in that hope he named her as his heir.[36]

The economic status of a family would have mediated the experience of these *mestizo* children in Spain. So, too, would their status at birth as children born to unmarried parents, known as *hijos naturales*. However, they faced a less arduous path toward legitimation than those who were born to a married man or women in an illicit affair (and known as *bastardos*). Gerónimo de Aliaga, an *hijo natural* of Captain Gerónimo Aliaga de Santomayor, who was the secretary of the *Real Audiencia* (Royal Court) in La Plata, lived in Seville as a young adult. Since his parents had been unmarried at the time of his birth, he sought—and gained—legitimation. He pursued an inheritance from his father's estate in the Indies in 1570.[37] Another *hijo natural,* mother unnamed but likely indigenous, sought to benefit from his "rich mother" in Peru when, as a young adult, he set up a merchant business between Seville and Peru.[38] Again, these examples reveal the transatlantic ties that indigenous mothers and their children experienced in the sixteenth-century conquest-era world.

Those indigenous women who wrote wills or gave donations reveal how they tried to shape their children's lives. In Potosí, Leonor Chumbo, an indigenous native of Cuzco, Peru, set down her will in 1577.[39] Though Chumbo had never married, she did have several children. She had two sons, Juan and Diego, with her longtime master Diego Serrano. When Serrano returned to Spain, he took the boys with him. Chumbo also had a son and daughter, Pedro and Antonia, children of another master named Hernando de la Queba. Chumbo ordered proceeds from the sale of houses, estimated at 250 pesos, to go to her sons in Spain. To Pedro and Antonia, she left additional property in Potosí.

Having children out of wedlock *and* claiming them was something native elite women did in this era as they employed Spanish legal instruments to try and protect their children. Doña Francisca, a native elite with an *hija natural* in the city of Arequipa, had high-ranking parents on both the maternal and paternal lines. Her father, don Pedro Alvarado Cayatopa, governor of Chachapoyas, was appointed (so she claimed) by no less than the early sixteenth-century Inca emperor Huayna Capac. Her mother, Catalina Chuqui Tecla, was the sister of the *cacique* (indigenous chieftain) of Chacapoyas.[40] In 1574, doña Francisca gave birth to a daughter, Marequita, whose father was a Spaniard named Juan García. Only four months after the little girl's birth, doña Francisca turned to the task of making her will as she lay sick in Lima in the home of Juan de Saracho. Interestingly, she did not make any claims or connections in relation to indigenous relatives. She had a small land plot, or *solar,* in Chachapoyas along with debts and money owed her in Chachapoyas, so she may have been a recent transplant to Lima.

Doña Francisca employed the Spanish legal framework of the will to care for her daughter's future. In order to better locate the baby girl's father, she mentioned in the will that she had heard Juan García was presently in Chachapoyas. She named Saracho as the girl's guardian in the absence of her father, Juan García, and named Marequita as her universal heir. She clarified her daughter's identity as a *mestiza* and not an *india*. Doña Francisca stated García's paternity of Marequita at three distinct places in her will. In this direct manner she clearly hoped to use the will to force García to accept some responsibility for her.

These indigenous mothers who raised their children in Peru offer a detailed counterpoint to those *mestizos* who moved to Spain, as in the case of the Ortíz sisters. The Cuzqueña indigenous doña Ana Palla mothered three daughters to two different men and never married during her life.[41] Palla had two girls, Francisca de la Serna and Ana de la Serna, with Martín López de la Serna. Her third daughter, still young in 1586, was María de Corrales, fathered by Anton Díaz de Corrales. Both fathers had died by 1586. María inherited goods from her father, including the house in which Palla lived. Securing the houses cost Palla time and energy in a legal suit; keeping the houses in good repair cost her, in her words, "many more gold pesos." She argued that other heirs of Anton Díaz de Corrales still attempted to take the houses away, but since she had spent so much money on them and on raising his daughter, she was confident in her claim that María should keep them.

While Francisca had married a man named Luis de Vargas, it was Ana who stayed at home and helped her mother. Palla noted that Ana "has always been obedient" and honored her service with the bequest of her clothing and dresses and other goods.[42] By and large these goods were the traditional Andean female dress of *llicllas, anacos,* and *chumbes,* along with *topos*. She emphasized that María de Corrales should not have access to these goods, and "if necessary I will give them to her [Ana] by way of the *mejora* [one-fifth of the will the parent could award at their own discretion]."[43]

María was not without a special bequest from her mother, as she received bedding, a mirror, and two boxes.[44] Ana Palla appointed Ana de la Serna as one of her executors *and* made her the tutor of María de Corrales until María was married. Both these daughters were her universal heirs. Francisca, however, who was already married to Luis de Vargas, had received her part of the estate when she was married. Palla specified that she had a dowry letter that spelled out her share of the inheritance.

Doña Ana Palla did not lose her *mestiza* daughters to Spanish households within Peru or overseas. Palla used her will effectively to account for material obligations to her three daughters. She had dowered Francisca, she had initiated legal action to protect María's inheritance from her Spanish father, and she offered recompense to Ana through the clothes for her help and companionship through the years. Palla's will did not detail her relationship with the fathers of these girls, nor did she mention relationships with any other men. Yet she fulfilled her maternal and legal roles to them even as she lived her life outside of marriage.

CONCLUSION

The circumstances of conquest challenged long-standing family patterns as defined by Andean communities. Through their relationships with indigenous women, Spanish men affected the role of mothers, and their ties to their children. When Spanish fathers exerted their Iberian legal power over their mixed-race sons and daughters, indigenous mothers said goodbye to children who boarded ships to Spain and never returned. Others saw their children taken to Spanish households in the new cities of colonial Peru. Yet still other mothers raised their *mestizo* offspring in their own households in Peru. Women of all three family experiences typically received some financial assistance from the Spanish men to whom they bore children. And, one after another, these women used their financial means to provide for their families. For women who lived near their children, the intimacy borne of their proximity is detailed: Ana Palla favored one child over another in terms of bequests as well as in the clauses of her will that characterized the actions of one daughter in comparison to another. Mothers with children nearby in Peru could also leave bequests of items, such as a favorite dress or heirloom silver *topos,* for their children to have for the next generation. When children lived in Spain, however, mothers had no choice but to liquidate their belongings and send bequests of silver pesos across the ocean, as textiles and material goods with a sentimental value did not make the trip. Conquest affected family structure generally, and mothers' roles specifically. The very potential of a mother's role might be limited by the circumstances of her child's birth to a Spanish father in the sixteenth century. Still, mothers continued to serve as providers for the children as they funneled important material and financial provisions to their *mestizo* sons and daughters. They used Spanish legal institutions to do so and followed these norms whether their children lived down the street or across the ocean. Ultimately, indigenous mothers of *mestizos* played a transatlantic role from within the heart of the Andes.

NOTES

1. Archivo General de la Nación, Perú (hereafter AGNP), Protocolos 29, Testamento of Leonor india, fol. 234–235r, July 5, 1579. This essay is a piece of a larger study of family in mid-sixteenth century Peru and Spain. Generous support from the ACLS Ryskamp Fellowship and Davidson College facilitated archival research.

2. Select examples of this rich historiography include Irene Silverblatt, *Moon, Sun, and Witches: Gender Ideologies and Class in Inca and Colonial Peru* (Princeton: Princeton Univ. Press, 1987); Kimberly Gauderman, *Women's Lives in Colonial Quito: Gender, Law, and Economy in Spanish America* (Austin: Univ. of Texas Press, 2003); Karen Graubart, *With Our Labor and Sweat: Indigenous Women and the Formation of Colonial Society in Peru, 1550–1700* (Stanford: Stanford Univ. Press, 2007).

3. See Peter Gose, "The State as a Chosen Woman: Brideservice and the Feeding of Tributaries in the Inka Empire," *American Anthropologist* 102, no. 1 (March 2000): 84–97.

4. María Emma Mannarelli, *Private Passions and Public Sins: Men and Women in Seventeenth-Century Lima*, trans. Sidney Evans and Meredith D. Dodge (original Spanish edition, 1993; English translation, Albuquerque: Univ. of New Mexico Press, 2007), 17.

5. Karen Powers, *Women in the Crucible of Conquest: The Gendered Genesis of Spanish American Society, 1500–1600* (Albuquerque: Univ. of New Mexico Press, 2005), 71. See also, Catherine Julien, "Francisca Pizarro, la cuzqueña, y su madre, la *coya* Ynguill," *Revista del Archivo Regional del Cuzco* 15 (June 2000): 53–74.

6. Karen Powers argues that Pizarro arranged the marriage. See Powers, *Women in the Crucible of Conquest*, 75.

7. Mannarelli, *Private Passions and Public Sins*, 8.

8. In addition to Powers, see Susan Kellogg, *Weaving the Past: A History of Latin America's Indigenous Women from the Prehispanic Period to the Present* (New York: Oxford Univ. Press, 2005), 57–58.

9. Teresa Vergara has discussed the definition of fatherhood and paternal roles with regard to indigenous children in Lima. See Vergara, "Growing Up Indian: Migration, Labor and Life in Lima (1570–1640)," in *Raising an Empire: Children in Early Modern Iberia and Colonial Latin America*, ed. Ondina E. González and Bianca Premo, 75–107 (Albuquerque: Univ. of New Mexico Press, 2007).

10. This trend may be in contrast to the experience of illegitimate children in Spain, who would not be taken from their mothers for the same cultural motivations. Altman's work is important on this front as it provides some comparison with the Spanish experience before conquest. It would be helpful to have additional work on this question for Spanish society during the 1500s for a full comparison. For a study of illegitimate children in late sixteenth-century Spain, see Angel Sánchez Rodríguez, *Hacerse Nadie: sometimiento, sexo y silencio en la España de finales del siglo XVI* (Lleida: Editorial Milenio, 1998).

11. AGNP, Protocolos 160, Sebastián Vazquez, Poder Mateo Veneciano to Pedro Tomas Griego, fol. 271, 1552/02/15.

12. Gose, "The State as a Chosen Woman," 85.

13. AGNP, Protocolos 28, Alonso de la Cueva, Donación Antonio de Medina to Maria mestiza su hija natural, June 12, 1577, fol. 131–132v.

14. AGNP, Protocolos 28, Alonso de la Cueva, Donación Antonio de Medina to Maria mestiza su hija natural, June 12, 1577, fol. 131r. All translations from the original Spanish to English are the author's.

15. See Nancy E. van Deusen, "Diasporas, Bondage, and Intimacy in Lima, 1535–1555," *Colonial Latin American Review* 19, no. 2 (August 2010): 247–277.

16. AGNP, Protocolos 160, Sebastian Vazquez, March 6, 1553, fol. 864v–865.

17. AGNP, Protocolos 9, Simón de Alzate, Testament of Juan Flores, fol. 1114–1114v, March 10, 1554.

18. AGNP, Protocolos 127, Estevan Perez, Testament of Gonzalo Gutierrez Nombre de Pila, April 18, 1560, fol. 1r–3r.

19. AGNP, Protocolos 127, Estevan Perez, Testament of Gonzalo Gutierrez Nombre de Pila, April 18, 1560, fol. 2r. See also AGI, Contratación 256A, N1, R4, where Bartolomé Carmona gave a sum of 100 pesos to his natural daughter's indigenous mother, Luisa Tocta.

20. Archivo Regional de Arequipa (hereafter ARA), Protocolos 99, Juan de Vera, Testament of Francisco Ramirez, fol. 106v, May 30, 1568.

21. AGNP, Protocolos 9, Simón de Alzate, Testament of Francisco Martinez, fol. 994–995v, August 26, 1553.

22. ARA, Protocolos 33, Gaspar Hernandez, Testament of Francisco de Quiros, fol. 80v–fol. 83r, March 2, 1556.

23. AGNP, Protocolos 41, Testament of Catalina Anpo, fol. 949v–951, November 9, 1564.

24. AGNP, Protocolos 109, Testament of Simon Ginoves, fol. 915–916v, August 29, 1558.

25. ARA, Protocolos 33, Gaspar Hernandez, Power to testate, Costança india to Diego yndio, fol. 320(v), August 1, 1556.

26. For a discussion of colonial inheritance law, see Matthew Mirow, *Latin American Law* (Austin: Univ. of Texas Press, 2005).

27. See Graubart, *With Our Labor and Sweat*, 103–105.

28. AGNP, Protocolos 33, Testamento de Elvira, fol. 303–304, April 15, 1572.

29. On the significance of cocos (the silver version of keros), see Thomas B. F. Cummins, *Toasts with the Inca: Andean Abstraction and Colonial Images on Quero Vessels* (Ann Arbor: Univ. of Michigan, 2002).

30. AGNP, Protocolos 33, Testamento de María de Carvajal, fol. 298v–300v, January 17, 1572.

31. Archivo General de las Indias, Seville (hereafter AGI), Contratación 242 N.1 R.15, Herederos de Isabel Tocto yndio sobre cobro de bienes, 1579, fol. 23r–24r.

32. For analysis of the production of notarial archives, see Kathryn Burns, *Into the Archive* (Durham: Duke Univ. Press, 2010).

33. AGI, Seville, Contratación 242 N.1 R.15, Herederos de Isabel Tocto yndio sobre cobro de bienes, 1579, fol. 3r and 3v.

34. AGI, Seville, Contratación 242 N.1 R.15, Herederos de Isabel Tocto yndio sobre cobro de bienes, 1579, fol. 3v.

35. AGI, Seville, Contratación 242 N.1 R.15, Herederos de Isabel Tocto yndio sobre cobro de bienes, 1579, fol. 39r–40v.

36. Archivo Histórico de Protocolos, Seville (hereafter AHPS), Protocolos, Oficio 6, Signatura 4063, Francisco de Soto, fol. 278, November 24, 1569.

37. AHPS, Protocolos, Oficio 13, Signatura 7764, Francisco Díaz, fol. 1035, May 30, 1570.

38. AHPS, Protocolos, Francisco de Almonte, Signatura 5383, Oficio 8, Company, Pedro de Mollinedo and Diego de Mollinedo, fol. 470, October 11, 1570.

39. Archivo Histórico de Potosí—Casa de la Moneda, Escrituras Notariales 8, will of Leonor Chumbo, fol. 1145–1146v, October 27, 1577.

40. AGNP, Protocolos 150, Juan Salamanca, Testament of Francisca india, fol. 197–198v, March 29, 1574.

41. ARA, Protocolos 81, Diego Navarro, Testament of Doña Ana Palla, fol. 148r–150v, February 18, 1586.

42. ARA, Protocolos 81, Diego Navarro, Testament of Doña Ana Palla, fol. 149v, February 18, 1586.

43. ARA, Protocolos 81, Diego Navarro, Testament of Doña Ana Palla, fol. 149v, February 18, 1586.

44. ARA, Protocolos 81, Diego Navarro, Testament of Doña Ana Palla, fol. 150r, February 18, 1586.

WORKS CITED

Primary Sources

Archivo General de la Nación, Peru, Protocolos
Archival Regional de Arequipa, Protocolos
Archivo General de las Indias, Seville, Contratación
Archivo Histórico de Protocolos, Seville
Archivo Histórico de Potosí—Casa de la Moneda, Escrituras Notariales

Secondary Sources

Burns, Kathryn. *Into the Archive*. Durham: Duke Univ. Press, 2010.

Cummins, Thomas B. F. *Toasts with the Inca: Andean Abstraction and Colonial Images on Quero Vessels*. Ann Arbor: Univ. of Michigan, 2002.

Gauderman, Kimberly. *Women's Lives in Colonial Quito: Gender, Law, and Economy in Spanish America*. Austin: Univ. of Texas Press, 2003.

Graubart, Karen. *With Our Labor and Sweat: Indigenous Women and the Formation of Colonial Society in Peru, 1550–1700*. Stanford: Stanford Univ. Press, 2007.

Gose, Peter. "The State as a Chosen Woman: Brideservice and the Feeding of Tributaries in the Inka Empire." *American Anthropologist* 102, no. 1 (March 2000): 84–97.

Julien, Catherine. "Francisca Pizarro, la cuzqueña, y su madre, la *coya* Ynguill." *Revista del Archivo Regional del Cuzco* 15 (June 2000): 53–74.

Kellogg, Susan. *Weaving the Past: A History of Latin America's Indigenous Women from the Prehispanic Period to the Present*. New York: Oxford Univ. Press, 2005.

Mannarelli, María Emma. *Private Passions and Public Sins: Men and Women in Seventeenth-Century Lima*. Translated by Sidney Evans and Meredith D.

Dodge. Original Spanish edition, 1993. English translation, Albuquerque: Univ. of New Mexico Press, 2007.

Mirow, Matthew. *Latin American Law*. Austin: Univ. of Texas Press, 2005.

Powers, Karen. *Women in the Crucible of Conquest: The Gendered Genesis of Spanish American Society, 1500–1600*. Albuquerque: Univ. of New Mexico Press, 2005.

Sánchez Rodríguez, Angel. *Hacerse Nadie: sometimiento, sexo y silencio en la España de finales del siglo XVI*. Lleida: Editorial Milenio, 1998.

Silverblatt, Irene. *Moon, Sun, and Witches: Gender Ideologies and Class in Inca and Colonial Peru*. Princeton: Princeton Univ. Press, 1987.

Van Deusen, Nancy E. "Diasporas, Bondage, and Intimacy in Lima, 1535–1555." *Colonial Latin American Review* 19, no. 2 (August 2010): 247–277.

Vergara, Teresa. "Growing Up Indian: Migration, Labor and Life in Lima (1570–1640)." In *Raising an Empire: Children in Early Modern Iberia and Colonial Latin America,* edited by Ondina E. González and Bianca Premo, 75–107. Albuquerque: Univ. of New Mexico Press, 2007.

5

Women and Kinship in Spanish East Texas at the End of the Eighteenth Century

CARLA GERONA

In 1801 the Spanish governor of Texas interrogated Nacogdoches citizen Gertrudis de los Santos and her husband, Antonio Leal, about Santos's *mala amistad* (illicit affair). Under questioning, Santos admitted to being a *mujer fragile* (fragile woman) because she had slept with her husband's business partner. Next, the governor asked her husband what he knew about the matter. Leal stated that Santos took "care of [his partner's] personal assistance, and whatever other things he needed," but he "did not know what other things his wife did."[1] He had been trading with the Tonkawa when she perpetrated her *mala amistad*. As it turns out, Santos's lover was the famous Irish-American horse trader Philip Nolan, the subject of much historical and literary attention. Most scholars have depicted Nolan as a Texas filibuster—the first in a long line of heroes who sacrificed themselves to wrest Texas away from the tyrannical Spanish (and later Mexican) governments. Others, perhaps more accurately, have described him as a man without a country. But if Nolan was a man without a country, he nonetheless formed extensive kinship networks, which included ties to Spanish-American women such as Gertrudis de los Santos.

Despite scant sources, this essay attempts to recover the worlds of Santos and the other women of Nacogdoches, Texas, at the end of the eighteenth century. While Leal claimed that he did not know what his wife was up to, historians know even less about Santos and the other women of East Texas. By looking at Spanish government records and putting the accounts of the few women who appear in them front and center, this essay begins to shed light on women's lives by mapping the ways kinship worked on a distant Spanish frontier with neighboring indigenous, French, and Anglo villages. Because the Spanish-American women of the borderlands lived in this world of intersecting cultures, there was a great deal of intermarriage and other forms of sexual interrelations, across race and ethnicity—some voluntary and others not so voluntary. Santos offers just one example.

Historians have long understood that intermarriage, and other sexual interrelations, abounded in Spanish and other frontier areas. Indeed, interrelations began with the earliest conquistadors throughout Latin America and continued through the centuries. These relationships, however, remain hazy in East Texas's borderlands, where the church records have been lost and other documentation is slim. Moreover, as historian Antonia Castañeda has pointed out, much of the literature concerning Spanish women in places that became part of the United States bears the weight of Anglocentric stereotyping. This is partly due to the organization of Western women's history around "concepts, issues, categories, and language that belong to the history of middle-class white women" instead of "addressing how these [concepts] may differ."[2] Additionally, dichotomous images of noble princesses/savage squaws or Spanish señoritas/Mexican prostitutes have dominated discussions of interrelations on the frontier. These female stereotypes formed the basis of a mythology in which, according to Castañeda, "women reject their own kind, native men, in favor of their white saviors"; both Anglo-American contemporaries and later U.S. historians focused attention on the Anglo men who fell in love with the "dark-eyed Mexican beauties."[3] To date, this is how Santos appears in the historical record. Yet, when we situate the women of Nacogdoches in their proper Iberian Atlantic context, which included subjectivity to Spanish rulers and laws, a more complicated narrative emerges. This essay, therefore, challenges dichotomous stereotypes based on good and evil, Spanish and Anglo, white and of color, active and passive, male and female, legitimate and illegitimate, and this story begins long before the nineteenth-century Anglo invasion.

Stereotyping, of course, is not limited to historians of the United States. As Ann Twinam has pointed out, Latin American historians have also been influenced by a different set of caricatures, in particular, male machismo and female marianismo. Twinam's work on gender, honor, sexuality, and illegitimacy in colonial Spanish America has done much to change this picture. According to Twinam, the stories uncovered in her book *Public Lives, Private Secrets* "reveal a colonial Spanish America that was far more flexible, and infinitely more complex, than ever imagined."[4] As a rule, Iberian religious and legal traditions demanded monogamous marriages and discouraged interracial unions. But, as Allyson Poska's essay shows in this volume, this was not universally adhered to within the Iberian Atlantic. Further, in Latin America, cultures engaged in a stunning variety of practices that allowed people to cross ethnic, racial, and social boundaries. And, in contradistinction to Anglo-American public and private spheres, Hispanic public and private spheres permitted Spanish-American elites to hold different statuses concomitantly, opening avenues to move up the social ladder, for example, by requesting *cédulas de gracias al sacar,* or royal decrees that eliminated the "stain of illegitimacy." Although there are no records from East Texas for a *gracias al sacar* during this period, other Spanish documents, such as census reports and official correspondence, add even more texture to Twinam's findings in yet another part of Spanish America. Spanish women in East Texas readily formed kinship ties to people from different ethnicities and sometimes violated Spanish laws in order to do so. As in the Altman and Mangan essays, we see Atlantic-Iberian women playing a crucial role in developing a culture that brought together American and European worlds. The Iberian men and women who made their homes in Texas prioritized the formation of kinship ties across ethnic and national boundaries despite legal and religious norms that discouraged intermarriage.

Until recently, historians of the British Atlantic have dominated the new wave in Atlantic history, though as Amy Bushnell points out, this was hardly normative for the hemisphere because "for the descendants of nineteen out of twenty people living in the Americas in 1492, the Atlantic world was to be Iberian, and its centers, Spanish."[5] But if the Iberian Atlantic periphery extended into Nacogdoches, the small Spanish town also sat in the center of Caddoan territory. Bushnell further suggests that by depicting the Atlantic world as a series of European thrusts, scholars miss the opportunity to adequately consider indigenous perspectives. She writes: "The key variable was not the country from which the settlers came, nor even what they sought, but the character of the society they encountered."[6] Though the Spanish founded the town of Nacogdoches in the late 1770s, they had been in the region for almost a century and had already formed strong ties to Texas's indigenous nations. Making connections with others was crucial to Nacogdoches's survival as a trading entrepot, and many of Nacogdoches's inhabitants already had family in indigenous Texas. Of course, it is difficult to parse out indigenous influences given the fact that Spanish officials kept the books, but it is worth keeping in mind that Santos's husband, Antonio Leal, had been with the Tonkawa at the time of his wife's infractions. It would be unusual if Leal had not established his own kinship networks with the Wichita. While Santos and the other people of Nacogdoches lived in a Spanish village, different people met each other in the town and in the region with minimal oversight from central authorities in provincial capitals and Mexico City—even as metropolitan Spanish authorities sought to extend their reach during a period of Bourbon reforms. This meant that the men and women of Nacogdoches had more than one cultural model on which to draw.

In the nineteenth century, Anglo cotton planters would take over the Red River Valley and try to make it a black and white place, but before this happened mixed indigenous, Spanish, and French communities dotted the region, places that belong to what Gary Nash has called the "hidden history of *mestizo* America." Nash points out that more than the battleground "indelibly etched in our national consciousness," *mestizo* America was "also a cultural merging ground and a marrying ground."[7] Indeed, East Texas was a place where people both fought and loved—and made something new. To better understand the complicated connections in this extension of the Atlantic world we have to look at women's roles within the different cultural traditions of the region. The first part of this essay will examine the broader Spanish-Texas records on kinship, intermarriage, and interrelations in East Texas. The second part will look closely at women in the Nacogdoches legal record at the end of the eighteenth century, as it reveals how unorthodox relationships between men and women often arose in conjunction with contraband trade. I argue that the women of Nacogdoches developed another important variation in Spanish "private lives," one that emerged because of the economic desire to trade with other people, the metropole's difficulty of overseeing the village, and the multiple traditions that coexisted on the borderlands.

INTERMARRIAGE AND INTERRELATIONS IN EAST TEXAS

At the end of the eighteenth century most of the Spanish citizens of Nacogdoches had years of experience in Texas, and many had been born there. Spanish preachers and soldiers first arrived in East Texas during the 1690s, although they did not establish more permanent settlements until the 1720s. Two of these sites, San Antonio and Los Adaes, became important outposts, and many of the citizens of Nacogdoches, including its founders, originally hailed from Nuestra Señora del Pilar de Los Adaes. From its inception, this one-time capitol of Texas in the heart of Caddo country neighbored French Natchitoches and served as a center of contraband trade. Following the Seven Years War, France transferred Louisiana to Spain and the Bourbon government reexamined its border policies. In 1772 the Spanish government decided to close Los Adaes and the East Texas missions, including Nuestra Señora de Guadalupe de Nacogdoches, and the governor ordered the citizens to move to San Antonio. Finding little arable land in central Texas, the East Texans successfully petitioned to resettle a new town, Nuestra Señora del Pilar de Bucareli, on the banks of the Trinity River. By 1779, severe flooding and Comanche wars caused them to move again to the defunct Nacogdoches mission site, closer to their former village of Los Adaes. By moving to Louisiana, they returned to a place where they could easily continue their illicit trade with neighboring French and Caddo villages. This group of people and their descendants felt comfortable adopting interrelations and intermarriage as a way to expand their circle of kin beyond Spanish and Spanish-Mexican colonists.[8]

East Texas women first appeared in the earliest records as daughters and wives, especially when Spanish men and women formed kinship relations with others, whether *mestizo,* indigenous, French, or *métis.* The 1795 census offers a good starting point to explore this heterogeneity. Organized by families, the census recorded place of birth, occupation, age, and *calidad,* or "quality," which described people's *casta* (or race). The census showed more people (219) originated from the abandoned town of Los Adaes than anywhere else. Still others came from further afield in New Spain: La Bahia, San Antonio, New Mexico, Laredo, Saltillo, Monterrey, Havana, and New Orleans. There were several Canary Islanders, but very few *peninsulares* from Spain. Some individuals came from Philadelphia, Canada, Ireland, France, Virginia, England, and Italy. The census listed thirty-three black slaves but did not report their origins. Indians included Lipan and Natchez, among others. For *calidad* the census listed eighty-one *españoles,* sixty-three *mestizos,* forty *mulatos,* thirty-three *negros,* twenty *indios,* fourteen *callotes* (coyotes), six *lobos* (wolves), and five *castizos* (mixed caste).[9] Some people identified as *español* in the 1795 census were recorded as *mestizo* in later censuses (and vice versa), and more than one so-called *español* had clear non-Spanish ancestry. The census did not list the *calidad* of the other people with identifiable European backgrounds, whether they came from France, Italy, Great Britain, or the United States.[10]

In addition to showing diversity, the census provides a powerful testament to extensive intermarriages in Nacogdoches. Sixty-four marriages took place between people of different categories, and only thirty-three marriages were between two people in the same category, and being Spanish did not prevent either men or women from marrying others. Eleven *español* men and women married each other, but fourteen *español* women and twenty-four *español* men married outside of their group.[11] Most of the people in Nacogdoches married at some point in their lives. Of the 268 nondependent adults, 210 were married. There were twenty-one widows and nine widowers. Four women and one man had absent partners. Other unattached adults included nine men living with relatives or employers, five single men, two elderly women living with relatives, and two priests. Some of the single men may have formed relations with women outside of Nacogdoches in the Indian villages, though we have no record of this. Among the slaves, only those of Gil Y'Barbo had their marriage status listed: two had married, one was widowed, and one remained single. Seven nonmarried couples came from other places, and thus might have been married outside the Catholic Church.[12] Of course, the fact that a majority of people married across *calidad* does not mean that Spanish Texans paid no attention to caste. They did. *Calidad* mattered; but in Nacogdoches it was hardly fixed and did not preclude individuals from assuming elite positions or prevent intermarriages.

The Spaniards of East Texas formed relations with others long before they founded Nacogdoches. As early as the 1680s Spanish soldiers slept with indigenous women, though at least some of these encounters did not meet with Caddo approval. Spanish sexual aggression, as historian Juliana Barr argues, made the soldiers unwelcome, and the ensuing tensions contributed to the Spanish withdrawal at the time.[13] Franciscan priests complained that Spanish men disturbed Caddo women and entered their homes; even General Terán's African slave and trumpeter raped a young girl and another Caddo woman.[14] The slave, however, eventually ran away, and may have joined an indigenous *ranchería* (native village) or started a maroon colony; a 1703 map of the region labeled a village just north of present-day Nacogdoches as the "Canesi village of black Spaniards."[15] Other Spaniards also deserted. Joseph Urrutia fled the Spanish to live with the Tonkawa and Xaranames before returning to

New Spain seven years later, where he would became a prominent citizen and eventually the governor of Texas. Other deserters did not return. In 1736, Governor Sandoval noted that a forty-four-year-old woman born to a Spaniard in 1692 still lived among the "Asinays nation in the same land of her birth."[16]

The record is even clearer about early Spanish and French interrelationships, as the most elite families on the borderlands chose to marry these outsiders. In 1714, Commander Diego Ramón detained a prominent Louisiana trader, Louis Juchereau de St. Denis, for violating Spain's mercantile laws. Later, the French trader would marry Ramón's stepgranddaughter, Manuela Sánchez Navarro, thus beginning a frontier trade cartel that connected two prominent French and Spanish families for the next century. After his release and marriage, St. Denis continued to bring contraband into Texas, and authorities ordered that he and his family be exiled to Guatemala. Instead, he made his way back to Louisiana, and eventually the French appointed him commander of Natchitoches. Despite continuing troubles, both St. Denis and his family continued to cultivate Spanish ties. Spanish priests baptized their firstborn at Los Adaes, and when their daughter, Marie des Neges de St. Denis, reached adulthood, Manuel Antonio de Soto Bermúdez, a Spanish soldier, deserted his post to marry her. National allegiances shifted easily for these multiethnic families who had more connections (and rivalries) with each other than with their more distant Crowns.[17]

While St. Denis wed a Spanish woman, his French partner François Derbanne married a former Chitimaca slave, Jeanne de la Grande Terre. Their wealthy *métis* (French word for *mestizo*) son, Jean Baptiste Derbanne, created a stir when he married the daughter of Joseph González, a Spanish commander at Los Adaes. In 1736 twenty-five-year-old Derbanne sought the advice of the Jesuit priest of French Natchitoches about how to pursue fifteen-year-old Victoria Margarita González. The priest suggested approaching the ministers at Los Adaes, but Franciscan Father Vallejo did not want to involve himself in the matter. Vallejo could see that this would be what he called an "injudicious marriage" because of the "inequality between the couple."[18] Thus rebuked, Derbanne went back to the Jesuit, who suggested petitioning her parents in person. When Derbanne approached González, the captain met him courteously, but did not give him an answer (or any hope). In a letter to the governor of Texas, González conceded that some might consider Derbanne a gentleman, and he did not wish to hurt his feelings, therefore González told the suitor he could not allow the marriage due to the governor's absence. But González's letter also reveals a different concern: he did not want his daughter to marry a Frenchman, even if he were nobility. Vallejo's and González's comments suggest three possible problems with the marriage. First, when Vallejo mentioned inequality he may have been referring to Derbanne's *mestizo calidad*. Second, González alluded to the Spanish law that required all officers and their families to have their marriages approved by the Crown. Third, and perhaps most important, González's comments suggest that the Spanish officer objected to Derbanne's French allegiance. Lacking González's approval, Derbanne and Victoria González eloped. The couple fled in a canoe to Natchitoches, arriving around midnight, leaving Father Vallejo to fume that the French Jesuit scorned Church laws when he performed "his rash wedding ceremony."[19] This case reveals that borderlands Spaniards could choose between different priests to legitimize their marriages.

Following the elopement, González proclaimed that Derbanne had sorely tried his patience. Or had he? It is possible that González masterminded the elopement plot to build ties to a powerful Natchitoches family without violating Spanish laws and losing his post. As Twinam has pointed out, what people said in public did not always match what they did in private. Or perhaps Victoria's mother and/or her side of the family supported the marriage. González accused his wife's foster brother, one de la Cerda, of abetting the plot, and locked up another Spanish accomplice, Juan de Mora. Indeed, Victoria and Jean Baptiste did not act alone; at the very least, some of the Spaniards sanctioned this "unequal" marriage in which Victoria may have obtained the better economic deal. Borderland matriarchs may have been especially keen on creating kinship ties—even if they violated official government policy. These women, and most of the people in East Texas, had a view of kinship that did not privilege nationality, at least not in an exclusive way.

Indigenous records on kinship, marriage, and interrelations are harder to recover. As countless Spanish critics noted, the East Texas missions failed to attract converts. Barr has argued that the Caddo did not depend on the Spanish for food, goods, or military support; if anything, the Spanish depended on the Caddo. Barr points out that among Texas's Native Americans, gender readily trumped the categories of class or caste as the main site to differentiate people within the group.[20] Texas Indians' marriages followed the model of "bride service." Men paid—and continued to pay—her family for her labor, a practice that worked in conjunction with serial monogamy. In the eighteenth century, Caddo villagers followed their own marriage rules and practices with little interference from Spanish priests, though certainly Spanish and other Europeans, including priests, traders, and refugees, went to Caddo villages and may have introduced new ideas.[21]

One of the earliest observers of Caddo marriage practices, Fray Francisco Casañas de Jesús María, commented on the economic and social aspects of Caddo marriages.[22] According to Casañas, most marriages were based on gifts. If a man wanted to marry a "maiden," he took the best things he had to her, and if her parents allowed her to accept the gift, they consented to the marriage. For previously married women, he only had to ask his bride if she wanted to be his "friend" and to give her something. This new arrangement might be for a few days or a lifetime. But to Casañas's dismay, few couples stayed married. Couples arranged their own divorces. When a woman sought a separation, she told the man she had appreciated his gifts, "but what he gave her was but little in comparison to what the new man offer[ed]." When a man sought a separation, he made a "difference between them," and if the first wife found that he had "another wife in view" she made it a "point of honor (a rare thing among them) to leave him at once and go away in search of another husband." Casañas concluded that casual attitudes toward adultery and divorce explained Caddos' lack of disputes and quarrels and thought it commendable that the Caddo never had more than one wife at a time. He approvingly noted that ruling families considered marriage contracts binding: "in *their* circles, no one dares to trouble another's wife." Yet there were some exceptions to Caddo monogamy. One priest wrote that following the death of a sister-in-law's husband, the sister's husband was to marry the sister-in-law.[23] After their initial encounters, Franciscan writings did not dwell on Caddo marriage practices, and they did not keep records of Caddo-to-Caddo marriages.

In the nineteenth century, the close Caddo allies, the Wichita, and various other indigenous groups moved into the area. It was then, in 1808, that American horse trader Anthony Glass described Taovaya Wichita marriage and sexual practices, noting that men bought their wives from an uncle or brother usually for one or two horses. Husbands dressed their wives as they pleased, and they were not jealous, as nothing was "more common than for a Man to loan or hire out his Wife; particularly to Strangers who visit the nation."[24] Strangers—that is, traders such as Glass—could also buy their own wife with a payment of straw, blankets, vermillion, and beads. About twenty years later, naturalist Jean Louis Berlandier recorded similar marriage practices. According to Berlandier, most Texas Indians practiced polygamy, except for the Caddo. Arapaho, Tawakoni, and Waco husbands "would offer their wives to strangers, and be deeply offended if their offer was refused."[25] More than the Franciscans, nineteenth-century observers such as Glass and Berlandier underscored the commoditization of indigenous wives. Was this because of European or Indian newcomers' influences? Or did European and indigenous involvement in the slave trade cause a shift in practice? All may have played a part in the changes.

Though the Spanish did not take censuses of the indigenous villages, it is clear that some Spaniards continued to live in them, with women, even at the turn of the eighteenth century. At that time Spanish authorities gave passports to several official traders, such as Leal, but in addition other Spaniards made their way to the indigenous nations covertly. During the 1790s officials began a concerted effort to track down military deserters and illegal traders, such as Alonso de León (named after the famous Spanish captain). A 1795 investigation found that León lived with the Tawakoni, with his two Indian wives and a daughter. In addition, León's two Spanish sons, Manuel and Ignacio, were also in Wichita villages. Other Spaniards among the Wichita included Patricio and his son, and two others, one from Coahuila and another from Bexar. When Spanish officials sent out notices to arrest three deserters: Manuel de León (Alonso's son), Francisco Chávez, and José Antonio Munive, they captured León but not Chávez and Munive, who had moved on to the Comanche. And after Spaniards extradited León's other son, Ignacio, the Wichita from "Pueblo de la Tortuga" (Turtle Village) retaliated by assaulting the official trader.[26] Also, Apaches and Comanches captured and dispersed hundreds of Spanish children from Coahuila, Nuevo León, New Mexico, and elsewhere—and some of these boys and girls would marry within their adoptive nations.[27] The fact that Spanish men (some of whom were husbands, such as Leal) spent so much time in Indian nations, where different rules about marriage applied, may have opened a space for Spanish wives (such as Santos) to extend their kinship networks as well.

This analysis of Spanish women and kinship ties in East Texas's borderlands reveals an even more complex world than scholars have hitherto imagined. Until now most scholarship on East Texas interrelations has focused on French and Indian relations. David La Vere has documented extensive French and Indian intermarriages in the Texas-Louisiana region.²⁸ Barr has persuasively argued that Europeans would have to abide by Native American gender constructs and understand the importance of kinship ties. According to Barr, French traders readily understood this and wed indigenous women, but "Spaniards did not emulate their imperial rivals, rejecting Caddos' overtures of intermarriage."²⁹ My findings suggest that at least at the local level in Nacogdoches, Spaniards did understand the importance of forming kinship relations with indigenous people, including Caddos. Both census records and government sources show that the Spanish people of East Texas sought to extend kinship ties across cultures as they continued to expand their involvement in trade. By the turn of the century, Spanish intermarriages might have even outpaced the French, who were well on their way to constructing a more rigid slave plantation society in West Louisiana.³⁰

SPANISH WOMEN IN EAST TEXAS LEGAL RECORDS

As a general rule, female subjects appeared in late-eighteenth-century East Texas records only if there was a problem. In Nacogdoches these problems included: disturbing tranquility, property disputes, violent acts, and—most frequently—illicit sex and contraband trade. Some Texas women clearly benefitted from Spanish legal protections. Historians Donald Chipman and Harriet Denise Joseph write that Texas's legal record of wills, lawsuits, estate settlements, and petitions reveals that "even unlearned females on the frontier demonstrated an osmotic knowledge of Castilian law, passed down generation after generation from grandmother to mother to daughter."³¹ As in other parts of New Spain, women in Texas could own property in their own name; laws protected bridal property brought into marriage; married couples shared new assets as community property; and daughters could inherit equal to sons. Chipman and Joseph further state that women of all classes could access the legal system, giving the example of *mulata* Antonia, who successfully petitioned to retrieve her son from a former employer in San Antonio. Chipman and Joseph also note, however, that in the eyes of the judicial system women did not have equal status with men and were encouraged to marry and have children. In the end, the historians conclude that Texas women "had more legal rights and protections than their counterparts in English colonies, or in the early United States."³²

Contemporary Anglo-American commentators did not see Spanish law in such a beneficial light. According to Charles Cutter, the foremost legal scholar of the borderlands, Anglo-Americans believed the Spanish legal system was "ponderous, tyrannical, arbitrary, and corrupt."[33] One traveler to New Mexico, Josiah Gregg, complained that "scarcely one alcalde in a dozen" knew "what a law [was]."[34] Cutter, however, proposes that Spanish law drew on both Castilian and Indian traditions to allow just mediations between diverse elements of colonial society. Imperial administrators guarded the dominant culture, but a "consensual hegemony" emerged due to constant negotiations and "local particularism."[35] The success of Spain's frontier laws, as scholar Alfredo Jiménez suggests, was rooted in the idea and actuality that ultimately the monarch dispensed justice—anybody could appeal to the Crown, though it might take a long time and a large expense.[36] As in other parts of Spanish America, Texans developed an extensive written record whereby all clerical, governmental, and military officials ultimately reported to the king of Spain. But unlike the more settled parts of colonial Spain that had established courts, full-time judges, and accessible lawyers, newly settled places had no formal full-time legal officers.[37] In Nacogdoches the lieutenant governor had the last word in terms of dispensing everyday justice. Occasionally, if this commander could not resolve a dispute, he collected evidence and sent it to the governor. In especially egregious cases, Spanish soldiers brought suspects directly to San Antonio. The commander-general, the highest figure on the North American frontier following the Bourbon reforms, rarely interceded in local affairs.

The government records suggest that some governors and commanders attempted to control illegitimate sex despite its widespread practice in Spanish East Texas. The case of trader Andrés Chirinos opens a window into how and when authorities chose to address such cases.[38] Chirinos had been sleeping with married Juana María Berbán, and to resolve the problem her husband (in consultation with family members, the priests, and the governor) decided that they should move from San Antonio to Los Adaes—away from Chirinos. When Chirinos requested a permit to trade in Nacogdoches, Governor Jacinto de Barrios y Jáuregi refused, citing the need to prevent any further adultery. Chirinos ignored the governor's orders, and it was not long before he was confronted by a priest who discovered him hiding near the mission. When a villager later accused Chirinos of illegally selling his cow in 1755, Barrios y Jáuregi confronted Chirinos, who proclaimed that he could never expect a fair trial from the governor. For this insubordination Barrios y Jáuregi put Chirinos in jail, collected evidence, and eventually released him with no other punishment than time served and an admonishment to reform.

In 1762, Chirinos was in an amorous relationship with a different married woman, María Padilla, the wife of future commander of Nacogdoches Antonio Gil Y'Barbo. The new governor Ángel de Martos y Navarette exiled Chirinos to La Bahia on the Texas coast, but the trader continued to appear in Los Adaes. In 1766, Y'Barbo petitioned to have Chirinos exiled outside of Texas, "because it was publically known that my wife and I were living in a constant state of vexation, anxiety, and discord on account of Andrés Chirinos."[39] Governor Martos y Navarette ordered Chirinos to be committed at El Moro prison in Cuba, but Chirinos fled to the Louisiana. When Hugo Oconór succeeded Martos y Navarette as governor in 1767, Chirinos returned to Texas and asked for a reexamination of his case. According to Chirinos, Martos y Navarette had not punished him for adultery, but rather because of "the economical injury that I was causing him by soliciting license to obtain deer skins—the same deer skins, which he obtained by various means for the purpose of carrying on his transactions with the French at Nachitos."[40] Chirinos charged that the former governor illegally employed soldiers to trade with Native Americans for his own economic benefit. When Oconór reinterviewed the deponents, they all supported Chirinos; according to the new testimony their signatures on the court records had been either forced or forged.[41] The Chirinos case shows that despite strictures in the Spanish law, men and women engaged in extramarital relations in Texas, and that they could be prosecuted for those offenses. But Chirinos's more serious infraction consisted in challenging governors who sought to control the illegal but profitable contraband trade. Preventing the adultery, at least according to Chirinos, was simply a pretext to impede his business by an authority who hoped to monopolize trade.

When Y'Barbo became a commander in East Texas he also sought to control all trade, whether legal or contraband. He even developed and published his own set of laws.[42] Whether Y'Barbo published these laws (which included punishments for illicit sex) because he had been hurt by Chirinos' actions, to reform a corrupt town, or to increase his power (or all three of these reasons), the laws point to his active role in regulating the new town, including the inhabitants' sexual practices. The laws also suggest that many women formed relationships outside of their formal marriages during Nacogdoches's foundational years.[43]

The laws spoke almost exclusively to social order in Nacogdoches. They decreed punishments for arson, witchcraft, theft, jailbreaks, vagrancy, desertion, assisting vagrants, hiding deserters, insulting language, indecent songs, disrespecting masters, attending dances, playing cards, gambling in lotteries, and disrespecting the king and church. Ten out of the fifty-three laws addressed illicit relations of one kind or another. Ravishing a young girl, committing a rape, and carnal relations with an animal all carried the death penalty. Other forms of illicit sex carried less severe punishments. Women convicted of illicit intercourse or living with a married man would be expelled from Nacogdoches and receive monetary fines. At the third offence she would also receive one hundred lashes. A married man who did not live with his wife would forfeit one-half his property to the Royal Chamber. Involvement with prostitution did not carry the death penalty, but a man who prostituted his wife would be exposed in public; he would be rubbed with honey and feathered, wear a fool's cap, a string of garlic, and a pair of horns as well as being assigned ten years to the galleys. For the second offense he'd be sent to the galleys for life. The punishment for other pimps or procuresses was the same, except the first offense resulted in only six years. Bigamists would be exposed publically and sent away for life. The records do not reveal whether Y'Barbo punished or prosecuted anyone for adultery or any other illicit relations, and he did not forward any cases to San Antonio. But this does not mean that he did not punish anyone; as the commander he had the authority to discipline unruly inhabitants and settle minor disputes.[44]

A murder case from 1776 supports the idea Y'Barbo's laws did reflect real circumstances. María Refugio de Jesús Santa María, a baptized Ais Indian, had married Spanish José Antonio Calderón in Los Adaes. Calderón had a history of beating Refugio, and at one point she fled back to the Ais but returned when he promised to treat her better. The couple eventually moved to San Antonio as part of the larger evacuation of Los Adaes. A notorious drunkard and gambler, Calderón continued to assault Refugio and failed to supply her with adequate food and clothes. According to the father at Mission San José, Calderón repeatedly sold Refugio's sexual services to other men in order to pay off his debts. When someone murdered Calderón, the governor immediately called Refugio to testify. She claimed that a San José Mission Indian, Francisco Arocha, had given her husband two pesos so he could have an illicit relation with her, but when she refused to participate in their deal, Arocha killed Calderón. The governor next interviewed Arocha, who told a different story. Arocha's relative,

Angela Pacheco, informed Arocha that Refugio wanted her husband murdered. Although Arocha never intended to fulfill the request, he killed Calderón when he saw him abusing Refugio. Given the conflicting testimonies, the governor called Pacheco, Arocha, and Refugio before him for a confrontation. In the end, Refugio conceded to Arocha's version, and both Refugio and Arocha admitted to having had an illicit relationship.[45]

Ultimately, the behavior in the case both violated Spanish law and resembled the practices Y'Barbo's laws proscribed. Calderón sold his wife to other men. Refugio engaged in an adulterous relationship willingly, as did Arocha. Both she and Arocha colluded in a murder to resolve the problem. At one point Refugio had turned to the Spanish priests for protection, but they would not help her dissolve her marriage. So she created a new kinship circle around San José's Mission Indians to engineer her escape. Both Arocha's and Refugio's defenses cited Calderón's abuse as justification for the murder, and neither received the death sentence as the law required. Vicente Camaño, who defended Arocha, asserted that if he was "punished in a severe manner, according to the Royal Laws, all the Indians who have been converted to the Catholic Church, and others who are going to be converted, shall abandon these missions, which will cause lamentable consequences."[46] In the end, each received a punishment of seven years of exile and labor, which might not have been enforced. By the proceeding's conclusion, Refugio had married again—not Francisco Arocha, but instead one Santiago Saucedo, another San José resident. Thus, an Ais Indian who plotted the murder of her *vecino* husband through a San José Indian ended up marrying a different man from that same mission. Do the laws in Y'Barbo's code, Calderón and Refugio's marriage, and Refugio and Arocha's actions reflect indigenous practices? Did Refugio and Arocha draw on models of indigenous justice when they killed Calderón? What we know is that Spanish authorities complained bitterly about the people on the frontier whose behaviors resembled those of their indigenous neighbors.[47] Furthermore, this case provides a unique window for historians to view not only the intricacies of the legal system on the Texas borderlands, but also an indigenous woman's precarious situation with an abusive husband.

Most commanders did not write about marriages in their official records, but one Nacogdoches commander took an especially strong interest in regulating them. In August of 1797, José María Guadiana wrote to the governor complaining about the many couples that cohabited with someone other than their marriage partner. Although he and the friars had done everything possible to correct them with warnings and punishments, some "married heads of families" still "practiced sinful concubinage."⁴⁸ Guadiana singled out one couple in particular: Jacinto Mora and María de Jesús del Rio, who had been living together for more than twenty years, though each was married to someone else. Guadiana claimed this case had special urgency because the scandalous behavior reflected badly on both families. María Antonia de Berbán, Mora's legitimate wife, repeatedly complained about the matter. When she confronted her husband, Mora snapped that only God could take his love away. Guadiana noted Mora and Rio had a son living with his grandmother, and that Berbán had remained innocent throughout the desertion. Guadiana suggested that because neither family had any goods, except a house and a plot, one of the families should relocate to Bexar. Though none of these couples lived with their original marriage partners, the 1795 census listed them as still married. Jacinto Mora was listed as married to María Antonia Berbán, with two boys. And Pedro González was listed as married to María de Jesús del Rio, with a three-year-old son. A straight reading of the census would suggest that the people of Nacogdoches stayed with their original marriage partners, but other records show that this was not the case. Perhaps more than in other parts of New Spain, the people of East Texas entered into new relationships readily, whether they were wealthy or poor, male or female.

    Why was Guadiana so concerned over Berbán's petition? Perhaps she needed financial help. Or maybe Guadiana used his position to assert his power. Guadiana's support for Berbán was surely not due to a strong moral imperative. A few years later, Guadiana would come under suspicion for his own illicit relationship. In 1801, the commander-general of the interior provinces wrote a secret letter informing the governor of Texas that both Lieutenants Músquiz and Guadiana lived in scandalous relationships: Músquiz with the daughter of soldier Juan de la Cruz and Guadiana with the daughter of one Padilla. The commander-general cited the illegitimate relations in conjunction with a more serious investigation of the lieutenants' involvement in contraband trade, and both Guadiana and Músquiz lost their jobs, but only temporarily.⁴⁹ As both Guadiana's actions and comments suggest, many people lived with someone other than their marriage partner, and most were not prosecuted. Easy separations rather than strict adherence to Spanish and Catholic law marked the marriages of East Texas. In this way Spanish Nacogdochians acted like neighboring Caddos.

Now we have a better context to return to Gertrudis de los Santos. Like Guadiana and Chirinos, Santos had crossed a line, but not primarily because of her illicit affair. Spanish authorities feared her economic alliance with a powerful and wealthy Anglo-American trader who could challenge Spain's political domination in East Texas. Santos was about forty or fifty years old in 1801. A descendant of the Canary Island families that populated San Antonio in its earliest days, Santos married another Canary Island descendant and Indian agent, Antonio Leal. The two lived on a large ten- or fifteen-acre land grant near Nacogdoches in San Agustin. Leal had been gathering *mesteño* (wild) horses, and trading with indigenous villages in East Texas and toward Comancheria, partnering with Nolan for about ten years. A friend of American general James Wilkinson and correspondent of Thomas Jefferson, Nolan made several drives from Texas to the United States with Spanish consent. When Spanish authorities became increasingly suspicious of Anglo incursions in the late 1790s, they refused to issue a passport for Nolan's last run. He decided to go anyway, with a crew of armed Americans, Spaniards, and African slaves. After a deserter informed Spanish officials that Nolan planned to build a fort and take over Texas, the commander at Nacogdoches sent Santos and Leal to San Antonio. There the governor's questions focused on several points. Did they know about Nolan's military plans? Did they have secret correspondences with him? Had they introduced contraband trade items into Texas? And did Santos have illicit relations with Philip Nolan? The evidence suggests that Santos was unaware of Nolan's military designs (indeed, the record is not clear that he had any). But she did receive a secret letter, participate in contraband trade, and had an illicit relationship with the horse trader. In short, she broke the Spanish laws on several counts.[50]

Yet she was hardly alone. The political and ecclesiastic leaders in Nacogdoches helped build the Nolan-Leal-Santos trade network. One post commander enabled Leal and Santos to purchase the ranch used to stage Nolan's horses. Another commander refused 100 pesos when they came directly from Nolan, but accepted the money from Santos, supposedly as payment for a debt. Even the Nacogdoches priest, Father Gaitán, welcomed a gun from Nolan via Santos. If Santos acted illegally, she did so with the tacit complicity of these other powerful figures. Indeed, her actions did not violate local ideas of right and wrong, even when she became Nolan's lover.[51]

She certainly did not hide her affair. According to one informant, everyone knew about Santos' illegitimate relations with the trader—after all, they had traveled together on a cattle drive. During her testimony Santos readily admitted to being a "fragile woman," and the relationship did not seem to bother her husband either. When the governor asked Leal why his wife served Nolan, what she did for him, how much did she earn, and where did she go?—Leal responded that his wife served Nolan due to his own friendship with the trader, that she did not receive a salary, that she took care of his personal assistance and any other things Nolan needed. This is when Leal said that he did not know "what other things his wife did for Nolan, nor where they had traveled together, because he was absent trading with the Tonkawas, as per the former deceased governor's orders."[52] Antonio Leal had asked his wife to provide hospitality for his trading partner. Did he ask for more? Perhaps. As the Indian agent for the Wichita villages, Leal would have known some of the Wichita customs that Glass and Berlandier have described. He likely had sexual relationships, and perhaps even a wife, among the Tonkawa. It is also possible that Leal followed indigenous practices by loaning his wife to his friend and partner Nolan. Or was he acting according to other frontier practices, selling his wife as Calderón had done? At the very least, he turned the other way when his wife had an adulterous affair. Whatever the case, and despite being among the more wealthy families in Spanish East Texas, Santos and Leal acted like others on the borderlands who welcomed sexual relations with outsiders in order to extend kinship ties and economic opportunities.[53]

Scholars Noel L. Loomis and Abraham P. Nasitir have seen the Santos-Nolan affair as an unusually genuine moment of true romance. Jack Jackson describes the relationship as more of a business venture.[54] A manuscript letter from Nolan to Santos intersperses seemingly romantic touches with financial information.[55] Nolan assured Santos that his heart belonged to her and after he finished his horse run he would buy a house and call for her in his new home or she could send for him in Nacogdoches. He closed the letter by asking her to write "everything that she is thinking and wants," and if she found no one who could write a secret letter, she might confide all of her thoughts to their assistant, James Cook. Nolan also told a friend that he wanted to bring Santos to Natchez after he made his fortune. This letter ultimately cannot prove Santos' and Nolan's love for each other, though it might have been very strong. The letter does suggest that they had more than a simple business relationship; whether they loved each other or not, their affair provided a way for each to extend their circle of kin on the borderlands.

For Nolan, Leal, and Santos, kinship-building provided a way to create ties with other people, and it involved other members of the Leal-Santos clan. In San Antonio Nolan impregnated teenager Gertrudis Quiñones, the daughter of Juana María (Leal) Quiñones and god-child of Juan José and Josefa Leal—possible relations of Antonio Leal. Nolan's letter to Santos also mentioned two other women in the Leal household. He told Santos that *la negrita* (the little black girl) could expect the flowered silk and to send his love to "la Chepita."[56] The records do not show that Leal and Santos had any children together, although the Leals appear in the 1799 census with an eight-year old *criada* (servant). So who were these women? Was *la negrita* someone's slave? Was she someone's lover? Was she someone's daughter? The same questions apply to la Chepita, who may have been Antonio Leal's lover and slave. "Chepita" is a diminutive for Josepha, and Leal claimed to have bought a slave, María Josepha, at a Natchez auction in 1796. At about the time of the trial, Leal took María Josepha's *mulato* son to San Fernando to be baptized with the name of Antonio Leal. María Josepha also had another *mulato* child, Soledad. To what degree any of these women participated willingly in the trade networks can never be known, but Nolan's letter suggests that he thought of *la negrita* and la Chepita as friends or family; of course they might have been abused kin.

At the turn of the century, Spanish elites in Nacogdoches increasingly extended ties to incoming Americans, as they had done earlier with the French and Indians. Gertrudis de los Santos' brother, José de los Santos, for one, chose to marry Maria Hooper, an American. When the priests at Nacogdoches refused to marry them (perhaps because Hooper had a Protestant upbringing), he followed in the footsteps of earlier Spaniards who had crossed over to Natchitoches to make their marriage vows. At the turn of the century the Spanish citizens of Nacogdoches broke many laws, but they still aligned themselves with the Spanish government. However, it would not be long before some Spanish citizens from Nacogdoches colluded with Anglo-Americans to overthrow Spanish and Mexican rule, though most would come to regret that decision.[57]

CONCLUSION

At the end of their trial, Spanish authorities exiled Santos, Leal, and their slaves to Coahuila. However, María Josefa's son Antonio Leal would return to the area of the original land grant, and his descendants continued to live in what became known as the Edmund Quirk grant. Philip Nolan had worse luck. The Spanish military shot him at his East Texas corral. In addition to his Texas kin, Nolan left behind a pregnant widow in Mississippi. Shortly before his last journey to Texas he had asked for Frances Lintot's hand in marriage. Her family belonged to Natchez's slave-owning elites and objected to the match—so she too eloped. One wonders what would have happened had Nolan survived. Would he have returned to Frances Lintot and built a home for Gertrudis de los Santos? How many slaves and/or children would their households hold? By making familial connections with Anglo outsiders, the powerful clans of Spanish Texas increased their own slave holdings and wealth but helped to put an end to Spanish Nacogdoches. The new wave of Anglo-Americans had different family ideals that discouraged marriage or open relations with Spanish, indigenous, or African peoples. Ethnic cleansing, as Gary Clayton Anderson has argued, was the order of the day.[58] Of course, some Anglos defied cultural and legal restrictions, some Tejanos remained in East Texas, and slaveowners continued to sleep with their slaves; however, the exact contours of the change from Spanish Nacogdoches to Anglo Nacogdoches will require further research.

Instead of focusing on Nolan or other men, this essay has taken a different angle, searching for the less visible stories of borderlands women. Doing so raises as many questions as answers, but we can draw some conclusions. As in other parts of New Spain, Spanish men and women could have different public and private lives, though the fluidity might have been even greater in East Texas than in most other Spanish colonies. Historians have long known that the people in East Texas defied mercantile rules that prohibited trade with their Indian, French, and Anglo neighbors. I argue here that they likewise defied Spanish marriage laws. Indeed, contraband trade and extended kinship reinforced each other. Spanish women in East Texas married Texas Indians, Frenchmen, Anglos, Africans, and *mestizos,* and they had sexual relations with different people outside of their Catholic marriages as they extended their Atlantic world into an area of indigenous control. To what degree women encouraged all of these interconnections may have depended on individual situations. Santos might have desired a relationship with the wealthy Nolan more than Refugio welcomed the man who sold her services to pay off his gambling debts. But Refugio did team up with another man to kill her abusive husband. Though women inhabited a world in which diverse men from widely different cultures sought to control their labor and sexuality,

European, Indigenous, African, and *mestiza* women from Spanish East Texas made choices, too. Through their involvement in kinship-building and trade they participated in an ongoing Spanish expansion that connected Europe, Africa, and America, resulting in a world that was neither entirely Spanish nor entirely Indian. In East Texas exogamous relationships began early with Spanish soldiers and Caddo women; the late eighteenth-century fusion eventually included an Anglo Irishman and Canary Island East Texan, as well as her Canary Island husband and his African slave.

NOTES

1. "Criminal proceedings against Santiago Cook, Antonio Leal, his wife Gertrudis de los Santos, and Pedro Geremias Longueville, all accused of secret conspiracy with Felipe Nolan," January 23, 1801–September 13, 1801, Bexar Archives, Center for American History, University of Texas, Austin (hereafter BA). Translation from Spanish to English by the author.

2. Antonia I. Castañeda, "Women of Color and the Rewriting of Western History: The Discourse, Politics, and Decolonization of History," *Pacific Historical Review, Special Issue: Western Women's History Revisited* 61, no. 4 (November 1992): 501–533.

3. Ibid., 514–515, 518.

4. Ann Twinam, *Public Lives, Private Secrets: Gender, Honor, Sexuality, and Illegitimacy in Colonial Spanish Latin America* (Stanford: Stanford Univ. Press, 1999), 34.

5. Amy Turner Bushnell, "Indigenous America and the Limits of the Atlantic World, 1493–1825," in *Atlantic History: A Critical Appraisal*, ed. Jack P. Greene and Philip D. Morgan, 192–193 (New York: Oxford Univ. Press, 2009).

6. Bushnell, "Indigenous America and the Limits of the Atlantic World," 192–193.

7. Gary B. Nash, "The Hidden History of Mestizo America," *Journal of American History* 82, no. 3 (December 1995): 947.

8. For the Spanish Borderlands and East Texas, see Juliana Barr, *Peace Came in the Form of a Woman: Indians and Spaniards in the Texas Borderlands* (Chapel Hill: Univ. of North Carolina Press, 2007); Herbert Eugene Bolton, *Texas in the Middle Eighteenth Century: Studies in Spanish Colonial History and Administration* (1915; reprint, New York: Russel and Russel, 1962); Carlos E. Castañeda, *Our Catholic Heritage in Texas*, 7 vols. (Austin: Von Boeckmann-Jones, 1936–1958); Donald E. Chipman, *Spanish Texas: 1519–1821* (Austin: Univ. of Texas Press, 1992); Francis X. Galán, "Last Soldiers, First Pioneers: The Los Adaes Border Community on the Louisiana-Texas Frontier, 1729–1770" (Ph.D. diss., Southern Methodist University, 2006); Elizabeth A. H. John, *Storms Brewed in Other Men's Worlds: The Confrontation of Indians, Spanish, and French in the Southwest, 1540–1795* (Norman: Univ. of Oklahoma Press, 1996); David J. Weber, *Bárbaros: Spaniards and Their Savages in the Age of Enlightenment* (New Haven: Yale Univ. Press, 2005); David J. Weber, *The Spanish Frontier in North America* (New Haven: Yale Univ. Press, 1992).

9. On *castas* and *mestizaje* see, Douglas R. Cope, *The Limits of Racial Domination: Plebian Society in Colonial Mexico City, 1660–1720* (Madison: Univ. of Wisconsin Press, 1994); Susan Kellogg, "Depicting Mestizaje: Gendered Images of Ethnorace in Colonial Mexican Texts," *Journal of Women's History* 12, no. 3 (2000): 69–92; María Elena Martínez, *Geneological Fictions: Limpieza de Sangre, Religion, and Gender in Colonial Mexico* (Stanford: Stan-

ford Univ. Press, 2008); María Elena Martínez, "The Black Blood of New Spain: Limpieza de Sangre, Racial Violence, and Gendered Power in Early Colonial Mexico," *William and Mary Quarterly* 61 (July 2004): 479–520; Ilona Katzew, *Casta Painting: Images of Race in Eighteenth-Century Mexico* (New Haven: Yale Univ. Press, 2004); María Concepción García Sáiz, *Las castas mexicanas: un género pictórico americano* (Milan: Olivetti, 1989). *Callotes* and *lobos* also referred to people of mixed caste.

10. "General Census Report of Nacogdoches," December 25, 1795, BA; Patrick J. Walsh, "Living on the Edge of the Neutral Zone: Varieties of Identity in Nacogdoches, Texas, 1773–1810," *East Texas Historical Journal* 37, no. 2 (1999): 3–24; Alicia V. Tjarks, "Comparative Demographic Analysis of Texas, 1777–1793," *Southwestern Historical Quarterly* 77 (1974): 291–338; Tina Laurel Meacham, "The Population of Spanish and Mexican Texas, 1716–1836" (Ph.D. diss., University of Texas at Austin, 2000).

11. "General Census Report of Nacogdoches," December 25, 1795, BA.

12. Ibid.

13. Barr, *Peace Came in the Form of a Woman*, 86.

14. Damián Massent, "Carta del padre Damián Mazanet al Virrey sobre la situación en San Francisco de los Tejas," in *Primeras exploraciones y poblamiento de Texas, 1686–1694,* ed. Lino Gómez Canedo, 261–270, 264, 268, 269 (Monterrey, Mexico: Publicaciones del Instituto Tecnológico y de Estudios Superiores de Monterrey, 1968).

15. Guillaume Delisle, "Carte du Mexique et de la Floride . . . ," in *Maps of Texas and the Southwest, 1513–1900,* ed. James C. Martin and Robert Sidney Martin, 92 (Albuquerque: Univ. of New Mexico Press, 1984).

16. José Antonio Pichardo, *Pichardo's Treatise on the Limits of Louisiana and Texas,* ed. and trans. Charles Wilson Hackett (1941; reprint, Freeport, N.Y.: Books for Libraries Press, 1971), 3:503.

17. Patricia R. Lemée, "Tios and Tantes: Familial and Political Relationships of Natchitoches and the Spanish Colonial Frontier," *Southwestern Historical Quarterly* 101 (January 1998): 341–358; Ross Phares, *Cavalier in the Wilderness: The Story of the Explorer and Trader Louis Juchereau de St. Denis* (Baton Rouge: Louisiana State Univ. Press, 1952).

18. Pichardo, *Pichardo's Treatise,* 489.

19. Ibid., 484–485.

20. Barr, *Peace Came in the Form of a Woman,* 2, 82–83.

21. George Sabo III, "The Structure of Caddo Leadership in the Colonial Era," in *Native American History of the Caddo: Their Place in Southeastern Archaeology and Ethnohistory,* ed. Timothy K. Perttula and James E. Bruseth, 159–174 (Austin: Texas Archeological Research Laboratory, University of Texas at Austin, 1998).

22. Francisco Casañas de Jesús María, "Description of the Tejas or Aisnai Indians: 1691–1722," trans. Mattie Austin Hatcher, *Southwestern Historical Quarterly* 30 (April 1927): 283–284.

23. Ibid., 283–284.

24. Anthony Glass, *Journal of an Indian Trader: Anthony Glass and the Texas Trading Frontier, 1790–1810* (College Station: Texas A & M Univ. Press, 1985), 55.

25. Jean Louis Berlandier, *The Indians of Texas in 1830* (Washington, D.C.: Smithsonian Institution Press, 1969), 36.

26. "Bexar Cuaderno of Muñoz's letter to Nava," BA, January 4, 1796–July 10, 1796; Various BA records on deserters: June 4, 1795; June 4, 1795–June 22, 1795; September 13, 1797; October 17, 1797; April 19, 1795–May 5, 1795; July 10, 1795.

27. Joaquín Rivaya-Martínez, "Captivity and Adoption among the Comanche Indians, 1700-1875" (Ph.D. diss., University of California at Los Angeles, 2006).

28. David La Vere, "Between Kinship and Capitalism: French and Spanish Rivalry in the Colonial Louisiana-Texas Indian Trade," *Journal of Southern History* 64 (May 1998): 197-218.

29. Barr, *Peace Came in the Form of a Woman*, 88-89.

30. On this theme, see Jennifer M. Spear, "'They Need Wives': Métissage and the Regulation of Sexuality in French Louisiana, 1699-1730," in *Sex, Love, Race: Crossing Boundaries in North American History*, ed. Martha Hodes, 35-59 (New York: New York Univ. Press, 1999). Recent work from Sophie Burton and Kathleen DuVal suggest that Louisiana's métissage has been overstated. DuVal's work on the Quapaw, Apalachee, and Osage suggests that Louisiana failed to practice large-scale métissage as in other parts of New France, and insofar as Louisiana's indigenous villages allowed intermarriages, most of the women were young outsiders and slaves with little say. (Kathleen DuVal, "Indian Intermarriage and Métissage in Colonial Louisiana," *William and Mary Quarterly* 65 [April 2008]: 267-304; Sophie H. Burton, *Colonial Natchitoches: A Creole Community on the Louisiana-Texas Frontier* [College Station: Texas A & M Univ. Press, 2008].) On métissage more generally, see Susan Sleeper-Smith, *Indian Women and French Men : Rethinking Cultural Encounter in the Western Great Lakes* (Amherst: Univ. of Massachusetts Press, 2001); Lucy E. Murphy, *A Gathering of Rivers: Indians, Métis, and Mining in the Western Great Lakes, 1737-1832* (Lincoln: Univ. of Nebraska Press, 2000).

31. Donald E. Chipman and Harriet Denise Joseph, *Notable Men and Women of Spanish Texas* (Austin: Univ. of Texas Press, 1999), 263-264.

32. Ibid., 267-269.

33. Charles R. Cutter, *The Legal Culture of Northern New Spain* (Albuquerque: Univ. of New Mexico Press, 1995), 164-165.

34. Ibid., 38.

35. Ibid., 3.

36. Alfredo Jiménez, "Who Controls the King?" in *Choice, Persuasion, and Coercion: Social Control on Spain's North American Frontiers*, ed. Jesús F. De la Teja, 1-25 (Albuquerque: Univ. of New Mexico Press, 2005).

37. Susan Kellogg, *Law and the Transformation of Aztec Culture, 1500-1700* (Norman: Univ. of Oklahoma Press, 1985); M.C. Mirow, *Latin American Law: A History of Private Law and Institutions in Spanish America* (Austin: Univ. of Texas Press, 2004); Kenneth L. Karst and Keith S. Rosenn, *Law and Development in Latin America* (Berkeley: Univ. of California Press, 1975); Mark F. Fernandez, *From Chaos to Continuity: The Evolution of Louisiana's Judicial System, 1712-1862* (Baton Rouge: Louisiana State Univ. Press, 2001).

38. "Proceedings held by Jacinto de Barrios y Jáuregui, Juan Prieto, Angel de Martos y Navarette, and Hugo O'Conor against Andrés Chirinos, accused of theft, contempt of the authorities, and disorderly Conduct," BA, June 6, 1755.

39. Antonio Gil Y'Barbo, "A Criminal Code Published in Nacogdoches," 1783, in *Antonio Gil Y'Barbo: Father of Nacogdoches*, ed. Carolyn Reeves Ericson and Linda Ericson Devereaux, xvii-xxv, 181-186 (Nacogdoches, Texas: Carolyn Reeves Ericson, 1995).

40. Ibid., 181-186.

41. Ibid.

42. Ibid.

43. Ibid.

44. Ibid., 183.

45. "Case against María del Refugio de Jesús María and Francisco de Arocha for the murder of José Antonio Calderón," June 4, 1776, BA.
46. Ibid.
47. Ibid. A good discussion of Indians and Spanish justice on Spain's northern frontier is Steven W. Hackel, *Children of the Coyote, Missionaries of Saint Francis: Indian-Spanish Relations in Colonial California, 1769-1850* (Chapel Hill: Univ. of North Carolina Press, 2005), chapter 8, 321–366.
48. "Guadiana to Muñoz asking that certain troublesome people be deported to Bexar," August 18, 1797, BA.
49. "Pedro de Nava," July 21, 1801, BA.
50. "Criminal Proceedings," January 23, 1801–September 13, 1801, BA.
51. Ibid.
52. Ibid.
53. Ibid.
54. Noel M. Loomis and Abraham P. Nasatir, *Pedro Vial and the Roads to Santa Fe* (Norman: Univ. of Oklahoma Press, 1967); Maurine T. Wilson and Jack Jackson, *Philip Nolan and Texas: Expeditions to the Unknown Land, 1791-1801* (Waco: Texian Press, 1987); Jack Jackson, *Los Mesteños: Spanish Ranching in Texas, 1721-1821* (College Station: Texas A & M Univ. Press, 1986); Noel M. Loomis, "Philip Nolan's Entry into Texas in 1800," in *The Spanish in the Mississippi Valley, 1762-1804*, ed. John Francis McDermott (Urbana: Univ. of Illinois Press, 1974).
55. "Letter from Nolan to Gertrudis de los Santos, November 1799," Trial Documents, BA, November 1799.
56. Ibid.
57. For an overview of the later period, see Andrés Reséndez, *Changing National Identities at the Frontier: Texas and New Mexico, 1800-1850* (New York: Cambridge Univ. Press, 2005); "Criminal Proceedings," January 23, 1801–September 13, 1801, BA.
58. Gary Clayton Anderson, *The Conquest of Texas: Ethnic Cleansing in the Promised Land, 1820-1875* (Norman: Univ. of Oklahoma Press, 2005).

WORKS CITED

Primary Sources

Bexar Archives. Center for American History, University of Texas, Austin.

Secondary Sources

Anderson, Gary Clayton. *The Conquest of Texas: Ethnic Cleansing in the Promised Land, 1820-1875*. Norman: Univ. of Oklahoma Press, 2005.
Barr, Juliana. *Peace Came in the Form of a Woman: Indians and Spaniards in the Texas Borderlands*. Chapel Hill: Univ. of North Carolina Press, 2007.
Berlandier, Jean Louis. *The Indians of Texas in 1830*. Washington, D.C.: Smithsonian Institution Press, 1969.
Bolton, Herbert Eugene. *Texas in the Middle Eighteenth Century: Studies in Span-

ish Colonial History and Administration. 1915. Reprint, New York: Russel and Russel, 1962.

Burton, Sophie H. *Colonial Natchitoches: A Creole Community on the Louisiana-Texas Frontier*. College Station: Texas A & M Univ. Press, 2008.

Bushnell, Amy Turner. "Indigenous America and the Limits of the Atlantic World, 1493–1825." In *Atlantic History: A Critical Appraisal*, edited by Jack P. Greene and Philip D. Morgan, 191–221. New York: Oxford Univ. Press, 2009.

Canedo, Lino Gómez. *Primeras exploraciones y poblamiento de Texas, 1686–1694*. Monterrey, Mexico: Publicaciones del Instituto Tecnológico y de Estudios Superiores de Monterrey, 1968.

Casañas de Jesús María, Francisco. "Description of the Tejas or Aisnai Indians: 1691–1722." Translated by Mattie Austin Hatcher. *Southwestern Historical Quarterly* 30 (January 1927): 283–304.

Castañeda, Antonia I. "Women of Color and the Rewriting of Western History: The Discourse, Politics, and Decolonization of History." *Pacific Historical Review, Special Issue: Western Women's History Revisited* 61, no. 4 (November 1992): 501–533.

Castañeda, Carlos E. *Our Catholic Heritage in Texas*. 7 vols. Austin: Von Boeckmann-Jones, 1936–1958.

Chipman, Donald E. *Spanish Texas: 1519–1821*. Austin: Univ. of Texas Press, 1992.

Chipman, Donald E., and Harriet Denise Joseph. *Notable Men and Women of Spanish Texas*. Austin: Univ. of Texas Press, 1999.

Cope, Douglas R. *The Limits of Racial Domination: Plebian Society in Colonial Mexico City, 1660–1720*. Madison: Univ. of Wisconsin Press, 1994.

Cutter, Charles R. *The Legal Culture of Northern New Spain*. Albuquerque: Univ. of New Mexico Press, 1995.

Delisle, Guillaume. "Carte du Mexique et de La Floride . . . " In *Maps of Texas and the Southwest, 1513–1900*, ed. James C. Martin and Robert Sidney Martin. Albuquerque: Univ. of New Mexico Press, 1984.

DuVal, Kathleen. "Indian Intermarriage and Métissage in Colonial Louisiana." *William and Mary Quarterly* 65 (April 2008): 267–304.

Fernandez, Mark F. *From Chaos to Continuity: The Evolution of Louisiana's Judicial System, 1712–1862*. Baton Rouge: Louisiana State Univ. Press, 2001.

Galán, Francis X. "Last Soldiers, First Pioneers: The Los Adaes Border Community on the Louisiana-Texas Frontier, 1729–1770." Ph.D. diss., Southern Methodist University, 2006.

García Sáiz, María Concepción. *Las castas mexicanas: un género pictórico americano*. Milan: Olivetti, 1989.

Glass, Anthony. *Journal of an Indian Trader: Anthony Glass and the Texas Trading Frontier, 1790–1810*. College Station: Texas A & M Univ. Press, 1985.

Hackel, Steven W. *Children of the Coyote, Missionaries of Saint Francis: Indian-*

Spanish Relations in Colonial California, 1769–1850. Chapel Hill: Univ. of North Carolina Press, 2005.

Jackson, Jack. *Los Mesteños: Spanish Ranching in Texas, 1721–1821*. College Station: Texas A & M Univ. Press, 1986.

Jiménez, Alfredo. "Who Controls the King?" In *Choice, Persuasion, and Coercion: Social Control on Spain's North American Frontiers*, edited by Jesús F. De la Teja, 1–25. Albuquerque: Univ. of New Mexico Press, 2005.

John, Elizabeth A. H. *Storms Brewed in Other Men's Worlds: The Confrontation of Indians, Spanish, and French in the Southwest, 1540–1795*. Norman: Univ. of Oklahoma Press, 1996.

Karst, Kenneth L., and Keith S. Rosenn. *Law and Development in Latin America*. Berkeley: Univ. of California Press, 1975.

Katzew, Ilona. *Casta Painting: Images of Race in Eighteenth-Century Mexico*. New Haven: Yale Univ. Press, 2004.

Kellogg, Susan. "Depicting Mestizaje: Gendered Images of Ethnorace in Colonial Mexican Texts." *Journal of Women's History* 12, no. 3 (2000): 69–92.

———. *Law and the Transformation of Aztec Culture, 1500–1700*. Norman: Univ. of Oklahoma Press, 1985.

La Vere, David. "Between Kinship and Capitalism: French and Spanish Rivalry in the Colonial Louisiana-Texas Indian Trade." *Journal of Southern History* 64 (May 1998): 197–218.

Lemée, Patricia R. "Tios and Tantes: Familial and Political Relationships of Natchitoches and the Spanish Colonial Frontier." *Southwestern Historical Quarterly* 101 (January 1998): 341–358.

Loomis, Noel M. "Philip Nolan's Entry into Texas in 1800." In *The Spanish in the Mississippi Valley, 1762–1804*, edited by John Francis McDermott, 120–132. Urbana: Univ. of Illinois Press, 1974.

Loomis, Noel M., and Abraham P. Nasatir. *Pedro Vial and the Roads to Santa Fe*. Norman: Univ. of Oklahoma Press, 1967.

Martínez, María Elena. "The Black Blood of New Spain: Limpieza de Sangre, Racial Violence, and Gendered Power in Early Colonial Mexico." *William and Mary Quarterly* 61 (July 2004): 479–520.

———. *Geneological Fictions: Limpieza De Sangre, Religion, and Gender in Colonial Mexico*. Stanford: Stanford Univ. Press, 2008.

Meacham, Tina Laurel. "The Population of Spanish and Mexican Texas, 1716–1836." Ph.D. diss., University of Texas at Austin, 2000.

Mirow, M. C. *Latin American Law: A History of Private Law and Institutions in Spanish America*. Austin: Univ. of Texas Press, 2004.

Murphy, Lucy E. *A Gathering of Rivers: Indians, Métis, and Mining in the Western Great Lakes, 1737–1832*. Lincoln: Univ. of Nebraska Press, 2000.

Nash, Gary B. "The Hidden History of Mestizo America." *Journal of American History* 82, no. 3 (December 1995): 941–964.

Phares, Ross. *Cavalier in the Wilderness: The Story of the Explorer and Trader Louis Juchereau de St. Denis.* Baton Rouge: Louisiana State Univ. Press, 1952.
Pichardo, José Antonio. *Pichardo's Treatise on the Limits of Louisiana and Texas,* vol. 3. Edited and translated by Charles Wilson Hackett. 1941. Reprint, Freeport, N.Y.: Books for Libraries Press, 1971.
Reséndez, Andrés. *Changing National Identities at the Frontier: Texas and New Mexico, 1800–1850.* New York: Cambridge Univ. Press, 2005.
Rivaya-Martínez, Joaquín. "Captivity and Adoption among the Comanche Indians, 1700–1875." Ph.D. diss., University of California at Los Angeles, 2006.
Sabo, George, III. "The Structure of Caddo Leadership in the Colonial Era." In *Native American History of the Caddo: Their Place in Southeastern Archaeology and Ethnohistory,* edited by Timothy K. Perttula and James E. Bruseth, 159–174. Austin: Texas Archeological Research Laboratory, University of Texas at Austin, 1998.
Sleeper-Smith, Susan. *Indian Women and French Men: Rethinking Cultural Encounter in the Western Great Lakes.* Amherst: Univ. of Massachusetts Press, 2001.
Spear, Jennifer M. "'They Need Wives': Métissage and the Regulation of Sexuality in French Louisiana, 1699–1730." In *Sex, Love, Race: Crossing Boundaries in North American History,* edited by Martha Hodes, 35–59. New York: New York Univ. Press, 1999.
Tjarks, Alicia V. "Comparative Demographic Analysis of Texas, 1777–1793." *Southwestern Historical Quarterly* 77 (1974): 291–338.
Twinam, Ann. *Public Lives, Private Secrets: Gender, Honor, Sexuality, and Illegitimacy in Colonial Spanish Latin America.* Stanford: Stanford Univ. Press, 1999.
Walsh, Patrick J. "Living on the Edge of the Neutral Zone: Varieties of Identity in Nacogdoches, Texas, 1773–1810." *East Texas Historical Journal* 37, no. 2 (1999): 3–24.
Weber, David J. *Bárbaros: Spaniards and Their Savages in the Age of Enlightenment.* New Haven: Yale Univ. Press, 2005.
———. *The Spanish Frontier in North America.* New Haven: Yale Univ. Press, 1992.
Wilson, Maurine T., and Jack Jackson. *Philip Nolan and Texas: Expeditions to the Unknown Land, 1791–1801.* Waco: Texian Press, 1987.
Y'Barbo, Antonio Gil. "A Criminal Code Published in Nacogdoches." 1783. In *Antonio Gil Y'Barbo: Father of Nacogdoches,* ed. Carolyn Reeves Ericson and Linda Ericson Devereaux, xvii–xxv, 181–186. Nacogdoches, Texas: Carolyn Reeves Ericson, 1995.

6

Cloistered Women in Health Care

The Convent of Jesús María, Mexico City

NURIA SALAZAR SIMARRO AND SARAH E. OWENS

Recent studies have shed much light on cloistered convents and their relationship with the outside world.[1] Even though at first glance one might assume that cloistered nuns, having taken their solemn vows of poverty, shut the gate to the outside world for good, this simply was not the case. Not only did nuns maintain open communication with the lay population, but at times they allowed secular people to enter their nunneries. Convents, however, could differ greatly from one another, depending on their order, time period, and location within the Catholic Atlantic world. A discalced Carmelite Spanish nun, for example from the 1600s, had a very different way of living from a Conceptionist calced woman religious in Mexico City.[2] The former would eat together with other nuns in a single refectory, sleep on a simple bed in a common dormitory, live a life without servants or slaves, and when necessary take her turn in caring for sick nuns in the infirmary. The Mexican nun led a very different lifestyle. She could be the owner of her "cell," sometimes a large apartment with a bedroom, kitchen, and living area. If she came from a wealthy family she would bring with her servants and slaves to take care of the cooking and cleaning. She might also invite other family members, both young and old, to share her living spaces. Although like a discalced nun, she could also serve as a nurse in the infirmary, she would not need to stoop to the menial labor of cleaning bedpans or changing sheets (the servant class would be assigned those tasks). In sum, she had a very comfortable way of life, not too different from that of a wealthy woman outside of the convent. Although strict orders of nuns such as the Carmelites and Capuchins did exist in the New World, the majority of nuns in Mexico opted for calced orders, allowing them to maintain some of their wealth and status from their previous lives, even more so than the same types of communities back in Spain.

This well-to-do standard of living within calced convents of Mexico City is especially evident in the Conceptionist Convent of Jesús María, relatively one of the wealthiest and largest nunneries in New Spain.[3] Upon closer examination, this becomes particularly noteworthy when analyzing the health care provided to the nuns themselves. These women did not pinch pennies when it came to caring for sick sisters. They spent considerable sums of money on visits from doctors and surgeons. Secular medical personnel entered the inner confines of the cloistered environment and attended to a wide variety of maladies, anything ranging from simple infections to kidney stones. When necessary, the women bought medicines from local pharmacies and stocked their own medicine cabinet. They kept a large and clean infirmary. A staff of trained nurses (the nuns themselves) tended to the sick patients. Servants and slaves assisted the nurses and at times aided them with traditional remedies passed down from indigenous traditions.

This essay uses the Convent of Jesús María as a snapshot to illuminate health care provided to religious women in early modern Mexico and the greater Catholic Atlantic world. It also serves as a window to understanding how calced convents in Mexico provided a safe haven for women of African, mixed, or indigenous descent within colonial society. Further, it will discuss how a multiethnic community brought with them diverse notions of health care, providing the sick patients a combination of traditional medicine from the Iberian Peninsula with indigenous healing drawn from pre-Hispanic roots. The first part of the chapter will cover the origins of the Conceptionist order on the Iberian Peninsula and the founding of the first convents in New Spain. The second half will analyze convent life and health care in female religious orders, specifically exploring the case of Jesús María. The time period covered in this chapter corresponds to Jesús María's heyday, approximately from 1600 until the mid-1700s. Typically, only white women of Spanish descent could profess as black-veiled nuns, but these boundaries were blurred especially when it came to *mestizas* (women of indigenous and Spanish descent). Additionally, behind the cloistered walls lived many lay women. There were numerous servants and slaves (*mulatas,* indigenous, and African women),[4] but others were family members of the nuns, some young girls, and others widows or unmarried siblings. The combination of all these women living together behind the thick outer walls of the colonial convent weaves for us a colorful tapestry of the diverse society that made up calced convents like Jesús María.

These Amerindian women certainly were not present in the first Conceptionist convents founded in Spain, nor in the others established in France and Italy. Nonetheless, some African women (or women of African descent) did serve in the Spanish nunneries,[5] perhaps even sharing some of their knowledge of the natural world—a topic astutely discussed by Hugh Cagle, Timothy Walker, and Ras Michael Brown in this same volume. In 1484, doña Beatriz de Silva y Meneses, a Portuguese noblewoman, and a lady-in-waiting for Queen Isabel of Spain, first started the Order of the Immaculate Conception in Toledo, Spain. She began the order with a core of other religious women and became their first abbess. This small group of women lived as nuns in the Palacios de Galeana in Toledo, but did not receive official recognition as a religious order until after the founder's death. She died in 1490 and Pope Julius II approved the order in 1511.[6] By 1526 there were thirty-six Conceptionist convents in Spain and others in France and Italy, making a total of forty-six.[7]

It did not take long for the Conceptionist order[8] to spread to the New World. In fact, the very first convent founded in Mexico and all of the Americas was the "Monasterio de la Pura y Limpia Concepción de Nuestra Señora" (more simply known as La Concepción) in 1541. The impetus for this first female monastic community in Mexico came from the Bishop Juan de Zumárraga. He wanted nuns in his diocese who could provide young indigenous girls a Catholic education. The founding mothers did not come directly from a convent in Spain; instead, the base of the new convent stemmed from a *beaterio* (a religious lay community) in Mexico City called La Madre de Dios, established in 1531. Some of these *beatas* (religious lay women) hailed from Spain originally, but none of them had taken vows as nuns before leaving the Iberian Peninsula.

This first nunnery in the Americas emulated Spanish calced communities, especially when it came to the housing of the lay community. For example, the founder, Beatriz de Silva, had two maids that did not leave her service while she lived in the convent in Toledo.[9] She founded the first community, the Convent of Santo Domingo Real, with the purpose of educating young women in Toledo.[10] With this as their model, the Mexican nuns afforded both indigenous and young Spanish girls a place for lodging and education. In some cases, nuns offered refuge for unwed family members (young and old). If they themselves came from a wealthy family, they could bring with them servants and slaves. Lastly, this first Conceptionist convent allowed wealthy widows to spend their remaining years in the cloister.[11]

These flexible rules that allowed female members of the lay population to live behind the protected walls of the convent also applied to Jesús María (and other communities). At the time of the founding of Jesús María in 1581 there were already two other Conceptionist convents in the capital.[12] Yet, many families, especially descendants of the conquistadors, still did not have a safe place to house their unwed daughters. Some of these families were of noble standing but had fallen on hard times and did not have the dowry to marry their daughters or for religious profession (calced convents also required dowries). By 1577 several former conquistadors started working together to find the funding to establish the new convent. They received the support of Viceroy Martín Enríquez de Almanza and the necessary licenses from Archbishop Pedro Moya de Contreras. The ten original founding mothers came from La Concepción. They lived together with fourteen novices in some houses next to the Church of Santa Veracruz. These early living quarters proved unsuitable for convent life: they flooded easily and their location on the outskirts of the city left the women vulnerable. These circumstances changed for the better when King Philip II of Spain decided to grant the convent royal patronage in 1583. This turn of events elevated greatly the prestige of the convent and its financial status. The king himself had a young (but illegitimate) daughter, Micaela de los Angeles, who moved from La Concepción to live in Jesús María. She also happened to be the niece of Archbishop Moya de Contreras, who had brought her to New Spain in 1572 when she was just two years old.[13] Since the original purpose of the convent was to help the poor daughters and descendants of the conquistadors, the king established approximately fifteen (although this number varied with time) *capellanías reales*—essentially lifetime scholarships for these women to become black-veiled nuns.[14] These women had to prove that they were living a *vida ejemplar* (exemplary lifestyle) and they had to be *peninsulares* (born in Spain) or *criollas* (Spaniards born in the New World), but some *mestizas* (mixed race women) did make the cut.[15] The rest of the black-veiled nuns had to pay a dowry to enter the convent. Due to the royal patronage from the king we know a lot about this convent. In particular, the renowned Mexican writer, scientist, and professor Carlos de Sigüenza y Góngora, whose sister was one of the nuns, wrote a chronicle of the nunnery and the original founders called *Paraíso Occidental*. He states that by 1588 there were already eighty-four religious women living in the cloister: eight founders, thirty-four nuns with dowry, twenty-two *capellanas,* ten novices, and ten pupils (and this number does not include other family members, servants, or slaves).[16] Throughout the chronicle Sigüenza y Góngora records the names of all the noble and upperclass nuns. His list reads like a "Who's Who" of the most distinguished and wealthy families of Mexico City.

As a royal convent sponsored by the king, the women enjoyed other benefits, mainly the possibility to move to a much better location. The same year that the king authorized his royal patronage (1583), with the blessing and support of Archbishop Moya de Contreras, the community moved to higher ground. Unfortunately, the construction crew used poor building materials, forcing the convent to undergo many renovations throughout the seventeenth century.[17] Nonetheless, the number of nuns began to grow, and along with them the female secular population under their protection.

At first the expansion of the secular population increased slowly, since the Conceptionist order stipulated only one servant per nun. Yet, things changed considerably for the community when in 1672 Archbishop Fray Payo Enríquez de Rivera took over the administration of the convent. He decided that it would be to the nuns' advantage to let each one individually manage her finances. Previously he and other administrators managed the funds to purchase the food for the convent, but under the new system he distributed cash to each individual nun (depending on her dowry or *capellanía real*) so that she could buy her own foodstuffs and other goods to run her "cell." This resulted in the need to employ more cooks and other servants to take over the domestic tasks of cooking and cleaning. This new practice of allowing the nuns to manage their own finances worked well and Fray Payo's reforms stayed in effect for the next hundred years.[18]

An added benefit of these reforms was that the nuns were able to contract outside help to assist them in their later years. Often these cases involved nuns who did not have the benefit of younger family members to lend them a hand. The black-veiled nuns would give the lay women food, lodging, and a place to stay in exchange for their company and help. Although in general much of the convent's servant-class was not white, some of these women were classified as poor Spaniards. If these women did not have the funding for a dowry to marry or profess in the convent, this was a viable and safe option for them. For example, Sor Juana de la

Cruz,[19] who lived fifty-three years as a nun in Jesús María from 1679 till 1732, had five women living with her during the last three years of her life (two of whom were poor Spaniards). As an orphan, she had no family members to help her during her senior years.[20] In a similar case, an orphaned nun, Sor María Rosa, accepted five women to live with her at the time of her profession in 1713 (three *mestizas* and two *mulatas*). They stayed with her for many years, helping her until her death in 1735.[21]

The convent would request the admission of laywomen for several reasons. They might be admitted to take care of an infirm or elderly nun, or to replace another servant who had become ill and could not continue with this task. In addition to servants, family members would sometimes enter the convent to tend to their relatives. Some of what we know about the fluid movement of the lay population comes from correspondence from the nuns to their family members on the outside world. Moreover, we also have access to some of the actual petitions necessary for a laywoman to enter or leave the cloister. These requests had to first pass through the hands of the archbishop, bishop, or vicar (assigned to the convent). After reviewing the petition they then asked the opinion of the abbess and the *definidoras* (the abbess's advisors). Despite this bureaucratic process, it appears that for the most part the lay population had little to no problems entering or exiting Jesús María.[22]

As the community of Jesús María began to grow, so did its need for competent medical personnel. Every nunnery, whether located in Europe or the Americas, had an infirmary. Although to a certain extent convalescent or elderly religious women could be cared for in the privacy of their cells, when it came to serious or contagious illnesses, the abbess would send infected nuns to the infirmary. Nuns trained as nurses, the primary health care providers in the convent, ran the infirmary. The actual number of nurses at any given time varied in the convent of Jesús María. Two nuns became nurses in 1670 (for approximately fifty-seven professed nuns),[23] but this number increased to six in 1710 (they provided health care to ninety-five professed nuns)[24] and stayed that way for the rest of the century.

Like many convents, Jesús María rotated the position of nurse on a triennial basis. This allowed the women time to learn the skills necessary to learn their trade. There was no formal training as such. In cloistered convents, nuns learned apprentice-style, by watching and doing. Generally, nurses could be reappointed only once by the abbess (for a total of six years), but exceptions were made for highly skilled nurses. Health care providers held different positions in the infirmary depending on their experience and expertise. Much like a modern-day hospital, essentially a head nurse and her assistants (labeled as first through sixth nurses, depending on the time period) staffed the infirmary.

According to Jesús María's Rule (a document outlining their rules and regulations), the position of nurse only should be given to kind and loving nuns who would care for her sisters with patience and humility. This document stipulated that the abbess and nurses tend to everything related to the infirmary. Among other duties, they oversaw the bedding, clothing, and general cleanliness of the area. They needed to communicate with the doctor or surgeon and to follow their prescriptions of medications.[25] Oftentimes in the case of Jesús María a pharmacist would distribute the compounds to the convent and leave the nurses to the task of mixing different ingredients. During the seventeenth century all of the medications supplied to the convent came with detailed instructions. There were long lists of ingredients and instructions on how to prepare a purgative, syrup, or tonic. Nurses with knowledge of home remedies and medicinal herbs could use them on their patients. These cases point to the fact that some of the healing taking place in convents came from women's informal knowledge, at times a blending of remedies that they learned from their *mestiza* and *mulata* servants, most likely very different from that of formally trained physicians. In addition to their role in helping the nurses administer remedies, the servants tended to more menial tasks, such as emptying bedpans, changing sheets, cleaning linens, and food preparation.[26] In exchange for their services, not only did the convent provide the nurses' helpers room and board, but they set aside money in the budget to buy them a new wardrobe on a triennial basis.[27]

Some Conceptionist convents, like Regina Coeli in Mexico City, had their own in-house pharmacy where they fabricated medicines.[28] The nuns of Regina sold some of these remedies to the general public—in particular they had a secret formula for *polvos purgantes* (a powdered purgative). They also handed out, free of charge, a curative *agua* that would treat *el mal de ojos* (eye problems).[29] Jesús María, on the contrary, purchased their medicine from a local pharmacist. The community gave physicians and surgeons lifetime contracts (this will be discussed in the next section), and they did the same for pharmacists. On an interesting side note that would merit further study, the profession of pharmacist could be held by a woman. In general, widows would inherit the business from their defunct spouse. We know of several cases specific to the convent of Jesús María. For example, Francisca Josefa Serón took over for her deceased husband, Francisco López Moroso, in 1734. When the nuns hired her, they did so at an annual salary of 400 pesos, one hundred more than they had paid her husband. She stocked the convent with medical supplies for another eight years.[30]

As a practical and straightforward remedy, all religious communities viewed a nutritious diet as an important vehicle to recovery. Therefore, sick nuns assigned to the infirmary did not have to follow any of the dietary restrictions and fasting common to the liturgical calendar. The infirmary of Jesús María had its own kitchen and the nurses fed the ailing women a diet rich in protein and nutrients. Foremost, the sick nuns ate meat such as mutton, chicken, or pigeon.[31] Depending on the gravity of the illness, the nurses supplied the patients on average one to two chickens per week.[32] In addition to the staples of meat and bread, the nurses and servant staff used many other ingredients acquired on a weekly basis in meal preparation, such as oil, rice, cumin, pepper, cilantro, garlic, onions, honey, milk, eggs, rosemary oil, and chocolate.[33]

Other products used to treat sick nuns included borage water, caper tablets, aureate and agaric stones, apple and orange blossom ointments, maidenhair, hyacinth and other flowers in general, linseed or apple oil, yellow ointment, violet syrup of nine infusions, roses, cilantro, and licorice.[34] These ingredients reveal how convents began to change and adopt many of the exotic new ingredients of the new continent into their everyday diet, like chili peppers and chocolate. Likewise, studies of religious communities on the other side of the Atlantic show that some of these New World ingredients made it back to Spain—most notably chocolate, but later other common foodstuffs, including tomatoes and potatoes.[35]

Much of these new foods came from the indigenous population ubiquitous to calced convents like Jesús María. Not only did the cooks utilize these ingredients in their everyday cooking, but at times the convents would employ the services of a *curandera,* who would use indigenous remedies such as *pulque* (an alcoholic beverage derived from the maguey plant) to treat the servants themselves and often the nuns in the infirmary.[36] In general it appears that the community reserved the luxury of the infirmary mainly for the nuns and novices—however, exceptions were made, especially in the case of wealthy widows or other family members living with the nuns. The servant class, in contrast, had the opportunity to leave the cloister and to recover with their families, although as mentioned earlier this did require a petition. The convent paid all medical bills related to servants and slaves, evidence that they valued their work.

Records show that Jesús María had employed *curanderas* either as assistants to the head nurses or as personal maids to the nuns. During the sixteenth century a cough epidemic constantly plagued the women of Jesús María, and in 1592 on several occasions the convent hired a *curandera* to treat this epidemic—evidence that *curanderas* also cared for the nuns.[37] We know of at least two more specific cases of indigenous medicine in the cloister: in the first, a woman known as Melchora de la Tisil cured three convent servants, and in another case an indigenous healer (she is never named) treated the novice mistress, María de la Visitación.[38] These documented cases of *curanderas* occurred at the turn of the sixteenth century (late 1500s and early 1600s)—relatively early in the convent's existence.

As Jesús María began to grow in wealth and numbers, the nuns began to rely less on *curanderas* and more on outside care. To a certain extent this parallels the information covered in this volume by Timothy Walker's essay on Portuguese *curandeiras*. In essence, the professionalization of the medical field in the seventeenth and eighteenth centuries began to shun the less traditional knowledge of folk healers, many of whom were women. Although, as discussed above, nurses and their assistants provided the bulk of the medical care, the nuns also paid considerable amounts of money to bring in physicians and surgeons to look after the ailing sisters.[39] At the turn of the seventeenth century, the largest convents in New Spain each began to hire a permanent doctor and surgeon. These men had special permission to enter the inner confines of the cloister, but only to look after ill women in the infirmary. A long ringing of the cloister bell indicated the arrival of doctors, surgeons, barbers, or confessors, all collaborators with the convent nurses, in the health of the female community.[40] Two veiled nuns known as *severas* would accompany these specialists to the infirmary and then waited for them during the medical examination of the patient and prescription of care or medicine. They would then chaperone the medical personnel to the exit door of the cloister.

The community paid the physician a salary double that of the surgeon because he visited the infirmary much more frequently and they regarded him as superior. Unlike present-day society, which views surgeons with the utmost respect, the early modern world regarded them as tradesmen. Only physicians required studies at university to practice medicine, whereas surgeons needed no formal studies or university degrees. At the most, they underwent an apprenticeship to learn their trade and only were allowed to cure or treat the "outside" of the body. The subordinate position of surgeon did not change until the institutionalization of this specialty in the late 1700s: first with the establishment of the "Reales Colegios de Cirugía" in Cadiz and Barcelona, Spain, and later with the "Real Escuela de Cirugía" in Mexico City.[41] In contrast, a royal medical board, called the *Protomedicato* regulated the profession of physicians in Spain and its colonies.[42] The physicians dealt with the diagnosis and prescription of medicine and treatments—all based on precepts from Hippocrates and Galen.[43] The surgeons implemented the actual treatments, most often that of phlebotomy, or bloodletting. This explains why some surgeons often carried the interchangeable title of *barbero* (barber), *sangrador* (blood letter), or phlebotomist. The convent records of Jesús María show no clear distinction between these professions, oftentimes using several titles to refer to the same person.

Jesús María began hiring permanent medical personnel in the early 1620s. They hired four doctors in the 1600s at an annual salary of 150 pesos each, and five in the 1700s for 200 pesos (by the end of the 1700s this had increased to 300 pesos).[44] The community actively sought out the best physicians in Mexico City. Three of the convent doctors were presidents of the *Protomedicato*: Juan Torres de Moreno,[45] Marcos José Salgado,[46] and José Ignacio García Jove.[47] Surgeons, in contrast, received a much lower annual salary: 50 pesos until the mid-1600s and then 60 pesos for the next one hundred years. We should note that the nuns raised their annual salary to 150 pesos during the second half of the eighteenth century—more than likely an indicator that this profession had grown in status.[48] A total of eleven surgeons worked for the convent during the seventeenth and eighteenth centuries.

Since convent walls did not ward off illness, Jesús María called on these outside medical providers to treat a wide variety of diseases common to all segments of the early modern population. Archival documents offer a valuable lens, not only to view the different diseases that struck the nuns of Jesús María, but also the treatments prescribed by the physicians. As mentioned earlier, many of the treatments stemmed from a long tradition based on the teachings of Hippocrates and Galen, but some were unique to the Americas. We know that the women of Jesús María suffered from many maladies: everything from simple infections, sore throats, migraine headaches, hypertension, kidney stones, and diabetes to gout, heart palpitations, stomach problems, eye infections, and epilepsy. They also had medical conditions that now seem very strange. For example, an illness called *dolor de costado* (pain in the side)[49] seems to have afflicted the population at large on both sides of the Atlantic, particularly religious women.[50]

Good health was one of the necessary requirements for entrance into the cloister, but because most of these women spent the majority of their lives behind the thick walls, it is natural that at some stage each one of them would suffer from some sickness, including mental illness.[51] Others succumbed to ailments associated with old age, such as dementia. For example, one of the original founders (from the Convent of Regina), Juana de Salcedo, stated that she had lived more than twenty-three years in the convent and "the majority of that time spent in bed with many illnesses."[52] She attributed all her ailments to two main causes: old age and years in the nunnery (thus insinuating that in some way religious life contributed to her poor health, yet never explaining how). The fact that Juana de Salcedo failed to comment on specific illnesses or treatments was quite common. Often nuns would write in letters to family members or to confessors about their poor health (or that of others), but only in general terms, without specifying the actual disease or cure. They would use expressions such as "están enfermas" (they are sick), "que están muy malas" (they are very ill), or "en cama" (bedridden). Other times they would say "está muy mala y pobre" (she's in very poor health) or "sufrió de varios accidentes" (she's had several episodes) or "tuvo grandes enfermedades que sufrió con paciencia" (she's endured great illnesses with patience).

Fortunately, embedded in some archival documents (mostly accounting receipts) we do find details, albeit sparse, about the actual diagnoses and treatments prescribed by the physicians. In some cases these documents only reveal the malady—for example, that the Madre Felipa de Estefanía was blind.[53] Others offer more information on cures. We learn that the Madre Estefanía was sick and *tullida* (paralyzed) and that in 1622 she was given a *lavatorio* (a medicinal bath).[54] In July of 1659 the Madre María de la Asunción suffered from *erisipela* (erysipelas),[55] and the barber bled her.[56] When the vicaress became deathly ill in the mid-1600s, the barber applied *ventosas* (he cupped her)[57] and gave her *pulque* to drink[58]—proof that this indigenous drink had filtered its way into Western medicine, at least in colonial Mexico.[59]

Despite the professionalization of Western medicine mentioned earlier in this chapter, this combination of bloodletting and *pulque*, a syncretism of European and indigenous medicines, seems to have been quite common in Jesús María. For example, when the Madre Catalina de Jesús became very ill, the doctor prescribed nine days of *pulque, aguardiente* (hard liquor),[60] three rounds of *suero*,[61] and two sessions of bloodletting.[62] In another case, the Madre Ursula del Sacramento, who suffered from *dolor de costado* and gout, was given two different types of remedies. For the first, the convent bought milk for use in the preparation of the *emplastos* (poultices), and for the second, she drank *pulque* and was purged.[63]

Several epidemics plagued Mexico City in the early modern period and did not spare the nuns of Jesús María. Throughout 1659 the population at-large suffered from fevers, *dolor de costado*, and measles.[64] Most likely, the nuns Mariana de San Jerónimo and Luisa de San Nicolás contracted one of these diseases since they were described as "being sick with this contagious illness."[65] In 1692 another epidemic struck the community of Jesús María. On October 3 of that year Archbishop Alonso Núñez de Haro y Peralta ordered the convent's *mayordomo* (administrator) to give the nuns any extra funding that might be needed. He also told the *mayordomo* to invest 60 pesos in order to help the poor servants and to offset any costs to the infirmary.[66] It is important to point out that the administrator controlled the convent's general funds, so without his authorization, even if the nuns wanted to, they could not use that source to cover the medical costs of the servants. This document testifies to the quality of care given to the servant class.[67]

In conclusion, the convent of Jesús María provides a tantalizing glimpse into the diverse types of women, many from different ethnic and financial backgrounds, who took refuge in the community. This large Conceptionist nunnery was not only a place for the daughters of elite *criollo* and peninsular families, it was a melting pot of indigenous, African, and mixed-race women. As a royal convent, the monarchy sponsored special lifetime scholarships known as *capellanías reales*. With this extra funding, poor white Spanish women descended from conquistadors could find a place not only as servants but as nuns of Jesús María. The convent harbored this diverse group of women, offering them a protected environment inside the cloistered walls. The circumstances of Jesús María shed light on the complex social milieu in Mexico City's calced nunneries. Undeniably, the convent life revolved around a hierarchical structure, with black-veiled nuns at the top. Moreover, the gender and racial ideology transported from Spain marked indigenous women as inferior. Not until 1724 was the first convent established for indigenous women: Corpus Christi in Mexico City, and even then an aspirant nun had to demonstrate her *cacica* (female native ruler) lineage and fight with *criolla* nuns to eventually gain control of the convent's governance.[68] Nevertheless, this was also an arena where the women, whether they were servants, slaves, family members, or trained nurses, formed an intermeshing network of support. The nuns did not throw the servant class out on the street when they fell ill, but instead invested money in medicine and doctors' visits. Likewise, the servant women tended to the religious during times of illness and looked after elderly nuns as their hair grayed and their memory faded.

Furthermore, this Conceptionist community served as a microcosm for the agency of astute women who lived in the viceregal capital of New Spain. This is especially true when we study the health care provided within the walls of the cloister and the different roles that men and women played in the care of ill patients. These nuns demanded what they believed to be the best possible services available in early modern Mexico. For primary care they did not need to look any farther than their own nursing staff, who took care of sick women in the infirmary. Although these nurses had never taken any university classes and had no medical degrees, they did acquire considerable practical experience at their patients' bedsides. They saw to it that a sick nun had proper rest and a nutritious diet (probably the best remedy for any ailment of that time period). A head nurse took charge of the sick ward and had as many as five other nurses working under her supervision. They all held three-year positions, but if one of them particularly shined in this profession, the abbess could reappoint her for subsequent terms. These nurses did not work alone. They employed servants and slaves to perform more menial tasks. In the early years of the convent's existence they utilized the services of *curanderas,* sometimes indigenous servants themselves, also living in the convent. Later the community hired physicians and surgeons to treat the ailing nuns, showing a shift, with the nuns preferring standard masculine professional medicine. They bought medicine from local pharmacists, who supplied the nurses with necessary products to stock their medicine cabinet. These religious women did not insulate themselves from the outside world. Although they lived behind thick walls, they knew that they needed these close working relationships with men to ensure quality health care for their community. They believed that these trained male physicians and surgeons were truly qualified to provide diagnoses and remedies for the ill nuns. In fact, the convent made special efforts to hire the best physicians in the field, such as Juan Torres de Moreno, and they paid him and others well for their services. In sum, the privileged economic situation and agency of the nuns of Jesús María enabled them to demand the best possible health care available in the Atlantic world.[69]

NOTES

1. See Asunción Lavrin's introduction to *Brides of Christ: Conventual Life in Colonial Mexico* (Stanford: Stanford Univ. Press, 2008), 2–5, for an excellent overview of these studies. See also Elizabeth A. Lehfeldt, *Religious Women in Golden Age Spain: The Permeable Cloister* (Burlington, Vt.: Ashgate, 2005).

2. The discalced orders (barefoot) were normally much stricter than the calced (shod—wearing shoes).

3. Other convents were even wealthier than Jesús María (such as la Concepción and la Encarnación). Josefina Muriel's *Conventos de monjas en la Nueva España* (Mexico City: Editorial Jus, 1995), provides invaluable data on the finances of New Spain's convents.

4. According to scholars Electa Arenal and Stacey Schlau, in the context of New World convents, "Mestiza, Indian, mulatta, and Black women servants outnumbered those they served" (Electa Arenal and Stacey Schlau, eds., *Untold Sisters: Hispanic Nuns in Their Own Works*, trans. Amanda Powell [Albuquerque: Univ. of New Mexico Press, 1989], 339).

5. For one such example, see Baltasar Molinero, "La primera escritora afrohispánica: Chicaba o Sor Teresa Juliana de Santo Domingo," http://abacus.bates.edu/~bframoli/pagina/chicaba.html.

6. *Regla, y ordenaciones, de las Religiosas de la Limpia e Inmaculada Concepción de la Santísima Virgen Nuestra Señora, Que se han de observar en los Conventos del dicho Orden de la Ciudad de México* (México: Imprenta Matritense de Felipe de Zuñiga y Ontiveros, 1779), fols. 2v.–4.

7. María Concepción Amerlinck, *Regina Coeli en su 425 Aniversario de su Fundación* (México: Por las religiosas de Regina Coeli, 1998), 15.

8. Contrary to popular belief, Conceptionist nuns did not belong to the Franciscan order and they did not rely on Franciscan friars as priests or confessors. It was the local bishop who would assign the convent a certain number of priests and chaplains.

9. *Regla, y ordenaciones, de las Religiosas de la Limpia e Inmaculada Concepción . . .* , no page numbers.

10. Juan Meseguer Fernández, "Primeras constituciones de las franciscanas concepcionistas," *Archivo Ibero-Americano* 100 (October–December 1965): 25.

11. María Concepción Amerlinck de Corsi and Manuel Ramos Medina, *Conventos de monjas: Fundaciones en el México virreinal* (Mexico City: Grupo Condumex, 1995), 31–33.

12. Due to the popularity of the Conceptionist order, seven other convents were founded in the capital and six in other areas of New Spain, making a grand total of fourteen Conceptionist nunneries. This is a large sum, considering there were fifty-seven established in New Spain.

13. Kathleen Ross, *The Baroque Narrative of Carlos de Sigüenza y Góngora: A New World Paradise* (Cambridge: Cambridge Univ. Press, 1994), 87.

14. Muriel, *Conventos de monjas en la Nueva España*, 80–107.

15. According to Ralph Bauer and José Antonio Mazzotti, "Somewhere between 20 and 30 percent of all defined as criollo were in fact biologically mestizos whose assimilation as creoles was linked to their Spanish fathers' efforts to retain certain privileges in colonial society" (Introduction to *Creole Subjects in the Colonial Americas: Empires, Texts, Identities*, ed. Ralph Bauer and José Antonio Mazzotti, 34 [Chapel Hill: Univ. of North Carolina Press, 2009]).

16. Carlos de Sigüenza y Góngora, *Paraíso Occidental* (Mexico City: Consejo Nacional para la Cultura y las Artes, 1995), 78.

17. Amerlinck de Corsi and Ramos Medina, *Conventos de monjas*, 63.

18. José María Marroquí, *La ciudad de México. Contiene el origen de los nombres de muchas de sus calles y plazas, del de varios establecimientos públicos y privados, y no pocas noticias curiosas y entretenidas* (Mexico City: Jesús Medina, 1969), 68–69.

19. Not to be confused with the famous Mexican poet Sor Juana Inés de la Cruz.

20. Only one of the five women was a candidate to be a nun. At her death the eldest was a nun (age thirty-two) and the others were twenty-two, eighteen, sixteen, and fifteen years old.

21. For both cases see: Archivo General de la Nación de México. Ramos: Bienes Nacionales (hereafter AGNM, BN), leg. 474, exp. 5 and 13.

22. We have been unable to find any denied requests for the Convent of Jesús María.

23. AGNM, BN, vol. 259, exp. 22. By 1681 this number increased to seventy-three nuns (Archivo Histórico de la Secretaría de Salud [previously Salubridad y Asistencia] [hereafter AHSSA], vol. 18).

24. AGNM, BN, leg. 213, exp. 55.

25. *Regla, y ordenaciones, de las Religiosas de la Limpia e Inmaculada Concepción . . .*, 91–92.

26. In regard to these servants, the convent records from Jesús María cite the case of Juana de Dolores, a thirty-year-old *mestiza* (mixed race) servant woman, who was admitted into the convent in 1728 to help the acting head nurse, María Teresa de San José (AGNM, BN, leg. 474, exp. 5).

27. See the following documents from 1786: AHSSA, vol. 319, fol. 43, 61.

28. For convent pharmacies in Italy, see Sharon T. Strocchia, "The Nun Apothecaries of Renaissance Florence: Marketing Medicines in the Convent," *Renaissance Studies* 25, no. 5 (2011): 627–647.

29. Muriel, *Conventos de monjas en la Nueva España*, 70.

30. AHSSA, Fondo: Convento de Jesús María (hereafter FCJM), vol. 99, fol. 138; vol. 102, fol. 39; vol. 107, fol. 29; vol. 111, fol. 54; vol. 116, fol. 69.

31. Mutton was much more common in Jesús María in the first half of the seventeenth century, and poultry in the second half. Beef is never mentioned.

32. We can trace this same emphasis on the benefits of meat to sixth-century Europe when Anthimus, a Byzantine physician at the court of the Frankish King Theuderic, wrote a dietary manual called *De observatione ciborum* (Massimo Montanari, *El hambre y la abundancia. Historia y cultura de la alimentación en Europa*, [Barcelona: Editorial Crítica, 1993], 24–25).

33. AHSSA, FCJM, serie libros, vol. 12, fols. 80–86, June 1621–February 1622.

34. The following is the original Spanish version transcribed from the archival docu-

ment (mentioned by the convent doctor Cristóbal Hidalgo Bendaval). Some of these ingredients were difficult to translate, and we did not include all of them in the text of the chapter: "Agua de borrajas, trociscos de alcaparras, piedras aureas y de agárico, ungüentos de manzanas y azahar, diacinino en tabletas, culantrillo, jacintos, y flores en general; jarabe o agua de endivia, aceite de linaza o de manzanilla, ungüento amarillo, jarabes violados, de nueve infusiones, rosas, cilantrillo y orozuz" (AHSSA, FCJM, leg. 4, exp. 5, fols. 1–2).

35. For a detailed overview of convent infirmaries in Madrid, see María Elena del Río Hijas, "El desarrollo de las enfermerías en las órdenes religiosas en Madrid capital, durante los siglos XVII, XVIII y XIX," *Archivo Ibero-Americano* 53, no. 209/212 (February 1993): 325–421. This article also lists the basic food stuffs used in Madrid's infirmaries, such as chicken, ham, burro's milk, chocolate, and beer (344–345). For more information on convent food in the Atlantic world, see Sarah E. Owens, "Food, Fasting, and Itinerant Nuns," *Food and Foodways* 19, no. 4 (2011): 274–293.

36. *Pulque* can be traced to its Mesoamerican roots (the Aztecs considered it the drink of the Gods).

37. AHSSA, vol. 4, n.p.

38. For information on the indigenous healer, see: AHSSA, FCJM, serie libros, vol. 12, fol. 80v., July 1621. María de la Visitación represents an unusual case for the convent since she served as the novice mistress without having taken her vows of profession during the triennial of 1589–1591. She represents the flexibility of the convent in times of need (especially during the formative years). Apparently her knowledge and teaching abilities trumped her secular status, although on May 8, 1596, she did take her vows of profession. She died in 1638. (*Libro de Profesiones del convento de Jesús María,* private collection, fols. 66–78 y 91.)

39. At their death, some nuns donated considerable sums of money to the infirmary's budget. See Nuria Salazar Simaro, "Salud y enfermedad en epístolas de monjas novohispanas," in *Women's Voices and the Politics of the Spanish Empire,* ed. Jennifer L. Eich, Jeanne Gillespie, and Lucia G. Harrison, 216, 217 (New Orleans: Univ. Press of the South, 2008). Salazar Simarro references several examples of these charitable gifts. Her essay also includes other examples pertaining to the health care of Jesús María (some of which overlap with this chapter).

40. *Costumbrero del Real Convento de Jesús María* (México: 1685) (Private Collection, typed copy), 6–6v.

41. María Luisa Rodríguez-Sala points out that during the 1500s the citizens of Mexico City welcomed surgeons with open arms. They appreciated their services and paid them well—some were close to physicians in their socioeconomic status. This all changed, however, by the end of the 1500s when the "Real Tribunal del Protomedicato" began to enforce its rules and regulations. See María Luisa Rodríguez-Sala et al., "Los cirujanos privados del siglo XVI en las ciudades de México y Puebla, representantes de una actividad ocupacional en formación," *Relaciones* 105, no. 27 (winter 2006): 18–58.

42. In Mexico the *cabildo* (local government) had been appointing *protomédicos* (chief medical officers) since 1527, but this was not made into a formal process until a royal decree of 1646, which was later substituted by another one in 1831. (Efraín Castro Morales, María Concepción Amerlinck de Corsi, and Lorenza Autrey de Ziebe, *Farmacias y farmacéuticos en México* [Mexico City: Autrey, 1992], 41; José Rogelio Álvarez, dir., *Enciclopedia de México,* vol. 11. [Mexico City: Enciclopedia de México / Secretaría de Educación Pública, 1988], 6614.)

43. Hippocrates and Galen's influence on medieval and early modern medicine cannot be understated. First Hippocrates and then Galen embraced the "humoral" theory that the

body was made up of four basic humors: blood, phlegm, yellow bile, and black bile. When one of these basic humors became out of balance it could cause sickness, the most common ailments stemming from an excess of blood. Thus, the practice of bloodletting became the most widely used treatment up until the nineteenth century.

44. The physician Juan José Bermúdez de Castro received a pay raise in May of 1788. From that year onward all physicians received an annual salary of 300 pesos. (AHSSA, FCJM, vol. 324, fol. 64; vol. 325, fol. 22, 51; vol. 343, fol. 60.)

45. Juan Torres de Moreno was the most acclaimed physician of his time. He served the convent for a span of twenty-eight years, from 1656-1684.

46. Marcos José Salgado held the endowed chair of "Prima de Medicina" and was the president of the *Protomedicato* in 1737 when a plague epidemic waged war on the city. He worked at Jesús María from January 1717 until his death on May 12, 1740.

47. José Ignacio García Jove received his appointment as president of the *Protomedicato* in 1795, but it was not confirmed by royal decree until 1799. He served as the convent's doctor between 1812 and 1817.

48. AHSSA, FCJM, vols. 213, 224, fol. 49; vol. 300, fol. 52; vol. 301, fols. 22-24; vol. 305, fol. 51; vol. 306. fols. 23-25; vol. 312, fol. 51; vol. 313, fols. 25-27; vol. 319, fol. 51; vol. 320, fol. 22; vol. 324, fol. 53; vol. 325, fols. 23-25; vol. 331, fol. 51. vol. 338, fol. 52; vol. 343, fol. 48; vol. 350, fol. 47; vol. 357, fol. 48; vol. 364, fol. 48; vol. 365, fols. 23-25; vol. 371, fol. 48; vol. 372, fols. 21-23; vol. 378, fol. 48; vol. 387, fol. 49; vol. 388, fols. 20-22; vol. 394, fol. 49v; vol. 395, fols. 27-29.

49. According to Sherry Fields, "*Dolor de costado* must have specified a large group of symptoms common to many actual diseases, such as pleurisy, emphysema, pneumonia, or tuberculosis." *Pestilence and Headcolds: Encountering Illness in Colonial Mexico* (New York: Colombia Univ. Press, 2008), chapter 1, 32, www.gutenberg-e.org/fields/.

50. Saint Teresa of Avila mentions this ailment at least twice in her *Book of Foundations*. Saint Teresa of Avila, *The Complete Works of St. Teresa of Jesus,* vol. 3, *The Book of Foundations,* ed. and trans. E. Allison Peers (London: Sheed and Ward, 1973): See chapters 16 and 22.

51. In an extreme case, Sor María Gertrudis de San Lorenzo, a nun from the convent of San Bernardo in Mexico City, "was enclosed in her cell for thirty years and six months. They had built a cage inside of her cell since they believed her to be demented" (*Libro de Profesiones del convento de San Bernardo,* Private Collection, fol. 96).

52. AGNM, BN, vol. 78, exp. 37.

53. AHSSA, FCJM, serie libros, vol. 12, fols. 80v, 81, 82, 82v, 85v, 87. (1621-1624).

54. AHSSA, FCJM, serie libros, vol. 12, fols. 80v., 83v., 84, 86v., 87v., 131v.

55. This is a streptococcal infection of the skin which produces a reddish color.

56. AHSSA, FCJM, serie libros, vol. 21, fols. 49-57.

57. Like bloodletting, the practice of cupping was also based on the humoral theory that balance could be restored to the body by removing excess blood. The actual process involved applying evacuated glass cups to the skin in order to draw blood toward the surface.

58. AHSSA, FCJM, serie libros, vol. 20, fol. 94v; vol. 21, fol. 55v. (1652-1655).

59. An eighteenth-century advertisement in the newspaper *La Gaceta de México* touts "pulque blanco" as a cure for diarrhea (Fields, *Pestilence and Headcolds,* chapter 5, 13. www.gutenberg-e.org/fields/).

60. The belief in the medicinal qualities of alcoholic beverages has a long history (Montanari, *El hambre y la abundancia,* 122.)

61. This was some sort of liquid.

62. AHSSA, FCJM, serie libros, vol. 21, fols. 50v–51; vol. 20, fols. 94v, 95, 96v, 97. (1652–1660).

63. The first treatment was administered in December of 1657, and the second in August of 1659. (AHSSA, FCJM serie libros, vol. 21, fols. 51v., 57.)

64. Elsa Malvido, "Cronología de epidemias y crisis agrícola en la época colonial," in *Ensayo sobre la historia de las epidemias en México*, ed. Enrique Florescano and Elsa Malvido, 173 (Mexico City: Instituto Mexicano del Seguro Social, 1982).

65. They fell ill in February of 1659 (AHSSA, FCJM, serie libros, vol. 21, fol. 55v).

66. AHSSA, vol. 46, fol. 62.

67. At the time nuns also had to pay for their own medical bills, especially when medicines or other treatments exceeded the convent's budget. At their death, the sale of their possessions would be used to replenish the convent coffers.

68. For an outstanding analysis of the first indigenous convents in New Spain, see Mónica Díaz, *Indigenous Writings from the Convent: Negotiating Ethnic Autonomy in Colonial Mexico* (Tucson: Univ. of Arizona Press, 2010).

69. Everything changed drastically for the nuns in 1774, when Carlos III issued a royal decree imposing "la vida común" (common life). This decree ordered the expulsion of all of the "lay women" from the convent (that is, all the servant class, family members, and widows). Jesús María was allowed to keep the pupils under its tutelage, but only because this was one of the original reasons for the foundation. In addition to the expulsion of the secular population, the nuns had to embrace common life—that is, sleep together in one large dormitory and share all meals in the refectory. In essence, these new rules destroyed their unique way of life that had provided for a vibrant and diverse community. For a study of this time period, see Nuria Salazar Simarro, *La vida común en los conventos de monjas de la ciudad de Puebla* (Puebla, Mexico: Gobierno del Estado de Puebla, 1990).

WORKS CITED

Primary Sources

Archivo General de la Nación de México (AGNM), Ramos: Bienes Nacionales (BN).

Archivo Histórico de la Secretaría de Salud (AHSSA), Fondo: Convento de Jesús María (FCJM).

Costumbrero del Real Convento de Jesús María, México, 1685, Private Collection.

Libro de Profesiones del convento de Jesús María, Private Collection.

Libro de Profesiones del convento de San Bernardo, Private Collection.

Secondary Sources

Álvarez, José Rogelio, dir. *Enciclopedia de México,* vol. 11. Mexico City: Enciclopedia de México / Secretaría de Educación Pública, 1988.

Amerlinck de Corsi, María Concepción. *Regina Coeli en su 425 Aniversario de su Fundación.* Mexico City: Por las religiosas de Regina Coeli, 1998.

Amerlinck de Corsi, María Concepción, and Manuel Ramos Medina. *Conventos de monjas: Fundaciones en el México virreinal.* Mexico City: Grupo Condumex, 1995.

Arenal, Electa, and Stacey Schlau, eds. *Untold Sisters: Hispanic Nuns in Their Own Works*. Translated by Amanda Powell. Albuquerque: Univ. of New Mexico Press, 1989.

Bauer, Ralph, and José Antonio Mazzotti, eds. *Creole Subjects in the Colonial Americas: Empires, Texts, Identities*. Chapel Hill: Univ. of North Carolina Press, 2009.

Castro Morales, Efraín, María Concepción Amerlinck de Corsi, and Lorenza Autrey de Ziebe. *Farmacias y farmacéuticos en México*. Mexico City: Autrey, 1992.

Díaz, Mónica. *Indigenous Writings from the Convent: Negotiating Ethnic Autonomy in Colonial Mexico*. Tucson: Univ. of Arizona Press, 2010.

Fields, Sherry. *Pestilence and Headcolds: Encountering Illness in Colonial Mexico*. New York: Colombia Univ. Press, 2008.

Lavrin, Asunción. *Brides of Christ. Conventual Life in Colonial Mexico*. Stanford: Stanford Univ. Press, 2008.

Lehfeldt, Elizabeth A. *Religious Women in Golden Age Spain: The Permeable Cloister*. Burlington, Vt.: Ashgate, 2005.

Malvido, Elsa. "Cronología de epidemias y crisis agrícola en la época colonial." In *Ensayo sobre la historia de las epidemias en México,* edited by Enrique Florescano and Elsa Malvido, 171–178. Mexico City: Instituto Mexicano del Seguro Social, 1982.

Marroquí, José María. *La ciudad de México. Contiene el origen de los nombres de muchas de sus calles y plazas, del de varios establecimientos públicos y privados, y no pocas noticias curiosas y entretenidas.* Mexico City: Jesús Medina, 1969.

Meseguer Fernández, Juan. "Primeras constituciones de las franciscanas concepcionistas." *Archivo Ibero-Americano* 100 (October–December 1965): 1–29.

Molinero, Baltasar. "La primera escritora afrohispánica: Chicaba o Sor Teresa Juliana de Santo Domingo." http://abacus.bates.edu/~bframoli/pagina/chicaba.html.

Montanari, Massimo. *El hambre y la abundancia. Historia y cultura de la alimentación en Europa*. Barcelona: Editorial Crítica, 1993.

Muriel, Josefina. *Conventos de monjas en la Nueva España*. 1946. Reprint, Mexico City: Editorial Jus, 1995.

Owens, Sarah E. "Food, Fasting, and Itinerant Nuns." *Food and Foodways* 19, no. 4 (2011): 274–293.

Regla, y ordenaciones, de las Religiosas de la Limpia e Inmaculada Concepción de la Santísima Virgen Nuestra Señora, Que se han de observar en los Conventos del dicho Orden de la Ciudad de México. México: Imprenta Matritense de Felipe de Zuñiga y Ontiveros, 1779.

Río Hijas, María Elena del. "El desarrollo de las enfermerías en las órdenes religiosas en Madrid capital, durante los siglos XVII, XVIII y XIX." *Archivo Ibero-Americano* 53, no. 209/212 (February 1993): 325–421.

Rodríguez-Sala, María Luisa, et al. "Los cirujanos privados del siglo XVI en las ciudades de México y Puebla, representantes de una actividad ocupacional en formación." *Relaciones* 105, no. 27 (winter 2006): 18–58.

Ross, Kathleen. *The Baroque Narrative of Carlos de Sigüenza y Góngora: A New World Paradise*. Cambridge: Cambridge Univ. Press, 1994.

Salazar Simarro, Nuria. *La vida común en los conventos de monjas de la ciudad de Puebla*. Puebla, Mexico: Gobierno del Estado de Puebla, 1990.

———. "Salud y enfermedad en epístolas de monjas novohispanas." In *Women's Voices and the Politics of the Spanish Empire*, edited by Jennifer L. Eich, Jeanne Gillespie, and Lucia G. Harrison, 201–233. New Orleans: Univ. Press of the South, 2008.

Sigüenza y Góngora, Carlos de. *Paraíso Occidental*. Mexico City: Consejo Nacional para la Cultura y las Artes, 1995.

Strocchia, Sharon T. "The Nun Apothecaries of Renaissance Florence: Marketing Medicines in the Convent." *Renaissance Studies* 25, no. 5 (2011): 627–647.

Teresa of Avila, Saint. *The Complete Works of St. Teresa of Jesus*, vol 3. *The Book of Foundations*. Edited and translated by E. Allison Peers. London: Sheed and Ward, 1973.

7

The Role and Practices of the Female Folk Healer in the Early Modern Portuguese Atlantic World

TIMOTHY D. WALKER

As in many early modern societies, specialized women healers in the Lusophone Atlantic world often provided the first—and usually the only—source of health care for their own families and people in their immediate vicinity. In rural agrarian peasant communities (be they in continental Portugal or the diverse transatlantic colonial hinterlands), where trained conventional physicians and surgeons were virtually unknown (or, due to the expense, were the exclusive recourse of elites), the practical ability to treat sickness or injuries had its origins in ancient folkways and practical knowledge about curative plants. In these contexts, women of any race who kept such lore and applied it with apparent success gained widespread reputations for their healing prowess and neighbors sought their skills whenever need arose.

Portuguese Inquisition trial records from the seventeenth and eighteenth centuries provide us with unparalleled insights into the cosmology and practices of female folk healers within the Portuguese cultural tradition. While most cases are drawn from events in continental Portugal, several of the accused had come to the metropole from Brazil and the Atlantic islands; still others were banished to the colonies as punishment for unlawful superstitious healing practices. Wherever Portuguese immigrants established colonial communities, the culture and circumstances of popular healing were present and their procedures broadly consistent—though outside of Portugal such practices tended to mingle quickly with local indigenous folk healing traditions, in part because comparatively few continental Portuguese peasant women traveled to imperial enclaves (Brazil excepted, after circa 1690).[1] As Brazilian medical historian

Alceu Maynard Araújo has written, "Rustic medicine is the result of a series of acculturations of popular medicine from Portugal with indigenous and black [African] healing."²

Women's social roles throughout the Portuguese Atlantic world (continental or colonial) encompassed many tasks and duties, but that of a healer was among the most important. Simultaneously, the role of folk healer and nurturer of the sick could also put a woman in a precarious position.³ Beginning in the 1530s with the commencement of Holy Office activities in Portugal, Inquisitorial law condemned many basic age-old traditional healing practices.⁴ In time, with the advent of the vigilant Holy Office, *familiares* (lay collaborators of the Inquisition), resident in communities on the continent and in the colonies, put the healing women in jeopardy. They viewed these women as trespassing on newly enforced social norms defined by Church and Inquisition policies. Across Portugal in the seventeenth and eighteenth centuries, an appreciation for the concepts of rational medicine spread among Portuguese physicians, surgeons, and other elites. Thus, what had been commonplace and popular curative practices met the Inquisition's crackdown on traditional medicine, making women folk healers extremely vulnerable to denunciation and Holy Office prosecution.⁵ The following case serves as a representative example.

In the mid-1740s, Joana Baptista, a *curandeira* (folk healer) living in the village of São Marcos near the important regional market town of Évora, was known to her neighbors as *a Ratinha,* or "the Little Mouse." She had moved to Évora, located on the plains of the Alentejo province in southeast Portugal, a number of years before from the country's far north, near Chaves in the Archbishopric of Braga. She lived with her husband, who was a common laborer. On June 15, 1747, the day *familiares* of the Holy Office arrested her, she claimed to be over thirty years old; like most of her contemporaries, she did not know her exact date of birth.⁶

By profession, Joana Baptista was also a recognized practicing *parteira,* or midwife. Her highly questionable methods, however, resulted in her being denounced to Inquisition authorities. The charges brought against her included practicing sorcery, disseminating superstitions, and having entered into a pact with the Devil. Before her arrest, her neighbors had provided the Holy Office with damaging testimony about her magical healing techniques.⁷

Consistent with her position as a midwife, Joana Baptista's illicit healing practices focused on the maladies of childhood. Among the superstitious cures she was said to perform was the following ritual, meant to extract sickness from patients who were, of necessity, quite small and therefore very young. Joana Baptista cured children by passing them through a special circular loaf of bread, called a *rosca*. The loaf was formed by twisting and braiding together three long strings of dough. This particular bread dough was to be made from flour provided from the households of three different women, each named Maria. Once the dough had been baked into a big wreath or hoop, Joana Baptista would pass the ill child through this *rosca de três Marias* three times in an unbroken sequence, all the while reciting a special incantation that addressed the sickness or disorder in question.[8]

Joana Baptista remained in the custody of the Évora tribunal of the Portuguese Inquisition, enduring interrogation and periodic torture, for over two years. According to the terms of her final punitive sentence, she was exiled for two years to the Bishopric of Portalegre, obliged to receive religious instruction, again imprisoned for an arbitrary length of time determined by the whim of her Inquisitor jailers, and made to pay all costs stemming from her trial and incarceration. She was released from prison on October 31, 1749—the eve of All Saints' Day—eleven days after her public act of faith, or *auto-de-fé,* which occurred on October 20, 1749.[9] She was then dispatched to travel northward to begin her term of banishment.

In many ways, Joana Baptista's experience fits a scenario typical among popular healers in early modern Portugal, Brazil, and the Atlantic islands. Like most other *curandeiras* (and male *curandeiros*), she was a member of Portugal's poorest social class; she lived as an outsider to the community in which she resided; and, at the time of her arrest, which occurred during the Portuguese Inquisition's most active period of prosecuting magical criminals, she was a relatively young adult. In gender terms, just over half the illicit healers brought to trial in the region under the Évora tribunal's jurisdiction were women (though this ratio was higher for the nation as a whole). Further, like nearly half of the women arrested for magical crimes in Portugal in the eighteenth century, Joana Baptista was married. Finally, as a first-time offender, her sentence was light; she was not required to travel an extraordinary distance from her home (Portalegre lies just eighty-five kilometers north of Évora) and a two-year banishment was brief by the standards of the Portuguese Holy Office.[10]

What Joana Baptista's case illustrates most clearly, though, is that superstitious healing, especially as performed by women, was perfectly commonplace in Portuguese peasant society, even in the middle of the eighteenth century after decades of active repression at the hands of Holy Office authorities and other elites. Although she may have worked behind closed doors, this *curandeira* and midwife employed healing methods (apparently for many years) that a substantial proportion of the people in her village were aware of and must have condoned, at least in practice if not in theory. Once denounced, however, this illicit healer's position was revealed as a fragile one. Joana Baptista's case also illustrates that the transition from being an oft-patronized and even respected local authority on remedies among one's peers to being a moral criminal under prosecution by the Inquisition could be a very rapid one.

Who, then, were the female popular healers of the Lusophone Atlantic, those common women who cured by common superstitious means? What was their place in Portuguese society, and how did their neighbors perceive them? What kinds of curative services were *curandeiras* expected to provide, and who were their clients?

First, how may we explain the parallels between folk healing concepts reported by the Inquisition in Portugal and in colonized regions in Africa and South America? Core characteristics of any colonial society are shaped by the beliefs, cosmology, and expectations of the colonizers, who establish the ascendant social paradigm within areas they control. In Portuguese settlements in Africa and Brazil, the social paradigm regarding healing was heavily influenced by European immigrants of every socioeconomic class, despite how few their numbers actually may have been in the colonial community.[11] Popular healers anywhere, whatever their ethnic origin, sought to profit from those who had wealth or power; in the colonies that meant mainly Europeans. Thus, in any geographical context (Portugal or its colonies), there was an incentive for folk healers of any cultural background to shape or tailor their practices to fit the expectations of their European clientele (even if the healers' cures employed African or Brazilian medicinal or ritual components). Moreover, illicit healers entered the historical record when their activities came under the scrutiny of European elites. European authorities interpreted and recorded, according to their own cultural terms, contemporary popular healing methods. Of course, the preexisting healing culture of majority indigenous populations did continue to flourish in colonized regions of Africa and Brazil, and elements of their beliefs did cross over to influence those of European colonists. But colonial regions ruled under Portuguese authority reflected European influence, even if the culture developing therein was a hybridized one.[12]

In addition, we must not forget the role of *degredados* (exiled convict folk healers), whom the Inquisition typically sent to the Atlantic colonies for committing a repeat offense; they too shaped the character of popular healing in the Portuguese empire. Examples include relapsed *curandeiras* Antónia Nunes da Costa, whom the Coimbra tribunal exiled to Brazil for three years in 1716, and Maria Gomes, exiled to Angola for seven years by the Évora tribunal in 1747.[13] Such unrepentant healers, though few in number, had very little oversight once they reached their exile destinations in Angola or Brazil. Hence, they were in a position to significantly influence the popular healing culture of their new residence communities. Alongside them, we may add the influx of significant numbers of women from northern Portugal who immigrated to Brazil with their families throughout the eighteenth-century gold boom.[14] Those women brought with them the rich healing traditions of female folk healers typically found in continental peasant society of the northernmost provinces: Minho, Douro, Trás-as-Montes, and the Beiras.[15]

These examples of convicted female healers mask the larger gendered ratios of magical criminals in early modern Portugal. To better understand how gender determined who was a Portuguese folk healer, we will consider the statistical significance of Holy Office trials conducted only against popular healers, *curandeiros* or *saludadores,* all of whom were considered *mágicos* (magical offenders). The 442 Inquisition trial dossiers viewed for this study represent all types of magical crimes, including healing, between 1680 and 1805 across Portugal and its Atlantic colonies.

Among Inquisition trials of Portuguese folk healers specifically, 40.3 percent were men, while women account for 59.7 percent overall, combining the figures for all three tribunals (Coimbra, Lisbon, and Évora).[16] To do so, however, distorts the true historical picture, since the three tribunals prosecuted *curandeiras* at widely varying rates. For example, in Évora (the Inquisition tribunal responsible for the southern third of the country), the ratio was nearly even, with a total of thirty-four female folk healers tried during the period in question, as compared to thirty-two males (51.5 percent and 48.5 percent, respectively). These were drawn from a body of 184 total cases conducted by the Évora tribunal between 1668 and 1802 in which the accused's crime was a magical one.

In Lisbon's tribunal (responsible for the middle third of the country, the Azores and Madeira Islands, and all of the Portuguese Atlantic world colonies in Brazil and West Africa), healing men outnumbered healing women thirteen to nine, or 59.1 percent male as compared to 40.9 percent female (figures which neatly reverse the national male-to-female ratio for all magical offenders).

Conversely, the Holy Office tribunal of Coimbra (responsible for the northern third of the country) prosecuted a far larger percentage of women healers: *curandeiras* account for 69.8 percent of the trials against popular healers, while *curandeiros* make up only 30.2 percent (sixty-seven women and twenty-nine men were tried for illicit healing in Coimbra; these were culled from a body of 203 total magical crimes cases compiled by the Coimbra tribunal between 1693 and 1796).

Note that these figures are not necessarily representative of the actual gender ratio of popular healers functioning at large in contemporary Portuguese society. It is possible, for example, though difficult to prove, that Inquisitors in Coimbra were specifically targeting female healers for arrest. However, in the north of Portugal, as elsewhere in the northern Iberian Peninsula, women played a stronger social role as folk healers than they did in the south. Modern scholarship has indicated that women shaped and controlled the general expression of popular culture paradigms in northern Portugal and Galicia to an extent far greater than did men.[17] An elevated number of arrests among female healers by the Coimbra Inquisition tribunal, then, may be related to this point as well.

Although the focus of this essay is on female healers, it must be noted that one of the most striking aspects to emerge in this study is the high percentage of men whom the Portuguese Holy Office prosecuted for general magical crimes (including healing) between 1662 and 1802.[18] The Inquisition arrested surprisingly large numbers of men, not only for such crimes as conducting acts of simple sorcery and divining the future, but also for curing illness. By European-wide standards, men made up a very large proportion of the popular healers in Portuguese society, particularly in the southern region of the country. This is clearly reflected in the ratio of men to women among *mágicos* tried by the Inquisition across the whole of Portugal, including both healers and those accused of other magical crimes: 41 percent male to 59 percent female.[19]

The masculine folk healer was a well-entrenched figure in Portuguese peasant society. Of the twelve *saludadores* and *curandeiros* whom the Portuguese Inquisition arrested in the sixteenth century, as documented by Portuguese historian Francisco Bethencourt, ten of them were men.[20]

But the tradition of men acting as folk healers in the south of Portugal was at least as old as the six hundred-year Muslim occupation of the Iberian Peninsula, beginning in the eighth century. North African Muslim society generally placed men in the position of being agents of healing, even at the popular level; this seems to be the historical genesis of the similar Portuguese practice, particularly south of the River Tagus.[21]

Still, there are no easily identifiable patterns to the persecution of magical crimes in the eighteenth-century Portuguese world. As the relative flood of trials against *mágicos* between 1715 and 1755 indicates, Lusophone elites in the eighteenth century lost their long-standing tolerance for *all* types of peasant beliefs that ran contrary to empirical reason. As lettered and cultured Portuguese grew gradually more influenced by the rationalistic culture that prevailed among elites in other parts of Europe (especially northern countries like England, France, and the Netherlands), popular practices that relied on superstitious rituals and had no basis in rational science became increasingly distasteful to them. Conventional medical practitioners, motivated by a desire to spread Enlightenment principles, but spurred additionally by material and professional interests, became instrumental in initiating a new campaign of repression against superstitious folk healers (*curandeiras* and *saludadores*).[22]

The broad and even distribution of prosecutions in Portuguese Atlantic territories against all types of magical practitioners, regardless of their gender or specialty, indicates that elites were more concerned with curbing the superstitious beliefs and practices themselves, because of their fundamental irrationality, than with furthering a more subtle and sinister gender-based agenda. Generally, accused practitioners, male or female, went to trial and suffered equally. Elites had nothing to gain by persecuting one sex over another. To have done so would have risked discrediting the basic point of the prosecution in any trial for magical crimes: that no common mortal could possess supernatural, extra-human powers for healing or anything else.

These trials all took place within an early modern Portuguese society that held the female folk healer in an ambivalent place. From the outset, it is important to establish that female *curandeiras* provided health care services to mostly rural people of commoner status (though popular healers certainly worked in cities, too, and counted elites among their patrons), all of whom both desired and needed these services. To that extent, popular healers must be seen, at least at the level of their client base, as being purveyors of a socially approved body of magical beliefs and practices. Borrowing from anthropologist Raymond Firth's analysis of the different types of social functions that practitioners of magic can fulfill (productive, protective, or destructive), we see that the healer's magical art falls squarely in the realm of what Firth calls *protective* magic.[23] Protective magic is performed for the good of the community; besides curing illness, its intent is to guard property, avert misfortune, provide security while traveling or hunting, and otherwise assist the activities of the social group for which it is generated.

Superstitious popular healing, then, had a socially positive function; its practice was not ill-intentioned. On the contrary, the earnest healer performed a service meant to aid individuals in the community, as "a stimulus to [general social] effort."[24] (Of course, this ignores the inevitable cynical charlatans; still, the majority of folk healers in Portugal appear to have had a sincere faith in their own stated abilities.) Popular remedies by design were aimed at restoring members of a social organization—a village or neighborhood community—to their full productive capacity, not to cause harm to the social fabric. Further, a folk healer did not intend her curative acts to be a divisive social or religious matter for her elite or commoner neighbors; most *curandeiras,* in fact, reacted with indignation when accused of acts repugnant to the Church.[25]

Regardless of gender, a magical folk healer's position was precarious. Once accused or denounced, authorities could usually count on their social inferiors, commoners, to line up and give testimony against the illicit healer in their community. Such behavior suggests that superstitious healing practices occupied a zone of beliefs that most people understood to be "wrong" at some level, but which desperation drove them to use in the event of illness.[26] Thus, the local *curandeira* occupied an ambivalent position in her community, and an insecure one. Friends and neighbors could (and did) turn on a folk healer in an instant if the *curandeira's* remedies were perceived to be ineffectual or harmful, or once the healer had been made a pariah due to Inquisition scrutiny.

By comparison, note that the cloistered women in holy orders described in this volume by Nuria Salazar Simarro and Sarah E. Owens suffered none of the above disadvantages or dangers associated with their healing work. As socially sanctioned health care providers, the women of the Convent of Jesús María in Mexico City interacted freely with elites: colonial authorities or conventional licensed physicians and surgeons. Though often employing similar medicinal substances and methods, the nuns' wealth and privileged position protected them, creating an experience radically different from that of poor, uneducated commoners, the *curandeiras,* who had no institutional support or fixed facilities in which to conduct their work.

What were some of the traditional female healers' sources of power, the unorthodox magical means on which they relied? During the seventeenth and eighteenth centuries, one could encounter a range of female popular healers in Portuguese-ruled territories. Popular folkways provided an abundance of home remedies, treatments that drew on the accumulated experience of untold agrarian generations. To that extent, virtually every household included someone who attended to common human complaints, pains, and ailments, and every community relied on *parteiras* (midwives), many of whom resorted to superstitious rites in the conduct of their craft. Using well-known natural remedies, the animal, vegetable, or mineral ingredients for which were readily available, old wives and cunning women could employ their broad knowledge of floral and faunal characteristics—unscientifically gained but often effective—to address all manner of common maladies.[27] Typically, such cures would be administered in combination with a prayer, incantation, prolonged healing ritual, or dietary regimen.[28] Thus, to be effective, these folk healing practices usually required a tangible, practical remedy combined with a superstitious or "magical" act.

In addition, there were also in Portugal those *curandeiras* and *saludadoras* who firmly believed that they had been given a divine gift: an inherent healing "virtue" that empowered them with the capacity to cure humans or animals with nothing more than a touch, or with rituals and the aid of an intangible internal "holy" power. Of course, charlatans could and did make this same assertion, but Inquisition cases provide numerous examples of illicit folk healers who, when pressed or tortured, would not easily back away from their conviction that God had imbued them with a special personal restorative power.[29]

These were the types of *saludadores,* or healers (male or female), who most concerned and challenged the ecclesiastical officers of the Inquisition. True, the attention of the Holy Office was much occupied with those *curandeiras* who applied superstitious folk remedies founded on horticultural lore—conventional physicians and surgeons who worked within the Inquisition particularly opposed their competition—but in terms of a theological challenge to the Church, *saludadores* who claimed to have a divine gift represented the greater threat. The assertion of possessing "divine virtue" made *saludadores* and *curandeiras* a threat to the medical profession, as well, by discounting the value of the *médicos'* conventional training.³⁰

Antónia Pereira, for example, was a sixty-five-year-old *curandeira* whose nickname, *a Galinheira,* meant "the Chicken Lady." After the Coimbra tribunal arrested her on October 8, 1722, she maintained that God had bestowed a divine virtue upon her that empowered her to heal people. State-licensed medical personnel working within the Inquisition, however, confirmed that "her cures were faked." Further, they asserted in the trial summary that Antónia Pereira's remedies had not resulted in any healing effect, and that "such effects could not proceed from any 'natural virtue'" which Antónia Pereira claimed to have. The "attacks" of illness that she treated without medicine, the Holy Office maintained, could only have been "cured by Doctors, not by 'divine virtue.'"³¹

A short Holy Office treatise concerning healers called *Dos Saludadores* ridicules Portuguese folk healers' often-claimed power to cure people by divine virtue.³² This brief but influential work, effectively an internal policy memo of the Portuguese Inquisition, was written during the second decade of the eighteenth century. In subsequent trials against illicit superstitious healers, the Inquisitors took the opportunity to drive home the point that folk medicine had no efficacy because God no longer provided mere mortals with healing powers. Official trial summaries often reiterated the language of *Dos Saludadores* almost verbatim.³³

By all appearances, however, many popular healers genuinely believed that their capacity to heal came from God's hand, and that such "divine virtue" did not empower them to do anything else. Indeed, Holy Office personnel seemed to have been, if possible, the most agitated, even unnerved, when they occasionally encountered *saludadores* who asked for no specific sum in return for their services, asserting that it was unseemly for a man of God to solicit remuneration.³⁴ The *Inquisidores* were on firmer legal and theological ground when confronted by cases they could classify as straightforward charlatanism. "True" *curandeiras,* though, who typically did not indulge in fortune telling, love magic, or any practice other than the healing of human or animal bodies, caused a problem, especially if they refused to accept any but voluntary donations for their work. Such behavior, modeled on the lives of Christ and the Saints, raised in the Inquisitors' minds the unwelcome possibility that the *saludador*'s claim to possessing divine virtue might not be false.

Generations of exposure to clerical remonstrances about the moral dangers of superstitious practices had, by the mid-seventeenth century, rendered any popular healer's activities somewhat suspect in the eyes of common folk. That notwithstanding, the circumstances of life in the countryside during the early modern period (agrarian, isolated, and conservative) dictated that the services on offer from *curandeiras* continued to be in broad demand. Poor rustics required relief for their health problems, too, and traditionally such succor was to be found in the person of a local or itinerant folk healer.[35] Either because of the traditional remedies used or because of a person's natural ability to heal or fight infection, the folk healers' patients often recovered. Those successes would have cemented the individual folk healer's reputations for those patients and their immediate families, and perhaps for others within their social circle. In any case, state-licensed surgeons and physicians were universally male. The circumstances under which they could effectively examine female patients were at best extremely restricted—reason enough for many early modern Portuguese women to turn to a familiar *curandeira* to address their physical complaints.[36] Further, licensed conventional medical practitioners were exceptionally few in Portugal's rural areas during the seventeenth and eighteenth centuries. If one could be found, peasants of pitiably small financial means could rarely afford the fees an educated surgeon or physician was likely to charge. Moreover, merely citing peasants' inability to pay does not address the profound cultural differences that separated the medical treatment of elites from that of commoners, nor the barrier of perception that divided each group's ideas about healing. Peasants often simply did not trust the "learned cures" of conventional practitioners. Such differences would become increasingly divergent as the eighteenth century progressed and enlightened ideas about science and healing spread through elite groups, leaving the poor increasingly outside and isolated from the intellectual currents of rationalized medicine.

Even as this distinction between science and healing grew, female healers served a popular clientele in Portugal and the colonized Portuguese Atlantic territories. As we might expect, rural peasants complained of a multitude of ailments and maladies. Living as they did in damp houses, working long hours out of doors, performing intensely physical labor, and subsisting on a nutritiously meager diet, Portugal's rural poor developed numerous health problems, suffering disproportionately from seasonal fevers, influenza, colds, and respiratory ailments. Substandard hygiene and unsanitary conditions compounded health problems; simple injuries became infected; gangrene often set in.[37] Female folk healers naturally addressed health issues particular to women in early modern Portugal, albeit with little apparent success. Continued heavy labor and poor diet during pregnancy contributed to a miscarriage rate estimated at 25 percent.[38] Mortality rates soared due to complications in childbirth; this was the leading cause of death for young Portuguese women (ages nineteen to thirty-two). Childhood diseases also took their toll: one third of all children born in seventeenth- and eighteenth-century Portugal died before reaching their first birthday, and only half reached the age of seven.[39]

Maladies that a *curandeira* might be called on to cure included the following broad range of common ills:

- *Ar* ("air"): Paralysis of the body or parts thereof, thought to be provoked by corruption in the air. This sickness had many potential treatments, most of which involved the recitation of special words or verses.[40]
- *Espinhela* ("spinal disorder"): This malady could refer to backache, stomachache, heartburn, or any painful internal disorder, or "oppression," in the trunk of the body or abdomen. Healers addressed this condition with a combination of medicinal preparations, rituals, and prayers.[41]
- *Quebranto* ("weakness," also known as *trespasso,* meaning to magically hurt, wound, or otherwise incapacitate): Often attributed to *mau olhado,* or the evil eye, this malady name designated a general state of indolence, apathy, and sadness or depression. This indistinct set of afflictions was among those for which the services of a popular healer were most frequently sought.[42]
- *Mal do Sentido* (literally, "feeling bad or poorly"): This category of malady included such common health problems as dislocated joints, bone fractures, and sprains, as well as skin lesions. Because of the frequency of such injuries among Portuguese agricultural workers, *curandeiras* had many methods of addressing them: the ingestion of formulas consisting of herbs and other ingredients; the application of lotions, ointments, and unguents; the performance of certain ceremonial rites over the affected body part; or simply reciting a healing prayer or incantation.[43]
- *Cobrão* ("big snake"): This malady referred to skin irritations attributed to "the passing of a repellent animal"—snakes, spiders, lizards, scorpions, and the like—over or near an afflicted person's body. Popular healers addressed this illness with what anthropologists call "sympathetic magic": words to attack or thwart the animals in question. Rituals to cure this malady typically included using a knife to cut and

kill an actual representative creature of the offending species; however, an effigy of the animal rendered in paper or clay might also have been sacrificed.[44]

- *Fogo* ("fire," also known as *osagre*): Like *cobrão*, *fogo* was a complaint characterized by irritated skin that produced great burning pain. Because of this similarity, many of the treatments *curandeiras* used were the same for both types of illness.[45]
- *Mordeduras de répteís e de "cães danados"* ("bites from reptiles and 'mad dogs'"): Animal bites, certainly not limited to dogs and reptiles, were a frequent complaint in rural areas with many domesticated animals, a proportion of which inevitably carried some form of disease. Local superstitious healers were often called on to treat such injuries; indeed, the reputations of many *curandeiras* rested specifically on their proficiency in addressing this variety of ills.[46]
- *Carne talhada ou rendida* ("cut or broken flesh"; wounds): Normally, *curandeiras* dealt with flesh wounds by applying cloth bandages, typically in a configuration representing a cross, over the affected area. Popular healers employed olive oil "with insistence" to clean and purify open wounds, or as an application to cloth dressings. Further, the *curandeira* was often said to blow on the wound, warming it with her breath, or to caress it with her touch,[47] thus imparting a personal healing quality upon the injury.
- *Dores variadas e "febres"* ("various pains and 'fevers'"): This set of maladies included toothaches, headaches, and backaches, as well as various kinds of fevers. The folk healers' repertoire included numerous plant remedies that acted as pain relievers and febrifuges.
- *Controle da natalidade* ("birth control methods," including abortion): Community *parteiras* and healers in the seventeenth and early eighteenth centuries usually possessed accumulated experience far superior to what contemporary conventional medicine taught concerning contraception and abortion. Still, practitioners of folk medicine employed a range of unorthodox methods—magical, mechanical, and medicinal—intended to prevent pregnancy (or facilitate it, for that matter). These included the wearing of special amulets, the performing of particular rituals, and the ingestion of herbal or mineral preparations.[48]

Portuguese Inquisition sources dating from the sixteenth century provide documentary evidence confirming the existence of a solid popular understanding of how to induce abortion. To be sure, some of the means *curandeiras* are known to have used certainly put their clients' lives in danger; even so, female folk healers' skills were such that abortions were performed successfully and with some regularity. The exact chemical composition of beverages drunk to induce a miscarriage is difficult to assess, but reported ingredients of uterine "purgatives" include camphor, almond, pennyroyal, rue, and a substance called *marbejas,* which may have a mineral provenance.[49] The efficacy (and hazards) of an herbal extract made from the pennyroyal plant, at least, in achieving the desired result of this treatment has been demonstrated by modern pharmacology.[50]

By the late seventeenth century, the Portuguese state had begun to certify and license *parteiras*. Practical training manuals especially for midwives, written in Portuguese, began to circulate in manuscript at least as early as the mid-eighteenth century, though not widely. An example produced during the second half of the eighteenth century included nearly 150 technical questions with didactic responses concerning female anatomy, giving birth, and the proper midwife's procedure for every stage of childbirth. Illiteracy among *parteiras* no doubt caused a problem for effective consultation of these unillustrated handbooks. Still, extant copies indicate that the level of obstetrical knowledge among midwives in eighteenth-century Portugal was quite high.[51]

If gender differentiated who might have access to state licenses or books on state-of-the-art medical knowledge, race emerges as a factor in the practices and prosecutions of healers. Specifically, Luso-African *curandeiras* enjoyed a mystique because of the perception that their origins enhanced their power. Illicit Afro-Portuguese folk healers could command great respect across the social strata of early modern Portuguese society, whether in the metropole or the colonies. A selection of cases involving well-regarded, often-patronized female Afro-Portuguese and Afro-Brazilian folk healers illustrates this additional dimension of the role and practices of *curandeiras* in the seventeenth- and eighteenth-century Portuguese Atlantic world.

Statistically, persons of African descent made up only a small percentage of the total cadre of folk healers encountered in early modern Portugal. At most, the Portuguese Holy Office tried only fifteen or twenty Luso-Africans as *curandeiros* during the late seventeenth and eighteenth centuries, amounting to less than 10 percent of all prosecuted contemporary folk healers.[52] Yet blacks were some of the most renowned and notorious purveyors of superstitious remedies in the country. Healers of African origin (whether from the African colonies, Brazil, or born in the home country) seem to have been surrounded by a mystique that benefited their commerce in folk remedies. Many whites accorded black healers respect and power based on their perceived singular exoticism, assuming that their origins in Africa or Brazil had provided them with healing knowledge to which white *médicos* or *curandeiras* did not have access.

This dynamic is especially true regarding black women. Of the twelve positively known cases in which the Portuguese Inquisition prosecuted blacks as healers, two-thirds (eight) were women. Four of the twenty-two popular healers tried in Lisbon—two women and two men—were of African descent (most had been born in Brazil, one had been born in Angola). The Évora tribunal tried five Luso-Africans. This number is higher because the southernmost Algarve province, where the enslaved and free black population was greater, was in Évora's jurisdiction.[53]

In 1754, Inês de Carmo was a recently freed slave from Tavira, a fishing town and trading port on the southern coast of Portugal. She had gained her freedom after the death of her owner, an Anglo-Portuguese sea captain named John Pires; the terms of his will provided for her manumission. Inês de Carmo was an illegitimate child but, because her mother had been a slave to the same master, she was probably the daughter of her owner. At the time of her arrest, she was forty-eight years old and married to a local mariner. Among her neighbors she was known as *a Palita* ("the Toothpick") or *a Viva* ("the Lively").[54]

Although the Portuguese Inquisition first arrested her in 1754, the earliest set of denunciations against Inês de Carmo had been collected in 1738. Over a period of fifteen years, the Évora tribunal of the Holy Office had collected testimony about her activities as a *curandeira* from dozens of residents of Faro and Tavira. Among other things, Inês de Carmo was accused of pronouncing superstitious incantations, employed in the curing of a neighbor's child.[55]

Predictably, some denunciations had come from state-licensed medical professionals. João de Deos, a *sangrador* (phlebotomist) and *barbeiro* (barber) of Faro, gave evidence against Inês de Carmo in June 1753. He was followed by João Baptista Marçal, licensed in the same professions but practicing in Tavira. That year the Inquisitorial commissioners interviewed twenty-eight people over nearly two months (May 30 to July 25, 1753), building a solid case against the accused Luso-African folk healer.[56]

In late April of 1755, after sixteen months in the Holy Office prisons, Inês de Carmo learned that the Évora Inquisitors had found her guilty of committing magical crimes. For a first-time offender, Inês de Carmo received a surprisingly severe sentence. Besides being whipped on the streets of Évora, the Inquisition banished her for four years to Viseu, a cold, isolated mountain town nearly five hundred kilometers to the north of her home, and they forbade her to return to Tavira or its environs.[57] What accounts for this exceptional penalty?

The death of Captain John Pires, Inês de Carmo's master, had left her suddenly vulnerable. While the Holy Office had obviously been reluctant to prosecute and banish her while Pires was alive, hence denying an owner of a valuable slave, once he had died the Inquisitors no longer felt any deterrent. With no master (who was likely also her father) to protect her, Inês de Carmo's position in her community, already weakened by years of accusations, became untenable. To both secular and Holy Office authorities, a newly freed, masterless ex-slave constituted a different matter entirely from an enslaved, supervised laborer.

The *curandeira* Inês de Carmo, after being released from her bonds of servitude, presented a three-fold affront to the established social order. First, her presence in the community was a daily reminder to local enslaved Luso-Africans of the arbitrary nature of their situation. Second, her continued residence in Tavira constantly called to mind the precedent that John Pires had set by freeing her; certainly this outcome was inconvenient and unpopular among whites. Third, she placed herself in jeopardy by conducting superstitious cures, a practice which local state-licensed healers and the Holy Office would not abide. Therefore, local residents, medical professionals, and the Inquisition authorities combined to act decisively against Inês de Carmo, shackling her with the stigma of an Inquisition condemnation, a sentence guaranteeing that she would cause their community no further trouble.

Inês de Carmo's misfortune with the Inquisition, and her experience of being especially harshly treated because she was a free person of color, was not unique. Luso-Africans convicted by the Portuguese Inquisition for illicit folk healing during the late seventeenth and eighteenth centuries experienced punishment patterns that were very different from those of their white counterparts. Moreover, Inquisition sentencing patterns reveal a stark disparity between the castigation of enslaved blacks and *pretos forros* (literally, blacks outside the condition of bondage). Simply put, there is a demonstrable relationship between the severity of a sentence and whether the accused person of African descent was a slave or free.[58]

In an earlier, similar case, *familiares* of the Évora Inquisition arrested the *curandeira* Maria Grácia on October 7, 1724. The crimes alleged against her were many: pact with the Devil, sorcery, superstitions, sacrilege, and "practicing false arts." This accused healer was a slave, born in Angola; she is described in the trial record as being unmarried, forty years old, and *preta retinta* (pitch black). Her master was Felipe Rodrigues Vitório, a wool contractor who lived on the Travessa de Alegría in Évora. The trial record explains that because she had been taken from Angola when she was very young, the accused did not know the names of her parents. Maria Grácia was taken into custody in the dispensary house of the Évora Inquisition palace and was not incarcerated with white offenders in the official prison.[59]

She was said to cure the malady of "weakness" (*quebranto*) and the "malady of the moon," which she achieved with superstitious chants (*orações*). At other times, Maria Grácia conducted a remedy that involved the use of simple sorcery and mechanical healing methods. She would employ the following chant, using a cup of cool, clean water that she had blessed:

> When the Virgin, Our Lady, walked through the world curing
> She cured with a cup of cold water.
> Jesus gives life to Santa Ana
> Santa Ana gives life to Jesus
> In the name of the Father, Son and the Holy Spirit, Amen.[60]

Additionally, in order to cure carbuncles she would exclaim:

> I bless you, carbuncles, in the name of the Father, Son and the Holy Spirit!
> When the Virgin, Our Lady, passed by here, snakes and lizards were killed
> In this way I beg God and the Virgin Mary for that which has begun to go back![61]

Maria Grácia "completed her confession of guilt" only after being tortured on September 10, 1725, nearly a year after her date of arrest. She performed her *auto-de-fé* on December 16, 1725, after which she was banished to Faro, in the Algarve, for three years.[62]

A good deal of the popular esteem given to black women as healers is, once again, in part attributable to North African influences on Portugal's past. Folktales of mysterious, alluring *mouras encantadas* (enchanted Moorish women) originated during the medieval *Reconquista*. Such stories abounded in early modern Portugal, particularly in the southern provinces (the Algarve and Alentejo); they spread powerful images that resonated in the popular mind. Beautiful dark women from North Africa were said to entrance, seduce, or spirit away lone travelers in the Portuguese countryside. Peasants commonly believed these *mouras encantadas* were ageless; they had been left behind to guard treasures hidden by the retreating Muslims.[63] Such women were said to have uncommon powers to charm and to heal Christians. In context, that unlettered rustics should project the powers of characters in folktales on to living Luso-Africans is not so difficult to understand.

Luso-African healers were also popular further north in Portugal. For example, one of the most famous *curandeiras* in the diocese of Coimbra, Antónia Nunes da Costa, was certainly a woman of Afro-Portuguese origins. Her nickname, *a Preta*, was and remains a pejorative term for women of African descent.[64] Still, she earned widespread notoriety for her ability to alleviate many types of illness. She may have been born in Portugal to a free black family, or she might have been a manumitted slave; it is possible that she arrived in Portugal from any one of the Portuguese Atlantic world colonies. In any case, though she brought to her profession a sensibility derived from her experience as an Afro-Portuguese woman, she shaped her folk remedies according to the expectations of her white clientele in the metropole.

In order to care for the numerous clients of all social classes who summoned her, da Costa would travel great distances on foot to various communities scattered across Portugal's midlands. To treat a headache, for example, she would "apply the hot entrails of a male sheep, opened, at the base of [the patient's] neck, and put milk from the breast of a woman into [the patient's] ears, along with some small sprigs of wormwood, increasing the amount until a good result is achieved."[65] Or, for a toothache, she applied hot embers from the hearth fire soaked in wine, affixed inside the mouth, above the jawbone and teeth of the sufferer.[66] During her travels to cure patients, Antónia Nunes da Costa eventually became well known to Church officials; her name as an illicit healer surfaced repeatedly during ecclesiastical visitations through the countryside in 1694, 1698, 1699, 1707, and 1712.[67] She would endure two Inquisition trials, in 1711 and 1716.[68]

The historical record reveals two additional *curandeiras* of color in the Coimbra district later in the century. In 1731, the Inquisition arrested forty-year-old Joana Baptista, resident of a village outside Oporto. She was described as a *parda* (woman of mixed race or *mulata*).[69] Also, in 1754–1755, the Holy Office tried one Maria Teresa, who lived inside the city walls of Oporto. Inquisition records describe her as a *mulata*—her father was a priest (a *sacerdote* of the habit of Saint Peter who lived in the Abbey of Estorãos) and her mother was a black slave owned by another priest.[70]

Luso-African *curandeiras* commanded their own peculiar authority as healers. This was due in part to the color of their skin, and in part by the authority accorded to them by their customers, some of whom were social elites. Even if few in number among the larger set of Portuguese folk healers, their popularity and prestige was perpetuated by those who chose to patronize them when stricken by illness. However, practicing their craft came with grave risks. If caught, enslaved and free black *curandeiras* suffered far worse penalties at the hands of the Inquisition than their fellow white folk healers.[71]

As Hugh Glenn Cagle points out elsewhere in this volume, African and Amerindian women were often the "healers of first resort" for Portuguese sailors and colonists during the early stages of Atlantic exploration and settlement. Furthermore, native women became exceptionally important sources of indigenous knowledge about medicinal plants throughout the global empire. Cagle also asserts that, in the confrontation of medical cultures (indigenous versus European) in a colonial context, no Western intellectual dominance is possible; instead, colonial exchanges result in a tenuous creative compromise between healing cosmologies.[72] While accurate for early colonial encounters, the seventeenth- and eighteenth-century *curandeiras* whose cases we have seen were the product of a long process of cultural blending; they drew their hybridized remedies, beliefs, and methods from geographically diverse sources throughout the Atlantic world. By the time Inquisition authorities turned their attention toward superstitious folk healing, the ideological split they addressed was not between Western and non-Western cultures, but between elite and peasant beliefs within a common culture found not only in the metropole, but also overseas in long-colonized Portuguese enclaves.

In conclusion, the arts of popular healing, whether practiced by women or men, Europeans, Africans, or Amerindians, were abhorrent both to the Portuguese Inquisitors and university-trained *médicos,* but for different reasons. Both groups within the Holy Office—licensed physicians or surgeons working as *familiares* and *Inquisidores* occupying the upper echelon of power—sought a policy of repression against illicit folk healers during the first half of the eighteenth century. Superstitious practices and heresies committed by illicit healers were anathema to Inquisitors because such behavior clashed with the Church orthodoxy they had pledged themselves to uphold. Licensed physicians and surgeons, meanwhile, who worked within the institution of the Holy Office, harbored an additional double-edged grievance against the purveyors of folk remedies. *Curandeiros* and *curandeiras* represented an obstacle to the conventional health practitioners' trade, insofar as most commoners preferred to patronize popular instead of state-sanctioned healers. Beyond that, though, for those conventional *médicos* whose professional outlook included innovative, rationalized medicine as it was beginning to be practiced in northern Europe, an additional benefit to persecuting folk healers was that the discrediting of popular healing methods opened the door to the practice of enlightened, scientific medicine at all levels of Portuguese society. To these forward-looking conventional *médicos,* convincing the general populace of the futility of superstitious healing was just one facet in a comprehensive program of long-term medical reform in Portugal.

Each of these groups within the structure of the Inquisition—ecclesiastical administrators and the professional medical practitioners who served as functionaries under them—had a clear set of motives for their antagonism toward male and female *curandeiros*. *Médicos* and *Inquisidores* acted cooperatively, fashioning a policy of widespread, systematic repression against illicit folk healers in early modern Portugal.

Female folk healers across the Portuguese colonial Atlantic world, for their part, merely continued trying to get by as they always had by treating the sick, delivering babies, dressing wounds, and mixing herbal remedies with traditional rites or incantations. For their clients, turning to a local, accessible, and affordable *curandeira* remained the only practical and viable option. More than a century of persecution by Inquisitors and medical elites did not change the social circumstances of women healers, nor did it change their practices. The poor remained poor and, in the countryside, necessity created demand for the folk healers' services, illicit or otherwise. *Curandeiras* continue to meet this demand within Portuguese rural and urban society well into the twenty-first century.

NOTES

I am grateful to the Instituto Camões, the Fundação Luso-Americano para Desenvolvimento, and the William J. Fulbright program for grants that made the research for this essay possible. I would like to thank professors José Pedro Paiva, Francisco Bethencourt, and the late A. H. de Oliveira Marques for their generous help over the years. In addition, for much assistance and patience, I would like to express my gratitude to the staff of the Arquivo Nacional de Torre do Tombo in Lisbon.

1. See Luiz Mott, "Feiticeiros de Angola na Inquisição portuguesa," *Mneme—Revista de Humanidades* 11, no. 29 (2011): 2–22; and Diádiney Helena de Almeida, "Um estudo das interações culturais entre curandeiros e medicos acadêmicos no Rio de Janeiro Oitocentista," in *Proceedings of the XIII Encontro de História, ANPUH*, 1–10 (Rio de Janeiro, 2008).

2. In the original Portuguese: "A medicina rústica é o resultado de uma série de aculturações de medicina popular de Portugal, indígena e negra. . . ." See Alceu Maynard Araújo, *Medicina Rústica*, 2nd ed. (São Paulo: Educação Nacional/INL, 1977), 43

3. For valuable recent studies of this topic, see António Lourenço Marques, ed., "As Mulheres e a Medicina Popular," *Cadernos da Cultura: Medicina na Beira Interior da Pre-História ao Século XX* 10 (1996); and Joao Ribeiro Nunes and Donizete Rodrigues, "Medicina popular: Curandeiros e plantas medicinais em Portugal," *Educación, salud y trabajo: Revista iberoamericana* 10 (1999): 91–98.

4. See Francisco Bethencourt, "Portugal: A Scrupulous Inquisition," in *Early Modern Witchcraft; Centres and Peripheries,* ed. Bengt Ankarloo and Gustav Henningsen, 403–422 (New York: Oxford Univ. Press, 1990); and Timothy D. Walker, *Doctors, Folk Medicine and the Inquisition: The Repression of Magical Healing in Portugal during the Enlightenment* (Leiden, The Netherlands: Brill Academic Publishers, 2005), 221–227.

5. See the discussion in Isabel M. R. Mendes Drumond Braga, "Medicina popular versus medicina universitaria en el Portugal de Juan V (1706–1750)," *Dynamis: Acta Hispanica ad Medicinae Scientiarumque Historiam Illustrandam* 22 (2002): 209–233; and Walker, *Doctors, Folk Medicine and the Inquisition*, 33–35, 395–403.

6. National Archives of Portugal (hereafter ANTT), Inquisition Tribunal of Évora, case number 6206.

7. Ibid.

8. Ibid.

9. Ibid.

10. See the tables of penalties provided in chapter 8 of Walker, *Doctors, Folk Medicine and the Inquisition*.

11. See Oswaldo Martins Ravagnani, "Subsídios para o estudo da medicina popular no Brasil," *Perspectivas: Revista de Ciências Sociais* 4 (1981): 65–73.

12. Three brief studies that consider this matter include Virginia Maria Almeida de Freitas, "Colonização Brasileira e Divisão entre Conhecimento Médico Científico e Medicina Popular," in *Proceedings of the XII Encontro Regional de História, APERJ*, 1–6 (Rio de Janeiro: XII Encontro Regional de História, APERJ, 2006); Lenina Lopes Soares Silva, "As 'misturas do humano com o divino' na medicina popular do Brasil colonial," *Mneme—Revista de Humanidades* 9, no. 24 (2008): 1–8; and Maria Regina Cotrim Guimarães, "Chernoviz and Popular

Medical Manuals in the Days of the Empire," *História, Ciências, Saúde-Manguinhos* 12, no. 2 (2005): 501–514.

13. ANTT, Inquisition Tribunal of Coimbra, case number 7199, and Inquisition of Évora, case number 10865.

14. A.J.R. Russell-Wood, "Patterns of Settlement in the Portuguese Empire (1400–1800)," in *Portuguese Oceanic Expansion, 1400–1800*, ed. Francisco Bethencourt and Diogo Ramado Curto, 172–179 (New York: Cambridge Univ. Press, 2007).

15. Walker, *Doctors, Folk Medicine and the Inquisition*, 80–82.

16. On this score, Paiva reports a larger ratio of men to women: 42 percent and 58 percent, respectively. See José Pedro Paiva, *Bruxaria e Superstição num País Sem "Caça às Bruxas": Portugal 1600–1774* (Lisbon: Editorial Notícias, 1997), 162.

17. Jaime Contreras, *El Santo Oficio de la Inquisición en Galicia, 1560–1700: poder, sociedad y cultura* (Madrid: Akal, 1982); see the discussion on pages 571–579 and 685–687.

18. Please refer to the data tables (sex, age, date of arrest, civil status) provided in chapter 8 of Walker, *Doctors, Folk Medicine and the Inquisition*.

19. See the demographics tables in chapter 8 of Walker, *Doctors, Folk Medicine and the Inquisition*. In *Bruxaria e Superstição*, Paiva supplies only marginally different figures for a substantially different chronological period: 61 percent women and 39 percent men. See Paiva, *Bruxaria e Superstição*, 162. Maria Luísa Braga, *A Inquisição em Portugal: primeira metade do séc. XVIII: O Inquisidor Geral D. Nuno da Cunha de Athayde e Mello* (Lisbon: Instituto Nacional de Investigação Científica, 1992), reports that she also found 41 percent men and 59 percent women among the magical crimes trials she studied, which all occurred between 1682 and 1750 (tables, 322–331).

20. Francisco Bethencourt, *O Imaginário da Magia: feiticeiras, saludadores e nigromantes no século XVI* (Lisbon: Universidade Nova, 1987), 177, 302–307.

21. Anwar G. Chejne, *Islam and the West: The Moriscos, A Cultural and Social History* (Albany: State Univ. of New York Press, 1983), 115–131. See also Bethencourt, *O Imaginário da Magia*, 182–183, and Paiva, *Bruxaria e Superstição*, 159–160.

22. Walker, *Doctors, Folk Medicine and the Inquisition*, 7–11, 31–35. Persecutions began anew in Portugal when *médicos* started to denounce popular healers to the Coimbra tribunal at the end of the seventeenth century.

23. Raymond Firth, "Reason and Unreason in Human Belief," in *Witchcraft and Sorcery*, ed. Max Marwick, 38–40 (New York: Penguin Books, 1990).

24. Ibid., 38.

25. For examples, see the following trials: ANTT, Inquisition Tribunal of Coimbra, cases 6217, 6306, 7186, 7229, 7346, 7809, 8093, 8574, and 8899; ANTT, Inquisition Tribunal of Évora, cases 516 and 372. See also the discussion concerning magical Portuguese healers in Paiva, *Bruxaria e Superstição*, 96–112.

26. Walker, *Doctors, Folk Medicine and the Inquisition*, 243–252.

27. Maria Benedita Araújo, *O Conhecimento Empírico dos Fármacos nos Séculos XVII e XVIII* (Lisbon: Edições Cosmos, 1992), 19–26.

28. See Maria Benedita Araújo, "A medicina popular e a magia no Sul de Portugal: Contribuição para o estudo das correntes mentais e espirituais (fins do século XVII a meados do século XVIII)," 3 vols. (Ph.D. diss., Faculdade de Letres da Universidade de Lisboa, 1988), 2:293–335.

29. For examples, see the following trials: ANTT, Inquisition Tribunal of Coimbra, cases

6217, 6306, 7186, 7229, 7346, 7809, 8093, 8574, and 8899; ANTT, Inquisition Tribunal of Évora, cases 516 and 372.

30. See Bethencourt, *O Imaginário da Magia*, 55–57.

31. ANTT, Inquisition Tribunal of Coimbra, case 7346: *Forão visto*, pages unnumbered.

32. "*Dos Saludadores*," ANTT: Santo Ofício Tomo XXVIII, Conselho Geral, Livro 269 (Lisbon: 1719), 15 (*recto* and *verso*).

33. ANTT, Inquisition Tribunal of Évora, case 516, 166.

34. Such was the case with popular healer Francisco Martins (ANTT, Inquisition Tribunal of Coimbra, case 33). According to the licensed physician who testified against him, this *saludador* claimed to cure by divine virtue, and "would accept no payment except what clients wanted to give."

35. Araújo, introduction to "A medicina popular," 1:1–18. See also Paiva, *Bruxaria e Superstição*, 60–62, and Bethencourt, *O Imaginário da Magia*, 55–57.

36. Teresa Veiga, *Cinco Séculos de Quotidiano: A vida em Lisboa do século XV aos nossas dias*, Collecção História, Nº 21 (Lisbon: Edições Cosmos, 1997), 121–135.

37. Teresa Ferreira Rodrigues, ed., *História da População Portuguesa* (Lisbon: Edições Afrontamento, 2008), 222.

38. Ibid., 201.

39. Ibid., 221. See also Mário Leston Bandeira, *Demografia e Modernidade: Família e Transição Demográfica em Portugal* (Lisbon: Imprensa Nacional/Casa da Moeda, 1996), 139–142.

40. Cited in José Pedro Paiva, *Práticas e Crenças Mágicas . . . na Diocese de Coimbra (1650–1740)* (Coimbra: Minerva, 1992), 81–82.

41. Ibid., 85.

42. Paiva, *Práticas e Crenças Mágicas*, 89. See also Maria Benedita Araújo, *Magia, Demónio e Força Mágica na Tradição Portuguesa (Séculos XVII e XVIII)* (Lisbon: Edições Cosmos, 1994), 15–30.

43. Paiva, *Práticas e Crenças Mágicas*, 93.

44. Ibid., 97.

45. For more on similar treatments used for different diseases, and on the treatment of inflamed skin in the Portuguese tradition, see Bethencourt, *O Imaginário da Magia*, 57–59.

46. Paiva, *Práticas e Crenças Mágicas*, 102–103.

47. The verb that Inquisition scribes used for both of these actions was *befejar*.

48. Bethencourt, *O Imaginário da Magia*, 64–66.

49. ANTT, Inquisition of Évora, case 457, cited in Bethencourt, *O Imaginário da Magia*, 64–65.

50. For the use of pennyroyal in Portuguese folk medicine, see Araújo, "A medicina popular," 3:206. For the use of pennyroyal in illicit abortions, see Varro E. Tyler, *The Honest Herbal: A Sensible Guide to the Use of Herbs and Related Remedies*, 3rd ed. (New York: Pharmaceutical Products Press, an imprint of Hayworth Press, 1993), 243–244.

51. *Guia de parteiras por preguntas e respostas*, unsigned, unpublished eighteenth-century Continental Portuguese manuscript in the inventory of Richard Ramer, rare book dealer, catalog eight (New York, 1996), 83.

52. Certain cases include ANTT, Inquisition Tribunal of Coimbra, cases 2362, 7199, and 7807; ANTT, Inquisition of Évora, cases 372, 4333, 5940, 6390, and 7759; ANTT, Inquisition Tribunal of Lisbon, cases 252, 437, 2355, and 4260.

53. Walker, *Doctors, Folk Medicine and the Inquisition*, 82–87.

54. ANTT, Inquisition Tribunal of Évora, case number 5940.
55. Ibid., fols. 63(v)-65(v), Inquisitors' final *acordão* (summary) of the trial. Apparently, de Carmo attributed the youngster's illness figuratively to invisible jumping fleas. Given that illnesses at this time were frequently blamed on an invasion of foreign entities—either spiritual or physical, representing either a real or imagined type of creature—that Inês de Carmo would have singled out fleas to blame should not be considered unusual. See also Araújo, *O Conhecimento Empírico*, 17–30.
56. ANTT, Inquisition Tribunal of Évora, case number 5940.
57. Ibid.
58. Timothy Walker, "Slaves, Free Blacks and the Inquisition in Early Modern Portugal: Race as a Factor in Magical Crimes Trials," *Bulletin of the Society for Spanish and Portuguese Historical Studies* 25, no. 2 (2000): 5–19.
59. ANTT, Inquisition Tribunal of Évora; case number 4333.
60. Ibid.
61. Ibid.
62. Ibid.
63. Paiva, *Práticas e Crenças Mágicas*, 159–160.
64. ANTT, Inquisition Tribunal of Coimbra, case 7199.
65. See Araújo, *O Conhecimento Empírico*, 39–54.
66. Cited in Paiva, *Práticas e Crenças Mágicas*, 106.
67. Ibid.
68. ANTT, Inquisition Tribunal of Coimbra, case 7199.
69. ANTT, Inquisition Tribunal of Coimbra, case 7807.
70. ANTT, Inquisition Tribunal of Coimbra, case 2362.
71. Walker, *Doctors, Folk Medicine and the Inquisition*, 6–9.
72. See Hugh Glenn Cagle's essay in this volume.

WORKS CITED

Primary Sources

NATIONAL ARCHIVES OF PORTUGAL (ANTT)

Inquisition Tribunal of Coimbra
Inquisition Tribunal of Évora
Inquisition Tribunal of Lisbon
Santo Oficio Tomo XXVIII, Conselho Geral, Livro 269

Secondary Sources

Almeida, Diádiney Helena de. "Um estudo das interações culturais entre curandeiros e medicos acadêmicos no Rio de Janeiro Oitocentista." In *Proceedings of the XIII Encontro de História, ANPUH*, 1–10. Rio de Janeiro, 2008.

Araújo, Maria Benedita. *Magia, Demónio e Força Mágica na Tradição Portuguesa (Séculos XVII e XVIII)*. Lisbon: Edições Cosmos, 1994.

———. "A medicina popular e a magia no Sul de Portugal: Contribuição para o estudo das correntes mentais e espirituais (fins do século XVII a meados do século XVIII)." 3 vols. Ph.D. diss., Faculdade de Letres da Universidade de Lisboa, 1988.

———. *O Conhecimento Empírico dos Fármacos nos Séculos XVII e XVIII*. Lisbon: Edições Cosmos, 1992.

Bandeira, Mário Leston. *Demografia e Modernidade: Família e Transição Demográfica em Portugal*. Lisbon: Imprensa Nacional/Casa da Moeda, 1996.

Bethencourt, Francisco. *O Imaginário da Magia: feiticeiras, saludadores e nigromantes no século XVI*. Lisbon: Universidade Nova, 1987.

———. "Portugal: A Scrupulous Inquisition." In *Early Modern Witchcraft: Centres and Peripheries*, edited by Bengt Ankarloo and Gustav Henningsen, 403–422. New York: Oxford Univ. Press, 1990.

Braga, Isabel M. R. Mendes Drumond. "Medicina popular versus medicina universitaria en el Portugal de Juan V (1706–1750)." *Dynamis: Acta Hispanica ad Medicinae Scientiarumque Historiam Illustrandam* 22 (2002): 209–233.

Braga, Maria Luísa. *A Inquisição em Portugal: primeira metade do séc. XVIII: O Inquisidor Geral D. Nuno da Cunha de Athayde e Mello*. Lisbon: Instituto Nacional de Investigação Científica, 1992.

Chejne, Anwar G. *Islam and the West: The Moriscos, A Cultural and Social History*. Albany: State Univ. of New York Press, 1983.

Contreras, Jaime. *El Santo Oficio de la Inquisición en Galicia, 1560–1700: poder, sociedad y cultura*. Madrid: Akal, 1982.

Firth, Raymond. "Reason and Unreason in Human Belief." In *Witchcraft and Sorcery*, edited by Max Marwick, 38–40. New York: Penguin Books, 1990.

Freitas, Virginia Maria Almeida de, "Colonização Brasileira e Divisão entre Conhecimento Médico Científico e Medicina Popular." In *Proceedings of the XII Encontro Regional de História, APERJ*, 1–6. Rio de Janeiro: XII Encontro Regional de História, APERJ, 2006.

Guimarães, Maria Regina Cotrim. "Chernoviz and Popular Medical Manuals in the Days of the Empire." *História, Ciências, Saúde-Manguinhos* 12, no. 2 (2005): 501–514.

Marques, António Lourenço, editor. "As Mulheres e a Medicina Popular." *Cadernos da Cultura: Medicina na Beira Interior da Pre-História ao Século XX*, no. 10 (1996).

Mott, Luiz. "Feiticeiros de Angola na Inquisição portuguesa." *Mneme—Revista de Humanidades* 11, no. 29 (2011): 1–22.

Nunes, Joao Ribeiro, and Donizete Rodrigues. "Medicina popular: Curandeiros e plantas medicinais em Portugal." *Educación, salud y trabajo: Revista iberoamericana* 10 (1999): 91–98.

Paiva, José Pedro. *Bruxaria e Superstição num País Sem "Caça às Bruxas": Portugal 1600–1774*. Lisbon: Editorial Notícias, 1997.

———. *Práticas e Crenças Mágicas . . . na Diocese de Coimbra (1650–1740)*. Coimbra: Minerva, 1992.

Ravagnani, Oswaldo Martins. "Subsídios para o estudo da medicina popular no Brasil." *Perspectivas: Revista de Ciências Sociais* 4 (1981): 65–73.

Rodrigues, Teresa Ferreira, ed. *História da População Portuguesa*. Lisbon: Edições Afrontamento, 2008.

Russell-Wood, A.J.R. "Patterns of Settlement in the Portuguese Empire (1400–1800)." In *Portuguese Oceanic Expansion, 1400–1800,* edited by Francisco Bethencourt and Diogo Ramado Curto, 161–196. New York: Cambridge Univ. Press, 2007.

Silva, Lenina Lopes Soares. "As 'misturas do humano com o divino' na medicina popular do Brasil colonial." *Mneme—Revista de Humanidades* 9, no. 24 (2008): 1–8.

Tyler, E. Varro. *The Honest Herbal: A Sensible Guide to the Use of Herbs and Related Remedies,* 3rd ed. New York: Pharmaceutical Products Press, an imprint of Hayworth Press, 1993.

Veiga, Teresa. *Cinco Séculos de Quotidiano: A vida em Lisboa do século XV aos nossas dias.* Collecção História, Nº 21. Lisbon: Edições Cosmos, 1997.

Walker, Timothy D. *Doctors, Folk Medicine and the Inquisition: The Repression of Magical Healing in Portugal during the Enlightenment.* Leiden, The Netherlands: Brill Academic Publishers, 2005.

———. "Slaves, Free Blacks and the Inquisition in Early Modern Portugal: Race as a Factor in Magical Crimes Trials." *Bulletin of the Society for Spanish and Portuguese Historical Studies* 25, no. 2 (2000): 5–19.

8

The Botany of Colonial Medicine
Gender, Authority, and Natural History in the Empires of Spain and Portugal

HUGH GLENN CAGLE

At the end of the sixteenth century, and nearing the end of his life, the Portuguese physician Cristovão da Costa composed a long and reflective essay, "In Appreciation of Women." He drew up a list of what he considered to be the most desirable qualities a woman could possess, chose five—chastity, honesty, resolve, silence, and fairness—and placed them in the title of his essay, where they could not possibly be overlooked by his readers.[1] A woman was at her best, Costa urged, when she embodied all of these. But that was no minor feat. The very "complexion" of women in general—that particular combination of the four humors that composed the female body—produced a distinctive feminine psychology. It predisposed women to mendacity, lust, and licentiousness, and it made them, as Costa put it, "prone to gossip." Quite simply: women spread misinformation. So strong was their impulse toward this peculiar "vice" that Costa thought it laudable that they should be able to quiet themselves at all. Women, he suggested, should strive to be "as with doors and locks upon their mouths."[2]

Here was the gendered architecture of an idealized intellectual order laid bare. And it was fitting that Costa should have written a defense of it. Among his peers, Cristovão da Costa was no chauvinist hack.[3] He was a prominent member of the Iberian medical establishment. A man with a keen interest in medicinal plants from the overseas world, Costa was both widely traveled and well published. As a young physician he had made his way across Portugal's empire. In the Castilian city of Burgos after his return, Costa published a popular Spanish translation of a Portuguese book on Asian *materia medica*.⁴ His work circulated among physicians and apothecaries throughout early modern Europe.⁵ He was a man of considerable experience and reputation. In Costa's view, the accumulation of knowledge about such things as the curative properties of plants required long and disciplined study. The articulation of truth claims concerning the natural world demanded integrity and focus. Women's uncontrollable appetites and predilection to lie made them distinctly ill-suited to the task. In this way, for Costa and his contemporaries, gender determined who could study the natural world and who was authorized to speak about it. And yet, as Costa well knew—indeed, what may have compelled the aged physician to write an essay on women in the first place— was that Iberian sailors, settlers, and explorers overseas found this intellectual order impossible to sustain.

Women of African and Amerindian descent were the healers of first resort for Iberians throughout the Atlantic.⁶ At the São Jorge da Mina castle—the Gold Coast redoubt that would become notorious as an embarkation point on the Middle Passage—Portuguese officials had begun to rely on the curative knowledge of enslaved African women as early as the 1480s. That care entailed the selection, cultivation, marketing, preparation, and ministration of medicinal recipes using plants from throughout the Guinea coast. Their pharmacopoeia included some of the region's 150 green, leafy comestibles—plants like hibiscus and baobab that were unfamiliar to most Iberian travelers. A few years later, in 1493, Alvaro de Caminha, the Portuguese governor of the island of São Tomé, reported that the survival of the Portuguese settlement there depended on the agricultural, culinary, and medicinal knowledge of enslaved African women.⁷ It was a consequence of the work of women like these that fruits, vegetables, and various *materia medica* were readily available in the markets that had sprung up along Africa's Atlantic littoral. Vendors—here again often African women—profited by selling to resident Portuguese and to the growing number of ships that visited western Africa's Atlantic ports. As slave ships traveled back and forth across the Atlantic, enslaved African women of the Senegambia region were often the ones who prepared the tamarind that made palatable the warm, foul water carried aboard ship—an additive believed to lend the water a curative quality. Sailors and slaves alike drank of it.⁸ African and African-descended women became prominent healers on the sugar plantations of Brazil's Atlantic littoral, from Recife in the north to Rio de Janeiro further south.⁹ In the far north, the regions of Grão Pará and Maranhão, where African slaves supplanted

Amerindian labor much more slowly, Native American women were especially prominent—and at times perhaps even dominant—players on the colonial medical stage. One such specialist lived along the Acará River in a small corner of Grão Pará. Sabina, an indigenous woman of unspecified extraction, had become so well known among the area's eighteenth-century smallholding cane farmers that the province's governor and military officers sought her out for treatments that involved tobacco and capsicum peppers, and the remains of various native birds, fish, and lizards.[10]

The pattern was repeated throughout the Iberian Atlantic. In Spain's American colonies, men looked to their Native American wives, slaves, and domestic servants to cultivate and collect medicinal plants and prepare the curative recipes that kept them, their families, their households, and even their finances in good health.[11] Facing frequent and debilitating fevers, the first Spanish settlers on Hispaniola took a keen interest in the medicinal plants wielded by Taino women. Encomendero Antonio Villasante learned from his wife, Catalina de Ayahibex—a converted *cacica* (female native ruler) from a Taino community near Santo Domingo—of the medicinal properties of a certain kind of tree. Calling the wood "balsam" after a well-known Old World medicinal, Villasante wasted no time in advertising the wood, hoping to profit from the remarkable natural knowledge of his wife.[12] At about the same time, the first generation of conquistadors began to settle on the American mainland, where through interaction, enslavement, and intermarriage they learned of the social, economic, and medicinal value of such plants as cacao and tobacco from Mesoamerican women.[13] Indeed, as Nuria Salazar Simarro and Sarah E. Owens discuss in their essay here, professed women in colonial Spanish American convents soon came to rely on Amerindian women to supply and administer these and many other New World medicinal plants. And in an episode that highlights the complex and thickly layered character of natural knowledge in the Atlantic basin, Gonzalo Fernández de Oviedo, the noted Spanish chronicler and naturalist, learned of the medicinal value of cacao from an enslaved African woman on the Mesoamerican coast, who in turn had learned of its applications from Amerindian healers she met while traveling in Oviedo's retinue.[14]

Women of African and Amerindian descent controlled access to, knowledge about, and the uses of sub-Saharan and New World nature. The prominent role of non-European and often non-Christian women in the production of new knowledge about the natural world was a defining feature of the practice of natural history in the Iberian Atlantic. And this served to distinguish colonial natural history from its metropolitan counterpart. The knowledge of these women not only found its way into the reports of officials like Caminha, the letters of merchants like Villasante, or the published accounts of men like Oviedo, it became the basis for the natural histories of a generation of Iberian writers—men like the Portuguese chronicler Duarte Pacheco Pereira and the Spanish physicians Francisco Hernández and Nicolás Monardes.[15] Throughout Europe and across the Iberian Atlantic, the first half of the sixteenth century was a transformative period in the writing of natural history, as voluminous new catalogs of an increasingly diverse array of flora and fauna came into circulation. Earlier accounts of nature usually took the form of commentaries on the centuries-old texts of ancient authors like Pliny and Dioscorides. But in the early and mid-sixteenth century, natural histories were based increasingly on reports and correspondence generated by expanding networks of friendship, patronage, and commerce. The study of nature was no longer restricted to university-trained physicians. Lawyers, merchants, craftsmen, and apothecaries like Costa now counted themselves as serious students of the natural world. And for many of these naturalists, the descriptions of plants and animals penned by their friends and colleagues possessed an authority that trumped that of the ancients.[16] Yet even as the ranks of those committed to the study of nature grew more diverse, and as definitions of authority began to change, the gendered division of intellectual labor grew more profound.

Cultures of natural history varied widely throughout early modern Europe.[17] But everywhere, gender influenced intellectual inquiry in fundamental and lasting ways. Among naturalists who traveled within—and who were often principally concerned with—the flora and fauna of Europe itself, women were rarely taken as credible contributors to the expanding corpus of natural knowledge and their work was often viewed with skepticism.[18] Within the field of medicine, professionalization increasingly circumscribed the curative work of women and eroded the authority they wielded on matters of reproduction, health, and healing. Costa's unflattering view of his female contemporaries was more than a reaction to events on the ground overseas. While it served to buttress his own claims to authority and expertise, his opinion also reflected the attitudes of a generation of physicians, apothecaries, and surgeons who used the increasingly centralized and standardized procedures of training, examination, and licensure to secure clinical primacy for themselves at the expense of other caregivers. The institutionalization of medical practice installed professional hierarchies that subordinated specialists such as midwives to those who, like Costa, were men with more formal certification.[19] Indeed, Timothy Walker's essay in this volume charts the process in considerable detail for both Portugal and Brazil, where the Inquisition played a significant role in reshaping medical practice. With the support of university-educated physicians, the Holy Office persecuted healers who lacked university training and a license and who relied on alternative forms of medicine.[20]

Across early modern Europe, the influence of gender ideologies was profound and pervasive. Its effects on the production, circulation, and exercise of natural knowledge went far beyond internecine struggles for professional recognition and clinical primacy. Gendered notions of authority and objectivity underwrote the development of a language, a conceptual apparatus, and an iconography that set women apart as targets of investigation. They linked femininity with passivity and with a peculiar susceptibility to mechanical manipulation and experimentation. So while the producers of knowledge were male and the pursuit of knowledge conceived of as a masculine endeavor, the objects of study—those things on which investigation and experimentation were performed—were conceived as feminine.[21] Gender shaped both what was known about nature and how far that knowledge circulated. An abiding concern for gendered notions of sexual propriety helped privilege sexual difference as a principal of plant and animal classifications.[22] Similar tensions shaped the development of the medical marketplace in metropolitan capitals and overseas colonies. Merchants' refusal to trade in such exotic *materia medica* as abortifacients and aphrodisiacs was rooted in a fear that these would give women too much control over their own fertility and over the passions of men.[23] Gendered modes of intellectual inquiry and investigative practice such as these supported the exclusion of women from the fields of professionalized medicine and natural history long after Spain and Portugal lost their empires.[24] In short: within early modern Europe, men produced authoritative accounts of nature. Women, though often the objects of investigation, generally did not.

Overseas, the intertwined endeavors of medicine and natural history participated in that ineluctable contradiction of colonialism: they depended on transgressing the very same ethnic divisions and gender hierarchies that colonial rule was meant to import, instill, and strengthen. The result was a litany of controversy. And Iberian policymakers, naturalists, and colonists throughout the Atlantic were all drawn into the fray.

In São Tomé, Governor Caminha faced criticism from the local bishop for allowing Portuguese Christians to consort all too freely with the non-Christian African women on whom they depended. In Brazil, increasingly over the seventeenth century and after, medical specialists like Sabina, be they of African or Amerindian decent, faced vitriolic attacks from university-trained physicians and frequent persecution at the hands of the Inquisition. In Santo Domingo, as Villasante advertised the remarkable medicinal value of American balsam, he took pains to explain to audiences on both sides of the Atlantic that his wife and erstwhile collaborator was a *Christian* woman. It was a reminder meant to bolster her credibility, buttress his authority, and mitigate suspicion that his knowledge might be the ill-begotten fruit of his participation in pagan rituals.[25]

These tensions and contradictions shaped the portrayal of women in reports and publications concerned with natural knowledge. Precisely because they were most vulnerable to suspicion and accusation, those writers best able to detail the intellectual work of countless women throughout the Atlantic were least inclined to do so. Portuguese and Spanish authors tended to diminish or deemphasize the role of women in certifying specific claims, to criticize them for being unforthcoming, or to occlude their contributions altogether. When Duarte Pacheco Pereira wrote his description of the overseas world of coastal West Africa, he never specified which aspects of local *materia medica* he learned from the women there. Contemporaries merely commented on the activities of local women and indicated that it was in the company of women that European travelers like Pereira ate, slept, and convalesced. When Villasante assured his correspondents in Iberia of the veracity of his claims about balsam, he insisted that he had not relied solely on his wife. He claimed instead that he had verified her assertions through his own trials of the drug.[26] And while Monardes—writing from Seville without ever having traveled to Spain's colonies—could offer vague acknowledgments of the superb skills of distant Mesoamerican women, his correspondents on the other side of the Atlantic could not. Lest they become targets of suspicion and accusation, their letters were often bereft of potentially incriminating details; they registered the knowledge of native peoples through sharp criticism.[27] To be sure, the same tendency toward criticism or outright omission characterized Iberian writing on the work of indigenous medical specialists more broadly—men or women—and the issue was not solely one of gender but of ethnicity too: Hernández, for example, was critical of Mesoamerican peoples generally for what he claimed was their unwillingness to share what they knew. But so many fleeting references to native expertise indicate that women were often the sources of what Iberian travelers learned about the natural world overseas.

The intellectual contributions of countless women to an expanding corpus of natural knowledge are traceable only through scattered letters, journal entries, Inquisition records, and a relative handful of publications. The full influence that any one of them might have had on the practice of colonial medicine and the production of natural knowledge remains—just as Iberian correspondents hoped it would—vague and uncertain. Yet the frequency with which Iberians came to depend on them and the accumulation of so many varied examples of their agricultural and curative insight suggest that these women were more important to colonial medical and scientific practice than the extant Atlantic sources make clear. They raise the possibility that at least some of these women were pivotal not just as native informants who relayed information but as specialists possessed of recognized intellectual expertise—women whose evident knowledge allowed them to participate in the certification of truth claims about both the contents of the natural world and the properties that specific plants possessed.

My aim here is to show that this was indeed the case and to provide a sketch of how it unfolded in one of Portugal's most important tropical colonies. The single most detailed source linking women, medicine, and natural history in the Iberian colonial world came not from the Atlantic but from the Indian Ocean basin—that other arena of intensive Iberian, and particularly Portuguese, activity. Indeed, from the point of view of Portuguese policymakers, merchants, traders, sailors, settlers, and missionaries, between the 1440s and early 1600s, the Atlantic was most important as a passage to Indian Ocean Asia. There, Portugal established an empire whose emphasis was on the control of maritime commerce rather than on extensive territorial conquest (as in the Spanish Americas) or on plantation agriculture (as in São Tomé or Brazil).[28] The political and administrative center of this maritime empire was Goa, a small port city on India's southwestern coast. This colonial enclave quickly became the favored destination for Portuguese migrants, the principal gateway for Asia-bound Catholic missionaries, and—what was unique in Portugal's empire—home to its own Inquisitorial tribunal.[29] In many ways, sixteenth-century Goa was the target of Portugal's earliest and most concerted attempt at full colonial control. Toward that end, for some three centuries Goa was also home to the only press permitted to operate anywhere in the Portuguese overseas world. Most of its publications were religious texts meant to buttress the work of the Jesuits and other Catholic missionaries in Asia. But in the spring of 1563 it printed the *Coloquios dos simples, e drogas e cousas medicinais da India* by Garcia de Orta, a university-trained physician with degrees from Salamanca and Alcalá de Henares.[30]

It was this Portuguese book on Asian *materia medica* that Cristovão da Costa would translate into Spanish and publish in Burgos.[31] Costa was not, however, the book's only translator. Rather, there were many and the *Coloquios* circulated in various guises—so much so that even if Orta's *Coloquios* was not a text *of* the Atlantic, it certainly had an influence *within* it. In the *Coloquios,* Orta sought to clarify with as much certainty as possible the identity of dozens of Asian plants, and to account for their origins, medicinal properties, and commercial value. It was a book meant for Portuguese residents in Goa as well as for readers in metropolitan Lisbon. That it was the very first secular text to be printed by the Portuguese in Goa was a testament to the importance that Orta's contemporaries attributed to the book and its aims. The more accurately the Portuguese could identify potent medicinal plants and prized commodities, the better prepared they were to stave off disease and buttress trade. The influence of the *Coloquios* stretched far beyond Goa. Copies arrived in Lisbon in the spring of 1564. And one of these soon found its way into the hands of the prominent Flemish naturalist Carolus Clusius, then visiting the Portuguese capital. Well before Costa's Spanish edition, Clusius translated Orta's book into Latin, making a number of substantial changes to it in the process. The Latin edition of the *Coloquios* went up for sale at the Frankfurt book fair of 1567. It brought Clusius widespread acclaim and made Orta into sixteenth-century Europe's most formidable authority on Asian flora.[32] Orta's book would help influence the investigation of nature throughout the European colonial world.

The Atlantic world was always part of a wider field of activity for every one of the major early modern European empire-builders. And as the endeavors of the Portuguese, Spanish, Dutch, English, and French intersected and overlapped in the Atlantic, they channeled exogenous human, material, and intellectual capital into and across their respective focal points of Atlantic activity.[33] As a consequence of the travels of Orta's book and the interconnectedness of the Atlantic, bits and pieces of the *Coloquios* informed the work of naturalists and physicians from Venice to Buenos Aires.[34] Certain knowledge of commodified Asian plants like cinnamon and ginger made possible their transplantation to and cultivation in Brazil. So rapid and prolific was this transfer that, fearing Brazilian suppliers might flood European markets, the Portuguese Crown put a stop to it with a series of decrees in the early sixteenth century. When the Dutch occupied northern Brazil, naturalists Willem Piso and Georg Marcgraf drew on the *Coloquios* in their investigations of Amazonian flora. And to revive the colonial economy in the wake of the Dutch invasion and the consequent devastation of Brazil's sugar sector, the Jesuit Antonio Vieira advocated in the 1680s the reintroduction, cultivation, and export of cinnamon—a proposal that depended on a Portuguese familiarity with cinnamon that emerged from the work of Orta and his contemporaries in South Asia a century earlier. In these and many other ways, Atlantic endeavors were underwritten by Indian Ocean encounters.[35]

In Goa, Garcia de Orta carried on much of his medical practice and most of his investigative work at home. This was, in part, a practical solution to the twin problems of botanical diversity and medical specialization that characterized Goa's medical marketplace. Orta's arrival to the subcontinent in 1534, his subsequent travels there, and his final settlement in Goa in 1538 brought him into contact with the enormity of South Asian *materia medica* and into conversation with specialists from throughout the region. In Gujarat, far to Goa's north, and in Bijapur, the kingdom that flanked Goa to the east, Orta met Muslim physicians, *hakims,* who practiced an Islamic form of humoral medicine. In and around Goa, Orta conversed with Hindu *vaidyas*—specialists in Indian Ayurveda. The pharmacopoeia they commanded included such diverse items of dispersed origins as salt from the Middle East, opium from Central Asia, rhubarb from China, cinnamon from Ceylon, and neem—a local medicine that was entirely unfamiliar to Western physicians. As a consequence of the tremendous range of medicinal plants, their widely dispersed origins, and their varied uses among specialists working within diverse medical traditions, any attempt to construct a single, comprehensive account of South Asian flora and its uses simply could not rely on a lone contact or on the knowledge of a single community of practitioners. Instead, it required the cultivation and maintenance of contacts with merchants, traders, and medical practitioners from throughout the subcontinent and beyond.

Orta's household was—like Goa itself—a point of convergence for these expansive commercial and intellectual networks. And it was at home and through the combined collection of both people and things that

Orta managed to identify medicinal plants and describe their properties. There, Orta could gather all manner of medicinal substances, compile the letters he received about them, and compare these reports with his own observations and with those of his frequent guests. In this way he set about resolving such quandaries as whether black and white pepper were the same and came from the same plant, or how to distinguish the true cinnamon from Ceylon from the rest that was grown elsewhere. His household bore all of the markers of a private and even cloistered scientific workshop. He had a library stocked with standard herbals and a few of the latest botanical texts from northern Europe. He also had a cabinet that contained such varied specimens of nature as amber, mace, and bezoar stones. That cabinet contained at least one locked compartment, where Orta kept valuable medicinal items, such as his prized rubies and diamonds.[36] The facade of the house stood like a sentinel over a garden that lay behind it. Enclosed from the outside by high walls, that hidden plot of land contained some of Goa's most commonly used medicinal plants.

Situated on Rua dos Namorados, two blocks from Goa's main thoroughfare, Rua Direita, Orta's household was often abuzz with the chatter of visitors.[37] It was within the protected confines of his home that Orta and the *vaidya* Malupa debated the origins of turbit and the uses that might be made of it when mixed with ginger.[38] Within these same walls, a Milanese lapidary named André visited briefly to arrange the sale of some of Orta's emeralds and, in the course of conversation, related what he had seen of a hunt for elephants and their ivory during a recent journey to Pegu.[39] Ivory, being of dubious medicinal worth but of substantial commercial value, was of particular interest to Orta, whose investigations were underwritten by commerce. And it was at home that one of Orta's younger colleagues and countrymen, the Portuguese physician Dimas Bosque, came to share word of a vermilion stone that—according to travelers—was more efficacious than even bezoar stones as an antidote to poison.[40]

Orta's assemblage of slaves and servants was still more diverse. In fact, it seems that in addition to collecting nature, Orta had a penchant for collecting people—and especially women—into his household. They came from Goa, from the expansive Deccan Plateau of the subcontinent's interior, and from Java far to the southeast and beyond the Strait of Malacca.[41] Standing between the patriarch Orta and his cabinet of medical curiosities, his numerous visitors, and his contingent of domestic workers was a domestic servant named Antonia. It was Antonia who haggled with Goa's apothecaries for the best locally available *materia medica*. She arranged and retrieved them from Orta's cabinet. She tended to the medicinal plants that grew in his garden. She retrieved and prepared the medicines that Orta prescribed. And she met the daily visitors at the door—patients and guests alike—and accompanied them into the protected confines of the household. It was also Antonia who introduced the newly recruited women to the daily goings-on of the Orta household. She oversaw their work and tended to them when they fell ill. In short, Antonia not only mediated Orta's exposure—and even access—to the unpredictable hubbub of Goa and its extensive pharmacopoeia, she ensured that the household remained an ordered, well-stocked, and cloistered arena for intellectual work. Her own networks, extending as they did across the wider world of Goa and throughout the otherwise insulated household, made all of that possible.

If the bits and pieces of nature that grew in his garden and populated Orta's cabinet are all reminders of the syncretic character of colonial material culture, medical practice, and natural inquiry, Antonia's relationship to Orta and her work among all of these artifacts is a reminder of the ethnic and gendered violence and of the stringent hierarchies that helped constitute European colonialism even in this early period and even in so tightly circumscribed an Iberian enclave as Portuguese Goa was in the middle of the sixteenth century. As in the Atlantic, intermarriage and cohabitation had been a common feature of Portuguese settlement in South Asia from the beginning.[42] With the arrival of increasing numbers of Portuguese, then of the Jesuits, and finally of the Inquisition came the expulsion or forcible conversion of Goa's Konkani-speaking Hindu communities. If they survived expulsion, uprooted Konkani villagers relocated to the region just beyond the pale of Portuguese settlement, where they rebuilt their temples and continued to worship much as they had before. The process of expulsion entailed the kidnapping of thousands of Konkani children. They were interned at missionary schools and compelled to learn the language, religion, and dress of metropolitan Portugal. Some converted. Others left. Many of those who eventually escaped found shelter as orphans in the newly established temples that ringed Goa's periphery. And converted or not, many orphaned Konkani children—and especially women—found work in the most intimate of all colonial spaces: the anterooms, corridors, kitchens, and bedrooms of Portuguese colonial households.[43] Antonia was almost certainly one of these women. Her

Christian name suggests that she grew up and was baptized in one of Goa's missionary schools.

As in the Iberian Atlantic, women who were often not even nominally Christian were healers of first resort. In Goa, Muslim Javanese women were particularly esteemed for their skill as midwives. These *daias* found work in institutions that were no less Catholic and no less critical to the production and reproduction of Portuguese colonialism than Goa's convents.[44] Taken together, Konkani villagers, Javanese *daias,* Hindu *vaidyas,* and Muslim *hakims* dominated the medical marketplace of Goa[45]— though as medical specialists, Goa's women far outnumbered the formally trained and male *hakims* and *vaidyas*. Over the course of a day in Goa, Hindu and Muslim men, women, and children moved back and forth across the domestic, geographic, and religious frontiers of the Portuguese colony.

When Cristovão da Costa left Lisbon in search of valuable medicinal plants, it was to Goa that he came. And when he worried about what he viewed as the pernicious influence of women in the production and circulation of natural knowledge, it was Goa and women like Antonia that he had in mind. In the colony, as in metropolitan Portugal, Costa was not alone. Fears of women ran high in Goa. The anxiety produced by Portuguese dependence on the principal objects of their ideological work helped generate vicious rumors about Goan women. One account told of a man whose longstanding bout with dysentery drove his exasperated wife to murder. Finding her husband's illness utterly abhorrent, she resolved to poison him, for which task she secretly acquired a small quantity of finely crushed diamonds. Her hope was that by mixing them with his food their toxic virtue would slowly drain him of life and put an end to their shared misery.[46] Another tale related the thievery exacted upon one unwed but wealthy Paula de Andrade. Her assailant was a young woman employed in Andrade's household. The servant had conspired with a lover to poison Andrade with the drug *datura*—common in Goa's streets—in order to steal as many of the matron's jewels as the two could carry in their escape.[47] Similar rumors of the use of poison in high diplomacy, low politics, and domestic intrigue were pervasive in Goa. Orta included these in his book—cautionary tales of the ways in which the expertise of Goan women threatened to upend the colonial social order.

Goa's hierarchy of medicinal knowledge was another matter. The example of Antonia demonstrates how the violence and compromise inherent in colonialism and colonial science combined to give individual women in Iberian colonies a distinctive hand in scientific transformation. Antonia was responsible for precise and quite detailed information about the parts and medicinal properties of some South Asian plants, as well as how medicines made from them could be administered or prepared and stored for future use. In the eighth chapter of the *Coloquios,* titled "Do bangue" ("On cannabis"), Antonia articulated the explanation of the plant, its parts, and the essential information required if European doctors wished to acquire it from a druggist in Goa: "this is one of the small trees, and you can see here the seeds that it yields, and you can see as well the readymade preparation that is sold by apothecaries."[48] Antonia later explained the differences between the varieties of *açafram da terra* ("saffron of the land") available in Goa—the fresh (*verde*) and the preserved, along with a description of its roots—which grew abundantly on the Malabar coast and were an invaluable treatment for cholera.[49]

While these exchanges explicitly portrayed Antonia as an authority on certain aspects of the region's *materia medica,* in a number of cases her influence must be inferred. In chapter 36, Orta explained that watermelons "are very good . . . for all kinds of choleric fevers, burning of the liver and kidneys . . . [although they] provoke a great deal of urine, and those [among the local inhabitants] who are healthy have the custom of eating them [about] four hours after lunch, at the hottest part of the day." Concerning the seeds, Orta added that they "elicit a feeling of sleepiness."[50] Antonia was not present during the discussion but, when Orta called for her to bring a slice of watermelon for a guest to taste, Antonia reminded Orta that watermelons "were not simply to eat," but that if Orta and his guest were to try the fruit, two varieties were available, one from Chaul and another, which, she added, was tastier and which came from Dabul—both small port cities to Goa's north.[51] Antonia thus had the authority to intervene in the physicians' exchanges and could expand the conversation into areas she deemed appropriate: it was Antonia who knew the varied provenance of the fruit in question and was compelled to remind her interlocutors of its many uses.

What Orta knew of the *mungo* (mung bean) and of tamarind was also due to his relationship with Antonia. Orta explained that throughout the subcontinent, from Gujarat to the Deccan, the small, round, green mung beans were potent remedies for various fevers. But they had to be administered properly, which usually meant they were to be taken only after a ten- to twenty-day period of fasting. Taken as a soup, Orta explained, *mungo* was particularly effective. Precisely how much of this Orta learned from Antonia is uncertain, but it was Antonia who knew that in order to render the mung beans effective, their hard outer shell had to be removed, and she, not Orta, knew how to produce the soup that Orta recommended to his readers.[52] The chapter on tamarind presented a similar situation. Orta noted that tamarind was a powerful medicine and was widely used in and around Goa. Native residents combined it with coconut oil and took it, according to Orta, as a purgative and digestive. Tamarind was a common ingredient in medicinal syrups and dentifrices as well. But when Orta noted of tamarind that, however effective it might be against choleric fevers, its major drawback was that it simply did not last long, Antonia provided the solution: she preserved it in salt. That was precisely the way that Antonia presented it to Orta. When, moreover, Orta said that he had "had tamarinds distilled," it was probably Antonia and the women she supervised who had actually carried out the procedure.[53]

Orta might readily have dismissed Antonia and all of his other South Asian collaborators as lacking proper university medical training, or as being inclined to deception, or both—and as therefore ill-equipped and insufficiently disciplined to offer credible accounts of the natural world, its contents, and their respective properties. And he might have been particularly inclined—as his metropolitan contemporaries were—to distinguish between his own university training and the culinary-cum-curative knowledge so effectively wielded by the women like Antonia whom he met in South Asia. But Portuguese throughout Goa relied on them; their expertise was never really in question. As with his other correspondents in Goa and beyond, Orta took Antonia's accounts seriously. They carried at least as much authority as those of any of the other individuals who participated in the making of the knowledge that found its way into Orta's book.

In the colonial world, Iberian colonists could never relegate women like Antonia or any of their other collaborators to the diminutive role of mere assistant or "informant." Even within metropolitan Europe itself at this time, the medicine of the universities was forced to jostle for adherents alongside of alternative approaches to sickness, health, and healing. It had no monopoly on authority and expertise. These conditions were all exacerbated in Iberia's colonies. Western medical and intellectual primacy was impossible. A close look at Orta's interactions with Antonia throws into sharp relief just how tenuous the colonizing endeavor could be, how very important non-Christian, non-European women were to scientific change, and reveals the profound degree to which colonial science was a creative compromise rather than the unproblematic projection of European procedures overseas. Goa—and by extension São Tomé, Bahia, Grão Pará, Santo Domingo, and Mexico City—was not London, Leiden, Lisbon, or Seville. Antonia's example suggests how very important it is for students of early modern colonialism and of science in the overseas world to attend to the process by which professional and intellectual distinctions were installed. They were part and parcel of the pursuit of cultural and intellectual hegemony; they helped constitute colonialism itself. Three years before the *Coloquios* went to press the Portuguese Inquisition arrived in Goa. Church officials began increasingly to persecute those members of the Portuguese community whom they felt affiliated too closely with Goa's Hindu physicians and apothecaries. Later, Goa's municipal council would enact laws that restricted the movement of *vaidyas* and native apothecaries.[54] The *Coloquios* is a window into a medical world in which professional and intellectual hierarchies had yet to correspond to the idealized order that Iberian colonizers envisioned and soon sought to construct.

NOTES

I would like to thank Michael Adas, Antonio Barrera-Osorio, Jodi Bilinkoff, James Delbourgo, Iona McCleery, Isabel dos Guimarães Sá, Timothy Walker, and two anonymous readers for their comments on ideas presented here. I would like to thank as well the Andrew W. Mellon Foundation, the Fundação Luso-Americano, and the Department of History at Rutgers University, each of which helped to fund the research on which this essay is based.

1. The treaty was published posthumously in Spanish by a printer in Venice. Cristovão da Costa [Cristoval Acosta], *Tratado en loor de las mvgeres. Y dela Castidad, Onestidad, Constancia, Silencio, y Iusticia: Con otras muchas particularidades, y varias Historias* (Venice: Giacomo Cornetti, 1592). Note the Hispanicized spelling of Costa's name. In the text I have used the Portuguese form under which the essay is cataloged at the Biblioteca Nacional de Portugal.

2. Ibid., 110–110v.

3. His views on women were entirely in line with those elaborated by Susan Migden Socolow, *The Women of Colonial Latin America* (New York: Cambridge Univ. Press, 2000), 5–15.

4. Cristovão da Costa [Cristoval Acosta], *Tractado Delas Drogas, y medicinas delas Indias Orientales, con sus Plantas debuxadas al bivo por Christoval Acosta medico y cirujano que las vio ocularmente* (Burgos: Martin de Victoria, 1578).

5. Joaquín Olmedilla y Puig, *Estudio histórico de la vida y escritos del sabio médico, botánico, y escritor del siglo XVI Cristóbal Acosta* (Madrid: Imprenta de los Hijos de M. G. Hernández, 1899).

6. In addition to the examples I have chosen here, see Daniela Bleichmar, Paula de Vos,

Kristin Huffine, and Kevin Sheehan, eds., *Science in the Spanish and Portuguese Empires, 1500–1800* (Stanford: Stanford Univ. Press, 2008). The same can be said for other European groups as well. See, for example, Karen Ordahl Kupperman, *Indians and English: Facing Off in North America* (Ithaca: Cornell Univ. Press, 2000), especially 133–135; Londa Schiebinger, *Plants and Empire: Colonial Bioprospecting in the Atlantic World* (Cambridge: Harvard Univ. Press, 2004); Susan Scott Parrish, *American Curiosity: Cultures of Natural History in the Colonial British Atlantic World* (Chapel Hill: Univ. of North Carolina Press, 2006), 259–306; and Harold J. Cook, *Matters of Exchange: Commerce, Medicine, and Science in the Dutch Golden Age* (New Haven: Yale Univ. Press, 2007), 203–205.

7. Ivana Elbl, "'Men without Wives': Sexual Arrangements in the Early Portuguese Expansion in West Africa," in *Desire and Discipline: Sex and Sexuality in the Premodern West,* ed. Jacqueline Murray and Konrad Eisenbichler, especially 72, 75 (Toronto: Univ. of Toronto Press, 1996); and James H. Sweet, "Mutual Misunderstandings: Gesture, Gender and Healing in the African Portuguese World," *Past and Present* 203 (2009, Supplement 4): 128–143.

8. Judith A. Carney and Richard Nicholas Rosomoff, *In the Shadow of Slavery: Africa's Botanical Legacy in the Atlantic World* (Berkeley: Univ. of California Press, 2009), 59–60, 69–70, 72–79, and 177–178.

9. Mary C. Karasch, *Slave Life in Rio de Janeiro, 1808–1850* (Princeton: Princeton Univ. Press, 1987); James H. Sweet, *Recreating Africa: Culture, Kinship, and Religion in the African-Portuguese World, 1441–1770* (Chapel Hill: Univ. of North Carolina Press, 2003), 154–160; Carney and Rosomoff, *In the Shadow of Slavery*, 182; and the essay by Timothy Walker in this volume.

10. Laura de Mello e Souza, *The Devil and the Land of the Holy Cross: Witchcraft, Slavery, and Popular Religion in Colonial Brazil,* trans. Diane Grosklaus Whitty (Austin: Univ. of Texas Press, 2003), 104–106.

11. See most recently Rebecca Earle, "'If You Eat Their Food . . .': Diets and Bodies in Early Colonial Spanish America," *American Historical Review* 3 (2010): 688–713.

12. Antonio Barrera-Osorio, "Local Herbs, Global Medicines: Commerce, Knowledge, and Commodities in Spanish America," in *Merchants and Marvels: Commerce, Science, and Art in Early Modern Europe,* ed. Pamela H. Smith and Paula Findlen, 166–167 (New York: Routledge, 2002).

13. Marcy Norton, *Sacred Gifts, Profane Pleasures: A History of Tobacco and Chocolate in the Atlantic World* (Ithaca: Cornell Univ. Press, 2008), 44–140.

14. Ibid., 59–60.

15. Duarte Pacheco Pereira, *Esmeraldo de Situ Orbis* (Lisbon: Typographia Universal, 1905). On his Spanish counterparts, see Norton, *Sacred Gifts, Profane Pleasures,* 122–129; and Daniela Bleichmar, "Books, Bodies, Fields: Sixteenth-Century Transatlantic Encounters with New World *Materia Medica*," in *Colonial Botany: Science, Commerce, and Politics in the Early Modern World,* ed. Londa Schiebinger and Claudia Swan, 83–99 (Philadelphia: Univ. of Pennsylvania Press, 2005).

16. Brian W. Ogilvie, *The Science of Describing: Natural History in Renaissance Europe* (Chicago: Univ. of Chicago Press, 2006); Antonio Barrera-Osorio, *Experiencing Nature: The Spanish American Empire and the Early Scientific Revolution* (Austin: Univ. of Texas Press, 2006); Francisco Contente Domingues, "Science and Technology in Portuguese Navigation: The Idea of Experience in the Sixteenth Century," in *Portuguese Oceanic Expansion, 1400–1800,* ed. Francisco Bethencourt and Diogo Ramada Curto, 460–479 (New York: Cambridge Univ. Press, 2007).

17. Nick Jardine, J. A. Secord, and E. C. Spary, eds., *Cultures of Natural History* (New York: Cambridge Univ. Press, 1996).

18. That such was the case for London is evident in Deborah E. Harkness, *The Jewel House: Elizabethan London and the Scientific Revolution* (New Haven: Yale Univ. Press, 2007); and Deborah E. Harkness, "Managing an Experimental Household: The Dees of Mortlake and the Practice of Natural Philosophy," *Isis* 88 (1997): 247-262. The same was true for northern Europe as portrayed by Ogilvie, *Science of Describing,* especially page 55, though the absence of women as naturalists is apparent throughout. There are exceptions, especially in the next century. Londa Schiebinger has covered women's pursuit of intellectual inclusion, their influence, and the shifting boundaries their male peers sought to construct in *The Mind Has No Sex? Women in the Origins of Modern Science* (Cambridge: Harvard Univ. Press, 1989). On the well-known example of Maria Sibylla Merian, see Natalie Zemon Davis, *Women on the Margins: Three Seventeenth Century Lives* (Cambridge: Harvard Univ. Press, 1995), 140-202; Schiebinger, *The Mind Has No Sex?,* 68-78; and Schiebinger, *Plants and Empire,* 107-113.

19. Mary Fissell reviews the historiography in "Introduction: Women, Health, and Healing in Early Modern Europe," *Bulletin of the History of Medicine* 82 (2008): 1-17. In addition to her piece and the other essays in the volume, see most recently Sharon Strocchia, "The Nun Apothecaries of Renaissance Florence: Marketing Medicines in the Convent," *Renaissance Studies* 25 (2011): 627-647.

20. Timothy D. Walker makes a strong case for Portugal in *Doctors, Folk Medicine and the Inquisition: The Repression of Magical Healing in Portugal During the Enlightenment* (Leiden: Brill, 2005).

21. Carolyn Merchant, *The Death of Nature: Women, Ecology, and the Scientific Revolution* (New York: Harper and Row, 1980); Evelyn Fox Keller, *Reflections on Gender and Science* (New Haven: Yale Univ. Press, 1985).

22. Londa Schiebinger, *Nature's Body: Gender in the Making of Modern Science* (New Brunswick, N.J.: Rutgers Univ. Press, 2004), 11-114.

23. Schiebinger, *Plants and Empire,* 226-241. I develop this idea for Portuguese Goa in Hugh Glenn Cagle, "Dead Reckonings: Disease and the Natural Sciences in Portuguese Asia and the Atlantic, 1450-1650" (Ph.D. diss., Rutgers University, 2011), 132-140.

24. Sweet, "Mutual Misunderstandings," illustrates just how pivotal gender could be in defining medical authority in the Portuguese Atlantic.

25. Elbl, "Men without Wives," 75; Sweet, *Recreating Africa,* 144-152, 154-160; Souza, *The Devil and the Land of the Holy Cross,* 106; Barrera-Osorio, "Local Herbs, Global Medicines," 167-168.

26. Elbl, "Men without Wives," 66-67; Barrera-Osorio, "Local Herbs, Global Medicines," 167-169.

27. Bleichmar, "Books, Bodies, Fields," 92-99, especially 95-96.

28. For a discussion of these differences, see Sanjay Subrahmanyam, "Holding the World in Balance: The Connected Histories of the Iberian Overseas Empires, 1500-1640," *American Historical Review* 5 (2007): 1359-1385; and Michael Adas and Hugh Glenn Cagle, "Age of Settlement and Colonization, 1500-1900," in *The Ashgate Companion to Modern Imperial Histories,* ed. Philippa Levine and John Marriott (Burlington, Vt.: Ashgate, 2012).

29. M. N. Pearson, *The Portuguese in India* (New York: Cambridge Univ. Press, 1987), 116-130.

30. Here I work from Garcia da Orta, *Coloquios dos simples e drogas da India*, 2 vols., ed. Conde de Ficalho (Lisbon: Imprensa Nacional, 1895) (cited hereafter as *Coloquios*). The original was published as Garcia d'Orta, *Coloquios dos simples, e drogas e cousas medicinais da India, e assi dalguas frutas achadas nella onde se tratam alguas cousas tocantes amediçina, pratica, e outras cousas boas, pera saber cõpostos pello Doutor garcia dorta: fisico del Rey nosso senhor, vistos pello muyto Reverendo senhor, ho liçenciado Alexo diaz falcam desenbargador da casa da supricacçã inquisidor nestas partes* (Goa: Joannes de Endem, 1563). Orta's name has been spelled several different ways. In the text, I follow that currently used by the Biblioteca Nacional de Portugal: "Garcia de Orta."

31. Costa, *Tractado Delas Drogas*.

32. Ogilvie, *The Science of Describing*, 244–245; Cook, *Matters of Exchange*, 96–99, 191–225.

33. The Atlantic framework itself has provoked a great deal of discussion and debate, much of which is represented among the contributions to Jack P. Greene and Philip D. Morgan, eds., *Atlantic History: A Critical Appraisal* (New York: Oxford Univ. Press, 2009).

34. Through Clusius's editions and publications based on them, Orta's book became part of a broader archive of the overseas natural world—the Indies, both East and West. That was precisely how Clusius conceived of Orta's work. Clusius's 1567 Antwerp original went through several editions—1573, 1574, 1579, and 1582. One of these was republished by the printers Viduus and Joannis Moretus in 1593. The seventh volume of Clusius's *Exoticorum libri decem* (Antwerp, 1605) also contains a version of the *Coloquios*. For a detailed discussion of Orta's book and its travels, see Maximiano Lemos, *Archivos de Historia da Medicina Portuguesa*, 2 vols. (Lisbon, 1887–1888), 2:90–92, and Augusto da Silva Carvalho, *Garcia d'Orta* (Coimbra: Imprensa da Universidade, 1934), 130–133.

35. A.J.R. Russell-Wood, *The Portuguese Empire in Asia, 1415–1808: A World on the Move* (Baltimore: Johns Hopkins Univ. Press, 1992), 152–156; Cook, *Matters of Exchange*, 191–225; and Daniela Bleichmar, "Atlantic Competitions: Botany in the Eighteenth-Century Spanish Empire," in *Science and Empire in the Atlantic World*, ed. James Delbourgo and Nicholas Dew, 230–232 (New York: Routledge, 2008).

36. Orta, *Coloquios*, 2:203. Orta kept these and other rare and precious stones on hand partly in order to evaluate commonplace claims about their medicinal value. The Spanish physician Andrés Laguna, for example, claimed that the humoral properties of diamonds naturally drew them into the walls of the stomach and bowels, where, because of their hardness, they would bore through these and other internal organs. Orta rejected such claims citing, examples of people he had seen swallow diamonds only to painlessly expel them later. He added that certain South Asian medical specialists used diamonds to break up kidney stones, though he did not say precisely how this was possible. For Orta, their dubious medical utility meant that precious stones were valuable primarily because of the price they could fetch on Goa's market. (Orta, *Coloquios*, 2:195–197.)

37. Carvalho, *Garcia d'Orta*, 31.

38. Orta, *Coloquios*, 2:332.

39. Ibid., 2:311–313.

40. Ibid., 2:382–384. On Bosque, see Jaime Walter, "Dimas Bosque, físico-mor da Índia e as Sereias," *Studia* 12 (1963): 261–271.

41. Orta, *Coloquios*, 2:139, 331–332.

42. On state concern with the domestic sphere in Goa, see Timothy J. Coates, *Convicts*

and Orphans: Forced and State-Sponsored Colonizers in the Portuguese Empire, 1550–1755 (Stanford: Stanford Univ. Press, 2001), 120–177; and Pearson, *The Portuguese in India,* 100–102.

43. Pearson, *The Portuguese in India,* 117–119; Paul Axelrod and Michelle A. Fuerch, "Flight of the Deities: Hindu Resistance in Portuguese Goa," *Modern Asian Studies* 30 (1996): 387–421, reconstruct this history through a combination of archival sources and oral history.

44. On the centrality of convents for Iberian colonial rule, compare Coates, *Convicts and Orphans,* 120–177, and Kathryn Burns, *Colonial Habits: Convents and the Spiritual Economy of Cuzco, Peru* (Durham: Duke Univ. Press, 1999).

45. João Manuel Pacheco de Figueiredo, "Goa Pré-Portuguesa," *Studia* 13/14 (1964): 157–180.

46. Orta, *Coloquios,* 2:197. The diamonds failed to do the trick and the ailing man succumbed to death only a long time later.

47. Orta, *Coloquios,* 1:295–296.

48. Ibid., 1:95.

49. Ibid., 1:280.

50. Orta, *Coloquios,* 2:133–134.

51. Ibid., 2:134.

52. Ibid., 2:139–140, 142–143.

53. Ibid., 2:321.

54. Cagle, "Dead Reckonings," 117–132.

WORKS CITED

Adas, Michael, and Hugh Glenn Cagle. "Age of Settlement and Colonization, 1500–1900." In *The Ashgate Research Companion to Modern Imperial Histories,* edited by Philippa Levine and John Marriott. Burlington, Vt.: Ashgate, 2012.

Axelrod, Paul, and Michelle A. Fuerch. "Flight of the Deities: Hindu Resistance in Portuguese Goa." *Modern Asian Studies* 30 (1996): 387–421.

Barrera-Osorio, Antonio. *Experiencing Nature: The Spanish American Empire and the Early Scientific Revolution.* Austin: Univ. of Texas Press, 2006.

———. "Local Herbs, Global Medicines: Commerce, Knowledge, and Commodities in Spanish America." In *Merchants and Marvels: Commerce, Science, and Art in Early Modern Europe,* edited by Pamela H. Smith and Paula Findlen, 163–181. New York: Routledge, 2002.

Bleichmar, Daniela. "Atlantic Competitions: Botany in the Eighteenth-Century Spanish Empire." In *Science and Empire in the Atlantic World,* edited by James Delbourgo and Nicholas Dew, 225–252. New York: Routledge, 2008.

———. "Books, Bodies, Fields: Sixteenth-Century Transatlantic Encounters with New World *Materia Medica.*" In *Colonial Botany: Science, Commerce, and Politics in the Early Modern World,* edited by Londa Schiebinger and Claudia Swan, 83–99. Philadelphia: Univ. of Pennsylvania Press, 2005.

Bleichmar, Daniela, Paula de Vos, Kristin Huffine, and Kevin Sheehan, eds. *Sci-*

ence in the Spanish and Portuguese Empires, 1500–1800. Stanford: Stanford Univ. Press, 2008.

Burns, Kathryn. *Colonial Habits: Convents and the Spiritual Economy of Cuzco, Peru.* Durham: Duke Univ. Press, 1999.

Cagle, Hugh Glenn. "Dead Reckonings: Disease and the Natural Sciences in Portuguese Asia and the Atlantic, 1450–1650." Ph.D. diss., Rutgers University, 2011.

Carney, Judith A., and Richard Nicholas Rosomoff, *In the Shadow of Slavery: Africa's Botanical Legacy in the Atlantic World.* Berkeley: Univ. of California Press, 2009.

Carvalho, Augusto da Silva. *Garcia d'Orta.* Coimbra: Imprensa da Universidade, 1934.

Clusius, Carolus. *Exoticorum libri decem: Quibus Animalium, Plantarum, Aromatum, aliorumque peregrinorum Fructuum historiae describuntur.* [Leiden]: Ex Officina Plantiniana Raphelengii, 1605.

Coates, Timothy J. *Convicts and Orphans: Forced and State-Sponsored Colonizers in the Portuguese Empire, 1550–1755.* Stanford: Stanford Univ. Press, 2001.

Cook, Harold J. *Matters of Exchange: Commerce, Medicine, and Science in the Dutch Golden Age.* New Haven: Yale Univ. Press, 2007.

Costa, Cristovão da [Cristoval Acosta]. *Tractado Delas Drogas, y medicinas delas Indias Orientales, con sus Plantas debuxadas al bivo por Christoval Acosta medico y cirujano que las vio ocularmente.* Burgos: Martin de Victoria, 1578.

———. *Tratado en loor de las mvgeres. Y dela Castidad, Onestidad, Constancia, Silencio, y Iusticia: Con otras muchas particularidades, y varias Historias.* Venice: Giacomo Cornetti, 1592.

Davis, Natalie Zemon. *Women on the Margins: Three Seventeenth-Century Lives.* Cambridge: Harvard Univ. Press, 1995.

Domingues, Francisco Contente. "Science and Technology in Portuguese Navigation: The Idea of Experience in the Sixteenth Century." In *Portuguese Oceanic Expansion, 1400–1800,* edited by Francisco Bethencourt and Diogo Ramada Curto, 460–479. New York: Cambridge Univ. Press, 2007.

Earle, Rebecca. "'If You Eat Their Food . . .': Diets and Bodies in Early Colonial Spanish America." *American Historical Review* 3 (2010): 688–713.

Elbl, Ivana. "'Men without Wives': Sexual Arrangements in the Early Portuguese Expansion in West Africa." In *Desire and Discipline: Sex and Sexuality in the Premodern West,* edited by Jacqueline Murray and Konrad Eisenbichler, 61–86. Toronto: Univ. of Toronto Press, 1996.

Figueiredo, João Manuel Pacheco de. "Goa Pré-Portuguesa." *Studia* 13/14 (1964): 105–225.

Fissell, Mary. "Introduction: Women, Health, and Healing in Early Modern Europe." *Bulletin of the History of Medicine* 82 (2008): 1–17.

Greene, Jack P., and Philip D. Morgan, editors. *Atlantic History: A Critical Appraisal*. New York: Oxford Univ. Press, 2009.

Harkness, Deborah E. *The Jewel House: Elizabethan London and the Scientific Revolution*. New Haven: Yale Univ. Press, 2007.

———. "Managing an Experimental Household: The Dees of Mortlake and the Practice of Natural Philosophy." *Isis* 88 (1997): 247–262.

Jardine, Nick, J. A. Secord, and E. C. Spary, eds. *Cultures of Natural History*. New York: Cambridge Univ. Press, 1996.

Karasch, Mary C. *Slave Life in Rio de Janeiro, 1808–1850*. Princeton: Princeton Univ. Press, 1987.

Keller, Evelyn Fox. *Reflections on Gender and Science*. New Haven: Yale Univ. Press, 1985.

Kupperman, Karen Ordahl. *Indians and English: Facing Off in North America*. Ithaca: Cornell Univ. Press, 2000.

Lemos, Maximiano. *Archivos de Historia da Medicina Portuguesa*. 2 vols. Lisbon, 1887–1888.

Merchant, Carolyn. *The Death of Nature: Women, Ecology, and the Scientific Revolution*. New York: Harper and Row, 1980.

Norton, Marcy. *Sacred Gifts, Profane Pleasures: A History of Tobacco and Chocolate in the Atlantic World*. Ithaca: Cornell Univ. Press, 2008.

Ogilvie, Brian W. *The Science of Describing: Natural History in Renaissance Europe*. Chicago: Univ. of Chicago Press, 2006.

Olmedilla y Puig, Joaquín. *Estudio histórico de la vida y escritos del sabio médico, botánico, y escritor del siglo XVI Cristóbal Acosta*. Madrid: Imprenta de los Hijos de M. G. Hernández, 1899.

Orta, Garcia de [Garcia da]. *Coloquios dos simples e drogas da India*. 2 vols. Edited by Conde de Ficalho. Lisbon: Imprensa Nacional, 1895.

Parrish, Susan Scott. *American Curiosity: Cultures of Natural History in the Colonial British Atlantic World*. Chapel Hill: Univ. of North Carolina Press, 2006.

Pearson, M[ichael]. N. *The Portuguese in India*. New York: Cambridge Univ. Press, 1987.

Pereira, Duarte Pacheco. *Esmeraldo de Situ Orbis*. Lisbon: Typographia Universal, 1905.

Russell-Wood, A.J.R. *The Portuguese Empire in Asia, 1415–1808: A World on the Move*. Baltimore: Johns Hopkins Univ. Press, 1992.

Schiebinger, Londa. *The Mind Has No Sex? Women in the Origins of Modern Science*. Cambridge: Harvard Univ. Press, 1989.

———. *Nature's Body: Gender in the Making of Modern Science*. New Brunswick, N.J.: Rutgers Univ. Press, 2004.

———. *Plants and Empire: Colonial Bioprospecting in the Atlantic World*. Cambridge: Harvard Univ. Press, 2004.

Socolow, Susan Migden. *The Women of Colonial Latin America*. New York: Cambridge Univ. Press, 2000.
Souza, Laura de Mello e. *The Devil and the Land of the Holy Cross: Witchcraft, Slavery, and Popular Religion in Colonial Brazil*. Translated by Diane Grosklaus Whitty. Austin: Univ. of Texas Press, 2003.
Strocchia, Sharon. "The Nun Apothecaries of Renaissance Florence: Marketing Medicines in the Convent." *Renaissance Studies* 25 (2011): 627–647.
Subrahmanyam, Sanjay. "Holding the World in Balance: The Connected Histories of the Iberian Overseas Empires, 1500–1640." *American Historical Review* 5 (2007): 1359–1385.
Sweet, James H. "Mutual Misunderstandings: Gesture, Gender and Healing in the African Portuguese World." *Past and Present* 203 (2009, Supplement 4): 128–143.
——. *Recreating Africa: Culture, Kinship, and Religion in the African-Portuguese World, 1441–1770*. Chapel Hill: Univ. of North Carolina Press, 2003.
Walker, Timothy D. *Doctors, Folk Medicine and the Inquisition: The Repression of Magical Healing in Portugal During the Enlightenment*. Leiden: Brill, 2005.
Walter, Jaime. "Dimas Bosque, físico-mor da Índia e as Sereias." *Studia* 12 (1963): 261–271.

9

Mother Nganga

Women Experts in the Bantu-Atlantic Spiritual Cultures of the Iberian Atlantic World

RAS MICHAEL BROWN

The great *madre nganga* known as Manga Saya lived in nineteenth-century Cuba during the days of slavery. She offered miraculous cures with her knowledge of plants and her cultivation of spiritual power. Even after her death, Manga Saya remained the empowering force for the ritual objects maintained by her spiritual descendants, and her vast expertise continued to shape those she initiated into her lineage. As a spiritual mother in both the visible physical world and the invisible spiritual world, Manga Saya has been a remarkable progenitor whose legacy resonates into the present.[1]

The enduring figure of Manga Saya brings into view an overlooked facet of the African-Atlantic diaspora. The roles of African women and their female descendants in African-inspired religions in the Americas have not received the level of scholarly attention commensurate with their importance in these spiritual cultures.[2] The general neglect of African-descended women as cultural agents remains the norm outside of key interventions treating the transmission of knowledge about rice cultivation, the assertion of reproductive identity, and the formation of collective identities in diaspora communities.[3] Nevertheless, Manga Saya and her spiritual siblings present a set of issues that invite much-needed inquiry. To begin with, who were these women identified as spiritual mothers (*madres ngangas* in Cuba and *mães de santos* in Brazil) in the diaspora religions inspired by West-Central Africans, particularly those from Kongo? Further, how did continuity and change in ideas about West-Central African women and spiritual power reflect continuity and change in cultures of the African-Atlantic diaspora? This essay attempts to answer these questions and offer direction for further research.

The first step entails locating West-Central African women throughout the Iberian-Atlantic realm, as they were dispersed widely and in substantial numbers for the duration of the transatlantic trade in captive Africans. The broad temporal boundaries of this traumatic relocation of peoples and cultures extended from the early sixteenth century through the middle decades of the nineteenth century. The largest proportion of people carried from West-Central Africa made the passage across the great sea after the late seventeenth century, with almost eight of every ten of these captives disembarking in Iberian-Atlantic ports, particularly in Brazil and Cuba. Second, this essay assesses the correlations of power and gender in the spiritual cultures of West-Central Africa, especially Kongo. Given the timing of the forced displacement of West-Central Africans to Iberian-Atlantic societies, it is appropriate that evidence for this section comes from the late seventeenth century and early eighteenth century, as this affords an invaluable view of the early manifestations of the spiritual cultures that accompanied captives to the Americas. This provides a basis for the third part of the essay, which explains the trajectories of continuity and change in the relationship between gender and spiritual power within the West-Central African-inspired religions of Brazil and Cuba. It appears that two divergent trajectories developed from the eighteenth century through the nineteenth century in which the spiritual status of women diminished in one case and retained high (though redefined) prestige in the other. Both trajectories drew from Bantu precedents, but took on local variations in the diaspora.

Pursuing these topics together raises theoretical matters that have to be addressed at the outset. The cross-currents of two interpretive trends addressing cultural processes in the African-Atlantic diaspora have coalesced to explain and also obscure the historical dimensions of cultural continuity and change. The North American trend, which typically has focused on the English-speaking societies of the Atlantic world, has been preoccupied with a dispute over the relative merits of "continuity" or "creativity" in describing the pedigrees of cultures of African-descended communities. The emphasis on African retentions derived from the work of historians, linguists, and anthropologists in the mid-twentieth century, who sought to counter politically charged assertions that African-descended people lacked valid cultural histories and heritages. This scholarly response was no mere academic exercise, but rather a collection of uncoordinated strikes against an interpretation of the past intended to deny social and political inclusion at that time. In the end, the identification of cultural continuity from Africa to the Americas indicated the resilience of African-descended people and their cultures in the midst of extreme oppression. More recent generations of scholars in this tradition have maintained this core ethos even as they have extended evidence and methods in new directions.[4] A number of scholars from the same range of disciplines took the early research in another direction beginning in the 1960s to devise what has become known as the "creolization" model. This approach has given primacy to radical changes in the social and cultural worlds of enslaved people in which the African backgrounds of captives contributed but did not remain central to the processes of establishing communities and cultures in the Americas. Instead, the principle cultural process centered on the generation of all things "new," including new communities, new cultures, and new identities fashioned from the diverse crowds that disembarked from the holds of slave ships. While the "creolization" model appropriately celebrates the agency and creativity of African-descended people in dire circumstances, it has also led many of the proponents of this approach to devalue, intentionally or not, the continued relevance of the lived experiences of millions of Africans before captivity and enslavement in the Atlantic world.[5]

The other interpretive trend that has concealed as much as it has revealed emerged from Latin Americanist studies of diaspora cultures. Rather than contest the degree of the influence of Africans as cultural agents in the Americas, this tradition has debated the subsequent development of African-inspired cultures as either maintaining "pure" African ways or descending into "degenerate" forms that mixed extensively with non-African cultures. This emerged most clearly in the process through which *candomblé* in Bahia became increasingly identified with and dominated by "pure Nagô" models promoted in competitions of authority among adepts beginning in the nineteenth century that influential scholars later canonized in their research in the twentieth century.[6] This has played out to some degree in Cuba, as the rise of the Lucumí *regla de ocha* (Santería) in the nineteenth century eventually engendered a spiritual hierarchy among African-inspired religions, with the *regla de ocha* emerging as preeminent, both in national discourses about culture and identity and in the work of scholars, based in part on success in differentiating it from so-called *brujería* (witchcraft).[7] The fundamental problem with the rigid opposition of "pure" and "degenerate" (as well as "religion" and "sorcery," which replicates the same relationship) usually reflects the rhetoric of presentist agendas to achieve legitimacy and prestige rather than to explain historical cultural processes of continuity and change. An unfortunate consequence has been the neglect of those African-inspired spiritual cultures demeaned as "degenerate" or as "sorcery" and, thus, unworthy of study.

Clashes between approaches that rely on the oppositions of continuity and creativity or purity and degeneration to describe African-Atlantic cultures have flared repeatedly over the past few decades despite excellent scholarship that routinely transcends these labels.[8] In the end, we would do well to see the confrontation of these dualistic interpretations as a false dilemma. Cultural processes entail the interaction of continuity and creativity in both normal and extraordinary circumstances. In most instances, it is practically impossible to delineate between the two because people think and act continuously in cultural dialogues that resist clear categorization. Further, when these dialogues occur in polycultural societies that experience the near constant comings and goings of people from diverse backgrounds, designations such as "pure" and "degenerate" (or even "mixed") tell us more about the perspectives of observers than of the cultural worlds named as such. Instead of imposing continuity and creativity as essentialist labels for larger cultural processes or for any of the particular ideas and practices within these processes, researchers have to assume the complementary workings of both and then explain how these interactions shaped cultures over time. And rather than presuppose that cultures slide along nonlinear continua from pure to degenerate, traditional to modern, homogeneous to mixed, or even old to new, scholars should acknowledge that Atlantic societies exhibited manifold cultural planes that people often intersected many times every day as they thought, talked, ate, sang, danced, moved between the *casa nganga* (Cuban-Kongo spiritual house) and the *iglesia* (church) and the home and the market, and so on in an endless interplay of relationships, institutions, languages, ideas, and things. Reconstructing connections in the cultural pasts of African-descended people dispersed throughout the Atlantic world demands consideration of these complex dynamics and supports innovations in the methods used to fulfill this intent.

The many contexts for the dispersal of West-Central African spiritual mothers into the Iberian-Atlantic cannot be readily synthesized in a short essay. Still, we can begin to examine the historical development of Bantu-Atlantic spiritual cultures by focusing on certain core features shared by all of these religions across space and time. To this end, this project explores the continuities and changes in meanings in the titles associated with spiritual experts, particularly those in positions of leadership. An examination of the evolving relationships between three key terms, *nganga* (expert), *ngudi* (mother), and *tata* (father), allows for a historical, comparative analysis of power and gender in Bantu-Atlantic spiritual cultures in West-Central Africa (Kongo/Angola) and the Iberian-Atlantic (Brazil and Cuba).

WEST-CENTRAL AFRICAN WOMEN IN THE IBERIAN-ATLANTIC WORLD

Women like Manga Saya arrived on the western shores of the Atlantic from West-Central Africa over three and a half centuries ago. They nurtured and instructed countless waves of African newcomers and generations of New World-born children as they aided families, communities, and cultures in forced exile. In many cases they were newcomers themselves, numbering among the millions of West-Central Africans carried as captives throughout the Atlantic basin. Those with the exceptional abilities and knowledge of spiritual experts numbered far fewer, yet this small cadre of women and men provided the essential foundations for the elaboration of African-Atlantic religions throughout the diaspora. The "Bantu" spiritual cultures of Kongo and Angola found expression in the Americas in a variety of forms, including the *reglas de congo* (Palo Monte, Palo Mayombe, among others) in Cuba and the *candomblé* in Brazil as well as in other manifestations often denoted generically and pejoratively as "witchcraft" in numerous Atlantic societies.

The spatial breadth of these expressions coincided with the pan-Atlantic dispersal of West-Central Africans to almost every region of the Americas that relied on the enslavement of African-descended people to any extent. In the Iberian-Atlantic context, this included Portugal and Spain, the first island colonies near Africa (Cabo Verde and São Tomé), the early American mainland colonies (New Spain and Brazil), as well as the remaining regions and islands of the Americas colonized by Spain in subsequent generations. Overall, between the years 1531 and 1866 as many as 3,899,700 West-Central Africans arrived in Iberian societies in the Americas and comprised more than 63 percent of all captive Africans landed in these locations for the entire duration of the transatlantic trade in people. Further, the predominance of West-Central Africans was even greater before 1800, when captives taken from this region represented almost two-thirds of African newcomers taken to Iberian-Atlantic societies.⁹

The extensive presence of West-Central Africans in the Iberian-Atlantic realm amplified larger patterns of the transatlantic trade in people. Estimates based on voyage data indicate that no less than 10,538,200 captive Africans disembarked in the Americas. Almost half (47 percent) of all captives transported across the Atlantic originated in West-Central Africa. Captives from the three contiguous regions of West Africa identified as the Gold Coast, the Bight of Benin (the "Slave Coast" in the parlance of the era), and the Bight of Biafra collectively included at least 3,982,700 people, or 38 percent of all Africans landed in the Americas.

These figures do more than detail demographic trends. They suggest that studies of the cultural lives of African-descended people in Iberian-Atlantic societies must consider the significance of West-Central Africans and their cultures more than has usually been case in the scholarly literature. An emphasis on Yoruba ("Nagô" in Brazil, "Lucumí" in Cuba) cultural influences has predominated for various reasons, in large part because these traditions gained greater prestige within African-descended communities and among the early academic investigators beginning in the late nineteenth century. This has typically undermined sustained efforts to understand the "Bantu" (West-Central African) influences in Brazil, Cuba, and other portions of the Iberian-Atlantic that had prevailed in earlier eras.¹⁰ The patterns of the transport of captive Africans, however, compel us to recognize that the Iberian-Atlantic and Bantu-Atlantic realms developed as worlds deeply intertwined from the early sixteenth century through the mid-nineteenth century.

The focus on women and gender in Bantu-Atlantic spiritual cultures in this essay requires us to consider the presence of women and girls among the West-Central Africans taken to Iberian-Atlantic societies as well. The voyage data does not offer as much information about sex ratios as that given for the number of people carried on individual vessels and ports or regions of embarkation and disembarkation. Nevertheless, the available information indicates that the proportion of women and girls taken from West-Central Africa to Iberian-Atlantic ports averaged almost 34 percent each voyage. This was slightly higher than the average of 33 percent aboard vessels that transported captives from all other African regions to Iberian-Atlantic destinations. Both figures stood below the average of 35 percent for the transatlantic trade overall. In any case, the averages do not reveal the remarkable fact that among the Africans dispersed through the Iberian-Atlantic realm the absolute number (1,322,200) of West-Central African women and girls alone exceeded the total number of male and female captives carried from ports along the Bight of Benin (the primary region of origin for those later identified as Yoruba/Nagô/Lucumí). As such, it appears fair to assert that the women of the Bantu-Atlantic diaspora deserve more attention than has been the case.

POWER AND GENDER IN WEST-CENTRAL AFRICAN SPIRITUAL CULTURES

Fundamental notions about the sources of spiritual power and their connections to gender roles originated in the deep past of Bantu societies in Central Africa. By the time that European explorers, missionaries, and merchants began arriving in West-Central Africa in the late fifteenth century, the kinds of people who became spiritually potent individuals and the knowledge they cultivated had been fully vested in the position of *nganga,* an "expert" or "knowing one" in valued disciplines. Although typically marred by biases and misunderstandings, accounts composed by European visitors provide documentary insight into the status and work of these West-Central African spiritual experts, especially during the period from the mid-seventeenth century through the early eighteenth century, when captives from Kongo and Angola were dispersed in rapidly expanding numbers throughout the Iberian-Atlantic realm.[11] It is in this time range and in these sources that we find early manifestations of powerful spiritual mothers who would extend their spiritual and biological lineages across the ocean over the next two centuries.

Any discussion of power must begin with a specific understanding of what the word "power" means. For the purposes of this essay, power refers to the ability to make things happen. A secular materialist approach to power commonly embraced by experts in academic studies treats power in instrumental terms only. The capacity to exert one's will through coercion, usually physical or economic force, reveals "real power." Other means of making things happen, particularly those that do not rely primarily on the corporeal strength of individuals or states, tend to be regarded as "merely" symbolic if not essentially superficial. Societies in West-Central Africa, however, have not employed this limited conception of power. Instead, power has encompassed a range of abilities that may be labeled "religious," "spiritual," or "creative." The effects of these abilities have been regarded as no less "real" than those generated by instrumental power. West-Central Africans have not separated these forms of power from the manifestations of political power that academic historians have afforded privileged status in the usual discussions of power. As such, no scholar can justifiably interpret power and gender in West-Central African societies without accepting a broader view of the sources and expressions of power.[12]

Linked with this instrumentalist bias in conceptions of power has been an assumption of male dominance. Certainly greater physical strength and the holding of positions of high status appear to confirm the notion that "real power" comes in largely masculine forms. Indeed, a familiar assertion of this masculine, physical power remains the ability to coerce and kill, often achieved through the internal workings of the state and warfare against external enemies. Thus, heads of state, formal institutions of governance, and wars matter most. Further, male power appears so "natural" that it is taken for granted as basic to human societies to the extent that only those women who have pursued or associated with these supposedly "male" forms of power have been seen as having any "real power." The most conspicuous example of this in West-Central Africa remains Njinga, the seventeenth-century ruler of Ndongo, who continues to draw the attention of scholars and laypeople alike, primarily because she redefined political leadership in her time and afterward.[13] The exclusive emphasis on the abilities of some to dominate and even take the lives of others ignores an equally potent source of power in West-Central African cultures: the ability to bring life into this world. So much of the effort of male leaders has entailed ensuring the imitation of this act in agriculture, commerce, diplomacy, spiritual institutions, and any other endeavor that may be regarded as the pursuit of "fertility" and "prosperity." Yet the core act has remained the birth of a child, which has served as both the symbolic foundation and the material basis of wealth and power in West-Central African societies. Because of this, motherhood has provided a source of power for those who could do it (women) or replicate its principle of generation (women and men).[14]

The most significant meaning of motherhood in much of West-Central Africa has been that it has provided the primary source of identity for every member of a community. The definition of a person's relationship to near and distant blood kin and to a considerable extent a person's status within the larger society derives from that person's connection to his or her mother and the mother's kin. Kongo communities and many other societies in Africa have maintained matrilineal descent to define kinship and have regarded this as the most important social institution undergirding all other institutions. The antiquity of this practice for Bantu-speaking societies (including Kongo groups) remains a matter of debate, although it certainly existed before the arrival of Europeans in the fifteenth century and the beginning of the transatlantic trade in captives.[15] Further, the profound significance of kinship and matriliny in much of West-Central Africa shaped the ways that people perceived the sources and transmission of spiritual power.

This foundation appears most clearly in the ways that West-Central Africans conceptualized relationships between experts and members within spiritual disciplines and initiation societies. Family structures and marital bonds have predominated as models for internal hierarchy and for the incorporation of neophytes, as senior males have typically carried the title *tata* (father), senior females *ma* or *ngwa* (mother), and novices *mwana* (child).[16] The idiom of kinship through motherhood carried especially potent meanings in these disciplines and initiation societies. This was seen most clearly in the title *ngudi,* which has had the primary meaning of "mother," and has carried the additional connotations of maternal kinship, high status, and the idea of origination. This range of meanings appears in a seventeenth-century dictionary of the Kongo language, which in addition to *ngudi/nguri* (mother) included the terms *ngudi yazitiswa* (respected mother), *ngudi muzitu* (venerable mother), *nguri a nsimba* (mother of twins), and *ngudi/nguri a nkama* (head, master/mistress, chief/chieftess, Mister/Madam).[17] The mixed gender references in this last title indicate that the meanings of motherhood could apply to men as well. It is essential to note that the fundamental connection of motherhood to power provided the basis for the broad use of the term and conferred the highly valued status of "mother" to the men who earned the privilege to bear the title.

The role of the *nguri (ngudi) a nsimba,* or ("mother of twins") provides a revealing example of the interplay between the idiom of kinship, biological sex, physical reproduction, and gendered meanings of spiritual power. As seen in more recent ethnography, the birth of twins required the mother and father to undergo initiation into a society dedicated to addressing the spiritual power of twins.[18] A missionary in Soyo (Kongo) during the eighteenth century described this institution, though without recognizing the larger spiritual significance, in noting that the birth of twins occasioned the gathering of other mothers and fathers of twins. The association formed by those affected by the birth of twins kept as powerful objects a knife, a hoe, and a small container of liquid. These objects had to be replaced if touched accidentally by outsiders in order to avoid some misfortune caused by the transgression. At the gathering, members of the group used the knife, hoe, and container in their communal meal in which the oldest woman placed a small amount of food in the hands of the members, each of whom positioned their hands "one on top of the other in the shape of a cross."[19] This proceeded in silence without the usual sounds of clapping or talking on such occasions. The ritual meal served to promote good health, as it prevented swelling and protected the participants from death. Further, members of this group did not consult outside experts in instances of illnesses, but rather treated each other. In another notable practice associated with twins, those who gathered the first harvest of vegetables conscientiously set aside a portion for the mothers of twins to eat to ensure their well-being and defend them from misfortune.[20] A later eighteenth-century account by a European missionary mentioned the spiritual power of the mothers of twins in stating that people respected them more than other spiritual experts and considered them infallible as oracles. Those who could not realize their desires through the work of the other experts then turned to these mothers. If the intercession of a mother of twins failed, people then resigned themselves to the fact that *"Nzambi nzolelequo,"* or "God does not want it," accepting the futility of pursuing the matter any further.[21]

The power associated with the mother of twins was such that this descriptive phrase functioned as a spiritual title for males, as the biological father of twins also acquired the distinction of *ngudi a nsimba*. An early twentieth-century source stated that the male *ngudi a nsimba* possessed special standing because he had "more magic power than the banganga, and he is accordingly sent for when some nkisi is to be made up. He must then come to prepare and bless the first medicine. No one, as a matter of fact, may complete a nkisi until a ngudi a nsimba has been present."[22] In sum, the occurrence of the birth of twins conferred to the biological parents an elevated status that affirmed both as exceptional "mothers." Given that the appearance of twins was perceived as an especially auspicious manifestation of fertility and a fortuitous intervention from the spiritual realm, the biological father's standing was enhanced to that of a "mother," which in a matrilineal society certainly represented far more than an honorary label. Further, this served as an acknowledgment that spiritual, procreative power relied on the complementarity of both female and male. The same principle appeared among the experts who operated shrines for nature spirits in seventeenth-century Angola, as the experts and the nature spirits they served worked as pairings of females and males.[23]

Ngudi as a title and the ideas of spiritual power associated with the concept and role of mother fit within a larger Bantu cultural context that assigned special status to those who possessed exceptional abilities and training in making things happen. Both women and men recognized as having this status earned the designation *nganga*, which in the most basic sense meant "expert" but had the additional connotation of expertise in spiritual matters particularly. The women and men who became *banganga* (plural of *nganga*) filled one of the most important positions in West-Central African communities. West-Central Africans routinely called on the *banganga* to assist them in the major phases of their lives. Women consulted these experts and received sacred objects to ensure that they would become pregnant and safely deliver children. Once children had arrived in the land of the living, the *nganga* provided them with objects to protect them from misfortune and ensure health and strength in their maturation. Experts supervised initiation schools that integrated young women and men into adult communities and introduced them to bodies of spiritual knowledge, which ensured the training of another generation of *banganga*. Just as they helped people through key stages of physical and spiritual growth, *banganga* assisted in the transition to the land of the dead. According to one account, the families of recently deceased people had *banganga* touch their dead relative on the face with an iron hammer, an object associated closely with the spirit world and its forces.[24]

The occasion of death required the services of an *nganga* for another purpose. If a death appeared "unnatural" for any reason, the family of the dead employed an *nganga ngombo* to discover the cause, which often was found to have emanated from maleficent use of spiritual power. The *nganga ngombo* acquired this knowledge through possession. The family seeking information, the expert, and the expert's assistants participated collectively in a private ritual in which singing and praying invoked a spirit to enter into the *nganga*'s head. Once possessed, the *nganga* could speak for the spirit and reveal the person responsible for the death. A public ritual led by the *nganga ngombo* also functioned to identify culprits in a suspicious death. This event began after the expert played a drum to call people together and continued with singing and dancing in a circle. The *nganga ngombo* became possessed, as evidenced by erratic dancing, and cast dust into the faces of individuals accused of causing the death. The accused then had to submit to an ordeal that consisted of consuming a drink prepared by the *nganga*. The physical response of the accused to the drink confirmed the original charge or in some cases resulted in exoneration. Additionally, people frequently consulted the *nganga ngombo* for access to other hidden information, such as the cause of an illness or the location of lost objects.[25]

Once the *nganga ngombo* had uncovered the source of misfortune, people sought the proper remedy. Numerous *banganga* possessed the knowledge and abilities to treat both the spiritual and biological aspects of a variety of illnesses, each with its specific expert. Their knowledge of the abundant roots, leaves, and barks in the region rendered notable biological cures for various afflictions.[26] This expert knowledge provided remedies for poisons injected by venomous creatures, consumed by accident, or administered by an *nganga* enlisted to cause harm.[27] Further, the knowledge of poisons allowed *banganga* to administer numerous ordeals, such as the one by the *nganga ngombo* described above.[28]

Many who benefited from the services of healing experts had to become apprentices to the *banganga* to learn to cure the very illnesses they had suffered, thus becoming *banganga* themselves. The rigorous training and obligations that accompanied apprenticeship typically comprised the core element of the remedy, in addition to payment of goods or currency. The method of treatment in which the afflicted received the cure and then became an *nganga* of the cure ensured that numerous people had specialized spiritual knowledge.[29]

The broad category of healing experts known in different regions as either *nganga mokisi* (*nganga nkisi*) or *nganga itiki* (*nganga iteke*) focused their work on harnessing power from the invisible spiritual world for a client by creating consecrated objects, often called *nkisi*, through a process that included singing, dancing, observing specific codes of behavior, and systematically assembling the objects with certain "medicines." These consecrated objects then embodied the coalescence of all the people, materials, activities, and energies employed to animate them, including the spirits that imbued every *nkisi* with spiritual power.[30]

As noted above, both women and men became experts in bodies of spiritual knowledge that were not usually restricted by sex or gender. Although European missionaries tended to give more attention to male *banganga,* they recorded the presence of female *banganga,* who held expertise in the same disciplines as their male colleagues. One missionary observed the practices of a female "nganga zagi" (*nganga nzazi*), an expert in a spirit with "power over thunder and lightning, which serve to defend and attack."[31] This *nganga* had been provoked by a male "sorcerer," who had approached her house without announcing his identity and then hastily fled. This provided sufficient grounds for the *nganga* to interpret the man's motives as malevolent, in that he likely intended to "kill her by witchcraft." She exited her house with her *biteke* (anthropomorphic statues) in her hands and "in the name of these idols, she cursed her enemy" by invoking the lightning to hit her target. The invocation involved the *nganga*'s striking the *biteke* together, which produced a fearful noise, while running throughout the town shouting words of attack.[32] Another missionary recorded that the "Nganganzasi" (*nganga nzazi*) caused thunder to rumble during the dry seasons when it did not normally occur and to resonate for exceptionally long times. Given the connection between thunder, lightning, and rain, people also believe that the *nganga nzazi* ensured the coming of rain with the help of consecrated objects.[33] This second description of the powers and duties of the *nganga nzazi* did not make reference to the sex of the experts, which suggests that we can assume the normal presence of both women and men in this discipline. Further, female and male *banganga* of the entity Nzazi possessed much prestige, as the spirit of thunder and lightening appears in oral traditions among the cohort of the most powerful nature spirits, including Mbumba Luangu and Mpulu Bunzi.[34]

Women were also initiated into the discipline of the *nganga ngombo* described above. A missionary witnessed a female *nganga ngombo* walking hastily through her village making "o, o, o" sounds and panting "ah, ah," as though "she carried a heavy burden." She had been sleeping and the *nganga*'s patron spirit possessed her to protect her from the attack of a male *nganga* who supposedly entered her house to poison her. The spirit woke the female *nganga* and led her to shout throughout the village, which not only repulsed the attacker from her home but also compelled him to flee and hide.³⁵

Another incident described both female and male *banganga* working together. A group of *banganga* gathered in the town of Sole in the Zombo province to heal a sick person. A Roman Catholic missionary heard their songs as they conducted their ceremonies and asked the leader (*mani*) of the area to allow him to attend the proceedings. The *mani* passed along this request to the *banganga*, who refused, stating that "they must heal this person on the point of death," with the implication being that the presence of the missionary would disrupt their efforts. The indignant missionary then sent a message through the town's leader to the *banganga* that the leader or even the missionary himself would send people to "capture them and chain them" if they did not terminate their "diabolical" rites. The *banganga*, however, had a spiritual status that did not require them to blindly obey the authority of political leaders, and they left the town that night. They returned on a night soon afterward to conduct their own attack on the meddling and arrogant European missionary and his *mani* ally. Well after the dark of evening had enveloped the town, the female *banganga* "commenced to throw their diabolical curses and strike their idols one against the other." The male *banganga* then joined in, "but with more noise and cries" as they "threw their curses in striking their idols with force." Following this, the *banganga* collectively intoned songs that included verses assuring that their attack would come true with the burning of the town and the missionary's hut.³⁶

This last example recalls the earlier observation of the complementarity of the female and male within motherhood captured in the title *ngudi*. Indeed, the most significant expression of the convergence of motherhood and spiritual ability appeared in the title *ngudi nganga*. As "mother experts" (the literal rendering), the *bangudi banganga* were considered the ultimate masters of spiritual ability, which gave them superior status and required them to oversee the initiation of new *banganga*.³⁷ The *bangudi banganga* included men and women, of course, and the inclusiveness of the title derived from the importance attached to maternal kinship and descent in West-Central African societies, which infused this application of the term with the idea that the *ngudi* class of *banganga* acted as the heads of an *nganga* lineage in the very direct sense of having given birth to spiritual children. As such, while the practical translation of *ngudi nganga* has usually been rendered as "master expert," the core notion of the *ngudi nganga* as the "mother expert" must remain central to our understanding of the principle of motherhood in the transmission of spiritual knowledge and power.

CONTINUITY AND CHANGE IN GENDER ROLES IN BANTU-ATLANTIC SPIRITUAL CULTURES

West-Central Africans who were dispersed throughout the Atlantic basin implanted their spiritual cultures in new lands, which have remained vital into the present. The descendants of these West-Central African progenitors retained key features of the familial structure of ancestral spiritual communities and the roles of women spiritual experts while transforming them in response to the unique demands and conditions of diverse Iberian-Atlantic contexts. An assessment of the uses of *nganga, tata,* and *ngudi* in the Bantu-Atlantic spiritual cultures of Brazil and Cuba reveals these dynamics and suggests additional avenues of research.

Of the three terms, the one most fundamental to West-Central African spiritual cultures, *nganga,* appears to have undergone extensive reworking in the Iberian-Atlantic setting. African-descended people throughout the African-Atlantic diaspora continued to link the term to spiritual experts, though not with the same general applicability that prevailed in West-Central Africa.[58] One of the earliest references from Brazil in the 1690s describes the work of one *nganga wisa* (*nganga* of power). An enslaved woman named Luzia operated from a "public house" in the town of Rio Real in Bahia providing cures for numerous people. Singing in the language of Angola (most likely Kimbundu) to the accompaniment of her assistants, who played scrapers called *canzás,* this *nganga* held animal skins while dancing. These actions and the events that followed led her to an altered state in which Luzia declared, "I am gangahuiza." Once she achieved this state (probably possession by a spirit of that name), Luzia could then help her clients. Also, records for early eighteenth-century Rio de Janeiro indicate the presence of "*Gangazambes*" (*nganga nzambi*), described as "witches," who apparently wielded great power to "kill or give life."[39]

No later than the mid-nineteenth century, women experts in the Kongo-Angola *candomblé* houses, such as the Angola-born Ana Maria of the Dendezeiro house in the 1860s, no longer carried the gender-neutral title *nganga* and appear to have taken the more general designation "mother of the saint" (*mãe-de-santo* in Brazilian Portuguese) or other titles, including *mameto-de-inquice* (our mother of the spirits) and *nêngua*, that applied to women only.⁴⁰ The title *nêngua* in this shift is particularly interesting, as it replicates the southern Kongo term *néngua*, which refers to a caring and protective woman (not necessarily a mother). The Kimbundu-speaking neighbors of southern Kongo communities employed the word *ngudi* to convey the same meaning.⁴¹ Given the large representation of Kimbundu-speaking captives in Brazil, the synthesis of Kongo and Mbundu understandings of *néngua* and *ngudi* within the Bantu-Brazilian term *nêngua* suggests that African-descended people in nineteenth-century Brazil chose to emphasize more gender-specific titles of both Bantu and Portuguese origin to name women experts and reserve *nganga/ganga* for men alone. While the historical and ethnographic evidence remains too thin to support firm conclusions, the shift in terminology may have represented a trend toward greater male authority in Kongo-Angola houses. Leadership of *candomblé* houses of all nations in nineteenth-century Bahia included a strong presence of women, though men appeared to hold a majority of these positions. By the mid-twentieth century, however, male dominance in the Kongo-Angola houses had become the norm.⁴² This went against the trend exhibited in the West African *candomblé* houses, especially the Nagô (Yoruba) houses, which came to assert that spiritual leadership should conform to a model of matriarchy. Overall, then, the transformation of *candomblé* houses from the nineteenth century into the twentieth century entailed the departure from the female-male complementarity basic to West-Central African and West African spiritual cultures toward the ascendancy of matriarchy in the West African houses and patriarchy in the West-Central African houses. The result of this process in the Kongo-Angola houses was that all those known by the title *nganga* were men, who held more or less exclusive control over the leadership of their spiritual families. Further, the notion of the "father" as the head of the spiritual lineage gained reinforcement through the preference for the title *tata* over the standard Kongo appellation *ngudi nganga*. Not only had *ngudi* been dropped as a reference to the highest levels of spiritual power, likely because of its meaning of "mother," but even the previously gender-neutral title *nganga* gave way to the clearly masculine *tata*. It is remarkable that members of Kongo-Angola *candomblé* houses thought it desirable that titles possess greater gender specificity to such an extent that both *ngudi* and *nganga*, terms so essential to West-Central African spiritual cultures, were relegated to the semantic periphery or dropped altogether. In any event, the linguistic shift reflected a profound reconfiguration of gender and power in the Bantu-Atlantic spiritual cultures of Brazil that developed over a long period from the seventeenth century through the mid-twentieth century.

A similar process appears to have occurred in other parts of the African-Atlantic diaspora, as African-descended people generally came to employ *tata* far more frequently than *nganga* to denote a male spiritual expert. The substitution of terms likely resulted from the fact that the basic combination of the *tata* form with the primary meanings of "father" and "elder male" represents what may be the most widespread Bantu lexical retention in the Americas. It has appeared in the vocabularies of African-descended communities in Brazil, Cuba, Belize, Antigua, Jamaica, the U.S. Virgin Islands, Trinidad, and the South Carolina Lowcountry.[43] The use of *tata* to label a male ritual expert, or more specifically the male head of a Bantu-Atlantic spiritual community, has occurred most clearly in Iberian-Atlantic contexts, as seen above in Brazil. Certainly, in both of these places the presence and influence of male experts in the Roman Catholic Church, also commonly referred to as "father," likely reinforced this usage as these spiritual cultures interacted in the daily lives of African-descended people. Although we find common ground in the continued use of *tata* and its Iberian glosses *pai* and *padre* across spiritual cultures in Brazil and Cuba, the retention of the female-specific title *ngudi nganga* appears in Cuba alone and with a uniquely Cuban meaning.

Those even casually familiar with the *reglas de congo* tend to be well aware of the reputation of Palo Monte as being intensely masculine and even hostile to women. Additionally, many perceive the *reglas de congo* as occupying the "magic" and "witchcraft" end of the spiritual continuum, with the *regla de ocha* (or Santería) and Catholicism toward the "religion" end. This last judgment stems from the assessment that the *reglas de congo* mainly serve to direct spiritual power for the individualistic interests of the initiated without regard to a greater moral purpose or concern for fostering a spiritual community.[44] Certainly, a more nuanced understanding of both issues is in order. This can be achieved in part by assessing the roles of women ritual experts in the *reglas de congo* and how those roles reveal transformations in the Bantu-Atlantic spiritual cultures of the Iberian-Atlantic realm.

The first step involves an appraisal of the Cuban use of *ngudi nganga*, the key title applied to leading women experts in the *reglas de congo*. The title derives its basic meaning from the original Kongo term, but it has connotations unique to the Cuban context.[45] It most commonly denotes the highest ranking woman in a house of initiates to the *reglas de congo* and employs both senses of *ngudi,* as a term of high status and of motherhood. However, *ngudi* has not been used in Cuba as an ungendered label for both male and female ritual experts, as with the original Kongo convention. Further, *nganga* in this title does not refer to the expert but to the physical object, usually an iron cauldron filled with diverse items, composed to contain the force of a spirit and the powers of its makers. The object made and empowered by an expert thus carries the name that in West-Central Africa identified the expert. For the sake of clarity in the following discussion, the compound term *nganga/prenda* will be used to identify the Cuban object, so as to distinguish this usage from the name given to the spiritual expert.[46] The compact meaning of the title *ngudi nganga* has been understood in Cuba to be "mother of the *nganga/prenda.*" The *nganga/prenda* with its forces has served as the ritual focus of the house, and the titles of members of the house have reflected this relationship, as in *ngudi nganga, tata nganga* (father of the *nganga/prenda*), and *muana nganga* (child of the *nganga/prenda*). Additionally, people have frequently replaced the Kongo term *ngudi* with the Spanish words *madre* or *madrina,* thus reinforcing its specific application to women ritual experts alone.

What accounts for this constriction of the meaning of *ngudi* in Cuba? Does it reflect some kind of historical change in the status of women experts? Or more precisely, does it represent a linguistic indicator of the imposition of limitations on the *madres* in relation to the status and activities afforded to male ritual experts? This seems like a promising direction of inquiry, considering that many perceive the *reglas de congo* as dominated by men and overtly masculine in their beliefs and practices. Indeed, some have idealized a patriarchal structure within the *reglas de congo*:

> The Casa Nganga, which is also called the Casa Mundo, comes to be like a tribe: there is the Chief or the King with his vassals. There is the wife of the King, the Head Padre [*Tata Nganga*], the Mfumo [*mfumu,* "chief" in Kongo], who is like a Queen. This Head Padre Nganga is addressed as Master. Head Master. Later in the order come his Mayordomo or his Mayordomos, and the Madrina of the Nganga—Fundamento [another term for the *nganga*]—the *Ngudi Nganga,* and the Madrina of Gajo, the *Tikantinka* or *Nkento Tikatika Nkisi.* Then there are the *Nkombos* or *Ngombes, Mbua,* the servants or dogs of the Nganga who are mounted by the Fumbi [the spirit of a dead person

who possess the "dogs" and serves the *Tata Nganga*] and the Moana [*muana*, "child" in Kongo].⁴⁷

While this model may have had a "King" and "Queen" coupled at the top of the hierarchy, the *tata nganga* clearly ruled as the master. Further, the *mayordomo* acted as a kind of "second chief" and was presumed in this kind of order to be a man, as well. Those who have continued to advocate for a male-dominated hierarchy have contended that a "disciplined" and "orthodox" house should prohibit the participation of women in key functions of the house. For example, in such a house only the *tata nganga* has had the authority to "scratch" (ritually incise) novices. In instances when the *tata nganga* has not been able fulfill this responsibility, the *mayordomo* has performed the task. According to this perspective, a *madrina,* regardless of her age, experiences, and the extent of her spiritual lineage (measured in the number of her godchildren), should not be allowed to act in this capacity. Similarly, women have not been permitted to conduct sacrifices of four-footed animals or participate in the creation of an *nganga/prenda*. Further, only a postmenopausal *madrina* has been allowed to own a *nganga/prenda*.⁴⁸ Ironically, the prohibitions regarding the *nganga/prenda* defy the fact that every *nganga/prenda* embodies female procreativity in that each one descends from an original *nganga/prenda,* which (not surprisingly) has often been called a "mother nganga" (yet another Cuban variation on "mother nganga.").⁴⁹

The patriarchal view of the *casa nganga* ignores the history of Bantu-Atlantic spiritual culture in Cuba and overlooks the enduring importance of female spiritual power in the *reglas de congo*. Indeed, stories told about the great *madres ngangas* known as Manga Saya, Ña Filomena, and Ña Secundina allow our knowledge of women ritual experts to take root. Manga Saya was an enslaved woman whose beauty, regal demeanor, and extensive knowledge of herbal medicine earned her much renown. These qualities also drew many men, both enslavers and enslaved, to her. Unfortunately, this attention eventually brought her misfortune after Manga Saya spurned the amorous demands of an overseer. He responded by ordering her to endure a public whipping. Other African-descended people, however, helped her to escape to the *palenque* in the hills of Cuzco, where many other runaways found refuge and where another famed *cimarrón,* Juan Gangá, had already established himself. Manga Saya and Juan Gangá used plants, particularly parts of the *ceiba* tree, and the pure waters of the local streams to concoct miraculous cures that earned them much fame. Their great powers and the intimidating terrain kept the slave-catchers away, although others made the journey to this rugged area to bring those seriously ill to Manga Saya and Juan Gangá in search of cures.[50] The other two celebrated *madres ngangas*, Ña Filomena and Ña Secundina, both born in Kongo, arrived as enslaved women to the Matanzas region in the nineteenth century. They eventually joined an old *cimarrón* town founded in the previous century that over the generations earned a reputation as a center for remarkable African-descended healers who possessed the knowledge and abilities to exploit the rich medicinal plants of the region. Their talents as healers, coupled with the power of their Kikongo prayers, were so potent, legends say, that Ña Filomena and Ña Secundina restored to life many people thought certain to die. These three *madres ngangas* are also credited with being the originators of especially strong *nganga/prenda* imbued with their healing powers which have been passed down from expert to expert, thus ensuring that the *madres ngangas* would continue to support their spiritual lineages.[51]

In addition to overlooking prominent *madres ngangas*, the patriarchal model of the *casa nganga* neglects the gender dynamics of leadership in the *cabildo de nación*, a key institutional antecedent of the *nganga* houses that flourished in the eighteenth and nineteenth centuries. The formal structure of many *cabildos*, especially those identified as "Congo," assigned titles such as "King" and "Queen" to the highest positions of male and female leadership.[52] While this terminology was replicated in the *casa nganga*, the labels did not necessarily imply a male-dominated hierarchy. Instead, as Matt D. Childs explains in this volume, women within the *cabildos* played essential roles in the governance and operations of these organizations even without the benefit of specific titles of leadership.

Also contrary to the patriarchal idealization of a *casa nganga*, women ritual experts have long played roles that were neither secondary nor subservient to male experts. Throughout Cuba in the past and present, women experts have led houses, composed and owned *ngangas/prendas*, and initiated many *muanas* (children). Indeed, in some places and times certain women have been the preeminent experts in the local *reglas de congo*, such as Ma Dolore Cabarnao, "an old black woman, gangá, [and] famous healer" in the nineteenth century.[53] Even in a house run by both female and male authorities, the *madrinas* have an especially powerful status derived in part from their relationship with the *nganga/prenda* and their ability to control the spirits that possess the "dogs" of the *ngangas/prendas*. *Madrinas* take care of the *ngangas/prendas* as though the women are nannies for the *ngangas/prendas,* which captures yet another maternal aspect of the meaning of the title *ngudi nganga.* Further, *madrinas* speak directly to possessing spirits, often for the purpose of protecting a "dog" whom a spirit does not wish to release from possession. They also serve as the final judge of the fidelity of the practices of the *tata nganga* and the *mayordomo,* so much so that they have the final word in disagreements over proper practices. Ultimately, as one practitioner put it, "The Madrina has much control in the casa Nganga."[54]

If we cannot explain the narrowing of the semantic range of *ngudi* as a function of male domination in high-status positions in the *reglas de congo,* how can we account for the change? One possibility is that the members found it desirable to amplify the connection of motherhood and female biology inherent in the older use of *ngudi* to the extent that this became the primary meaning. This appears reasonable when we recall that the familial model of the Cuban *nganga* house reflected in the titles (mother/*ngudi,* father/*tata,* and child/*muana*) has represented the fundamental conception of the house as a spiritual family. This replicated not only the basic social and power structure in spiritual communities in the home societies of captive West-Central Africans and West Africans, but also addressed key needs of captive newcomers and their descendants in the diaspora. Indeed, the disintegration of familial and other group ties embodied one of the most momentous traumas inflicted on generations of enslaved people during the Middle Passage and during the subsequent centuries of enslavement. The need to reform corporate bonds considered essential to conceptions of well-being and personhood in numerous African societies certainly figured prominently in the concerns of enslaved people in Cuba as in the rest of the diaspora. The importance of the *cabildos* within Afro-Cuban communities in the colonial era verifies the centrality of these concerns.[55] But perhaps more vital than the perceptions of national/ethnic identity, notions of familial bonds likely provided the most important idiom for enslaved people to create and maintain group associations based on both biological and social ties. The Bantu terms for these ties came across the Atlantic with captive West-Central Africans and may have taken on even greater meaning, as the use of the familial model represented a deliberate choice for recreating group associations. As such, the *ngudi* and the *tata* likely served not only as spiritual mentors, but also as adoptive parents and elders who played roles necessary in a setting in which fragile biological bonds could be broken easily according to the whims of enslavers. Spiritual communities, such as the *reglas de congo,* offered surrogate families, and the titles *ngudi* and *tata* identified women and men readily understood as mother and father figures for African-descended communities that increasingly relied on Spanish as their primary language. Further, the old gender-neutral term *nganga* to name spiritual parents simply did not supply the linguistic and emotional satisfaction people needed, and it too underwent a transformation in its meanings. In the end, the most literal rendering of *ngudi nganga* as "*madre nganga*" meant more to African-descended Cubans than did its other broader connotations. As in Brazil, this marked a reworking of gendered roles in small spiritual communities that operated within the larger patriarchal Cuban society.

West-Central African women dispersed throughout the Iberian-Atlantic world came from societies that envisioned spiritual power as being accessible to women and men in ways that were essential to their spiritual cultures. As neither men nor women had exclusive claim to the sources of spiritual power, the basic principle of the complementarity of female and male resonated in many of the ideas and activities that maintained the connections between the visible physical domain and the invisible spiritual realm. West-Central African women and girls were thus initiated into the disciplines and societies that directed spiritual power toward the interests of individuals and communities and earned the status as *banganga* in these bodies of knowledge and practice. The transatlantic trade in captive Africans reached deeply into West-Central African societies from the sixteenth century through the mid-nineteenth, carrying millions of people across to the Americas. Almost one-third of these unfortunate captives consisted of women and girls, some of whom carried their status and abilities as spiritual experts with them. They occupied leading positions in establishing the Bantu-Atlantic spiritual cultures that gave rise to the *candomblé* of Brazil, *reglas de congo* of Cuba, and other forms of African-inspired religious expression found throughout the Iberian-Atlantic.

This brief survey of the mother *ngangas* represents a starting point in the process of filling in large gaps in our knowledge of the historical roots and subsequent development of Bantu-Atlantic spiritual cultures by first documenting the roles and abilities attributed to women experts in West-Central Africa and in the Atlantic diaspora. The effort to assess transformations over time in the status accorded to women experts serves to stimulate further questions about the ways that members within African-inspired spiritual communities reconceptualized the composition of their groups' hierarchies as well as their relationships with each other and with spiritual communities of other proveniences. Given that African-descended people in Iberian-Atlantic societies have often participated in multiple spiritual cultures simultaneously, it seems reasonable to expect that the gendered roles and expectations associated with each of these cultures coexisted in combinations that shaped each internally and influenced how people approached them collectively. Such matters await further study. In any case, it is clear that the African mother *ngangas* taken to Iberian-Atlantic societies and the spiritual lineages they established deserve greater consideration in scholarly investigations of African-Atlantic spiritual cultures.

NOTES

1. Natalia Bolívar Aróstegui and Carmen González Díaz de Villegas, *Ta Makuende Yaya y las Reglas de Palo Monte* (Havana: Ediciones Unión—Unión de Escritores y Artistas de Cuba, 1998), 70–71; Lydia Cabrera, *Reglas de Congo: Palo Monte Mayombe* (Miami: Peninsular Print, 1979), 132–133.

2. Notable exceptions include Sheila S. Walker, "The Feast of the Good Death: An Afro-Catholic Emancipation Celebration in Brazil," in *Women in Africa and the African Diaspora: A Reader,* ed. Rosalyn Terborg-Penn and Andrea Benton Rushing, 203–214 (Washington, D.C.: Howard Univ. Press, 1996); Karen McCarthy Brown, *Mama Lola: A Vodou Priestess in Brooklyn* (Berkeley: Univ. of California Press, 2001); Miguel W. Ramos, "La división de la Habana: Territorial Conflict and Cultural Hegemony in the Followers of Oyo Lukumí Religion, 1850s–1920s," *Cuban Studies* 34 (2003): 38–70; Ina Johanna Fandrich, *The Mysterious Voodoo Queen, Marie Laveau: A Study of Powerful Female Leadership in Nineteenth-Century New Orleans* (New York: Routledge, 2005); Carolyn Morrow Long, *A New Orleans Voudou Priestess: The Legend and Reality of Marie Laveau* (Gainesville: Univ. Press of Florida, 2006); J. Lorand Matory, *Black Atlantic Religion: Tradition, Transnationalism, and Matriarchy in the Afro-Brazilian Candomblé* (Princeton: Princeton Univ. Press, 2005), 188–223; Kelly E. Hayes, "Wicked Women and Femmes Fatales: Gender, Power, and Pomba Gira in Brazil," *History of Religions* 48, no. 1 (2008): 1–21; Todd Ramón Ocha, *Societies of the Dead: Quita Manaquita and Palo Praise in Cuba* (Berkeley: Univ. of California Press, 2010); and Stefania Capone, *Searching for Africa in Brazil: Power and Tradition in Candomblé* (Durham: Duke Univ. Press, 2010), 143–170. My use of the term "African-inspired" comes from Ocha, *Societies of the Dead,* 8.

3. For an overview of the literature, see Sandra Gunning, Tera W. Hunter, and Michele Mitchell, "Introduction: Gender, Sexuality, and African Diasporas," *Gender and History* 15, no. 3 (2003): 397–408. See also Judith A. Carney, *Black Rice: The African Origins of Rice Cultivation in the Americas* (Cambridge: Harvard Univ. Press, 2001); Jennifer L. Morgan, *Laboring Women: Reproduction and Gender in New World Slavery* (Philadelphia: Univ. of Pennsylvania Press, 2004); Sandra Gunning, Tera W. Hunter, and Michele Mitchell, eds. *Dialogues of Dispersal: Gender, Sexuality and African Diasporas* (Malden, Mass.: Blackwell, 2004); and Judith A. Byfield, LaRay Denzer, and Anthea Morrison, eds., *Gendering the African Di-*

aspora: Women, Culture, and Historical Change in the Caribbean and Nigerian Hinterland (Bloomington: Indiana Univ. Press, 2010).

4. The literature for this approach is vast, but see as representative works W.E.B. DuBois, *The Negro* (New York: Henry Holt, 1915); Carter G. Woodson, *The African Background Outlined; or, Handbook for the Study of the Negro* (Washington, D.C.: Association for the Study of Negro Life and History, 1936); W.E.B. DuBois, *Black Folk, Then and Now: An Essay in the History and Sociology of the Black Race* (New York: Henry Holt, 1939); Melville J. Herskovits, *Myth of the Negro Past* (New York: Harper and Brothers, 1941); Lorenzo Dow Turner, *Africanisms in the Gullah Dialect* (Chicago: Univ. of Chicago Press, 1949); Sterling Stuckey, *Slave Culture: Nationalist Theory and the Foundations of Black America* (New York: Oxford Univ. Press, 1987); John K. Thornton, *Africa and Africans in the Making of the Atlantic World, 1400–1800*, 2nd ed. (New York: Cambridge Univ. Press, 1998); Michael A. Gomez, *Exchanging Our Country Marks: The Transformations of African Identities in the Colonial and Antebellum South* (Chapel Hill: Univ. of North Carolina Press, 1998); Gwendolyn Midlo Hall, *Slavery and African Ethnicities in the Americas: Restoring the Links* (Chapel Hill: Univ. of North Carolina Press, 2005); and Linda M. Heywood and John K. Thornton, *Central Africans, Atlantic Creoles, and the Foundations of the Americas, 1585–1660* (New York: Cambridge Univ. Press, 2007).

5. Of the many works that define or rely on this interpretation (though not always with the same emphases or to the same ends), see Edward Kamau Brathwaite, *The Development of Creole Society in Jamaica, 1770–1820* (Oxford: Clarendon Press, 1971); Sidney W. Mintz and Richard Price, *The Birth of African-American Culture: An Anthropological Perspective* (Boston: Beacon Press, 1992); Philip D. Morgan, "The Cultural Implications of the Atlantic Slave Trade: African Regional Origins, American Destinations and New World Developments," *Slavery and Abolition* 18, no. 1 (1997): 122–145; Michel-Rolph Trouillot, "Culture on the Edges: Creolization in the Plantation Context," *Plantation Society in the Americas* 1, no. 1 (1998): 8–28; Stephan Palmié, "Creolization and Its Discontents," *Annual Review of Anthropology* 35 (2006): 433–456; and Richard Price, "On the Miracle of Creolization," in *Afro-Atlantic Dialogues: Anthropology in the Diaspora*, ed. Kevin A. Yelvington, 115–147 (Santa Fe, N. Mex.: School of American Research, 2006).

6. Luis Nicolau Parés, "The 'Nagôization' Process in Bahian Candomblé," in *The Yoruba Diaspora in the Atlantic World*, ed. Toyin Falola and Matt D. Childs, 115–148 (Bloomington: Indiana Univ. Press, 2004); Matory, *Black Atlantic Religion*, 115–148; Kelly E. Hayes, "Black Magic and the Academy: Macumba and Afro-Brazilian 'Orthodoxies,'" *History of Religions* 46, no. 4 (2007): 283–315; and Capone, *Searching for Africa in Brazil*, 3–6, 194–196.

7. Stephan Palmié, *Wizards and Scientists: Explorations in Afro-Cuban Modernity and Tradition* (Durham: Duke Univ. Press, 2002), 159–200; David H. Brown, *Santería Enthroned: Art, Ritual, and Innovation in Afro-Cuban Religion* (Chicago: Univ. of Chicago Press, 2003), 62–162; Christine Ayorinde, "Santería in Cuba: Tradition and Transformation," in *The Yoruba Diaspora in the Atlantic World*, ed. Toyin Falola and Matt D. Childs, 223–225 (Bloomington: Indiana Univ. Press, 2004); Christine Ayorinde, *Afro-Cuban Religiosity, Revolution, and National Identity* (Gainesville: Univ. Press of Florida, 2004); and Matory, *Black Atlantic Religion*, 67.

8. For a thoughtful appraisal, see Kenneth Bilby, "African American Memory at the Crossroads: Grounding the Miraculous with Tooy," *Small Axe* 13, no. 2 (2009): 185–199.

9. All figures in this section come from the internet database *Voyages: The Trans-Atlantic*

Slave Trade Database (www.slavevoyages.org), using the "Examine Estimates of the Slave Trade" tool.

10. Jualynne E. Dodson, *Sacred Spaces and Religious Traditions in Oriente Cuba* (Albuquerque: Univ. of New Mexico Press, 2008), 2–9.

11. For cautionary words on the use of European-authored sources to interpret West-Central African spiritual cultures, see Anne Hilton, "European Sources for the Study of Religious Change in Sixteenth and Seventeenth Century Kongo," *Paideuma* 33 (1987): 289–312.

12. These ideas about power are informed by Edna G. Bay, *Wives of the Leopard: Gender, Politics, and Culture in the Kingdom of Dahomey* (Charlottesville: Univ. Press of Virginia, 1998); Eugenia W. Herbert, *Iron, Gender, and Power: Rituals of Transformation in African Societies* (Bloomington: Indiana Univ. Press, 1993); and Wyatt MacGaffey, *Kongo Political Culture: The Conceptual Challenge of the Particular* (Bloomington: Indiana Univ. Press, 2000). Contrast this interpretation with John K. Thornton, "Elite Women in the Kingdom of Kongo: Historical Perspectives on Women's Political Power," *Journal of African History* 47, no. 3 (2006): 437–460.

13. John K. Thornton, "Ideology and Political Power in Central Africa: The Case of Queen Njinga (1624–1663)," *Journal of African History* 32, no. 1 (1991): 25–40.

14. Phyllis M. Martin, *Catholic Women of Congo-Brazzaville: Mothers and Sisters in Troubled Times* (Bloomington: Indiana Univ. Press, 2009), 3–6, 20–31. See also Christine Saidi, *Women's Authority and Society in Early East-Central Africa* (Rochester, N.Y.: Univ. of Rochester Press, 2010)

15. The debate on the deep roots of matriliny in Bantu-speaking Africa can be found in Jan Vansina, *Paths in the Rainforests: Toward a History of Political Tradition in Equatorial Africa* (Madison: Univ. of Wisconsin Press, 1990), 152–155; Christopher Ehret, *An African Classical Age: Eastern and Southern Africa in World History, 1000 B.C. to A.D. 400* (Charlottesville: Univ. Press of Virginia, 1998); Kairn A. Klieman, *"The Pygmies Were Our Compass": Bantu and Batwa in the History of West Central Africa, Early Times to c. 1900 C.E* (Portsmouth, N.H.: Heinemann, 2003); Jan Vansina, *How Societies Are Born: Governance in West Central Africa before 1600* (Charlottesville: Univ. Press of Virginia, 2004); and Saidi, *Women's Authority and Society*, 12–19.

16. Léo Bittremieux, *La société secrète des Bakhimba au Mayombe* (Brussels: Librairie Falk Fils, 1936); Luc de Heusch, *Le roi de Kongo et les monstres sacrés: Mythes et rites bantous III* (Paris: Gallimard, 2000), 186–187; Ngoma Ngambu, *Initiation dans les societes traditionnelles Africaines (le cas Kongo)* (Kinshasa: Presses Universitaires du Zaire, 1981); and Joseph van Wing, *Études Bakongo: II, Religion et Magie* (Brussels: Académie Royale des Sciences d'Outre-Mer, 1938), 183–185.

17. Joseph van Wing and C. Penders, eds., *Le plus ancien dictionnaire bantu = Het oudste bantu-woordenboek: Vocabularium p. Georgii Gelensis* (Louvain: J. Kuyl-Otto, 1928), 254. See also K. E. Laman, *Dictionnaire Kikongo-Française avec une étude phonétique décrivant les dialectes les plus importants de la langue dite Kikongo* (1937; reprint, Ridgewood, N.J.: Gregg Press, 1964), 693.

18. Karl Laman, *The Kongo*, 4 vols. (Uppsala: Studia Ethnographia Upsaliensa, 1962), 2:6–8; Wyatt MacGaffey, *Religion and Society in Central Africa: The BaKongo of Lower Zaire* (Chicago: Univ. of Chicago Press, 1986), 85–88; Wyatt MacGaffey, "Twins, Simbi Spirits, and Lwas in Kongo and Haiti," in *Central Africans and Cultural Transformations in the American Diaspora*, ed. Linda M. Heywood, 211–226 (New York: Cambridge Univ. Press, 2002).

The spiritual significance of twinning is attested to in a mid-seventeenth-century source. See Giovanni Antonio Cavazzi da Montecuccolo, *Descrição histórico doe três reinos Congo Matamba e Angola,* trans. and ed. Graziano Maria da Legguzzano, 7 vols. (Lisbon: Junta de Investigações do Ultramar, 1965), vol. 1, nos. 200 and 255.

19. Lorenzo da Lucca, *Relations sur le Congo du Père Laurent de Lucques (1700-1717),* trans. and ed. J. Cuvelier (Brussels: Institut Royal Colonial Belge, 1953), 138-139.

20. Ibid.

21. Giacinto Hyacinthe, *La pratique missionnaire de PP. Capucins italiens, dans le royaumes de Congo, Angola et Contrées Adjacentes, 1747* (Louvain: Éditions de L'Aucam, 1931), 125-126.

22. Laman, *Kongo,* 2:8.

23. Cavazzi, *Descrição,* vol. 2, no. 64.

24. Buenaventura de Corella, "Relation sur le Congo par Buenaventura de Corella," in *L'ancien Congo et Angola, 1639-1655, d'après les archives romanes, portugaises, néederlandaises et espagnoles,* ed. Louis Jadin, 2 vols. (1649; edited edition, Brussels: Institute Historique Belge de Rome, 1975), 2:1156, 1157, 1161; Luca da Caltanisetta, *Diaire congolaise (1690-1701),* trans. and ed. François Bontinck (Louvain: Éditions Nauwelaerts, 1970), 132-133; Lorenzo da Lucca, *Relations sur le Congo,* 134; and Cavazzi, *Descrição,* vol. 1, no. 198.

25. Luca da Caltanisetta, *Diaire congolaise,* 102-103; and Cavazzi, *Descrição,* vol. 1, no. 182. For a recent perspective on interpreting death in Kongo culture, see Kimpianga Mahaniah, *La mort dans la pensée kongo* (Kisantu, Zaïre: Centre de Vulgarisation Agricole, 1980), 8-13.

26. Cavazzi, *Descrição,* vol. 1, no. 193.

27. Hyacinthe, *La pratique missionnaire,* 124-125; Raimundo de Dicomano, "Informação do Reino do Congo de Frei Raimundo de Dicomano," trans. António Brásio, *Studia* 34 (June 1972): 41.

28. Luca da Caltanisetta, *Diaire congolaise* , 117-8; and Cavazzi, *Descrição,* Vol. 1, Nos. 205-225.

29. Luca da Caltanisetta, *Diaire congolaise,* 103; and Lorenzo da Lucca, *Relations sur le Congo,* 131-132. For descriptions of the training of *ngangas* based on more recent Kongo sources, see John H. Weeks, "The Congo Medicine-Man and His Black and White Magic," *Folklore* 21, no. 4 (1910): 447-471; Laman, *Kongo,* 3:173-183; Wyatt MacGaffey, *Art and Healing of the Bakongo Commented by Themselves: Minkisi from the Laman Collection* (Stockholm: Folkens Museum—Etnografiska, 1991), 33-34; and A. kia Bunseki-Lumanisa Fu-Kiau, *N'Kongo ye Nza Yakun'Zungidila: Nza-Kôngo (le Mukongo et le monde qui l'entourait)* (Kinshasa: Office National de la Recherche et de Développement, 1968), 133-148.

30. Cavazzi, *Descrição,* vol. 1, no. 170; and Olfert Dapper, *Description de l'Afrique* (Amsterdam: Chez Wolfgang, Waesberge, Boom and van Someren, 1686), 336-338.

31. Luca da Caltanisetta, *Diaire congolaise,* 95.

32. Ibid.

33. Girolamo de Montesarchio, "Viaggi apostolici," 18, 22v-23, in *La prefettura apostolica del Congo alla metá del XVII Secolo: La relazione inedita dei Girolamo da Montesarchio,* ed. Calogero Piazza, 193, 199 (Milan: A. Giuffrè, 1976).

34. Bittremieux, *Société secrète,* 249-263.

35. Luca da Caltanisetta, *Diaire congolaise,* 101.

36. Ibid., 137-138.

37. This role is described in recent ethnographic sources only, although we can assume that this station existed in earlier times based on the continuity in meanings associated with the term *ngudi*. See Laman, *Kongo*, 3:173, and Buakasa Tulu Kia Mpansu, *L'impense du discours: "Kindoki" et "nkisi" en pays kongo du Zaïre* (Kinshasa: Presses Universitaires du Zaire, 1973), 252.

38. Lydia Cabrera, *Vocabulario Congo: el bantu que se habla en Cuba* (Miami: Colección del Chicherekú en el exilio, 1984), 32, 33, 34, 96, 97, 113, 142; Altair Pinto, *Dicionário da umbanda: contendo o maior número de palavras, usadas na umbanda no candomblé e nos cultos afro-brasileiros* (Rio de Janeiro: Editôra Eco, 1971), 91; Olga Gudolle Cacciatore, *Dicionário de cultos afro-brasileiros, com origem das palavras* (Rio de Janeiro: Forense Universitária, 1977), 133; Nei Lopes, *Bantos, malês, e identidade negro* (Rio de Janeiro: Forense Universitária, 1988), 173; Milo Rigaud, *La tradition voudoo et le Voudoo haïtien: Son temple, ses mystères, sa magie* (Paris: Édition Niclaus, 1953), 422; and Turner, *Africanisms in the Gullah Dialect*, 140.

39. James H. Sweet, *Recreating Africa: Culture, Kinship, and Religion in the African-Portuguese World, 1441-1770* (Chapel Hill: Univ. of North Carolina Press, 2003), 155.

40. Yeda Pessoa de Castro, *Falares africanos na Bahia (um vocabulário afro-brasileiro)* (Rio de Janeiro: Topbooks, 2001), 271, 297. See the detailed description of the Dendeziro house in Bahia in Dale T. Graden, "'So Much Superstition Among These People!': Candomblé and the Dilemmas of Afro-Bahian Intellectuals, 1864-1871," in *Afro-Brazilian Culture and Politics: Bahia, 1790s to 1990s*, ed. Hendrick Kraay, 68-69 (Armonk, N.Y.: M. E. Sharpe, 1998). For the evolving roles of women ritual experts in *candomblé* in general, see Rachel Elizabeth Harding, "É a Senzala: Slavery, Women, and Embodied Knowledge in Afro-Brazilian Candomblé," in *Women and Religion in the African Diaspora: Knowledge, Power, and Performance*, ed. R. Marie Griffith and Barbara Dianne Savage, 3-18 (Baltimore: Johns Hopkins Univ. Press, 2006); and Kelly E. Hayes, "Serving the Spirits, Healing the Person: Women in Afro-Brazilian Religions," in *Women and New and Africana Religions*, ed. Lillian Ashcraft-Eason, Darnise C. Martin, and Oyeronke Oladimo, 101-122 (Santa Barbara, Calif.: Praeger, 2010).

41. António da Silva Maia, *Dicionário complementar Português-Kimbundu-Kikongo*, 2nd ed. (Cucujães: Depositária Editorial Missoes, 1964), 434.

42. Rachel Elizabeth Harding, *A Refuge in Thunder: Candomblé and Alternative Spaces of Blackness* (Bloomington: Indiana Univ. Press, 2000), 72-74; and Edison Carneiro, *Candomblés da Bahia* (Rio de Janeiro: Tecnoprint Gráfica S.A., 1967), 128-129. A similar process of gender realignment within religious institutions supported by African-descended people appears to have occurred within some Roman Catholic brotherhoods that included women members. See Mariza de Carvalho Soares, "Can Women Guide and Govern Men? Gendering Politics among African Catholics in Colonial Brazil," in *Women and Slavery: The Modern Atlantic*, ed. Gwyn Campbell, Suzanne Miers, and Joseph C. Miller, 2:79-99 (Athens: Ohio Univ. Press, 2007).

43. Cabrera, *Vocabulario Congo*, 32, 33, 113, 142; Pinto, *Dicionário da umbanda*, 188; Cacciatore, *Dicionário de cultos afro-brasileiros*, 249; José Rodrigues da Costa, *Candomblé de Angola* (Rio de Janeiro: Pallas, 1989), 27; Arthur Ramos, *O Negro Brasileiro* (Rio de Janeiro: Civilização Brasileira S.A., 1934), 92-93; Turner, *Africanisms in the Gullah Dialect*, 202; Maureen Warner Lewis, *Central Africa in the Caribbean: Transcending Time, Transforming Cultures* (Kingston, Jamaica: Univ. of West Indies Press, 2003), 311; and Richard Allsop, *Dictionary of Caribbean English Usage* (Oxford: Oxford Univ. Press, 1996), 549.

44. Erwan Dianteill, *Des dieux et des signes: Initiation, écriture et divination dans les religions afro-cubaines* (Paris: Éditions de l'École des Hautes Études en Sciences Sociales, 2000), 151–163; Palmié, *Wizards and Scientists,* 159–200; and Mary Ann Clark, *Where Men Are Wives and Mothers Rule: Santería Ritual Practices and Their Gender Implications* (Gainesville: Univ. Press of Florida, 2005), 63, 80–81, 138–141, 158 n.6. Positing gendered characterizations of entire spiritual cultures requires caution (to say the least), as discussed masterfully by Matory in *Black Atlantic Religion,* 188–266.

45. Cabrera, *Vocabulario Congo,* 96, 97.

46. There are some instances of the use of *nganga* to identify an expert, but this appears to be far less frequent. For examples, see Cabrera, *Vocabulario Congo,* 32, 34, 142.

47. Ibid., 130.

48. Bolívar Aróstegui and González Dias de Villegas, *Ta Makuende Yaya,* 70.

49. María Teresa Vélez, *Drumming for the Gods: The Life and Times of Felipe García Villamil, Santero, Palero, and Abakuá* (Philadelphia: Temple Univ. Press, 2000), 16.

50. Bolívar Aróstegui and González Dias de Villegas, *Ta Makuende Yaya,* 70–71.

51. Ibid.; Cabrera, *Reglas de Congo,* 132–133.

52. Cabrera, *Reglas de Congo,* 15, 130.

53. Emilío Sanchez y Sanchez, *Recuerdos del tiempo viejo: tradiciones trinitarias.* (Cienfuegos: Imp. Papeleria y Rayados de L-F-Martín, 1916), 129, quoted in Lydia Cabrera, *La medicina popular de Cuba: Médicos de antaño, curanderos, santeros y paleros de hogaño* (Miami: Ultra Graphics, 1984), 140.

54. Cabrera, *Reglas de Congo,* 168. The importance of women ritual experts in the *reglas de congo* has received very little scholarly attention, an important exception being the informative linguistic and ethnographic study by Jesús Fuentes Guerra and Armin Schwegler entitled *Lengua y ritos del Palo Monte Mayombe: Dioses cubanos y sus fuentes africanas* (Madrid: Iberoamericana, 2005), 77–81.

55. Philip A. Howard, *Changing History: Afro-Cuban Cabildos and Societies of Color in the Nineteenth Century* (Baton Rogue: Louisiana State Univ. Press, 1998); and Matt D. Childs, "Pathways to African Ethnicity in the Americas: African National Associations in Cuba during Slavery," in *Sources and Methods in African History: Spoken, Written, Unearthed,* ed. Toyin Falola and Christian Jennings, 118–144 (Rochester, N.Y.: Univ. of Rochester Press, 2003).

WORKS CITED

Allsop, Richard. *Dictionary of Caribbean English Usage.* Oxford: Oxford Univ. Press, 1996.

Ashcraft-Eason, Lillian, Darnise C. Martin, and Oyeronke Olademo, eds. *Women and New and Africana Religions.* Santa Barbara, Calif.: Praeger, 2010.

Ayorinde, Christine. *Afro-Cuban Religiosity, Revolution, and National Identity.* Gainesville: Univ. Press of Florida, 2004.

———. "Santería in Cuba: Tradition and Transformation." In *The Yoruba Diaspora in the Atlantic World,* edited by Toyin Falola and Matt D. Childs, 209–230. Bloomington: Indiana Univ. Press, 2004.

Bay, Edna G. *Wives of the Leopard: Gender, Politics, and Culture in the Kingdom of Dahomey.* Charlottesville: Univ. Press of Virginia, 1998.

Bilby, Kenneth. "African American Memory at the Crossroads: Grounding the Miraculous with Tooy." *Small Axe* 13, no. 2 (2009): 185–199.
Bittremieux, Léo. *La société secrète des Bakhimba au Mayombe*. Brussels: Librairie Falk fils, 1936.
Bolívar Aróstegui, Natalia, and Carmen González Díaz de Villegas. *Ta Makuende Yaya y las Reglas de Palo Monte*. Havana: Ediciones Unión—Unión de Escritores y Artistas de Cuba, 1998.
Brathwaite, Edward Kamau. *The Development of Creole Society in Jamaica, 1770–1820*. Oxford: Clarendon Press, 1971.
Brown, David H. *Santería Enthroned: Art, Ritual, and Innovation in Afro-Cuban Religion*. Chicago: Univ. of Chicago Press, 2003.
Brown, Karen McCarthy. *Mama Lola: A Vodou Priestess in Brooklyn*. Berkeley: Univ. of California Press, 2001.
Buakasa Tulu Kia Mpansu. *L'impense du discours: "Kindoki" et "nkisi" en pays kongo du Zaïre*. Kinshasa: Presses Universitaires du Zaire, 1973.
Buenaventura de Corella. "Relation sur le Congo par Buenaventura de Corella." In *L'ancien Congo et Angola, 1639–1655, d'après les archives romanes, portugaises, néederlandaises et espagnoles*, 2 vols., edited by Louis Jadin, 2:1150–1165. Brussels: Institute Historique Belge de Rome, 1975.
Byfield, Judith A., LaRay Denzer, and Anthea Morrison, eds. *Gendering the African Diaspora: Women, Culture, and Historical Change in the Caribbean and Nigerian Hinterland*. Bloomington: Indiana Univ. Press, 2010.
Cabrera, Lydia. *La medicina popular de Cuba: Médicos de antaño, curanderos, santeros y paleros de hogaño*. Miami: Ultra Graphics, 1984.
———. *Reglas de Congo: Palo Monte Mayombe*. Miami: Peninsular Print, 1979.
———. *Vocabulario Congo: el bantu que se habla en Cuba*. Miami: Colección del Chicherekú en el exilio, 1984.
Cacciatore, Olga Gudolle. *Dicionário de cultos afro-brasileiros, com origem das palavras*. Rio de Janeiro: Forense Universitária, 1977.
Campbell, Gwyn, Suzanne Miers, and Joseph C. Miller, eds. *Women and Slavery: The Modern Atlantic*. 2 vols. Athens: Ohio Univ. Press, 2007.
Capone, Stefania. *Searching for Africa in Brazil: Power and Tradition in Candomblé*. Durham: Duke Univ. Press, 2010.
Carneiro, Edison. *Candomblés da Bahia*. Rio de Janeiro: Tecnoprint Gráfica S.A., 1967.
Carney, Judith A. *Black Rice: The African Origins of Rice Cultivation in the Americas*. Cambridge: Harvard Univ. Press, 2001.
Cavazzi da Montecuccolo, Giovanni Antonio. *Descrição histórico doe três reinos Congo Matamba e Angola*. Translated and edited by Graziano Maria da Legguzzano. 7 vols. Lisbon: Junta de Investigações do Ultramar, 1965.
Childs, Matt D. "Pathways to African Ethnicity in the Americas: African National Associations in Cuba during Slavery." In *Sources and Methods in African*

History: Spoken, Written, Unearthed, edited by Toyin Falola and Christian Jennings, 118–144. Rochester, N.Y.: Univ. of Rochester Press, 2003.
Clark, Mary Ann. *Where Men Are Wives and Mothers Rule: Santería Ritual Practices and Their Gender Implications.* Gainesville: Univ. Press of Florida, 2005.
Dapper, Olfert. *Description de l'Afrique.* Amsterdam: Chez Wolfgang, Waesberge, Boom and van Someren, 1686.
Dianteill, Erwan. *Des dieux et des signes: Initiation, écriture et divination dans les religions afro-cubaines.* Paris: Éditions de l'École des Hautes Études en Sciences Sociales, 2000.
Dicomano, Raimundo de. "Informação do Reino do Congo de Frei Raimundo de Dicomano." Translated by Antonio Brásio. *Studia* 34 (June 1972): 19–42.
Dodson, Jualynne E. *Sacred Spaces and Religious Traditions in Oriente Cuba.* Albuquerque: Univ. of New Mexico Press, 2008.
DuBois, W.E.B., *Black Folk, Then and Now: An Essay in the History and Sociology of the Black Race.* New York: Henry Holt, 1939.
———. *The Negro.* New York: Henry Holt, 1915.
Ehret, Christopher. *An African Classical Age: Eastern and Southern Africa in World History, 1000 B.C. to A.D. 400.* Charlottesville: Univ. Press of Virginia, 1998.
Falola, Toyin, and Christian Jennings, eds. *Sources and Methods in African History: Spoken, Written, Unearthed.* Rochester, N.Y.: Univ. of Rochester Press, 2003.
Falola, Toyin, and Matt D. Childs, eds. *The Yoruba Diaspora in the Atlantic World.* Bloomington: Indiana Univ. Press, 2004.
Fandrich, Ina Johanna. *The Mysterious Voodoo Queen, Marie Laveau: A Study of Powerful Female Leadership in Nineteenth-Century New Orleans.* New York: Routledge, 2005.
Fuentes Guerra, Jesús, and Armin Schwegler. *Lengua y ritos del Palo Monte Mayombe: Dioses cubanos y sus fuentes africanas.* Madrid: Iberoamericana, 2005.
Fu-Kiau, A. kia Bunseki-Lumanisa. *N'Kongo ye Nza Yakun'Zungidila: Nza-Kôngo (le Mukongo et le monde qui l'entourait).* Kinshasa: Office National de la Recherche et de Développement, 1968.
Girolamo de Montesarchio. "Viaggi apostolici." In *La prefettura apostolica del Congo alla metá del XVII Secolo: La relazione inedita dei Girolamo da Montesarchio,* edited by Calogero Piazza, 165–279. Milan: A. Giuffrè, 1976.
Gomez, Michael A. *Exchanging Our Country Marks: The Transformations of African Identities in the Colonial and Antebellum South.* Chapel Hill: Univ. of North Carolina Press, 1998.
Graden, Dale T. "'So Much Superstition Among These People!': Candomblé and the Dilemmas of Afro-Bahian Intellectuals, 1864–1871." In *Afro-Brazilian Culture and Politics: Bahia, 1790s to 1990s,* edited by Hendrick Kraay, 57–73. Armonk, N.Y.: M. E. Sharpe, 1998.

Gunning, Sandra, Tera W. Hunter, and Michele Mitchell, eds. *Dialogues of Dispersal: Gender, Sexuality and African Diasporas.* Malden, Mass.: Blackwell, 2004.

———. "Introduction: Gender, Sexuality, and African Diasporas." *Gender and History* 15, no. 3 (2003): 397–408.

Hall, Gwendolyn Midlo. *Slavery and African Ethnicities in the Americas: Restoring the Links.* Chapel Hill: Univ. of North Carolina Press, 2005.

Harding, Rachel Elizabeth. "É a Senzala: Slavery, Women, and Embodied Knowledge in Afro-Brazilian Candomblé." In *Women and Religion in the African Diaspora: Knowledge, Power, and Performance,* edited by R. Marie Griffith and Barbara Dianne Savage, 3–18. Baltimore: Johns Hopkins Univ. Press, 2006.

———. *A Refuge in Thunder: Candomblé and Alternative Spaces of Blackness.* Bloomington: Indiana Univ. Press, 2000.

Hayes, Kelly E. "Black Magic and the Academy: Macumba and Afro-Brazilian 'Orthodoxies.'" *History of Religions* 46, no. 4 (2007): 283–315.

———. "Serving the Spirits, Healing the Person: Women in Afro-Brazilian Religions." In *Women and New and Africana Religions,* edited by Lillian Ashcraft-Eason, Darnise C. Martin, and Oyeronke Oladem0, 101–122. Santa Barbara, Calif.: Praeger, 2010.

———. "Wicked Women and Femmes Fatales: Gender, Power, and Pomba Gira in Brazil." *History of Religions* 48, no. 1 (2008): 1–21.

Herbert, Eugenia W. *Iron, Gender, and Power: Rituals of Transformation in African Societies.* Bloomington: Indiana Univ. Press, 1993.

Herskovits, Melville J. *Myth of the Negro Past.* New York: Harper and Brothers, 1941.

Heusch, Luc de. *Le roi de Kongo et les monstres sacrés: Mythes et rites bantous III.* Paris: Gallimard, 2000.

Heywood, Linda M., ed. *Central Africans and Cultural Transformations in the American Diaspora.* New York: Cambridge Univ. Press, 2002.

Heywood, Linda M., and John K. Thornton. *Central Africans, Atlantic Creoles, and the Foundations of the Americas, 1585–1660.* New York: Cambridge Univ. Press, 2007.

Hilton, Anne. "European Sources for the Study of Religious Change in Sixteenth and Seventeenth Century Kongo." *Paideuma* 33 (1987): 289–312.

Howard, Philip A. *Changing History: Afro-Cuban Cabildos and Societies of Color in the Nineteenth Century.* Baton Rogue: Louisiana State Univ. Press, 1998.

Hyacinthe, Giacinto. *La pratique missionnaire de PP. Capucins italiens, dans le royaumes de Congo, Angola et Contrées Adjacentes, 1747.* Louvain: Éditions de L'Aucam, 1931.

Klieman, Kairn A. *"The Pygmies Were Our Compass": Bantu and Batwa in the His-*

tory of West Central Africa, Early Times to c. 1900 C.E. Portsmouth, N.H.: Heinemann, 2003.

Kraay, Hendrick, ed. *Afro-Brazilian Culture and Politics: Bahia, 1790s to 1990s.* Armonk, N.Y.: M. E. Sharpe, 1998.

Laman, Karl E. *The Kongo.* 4 vols. Uppsala: Studia Ethnographia Upsaliensa, 1962.

———. *Dictionnaire Kikongo-Française avec une étude phonétique décrivant les dialectes les plus importants de la langue dite Kikongo.* 1937. Reprint, Ridgewood, N.J.: Gregg Press, 1964.

Lewis, Maureen Warner. *Central Africa in the Caribbean: Transcending Time, Transforming Cultures.* Kingston, Jamaica: Univ. of West Indies Press, 2003.

Long, Carolyn Morrow. *A New Orleans Voudou Priestess: The Legend and Reality of Marie Laveau.* Gainesville: Univ. Press of Florida, 2006.

Lopes, Nei. *Bantos, malês, e identidade negro.* Rio de Janeiro: Forense Universitária, 1988.

Lorenzo da Lucca. *Relations sur le Congo du Père Laurent de Lucques (1700–1717).* Translated and edited by J. Cuvelier. Brussels: Institut Royal Colonial Belge, 1953.

Luca da Caltanisetta. *Diaire congolaise (1690–1701).* Translated and edited by François Bontinck. Louvain: Éditions Nauwelaerts, 1970.

MacGaffey, Wyatt. *Art and Healing of the Bakongo Commented by Themselves: Minkisi from the Laman Collection.* Stockholm: Folkens Museum—Etnografiska, 1991.

———. *Kongo Political Culture: The Conceptual Challenge of the Particular.* Bloomington: Indiana Univ. Press, 2000.

———. *Religion and Society in Central Africa: The BaKongo of Lower Zaire.* Chicago: Univ. of Chicago Press, 1986.

———. "Twins, Simbi Spirits, and Lwas in Kongo and Haiti." In *Central Africans and Cultural Transformations in the American Diaspora,* edited by Linda M. Heywood, 211–226. New York: Cambridge Univ. Press, 2002.

Mahaniah, Kimpianga. *La mort dans la pensée kongo.* Kisantu, Zaïre: Centre de Vulgarisation Agricole, 1980.

Martin, Phyllis M. *Catholic Women of Congo-Brazzaville: Mothers and Sisters in Troubled Times.* Bloomington: Indiana Univ. Press, 2009.

Matory, J. Lorand. *Black Atlantic Religion: Tradition, Transnationalism, and Matriarchy in the Afro-Brazilian Candomblé.* Princeton: Princeton Univ. Press, 2005.

Mintz, Sidney W., and Richard Price. *The Birth of African-American Culture: An Anthropological Perspective.* Boston: Beacon Press, 1992.

Morgan, Jennifer L. *Laboring Women: Reproduction and Gender in New World Slavery.* Philadelphia: Univ. of Pennsylvania Press, 2004.

Morgan, Philip D. "The Cultural Implications of the Atlantic Slave Trade: African Regional Origins, American Destinations and New World Developments." *Slavery and Abolition* 18, no. 1 (1997): 122–145.

Ngoma Ngambu. *Initiation dans les societes traditionnelles Africaines (le cas Kongo)*. Kinshasa: Presses Universitaires du Zaire, 1981.

Ocha, Todd Ramón. *Societies of the Dead: Quita Manaquita and Palo Praise in Cuba*. Berkeley: Univ. of California Press, 2010.

Palmié, Stephan. "Creolization and Its Discontents." *Annual Review of Anthropology* 35 (2006): 433–456.

———. *Wizards and Scientists: Explorations in Afro-Cuban Modernity and Tradition*. Durham: Duke Univ. Press, 2002.

Parés, Luis Nicolau. "The 'Nagôization' Process in Bahian Candomblé." In *The Yoruba Diaspora in the Atlantic World,* edited by Toyin Falola and Matt D. Childs, 185–208. Bloomington: Indiana Univ. Press, 2004.

Pessoa de Castro, Yeda. *Falares africanos na Bahia (um vocabulário afro-brasileiro)*. Rio de Janeiro: Topbooks, 2001.

Pinto, Altair. *Dicionário da umbanda: contendo o maior número de palavras, usadas na umbanda no candomblé e nos cultos afro-brasileiros*. Rio de Janeiro: Editôra Eco, 1971.

Price, Richard. "On the Miracle of Creolization." In *Afro-Atlantic Dialogues: Anthropology in the Diaspora,* edited by Kevin A. Yelvington, 115–147. Santa Fe, N. Mex.: School of American Research, 2006.

Ramos, Arthur. *O Negro Brasileiro*. Rio de Janeiro: Civilização Brasileira S.A., 1934.

Ramos, Miguel W. "La división de la Habana: Territorial Conflict and Cultural Hegemony in the Followers of Oyo Lukumí Religion, 1850s–1920s." *Cuban Studies* 34 (2003): 38–70.

Rigaud, Milo. *La tradition voudoo et le Voudoo haïtien: Son temple, ses mystères, sa magie*. Paris: Édition Niclaus, 1953.

Rodrigues da Costa, José. *Candomblé de Angola*. Rio de Janeiro: Pallas, 1989.

Saidi, Christine. *Women's Authority and Society in Early East-Central Africa*. Rochester, N.Y.: Univ. of Rochester Press, 2010.

Silva Maia, António da. *Dicionário complementar Português-Kimbundu-Kikongo,* 2nd ed. Cucujães, Portugal: Depositária Editorial Missoes, 1964.

Soares, Mariza de Carvalho. "Can Women Guide and Govern Men? Gendering Politics among African Catholics in Colonial Brazil." In *Women and Slavery: The Modern Atlantic,* 2 vols., edited by Gwyn Campbell, Suzanne Miers, and Joseph C. Miller, 2:79–99. Athens: Ohio Univ. Press, 2007.

Stuckey, Sterling. *Slave Culture: Nationalist Theory and the Foundations of Black America*. New York: Oxford Univ. Press, 1987.

Sweet, James H. *Recreating Africa: Culture, Kinship, and Religion in the African-*

Portuguese World, 1441–1770. Chapel Hill: Univ. of North Carolina Press, 2003.

Terborg-Penn, Rosalyn, and Andrea Benton Rushing, eds. *Women in Africa and the African Diaspora: A Reader.* Washington, D.C.: Howard Univ. Press, 1996.

Thornton, John K. *Africa and Africans in the Making of the Atlantic World, 1400–1800,* 2nd ed. New York: Cambridge Univ. Press, 1998.

———. "Elite Women in the Kingdom of Kongo: Historical Perspectives on Women's Political Power." *Journal of African History* 47, no. 3 (2006): 437–460.

———. "Ideology and Political Power in Central Africa: The Case of Queen Njinga (1624–1663)." *Journal of African History* 32, no. 1 (1991): 25–40.

Trouillot, Michel-Rolph. "Culture on the Edges: Creolization in the Plantation Context." *Plantation Society in the Americas* 1, no. 1 (1998): 8–28.

Turner, Lorenzo Dow. *Africanisms in the Gullah Dialect.* Chicago: Univ. of Chicago Press, 1949.

Vansina, Jan. *How Societies Are Born: Governance in West Central Africa before 1600.* Charlottesville: Univ. Press of Virginia, 2004.

———. *Paths in the Rainforests: Toward a History of Political Tradition in Equatorial Africa.* Madison: Univ. of Wisconsin Press, 1990.

Vélez, María Teresa. *Drumming for the Gods: The Life and Times of Felipe García Villamil, Santero, Palero, and Abakuá.* Philadelphia: Temple Univ. Press, 2000.

Voyages: The Trans-Atlantic Slave Trade Database. www.slavevoyages.org.

Walker, Sheila S. "The Feast of the Good Death: An Afro-Catholic Emancipation Celebration in Brazil." In *Women in Africa and the African Diaspora: A Reader,* edited by Rosalyn Terborg-Penn and Andrea Benton Rushing, 203–214. Washington, D.C.: Howard Univ. Press, 1996.

Weeks, John H. "The Congo Medicine-Man and His Black and White Magic." *Folklore* 21, no. 4 (1910): 447–471.

Wing, Joseph van. *Études Bakongo: II, Religion et Magie.* Brussels: Académie Royale des Sciences d'Outre-Mer, 1938.

Wing, Joseph van, and C. Penders, eds. *Le plus ancien dictionnaire bantu = Het oudste bantu-woordenboek: Vocabularium p. Georgii Gelensis.* Louvain: J. Kuyl-Otto, 1928.

Woodson, Carter G. *The African Background Outlined; or, Handbook for the Study of the Negro.* Washington, D.C.: Association for the Study of Negro Life and History, 1936.

Yelvington, Kevin A., ed. *Afro-Atlantic Dialogues: Anthropology in the Diaspora.* Santa Fe, N. Mex.: School of American Research, 2006.

10

Gendering the African Diaspora in the Iberian Atlantic

Religious Brotherhoods and the *Cabildos de Nación*

MATT D. CHILDS

In 1803 the captain general of Cuba (equivalent to an English governor), the Marques de Someruelos, received several petitions to intercede in a disputed election. After local judicial officials in Havana investigated the complaints, several women called on the captain general to take on the case himself. The disputed election centered on who should hold the position of second *capataz* (foreman, captain, or overseer) of the African religious and mutual aid society known as the *cabildo de nación* Carabali Induri del Santo Cristo de Buen Viaje. None of the parties contesting the election disputed the vote count. Free black Juan Echevarría had easily won by nearly a 2–1 margin. But the losing side, representing Mateo Villarte, challenged the election. They solicited the aid of attorney don Gabriel Aleman and argued that their candidate's loss was the result of the vast majority of women voting for Juan Echevarría.[1]

The disputed election had occurred on June 17, 1803. Following established procedures, the commissioner of Havana's Santa Teresa neighborhood, accompanied by a notary, went to the house of the *cabildo de nación* Carabali Induri to observe and record the election of second *capataz*. The other *cabildo de nación* societies throughout Cuba employed the same terminology to designate rights as did governmental *cabildos*. Under these rights, the free black male and female members who held the authority of *"voto y voz"* had the privilege to "vote" and "speak" at the meetings and cast their ballots. Among the seventy-one votes counted in the election, forty-seven were for Juan Echevarría and twenty-four were for Mateo Villarte. Under normal procedures, the sources documenting *cabildo* elections simply recorded the winner of the election. In this case, however, because Mateo Villarte and his supporters challenged the results, the vote tally for the disputed election listed the names—and by inference, the gender—of those who voted.[2]

Although males held the leadership titles of first, second, and third *capataz* of the *cabildo* Carabli Induri, the voting records indicate that women wielded decisive authority over who would hold the elected positions by their numerical superiority. Of the forty-seven votes cast in favor of Juan Echevarría, thirty-two came from females and fifteen from males. Of the twenty-four votes cast in favor of Mateo Villarte, eight came from females and sixteen came from males. The attorney representing Villarte requested that the election be considered null and void because when "they have elections for *capataz*, they should not admit the votes of women."[3] If the female votes could be thrown out, Mateo Villarte would win the election by one vote, rather than losing by a landslide. When the case reached Captain General Someruelos, he quickly dismissed the protests. The captain general concluded that it would be "absolutely" unjustified to dismiss "the votes of women when they routinely follow the opposite" procedure in the day-to-day operations of the *cabildos*.[4] Someruelos upheld Juan Echevarría as winner of the election for second *capataz*, and affirmed the women's influence and the ability to vote in *cabildo* elections.

The disputed election over who should hold the position of second *capataz* of the *cabildo de nación* Carabali Induri offers a gendered perspective of a colonial Cuban institution that served the spiritual and worldly needs of the population of African descent. Dating back to as early as the sixteenth century, Africans in Havana had the ability to form religious and mutual aid societies that had evolved over the centuries from lay religious brotherhoods into collective voluntary associations that emphasized a common place of origin in Africa. Africans organized these societies by stressing a shared place of family ancestry and culture, such as Kongo, Lucumi, Mina, and Carabali, among others. Often a *cabildo* took a name that reflected both a broad provenance region in West Africa, such as Calabar (known in Spanish-speaking Cuba as Carabali), and emphasized a specific locality or polity, such as Nri (known in Spanish-Speaking Cuba as Induri), which is located in the Bight of Biafra on the Niger River delta and was a major source for Caribbean slaves during the eighteenth and nineteenth century.[5] As these organizations became more prevalent in colonial society during the eighteenth century, they owned their own houses and took on the title *cabildos de nación* to reflect the grouping by a common identity—often referred to as "*nación*" in Spanish—of the numerous African "nations" forcibly imported to Cuba. These societies and their houses were labeled *cabildos de nacíon* because the Spanish term "*cabildo*" represents the English language equivalent of a town council or a town government. The naming of these societies as *cabildos de nación* provides some indication of how their houses functioned as representative bodies for Africans by providing a cultural, social, and political space for their members to meet and fraternize in Havana. As is common in the literature, I will refer to these societies and their houses as *cabildos* throughout this chapter.[6]

This chapter examines the *cabildos* with a focus on the gendered relations between members of these societies. In particular, special attention is given to analyzing the roles and occupations of the male and female leaders of these societies. The first part of the chapter investigates the origins and operations of these societies and how rights and privileges varied between the free and enslaved members, and the African-born and Cuban-born members. Unlike Catholic brotherhoods and lay confraternities, or West African secret societies, which most commonly segregated participation by gender into separate organizations, *cabildos* had both male and female members and disputes often broke out along gender lines. The second part of the essay turns attention to male and female leadership roles in these societies. The overall argument of the chapter in regard to the internal gender relations among *cabildo* members can be summarized as follows: while men served as the leaders of the societies, women influenced and shaped who ran the organizations since they often outnumbered the men, and flexed their numerical superiority through voting for leaders and deciding the financial affairs, often to the consternation of the male members.

In focusing on the Havana *cabildos,* my major historiographical contribution is to be in dialogue with the current debates over studying African culture in the Americas during the era of slavery, while emphasizing and inserting more prominently the crucial role of gender in constructing diasporic identities. For the sake of brevity, two interpretative paradigms can be identified for studying the African diaspora. In a widely influential essay first authored in 1976, Sidney Mintz and Richard Price argued that African slaves brought to the New World represented "crowds" of disparate groups and cultures, "and very heterogeneous crowds at that." Subsequently known as the "creolization model," Mintz and Price did not ignore and even highlighted the cultural traditions Africans brought with them, but they forcefully suggested that scholarship should examine the creation of Creole cultures and innovations in the New World in response to the fact that "[w]hat they [slaves] undeniably shared at the outset was their enslavement." Mintz and Price cautioned scholars against looking for similarities between Old World and New World African traditions. Instead, they encouraged focusing analysis on how diverse African cultures came together and began to form and invent new bonds of association and identity born out of slavery through the process of creolization.[7] Since the 1970s, a large body of literature on slavery in the Americas has followed the Mintz and Price creolization model with its emphasis on New World innovations.[8]

Beginning in the 1990s a new direction in the field of diasporic studies began to challenge the creolization model by employing the Atlantic Ocean as one unit of study. Scholars with a deep knowledge of African history, such as Joseph Miller, Paul Lovejoy, Michael Gomez, Robin Law, John Thornton, David Eltis, James Sweet, and others took an increasing interest in slavery in the Americas. Embracing an Atlantic model for diaspora studies, scholars emphasized that slaves forcefully transported to the Americas carried with them their own history, culture, and identity that decisively shaped their experience in the Americas.[9] As *cabildos* formed along lines of tracing ancestry to a geographic point of origin on the African continent, yet represented institutions that catered to the needs and experiences of Africans in Havana, they reflect both innovations in adapting to New World slavery and efforts to maintain connections with an African past. Consequently, the *cabildos* serve to illustrate the benefits and limitations of current historiographical paradigms for interpreting diasporic culture in the Americas.

Moreover, and in regard to the particular focus of this volume on studying women in the Iberian Atlantic, *cabildos* also show how women must be featured more prominently in the debate over African cultural continuities and innovations in the Americas during the era of Atlantic slavery. Put another way, if the scholarly debate over *cabildos* pivots between interpretations of the organizations as locations for New World cultural innovations tied to creolization, or sites of cultural continuity in African cultural practices, how does the debate change when gender is inserted more prominently into the discussion? While scholarship on enslaved women (and gender and slavery more broadly) has created a burgeoning specialized subfield over the last thirty years, these studies have most often contributed to historiographies particular to a specific colony or a country. As historians Claire Robertson and Marsha Robinson have recently stressed, despite scholarly innovations in linking Africa and the Americas in diasporic studies through the Atlantic history model, "this literature has paid scant attention to women's particular, gendered roles in the process of transmitting cultures from Africa."[10] Similarly, Stephanie Smallwood's penetrating analysis of diasporic culture formed through the torturous process of the Middle Passage can only suggest at the end of her study (in a point that she does not investigate in detail) that "it would be difficult to overestimate the difference made by women's presence in these embryonic groups" when Africans crossed the Atlantic and disembarked at American ports.[11] With a few notable exceptions, the specific role of women in debates and conceptual models for studying diasporic cultural formation throughout the Americas has been at best obliquely recognized, or minimized altogether due to the sexual imbalance of the slave trade that favored males.[12]

In addition to inserting the gendered dimension of *cabildos* into the larger historiographical debates about the African diaspora during slavery, this study complements and complicates the existing literature on these societies as they relate more specifically to Cuban history. Scholarly examinations of the *cabildos* have largely focused on two distinct topics: religion and rebellion. In regard to religious studies of the African diaspora in Cuba, the *cabildos* often serve as the starting point where the Yoruba-influenced religion of Santería was born. The *cabildo* house functioned as the location where the syncretism of Yoruba and Catholic belief systems merged to create Santería. *Cabildos* with Yoruba (referred to in Cuba as a Lucumí) members, however, represented only one of many different African groups in Havana. Consequently, the role of other African groups in the history of *cabildos* tends to be grafted onto the experience of the Yoruba. In addition, the *cabildos* have been featured in studies of rebellion and resistance, as they played important roles in some of the largest slave uprisings in Cuban history, such as the Aponte Rebellion of 1812, the La Escalera Conspiracy of 1843–1844, and the Wars for Independence. While it is certainly true that many *cabildos* members utilized their homes to strategize and engage in acts of resistance, they performed many other functions there as well, and it would be a mischaracterization to draw attention only to their acts of rebellion. This focus on rebellion and religion has been beneficial for our understanding of the *cabildos*. Scholars now have a much more detailed knowledge about how these societies operated by focusing their investigations on these topics. But the orientation of this literature also has some limitations for understanding the *cabildos*. What these approaches have in common is that they use the *cabildos* as a brush to illustrate the history of a different topic, rather than a focus on how the *cabildo* houses operated on a day-to-day basis.[13] In contrast with studies that focus primarily on religion and rebellion, by coupling gender with an examination of *cabildo* activities, this chapter reveals the central role women played in these diasporic societies.

IBERIAN ORIGINS OF THE BROTHERHOODS AND CUBAN *CABILDOS DE NACIÓN*

Havana's *cabildos* trace their origins to the Spanish and Portuguese practice of organizing Catholic subjects into religious brotherhoods on the Iberian Peninsula, in Africa, and in the New World. As the Portuguese led the Iberian charge out of Europe and first engaged in setting up colonies off the coast of Africa, they established a model for incorporating the population of African descent into Catholic religious brotherhoods. As historian Linda Heywood has concluded, "African folk Christianity" thrived among Lisbon's black population in the fifteenth and sixteenth centuries because, in part, the Church honored petitions to establish ethnic-based confraternities that reflected cultural groupings from their homelands.[14] In Portugal, slaves imported from the Catholic territories of the Kingdom of Kongo and Angola flocked to the Brotherhood of Our Lady of the Rosary. The common appearance of Angolan and Kongolese ethnicity among Catholic brotherhoods likely indicates religious traditions slaves took with them and transformed when they crossed the Atlantic.[15]

The presence of women of African descent in religious organizations and corporate institutional bodies of the Church has a long history that predates Iberian colonization of the New World, because Catholic rituals reserved important roles for females, whether they were nuns or were serving in confraternities. By at least the tenth century, women routinely participated in confraternities in Italy specifically and Europe more generally. Confraternity statues analyzed by historians for the fourteenth and fifteenth centuries in such locations as Florence, Padua, and Bologna, Italy, specify roles for women, albeit with restrictions against speaking at meetings and general prohibitions against voting for new leaders and deciding financial matters.[16] Historian Maureen Flynn's study of confraternities in medieval and early modern Spain found that the organizations rarely excluded women, as was becoming more common in some locations, such as France and Italy, in the sixteenth and seventeenth centuries. Flynn discovered that "any gender segregation that existed among Castilian organizations was just as likely to have been initiated by women as by men, for occasionally women designed their own confraternal programs to meet special needs such as assistance in childbirth."[17] However, unlike the *cabildos de nación* of Havana, women who participated in Spanish confraternities on the Iberian Peninsula were not allowed to routinely participate in elections or hold administrative positions. As Flynn emphasizes, "the only time women enjoyed all the rights of membership and fully exercised democratic principles was when they formed their own organizations."[18] And unlike trends documented for Havana brotherhoods from the sixteenth to the eighteenth centuries that would witness an escalating and more visible role for African women in confraternities and *cabildos*, the Catholic Reformation under Philip II required that women sit at separate tables and in silence during feast day banquets. Moreover, by the seventeenth century only men could participate in the Passion confraternities in Spain.[19] As a result, while women most certainly played instrumental roles in Old World Catholic confraternities, the right for women of African descent in Havana's *cabildo* organization to exercise "*voto y voz*" equally with men appears unique to the Iberian New World.

Because these corporate fraternal bodies dotted the religious landscape of colonial Latin America, various scholars have focused on the confraternities to examine African-Catholic belief systems and the pronounced presence of the Catholic Church in shaping the spiritual lives of the enslaved and free population of African descent. For Brazil, historian Mariza de Carvalho Soares's study of religious brotherhoods in Rio de Janeiro documents how Africans who shared a similar ethnicity often formed their own sodalities.[20] Through a detailed analysis of internal documentation particular to the brotherhoods, Carvalho Soares has shown the prominent role of women in these brotherhoods and even their direct challenges to male authority, which had no parallel in Portugal.[21] By the end of the sixteenth century the names of sodalities in Lima often reflected African ethnicity, such as the Dominican brotherhood for the "negros Congos," and the brotherhood of Nuestra Señora del Socorro for Angolans.²² In Mexico City, Africans outnumbered Spaniards two to one by the end of the sixteenth century. Unsurprisingly, religious brotherhoods populated by and catering to the population of African descent proliferated there, as historian Nicole von Germeten has shown. In particular, enslaved and free women of African descent often had a more visible public role in confraternity and *cabildo* functions than elite Hispanic women in the New World. Whereas it would be unseemly and even dishonorable for Hispanic women of status and rank to work in the street or beg for alms, the gendered and racial ideals of Spanish honor did not apply equally to the African population. As a result, confraternities made up of female members of African descent routinely petitioned ecclesiastical and colonial officials for licenses to beg for alms and often had these mendicant duties written into their statutes.²³ From the northern borderlands of Saint Augustine to the far southern extreme of Buenos Aires, Catholic brotherhoods included a notable and visible female African presence that could be found throughout the Spanish empire.²⁴

In Cuba the presence of Catholic brotherhoods that included the population of African ancestry can be traced to the sixteenth century. In 1573 the town council of Havana reported that Africans took part in the procession of Corpus Christi, and several wills indicate that Africans regularly made donations to sodalities.²⁵ Historian Jane Landers found that the Mandinga, Carabali, Lucumi, Arara, Ganga, and Kongo nations proliferated in Havana and organized important brotherhoods. Most of the organizations selected a patron saint that they honored on his or her feast day with elaborate festivals and ceremonies.²⁶ Likewise, historian Alejandro de la Fuente has shown that during the sixteenth century free blacks and slaves organized brotherhoods in Havana that often elicited complaints because of their loud festivities, which were described as "scandals."²⁷

In 1755, Havana bishop Morell de Santa Cruz wrote with shock at the lack of interest in Christianizing the slaves and free people of color: "these miserables have been left totally abandoned as if they were not Christians and incapable of salvation."²⁸ In particular, the bishop's report emphasized the "scandalous and grave disorders" created by the *"cabildos . . . when they congregate on festival days."*²⁹ Apparently, during the span of the sixteenth and seventeenth centuries some *cabildos* had separated from the brotherhoods and taken on a social role independent of the Church. The bishop planned to bring the "lost sheep of the flock to the

Good Shepherd [by] ... administering to the *cabildos* the sacrament of confirmation, reciting the Holy rosary," and appointing lay religious officials to instruct and supervise the societies.[30]

Despite the bishop's protest, it does not appear that all the nations became "converted to temples of the living God," as he optimistically predicted.[31] For example, although the *cabildo* Carabali Induri affiliated itself with the Catholic Church Nuestra Señora del Buen Viaje, it does not appear as if any religious officials closely monitored or oversaw their day-to-day activities. At least from judicial records documenting disputes over finances and elections, no priest or religious authority gave testimony on behalf of the organization when legal conflicts emerged.[32] Part of the reason that the mediating role of the Catholic Church is somewhat absent in the records of the *cabildos* is that a new urban code in 1792 required that the *cabildo* houses be relocated outside the city walls, often some distance from the churches where they were founded. Most articles of the 1792 urban code dealt with mundane matters related to markets, fines for illegal activities, and what parts of the city could be organized for certain types of commerce and industry. Article 39 of the urban code focused specifically on the *cabildo* houses and set in motion their relocation from inside the city walls (*intramuros*) to outside the city walls (*extramuros*). The new regulations required *cabildo* houses to be located away from the more wealthy inhabitants in the center of the city.[33] In the process of forcing the *cabildos* to vacate the inner city and all the challenges that came with selling their existing houses and finding new ones, some of these organizations became involved in a series of drawn-out legal disputes over how to dispose of their old property and acquire new property. An examination of these legal documents provides significant details into how these societies operated, what services they provided for their members, and how gender relations shaped the *cabildos*' activities.[34]

Various scholars have traced the origins of the *cabildos* to religious holidays and Catholic brotherhoods of Spanish origin, but Philip Howard was among the first to point out that analogous societies were common to West and Central Africa.[35] At the port of Old Calabar and surrounding regions in the Bight of Biafra, an all-male secret society known as Ekpe formed as early as the second half of the seventeenth century. Identified with the leopard, Ekpe members paid dues assessed by their rank in the organization. According to historians Paul Lovejoy and David Richardson, the Ekpe society created an "interlocking grid of secret associations

[that] served to regulate the behavior of members."[36] The secret organization crossed the Atlantic and resurfaced in nineteenth-century Cuba (although in an altered form and with a different purpose) as the Abakuá society.[37] Undoubtedly the Ekpe organization influenced both the formation and function of some of the *cabildos* operating in Havana, especially those with members classified as "Carabali" from Old Calabar. However, what needs to be emphasized is that while Ekpe and Abakuá were all-male secret societies, the Havana *cabildos* included both male and female members. Likewise, in the Yoruba Kingdom of Oyo there existed a semi-secret organization known as the Ogboni society that advised the king on religious and political matters. Scholars disagree about the founding date of the Ogboni society and the extent of its influence. However, it is almost certain that because the war-torn region of Yorubaland funneled thousands of Africans to Cuba in the nineteenth century, some knowledge of the organization likely crossed the Atlantic and influenced the Yoruba-based *cabildos*.[38] Yet again, the Ogboni society was an all-male organization, whereas the Havana *cabildos* included both men and women.

Associations, organizations, and secret societies in West and Central Africa provided an institutional framework that enslaved and free Africans could mold to their New World surroundings in Cuba. The Yoruba in West Africa, for example, operated mutual aid societies as early as the eighteenth century through the *Ajo* and *Esusu* saving institutions. Each member paid dues into a collective fund that would then be made available for individual loans. Unlike the all-male "secret societies" that often functioned as an advisory board to royal officials on religious, political, and judicial matters, the *Ajo* and *Esusu* saving institutions functioned as mutual aid societies and were open to female participation. Although men most commonly held the position of *alajo* (treasurer) in the *Ajo* and *Esusu* organizations, the job was open to women, who occasionally filled the post. When Yoruba slaves began to be exported across the Atlantic, the *Esusu* savings association emerged in the Caribbean.[39]

Spanish colonial administrators and Catholic priests regarded African *cabildos* in Cuba as a natural and safe extension of their own religious sodalities. The organizations for Africans, however, surely did not represent something entirely of Spanish or Cuban origin, but an Old World institution modified to a New World setting. While the institutional ancestry of these societies can be traced to a combination of Catholic brotherhoods on the Iberian Peninsula with religious and mutual aid societies common to West Africa, the elevated role of women in these organizations became far more pronounced in the New World. Indeed, although Catholic confraternities that catered to the spiritual well-being of women could be found in Europe, and political, religious, and cultural societies in Africa often included female participation, the degree to which women and men jointly participated in the Cuban *cabildos* stands in marked contrast with how men and women were often segregated by gender in Africa and Europe. At least from a cursory comparison of religious and mutual aid societies in Africa and Europe with those in Cuba, it appears the influence women had within the Havana *cabildos* was shaped by Cuba's experience with slavery.

THE GENDERED ROLES OF *CABILDO* LEADERSHIP

Within each *cabildo* several members held administrative positions that strengthened the *capataz*'s leadership. The *cabildo* Carabali, located in the city of Matanzas, elected Rafael as their new leader in 1814. They then decided on a general staff that resembled a king's court. They agreed that Rafael's wife would serve as queen mother; María Rosario Domínguez as princess; Diego as first minister, Nicario as second minister; Bernardo as first captain, Miguel de la Cruz as second lieutenant; Manuel del Portillo and Felipe as musicians; and Francisco as treasurer.[40] In addition to these titles, other *cabildos* created positions such as governor, emperor, sergeant of arms, queen of war, and captain of war.[41] Although denied voting rights within *cabildos,* slaves often attained leadership roles. The slave Patricio served as "captain of the Carabali slaves" and Alonso Santa Cruz held the position of "King of the Kongo slaves."[42] The captain general of Cuba sought to prevent the establishment of an elaborate leadership structure and insisted that "there should not be positions other than first, second, and third *capataz*."[43] The captain general attempted to restrict the *cabildos*' ability to provide members with titles because of the dangers of allowing slaves and free people of color to create their own hierarchical structures.

    Cuban authorities remained torn over how to deal with the leadership organization created by *cabildos*. They recognized the important role of *cabildos* for a rapidly expanding slave society, as they provided crucial cultural adjustment for slaves recently imported from Africa. Further, a single leader provided the important function of an intermediary between colonial officials and African laborers. Nonetheless, the Cuban government continually voiced concerns over the power that came with being a *capataz* of a *cabildo*. In 1759, the captain general of Cuba informed Spanish officials that "as a precaution for certain disorders, it has been established by this government to name for each [*cabildo*] a Captain to watch and supervise their functions and meetings, who is of the same nation, and of old and mature age."⁴⁴ By the late eighteenth and early nineteenth centuries, the previous policy of the colonial government appointing leaders had been replaced by the *cabildos* electing their own leaders. *Cabildo* elections ultimately required approval of the colonial government, which, in turn, shaped who would and would not be an acceptable candidate. However, in my research to date I have not encountered any extant examples of authorities overturning an election. The change in policy from a government-appointed to a *cabildo*-elected leadership reflects the ability of *cabildos* to create a leadership structure acceptable to colonial officials. *Cabildos* expanded their restricted autonomy to determine the internal affairs of their societies by selecting leaders who did not attract the government's close scrutiny.

While government officials referred to *cabildo* leaders as *capataz*, many societies came up with their own titles. The free black José Caridad Herrera described Antonio José Barraga, the leader of the Carabali *cabildo*, as "Captain General."⁴⁵ Authorities learned that "inside the house" of the Kongo *cabildo*, members called the *capataz* Joaquín "the Kongo King."⁴⁶ The difference between the government-given title of *capataz* and the chosen title by some *cabildo* leaders of captain general or king probably did not represent any vast difference in the function of nations. Nonetheless, the distinction does reveal the tension that informed the process of identification and self-identification for Africans in the diaspora. The decision by the Kongolese to give their leader the title of king might be considered as something more than a generic reference to monarchical authority. Throughout the eighteenth century one of the central claims to legitimate rule in the Kongo region was made by asserting: "I am the King of the Kongos."⁴⁷ Civil wars split the Kingdom of Kongo into various camps that claimed adherence to a military king or a blacksmith king, which may have informed who became selected as a leader of a *cabildo* in Cuba. Some *cabildos* eschewed the leadership title of *capataz* provided by the colonial government. Perhaps they did so in reaction to how colonial society disproportionately shaped the discourse of identity, from stripping Africans of their birth names to deciding what titles could be given to *cabildo* leaders.

Many of the male leaders of the *cabildos* earned their elected position by distinguishing themselves as militia soldiers. Manuel Blanco rose to a leadership role within the black militia by commanding a one hundred-man company that fought in the American Revolution. He also served as a leading force in directing the financial affairs of the *cabildo* Lucumi.[48] Tomás Poveda and Clemente Andrade, retired militia soldiers of the black battalion of Havana, served as the elected leaders of the *cabildo* Carabali.[49] Juan Gavilan, also a retired soldier, emphasized his military service when he wrote to the captain general to resolve a dispute within the *cabildo* Carabali Umugini.[50]

Military distinction and service helped to single out these male soldiers as leaders among people of color and within their own ethnic communities.[51] For many male soldiers, the militia represented an opportunity for social advancement and a stepping stone toward achieving what some scholars have regarded as "social whiteness" through the acquisition of legal rights denied to blacks and *mulatos*.[52] The acquisition of rights and special privileges accorded to soldiers, however, did not necessarily preclude identification with slaves and free people of color. The common appearance of militiamen as elected *cabildo* leaders likely indicates their military status did not automatically separate them from slaves and free people of color, but rather, could elevate them to leadership roles within their community.

Cabildo leaders tied to the militia would often have their military privileges (known as *fuero* rights) extended to their associations. The *fuero* consisted of access to military courts, exemptions from certain taxes, tribute payments, and labor levies, and the right to bear arms that had been denied to the population of African ancestry.[53] Domingo Acosta, the *capataz* of the Carabali Apapa *cabildo*, drew on his connections as a retired militia soldier to request that a military court settle a dispute within the *cabildo*.[54] Captain General Someruelos recommended a "military tribunal" investigate the financial affairs of the Mina Guagni society after leaders Esteban Torres and Salvador Ternero emphasized their militia service.[55] When Manuel Blanco became involved in a property dispute with the *cabildo* Lucumi over selling the nation's house, he hoped to win the case by mentioning his volunteer militia service and stressing that he did it "without receiving a salary or any gratification."[56] The election of male *cabildo* leaders from the ranks of the free people of color militia served to present colonial authorities with individuals they regarded as loyal subjects of the Spanish Crown. By electing male leaders known and acceptable to government officials, the *cabildos* would suffer less scrutiny and supervision.[57] The "public" and "visible" link between the free people of color militia as an all-male military colonial institution in service of the Spanish empire and the election of males to *cabildo* leadership positions, who then could extend the corporate rights of the *fuero* to these African organizations, has tended to obscure and conceal the important "private" and "invisible" role of females in the day-to-day operations of these societies.

An examination of the electoral process indicates that female members often guided the affairs of the *cabildos,* not the elected male *capataz* as Cuban officials believed. Because of their frequent numerical superiority among the *cabildo*'s voting members, women often decided the selection of new leaders. In 1804, when the *cabildo* Carabali Oquella compiled its roster of members who had the privilege of "*voto y voz,*" women outnumbered men three to one. Of the forty-two eligible voters who participated in the *cabildo* Carabali Oquella elections, thirty-one were women.[58] When the *cabildo* Kongo Macamba held elections for the new king of their society in 1807, the males backed the wrong candidate. Although the majority of males cast their votes for Cayetano García, Antonio Diepa won the Kongo Macamba crown by six female votes.[59] The *capataz* of the Carabali Oquella, Cristóbal Govín, shared the opinion of other male cabildo leaders that females should not be able to participate in elections because his rival Lázaro Rodríguez won the election with "only the assistance of Teresa Barreto's supporters."[60] While female members of *cabildos* could not run for *capataz,* we should not underestimate their ability to influence who held the elected offices. Because women often represented the majority of *cabildo* members who had the privileges of "*voto y voz,*" they often determined who won the elections.

As cabildos were above all urban institutions, and the free population of African descent exercised the rights of "*voto y voz,*" females had something of a demographic advantage over men when it came to membership and authority within the organizations. The Cuban plantation economy of the late eighteenth and nineteenth century produced a geographically gendered division of labor for the population of African descent. While men and women, both free and enslaved, lived and labored in both rural and urban areas, women and especially free women of color could be found most prominently in Havana. Census data for Havana from the

1790s through the 1860s consistently showed free women of color outnumbered men.[61] Foreign travelers who visited the bustling Atlantic port city in the nineteenth century often expressed amazement when they encountered free women of color and their opulent public displays of wealth and status. British traveler Robert Jameson, for example, described Havana's free black women dressed in "silk stockings, sateen shoes, muslin gowns, French shawls, gold ear-rings and flowers in their wollen headdress . . . these are your washerwomen."[62] While Jameson's description undoubtedly does not apply to all free women of color and most certainly reflects some embellishment to entertain his readers, his indication of status and wealth does hint at some of the material accomplishments made by formerly enslaved women after achieving their freedom.

From the early colonial era slaves had the right to initiate the purchase of their own freedom by making a down payment on their market value. In Cuba, as in other parts of Spanish America, the practice of self-purchase initiated by the slaves was most commonly referred to as *coartación*.[63] Contemporaries as well as historians have tended to concur that manumission by self-purchase largely represented an urban phenomenon and rarely extended to the plantations. Urban slaves had easier access to courts and notaries to initiate self-purchase, could market goods to earn money to buy their freedom, and could draw on free people of color to assist in the process.[64] Although there are few quantitative studies of manumission for Cuba and none which makes a systematic comparison between rural and urban areas, it appears that self-purchase in one payment or through a series of installments by a *coartación* agreement had become widespread by the nineteenth century. Especially important for understanding the role of free women of color in *cabildos*, historians Laird Bergad, Fe Iglesias, and María del Carmen Barcia have concluded "it was far more common for urban slaves to acquire their freedom, because female slaves were heavily concentrated in Cuba's cities and males in the rural zones."[65] Moreover, for the period 1790 to 1830 it was the female African-born population that represented the largest percentage of the enslaved population that gained their freedom compared to male Cuban-born slaves or male African-born slaves.[66]

The urban gendered patterns of *coartación* meant that African-born free women of color in the first half of the nineteenth century most often displayed the greatest degree of social mobility and material wealth when compared to the enslaved and free, African and creole, male and female, and rural and urban populations of African descent. In other words, among the very restricted and subordinated slave and free African populations of eighteenth and nineteenth century Havana, it was the African-born free women of color who exhibited a striking degree of financial and social versatility compared to the other people of color that inhabited the port city. Women of African descent's elevated demographic presence among Cuban slaves who had obtained their freedom by self-purchase perhaps explains their equally elevated role in *cabildo* associations, where they exercised the privileges of *"voto y voz."*

Enslaved and freed women most commonly found employment as domestic servants, water carriers, nurses, seamstresses, laundresses, midwives, and market vendors.[67] As elsewhere in the New World, wet-nursing became a racialized occupation as Cuba became more dependent on slavery. In the process, women of color derived a measure of economic freedom through serving as wet-nurses, and wet-nursing allowed slave women the opportunity to self-purchase their freedom. In addition, free women of color derived a substantial part of their economic livelihood by nursing.[68] Other sources of revenue for slaves and free women of color included selling foodstuffs and material goods at Havana markets at lower prices than imports, which all too often did not arrive as expected.[69] As elsewhere in the Americas, urban residents expressed alarm over the large number of urban slaves and suggested sending them to the disciplined labor regimes of the plantations and mines.[70] The Havana town council regularly checked markets for illicit goods and received complaints about the numerous black female vendors "uniting with others of their class" and "the trouble created by their clamor and obscenities."[71] Similarly, an assistant to the captain general of Cuba charged with investigating the urban markets recognized the dangers of allowing women to engage in street vending activities, writing that the risks "are very serious, resulting in the corruption of the slave by the liberty given to them by their masters."[72] Despite the recognition of the problems caused by the enslaved and free market vendors of African descent, the vendors performed a vital function without which a port city like Havana could not survive.

The important role freed black women played in the microeconomy of Havana often translated into earning respect and authority within their *cabildo* organizations. Although some *cabildo* leaders felt threatened by the power women could exert in shaping the leadership of African societies, as indicated by challenges to overturn their voting rights, other *capataces* singled out and recognized the central role of female leaders in maintaining the unity of the organizations. In 1805, José Arostegui of the *cabildo* Carabali Osso informed the captain general of the death of Rita Castellanos, who held the leadership position among the female members of the nation. Shortly thereafter, Barbara de Mesa "occupied her place with all the support of the nation for her recommendable" characteristics. Arostegui requested that the captain general "give his recognition to Barbara de Mesa as *capataza*" so that she could "govern the women of said *cabildo* with authority" to ensure "perfect peace and harmony."[73] Other *cabildos* went beyond recognizing the important role of women in governing female members and acknowledged their crucial role in promoting a unified organization. When the Queen of the Kongo Macamba nation, Rafaela Armenteras, died, the *cabildo* recognized that "disorder has increased" as a result of their loss of her leadership, and they could no longer resolve disputes by themselves, but required government intervention.[74]

Not only did females in *cabildos* exhibit considerable authority in determining leaders, but they also shaped the financial wealth of the organizations by raising revenues and deciding financial expenditures. Through membership dues, renting rooms, collecting alms, and hosting festivals, *cabildos* normally held savings in cash that varied from 300 to 1,000 pesos. These savings represented a significant amount, given that the prices for slaves in Havana newspapers usually ranged from 300 to 500 pesos.[75] Nearly half of all the money held collectively by the *cabildo* Carabali Umugini in 1805, which totaled over 500 pesos, came from donations made by female members of the organization.[76] Some *cabildos* developed strict regulations that required monthly donations for "*voto y voz*" privileges, which had the consequence of further underscoring the importance of women as financial agents in shaping the decisions and operations of the *cabildos*. For example, the *cabildo* Mina Guagni required members to pay 8 pesos a month to have the right to vote in elections of new leaders and help decide how to spend the organization's money. As a result, when an active voting list was compiled in 1794, women outnumbered men because of their financial contributions.[77] Beyond donations to exercise rights and privileges, women also made loans to aid their societies in hosting festivals and functions. In 1808, the *cabildo* Lucumi Llane account books recorded a payment of 542 pesos to the queen of the organization, who had loaned money to fund celebrations and functions.[78]

The important duty of guarding the safe that contained the *cabildo*'s money usually fell upon the queen. When the *cabildo* Carabali Osso became involved in a dispute that required paying a legal fine, Barbara de Mesa would not turn over the safe to the neighborhood commissioner, José Castillo, "until she had been threatened with prison."[79] When members of the *cabildo* Carabali Oquella challenged the financial expenses of the *capataz*, the whole nation went "to the house of Teresa Barreto, queen of said *cabildo*," to count the money in the safe. The *cabildo* leaders pulled from the safe "a bag full of money and in the presence of the nation . . . counted 946 pesos."[80] Most cabildos entrusted the queen of the nation with guarding their money, but they took precautions to ensure that it would take more than one person to open the safe.

Cabildos used a safe modeled on the Spanish coffer system. It required three different keys, so as to prevent one person from making a withdrawal.[81] The *cabildo* Carabali Induri distributed "three different keys" to the "First *Capataz*," the "Second *Capataz*" and "an elected person in consultation with all the nation." The three key holders could only open the safe in the presence of "twenty people, men or women, of the nation" and had to explain the purpose of withdrawals.[82] Likewise, the *cabildo* Kongo Macamba required its safe to be opened in the presence of its members to "avoid future disputes, objections, and suspicions of the *capataz*."[83] Female leaders of *cabildos* guarded the safe, but they did not hold the keys to open it. The Kongo Macamba nation stated very clearly that whoever "takes on the task of treasury," that person would have to be a "black male."[84] The leader of the *cabildo* Carabali Oquella, Cristóbal Govín, feared that having "the funds of the *cabildo* held by Teresa Barreto, a rebellious woman with bad ideas," would jeopardize the stability of the nation.[85] Govín feared that if she could get hold of "the common money of the nation," that would empower her to "move all of these machinations."[86] Whether through deciding elections or guarding the safe, females decisively shaped *cabildo* functions.

CONCLUSION

Members of *cabildos* chose to join associations to define themselves in cooperation with others who shared a similar ethnicity, often reflecting a common language and geographic origin in Africa. In this sense, a study of the *cabildos* shows the importance of understanding that Africans in the diaspora did not immediately or exclusively adopt a racialized identity of blackness. By providing a network of alliances and an institutional structure that resonated with Iberian models of organizing by religious corporations through brotherhoods, and paralleling West African models of religious and mutual aid societies, *cabildos* offered Africans and their descendants in Havana a degree of cultural continuity modified to an ever-changing New World setting.

Within *cabildos,* free African-born males held the elected leadership positions. Many of the male leaders often served in the free people of color militia and could thereby extend their special judicial status as militiamen to their organizations during times of need. As an urban phenomenon, free African-born female members often represented the majority of *cabildo* members. Their influence in shaping the societies became most powerfully expressed during elections, when they often chose the leaders through their numeric superiority in the voting process, often to the vexation of the males, who tried to limit their voting rights. In addition, the societies recognized the important role of females' financial contributions by entrusting the elected "queen" of the *cabildo* to guard the safe.

This chapter has demonstrated that *cabildos* functioned as sites where transplants and transformations in diasporic culture carried by the transatlantic slave trade created an institutional framework for multiple African cultures to thrive, representing Kongos, Lucumis, Carabalis, Minas, Mandingas, and other West and Central African peoples in Havana, Cuba. In particular, women's actions by making monetary donations through dues, participating in elections, performing tasks on festival days, and deciding the group's financial expenditures all served to give a powerful "*voz*" to African diasporic culture beyond *cabildo* meetings. Exercising their "*voz*" in *cabildo* activities gave women a "*voto*" in imprinting their experiences in the development of African diasporic culture in the Iberian Atlantic.

In closing, the *cabildos* offer us two broad lessons for looking at gender and diasporic cultural formations and transformations during the time of slavery. First, while slavery and the new identities created out of blackness and whiteness undoubtedly and overwhelmingly shaped the New World experiences of Africans, ethnic identities traced back across the Atlantic to their points of origin continued to have profound meanings to Africans long after their arrival in the New World. The ability to form *cabildos* allowed male and female Africans to meet, cope, and deal with their experiences in Cuba with people who shared a similar cultural ancestry rooted in West Africa. And second, by looking at gender, we can understand how Africans in Cuba structured relations between themselves when they formed societies of their own volition. Women exercised far more influence and control within these organizations than historians' focus only on male leaders had previously recognized. As women earned their rights of *"voto y voz"* by financially contributing to the *cabildos,* they shaped the governance, the direction, and the goals of these organizations. On both accounts, *cabildos* offer us a window into how people of the African diaspora identified themselves through African ethnic associations, and how they navigated and negotiated gender relations among themselves.

NOTES

1. "La nación Caravali Induri sobre nombramiento de capataz del cavildo del Santo Cristo de Buen Viaje" (1802–1806), Archivo Nacional de Cuba, Havana, fondo Escribania de Gobierno (hereafter ANC-EG), leg. 125, no. 3, esp. fols. 107v–115v.

2. Ibid., fols. 107v–108v.

3. Ibid., fol. 108v.

4. Ibid., fol. 115.

5. For the Bight of Biafra and the slave trade to the Caribbean in the second half of the eighteenth century, see Alexander X. Byrd, *Captives and Voyagers: Black Migrants Across the Eighteenth-Century British Atlantic World* (Baton Rouge: Louisiana State Univ. Press, 2008), 17–31. For the location of Nri, see the map on page 12 of Byrd, *Captives and Voyagers.*

6. For a discussion of the Cuban *cabildos de nación,* see María del Carmen Barcia Zequeira, *Los Ilustres Apellidos: Negros en la Habana Colonial* (Havana: Ediciones Boloña, 2008); Rafael L. López Valdés, *Pardos y morenos esclavos y libres en Cuba y sus instituciones en el caribe Hispano* (San Juan: Centro de Estudios Avanzados de Puerto Rico y el Caribe, 2007); Philip A. Howard, *Changing History: Afro-Cuban Cabildos and Societies of Color in the Nineteenth Century* (Baton Rouge: Louisiana State Univ. Press, 1998); Pedro Deschamps-Chapeaux, "Cabildos: Solo para esclavos," *Cuba* 7, no. 69 (January 1968): 50–51; Israel Moliner Castañeda, *Los Cabildos Afrocubanos en Matanzas* (Matanzas: Ediciones Matanzas, 2002); Carmen Victoria Montejo-Arrechea, *Sociedades de instrucción y recreo de pardos y morenos que existieron en Cuba colonial: 1878–1898* (Veracruz: Instituto Veracruzano de Cultura, 1993); Carmen Victoria Montejo-Arrechea , *Sociedades Negras en Cuba, 1878–1960* (Havana: Editorial de Ciencias Sociales, 2004), 13–45; Fernando Ortiz, *Los cabildos y la fiesta afrocubanos del Día de Reyes* (1921; reprint, Havana: Editorial de Ciencias Sociales, 1992); Fannie Theresa Rushing, "Afro-Cuban Social Organization and Identity in a Colonial Slave Society, 1800–1888," *Colonial Latin American Historical Review* 11, no. 2 (spring 2002): 177–201; Jane G. Landers, *Atlantic Creoles in the Age of Revolutions* (Cambridge: Harvard Univ. Press, 2010), 144–151. These societies had become so common that they received their own entry in an 1836 Cuban dictionary: see Esteban Pichardo, *Diccionario provincial de voces cubanas* (Matanzas: Imprenta de la Real Marina, 1836), 43.

7. Sidney W. Mintz and Richard Price, *The Birth of African-American Culture: An Anthropological Perspective* (1976; reprint, Boston: Beacon Press, 1992), 18–19.

8. See, for example, Richard Price, "The Miracle of Creolization: A Retrospective," *New West Indian Guide* 75, nos. 1–2 (2001): 35–64; and Richard Price, "On the Miracle of Creolization," in *Afro-Atlantic Dialogues: Anthropology in Diaspora,* ed. Kevin A. Yelvington, 115–147

(Santa Fe, N. Mex: School of American Research Press, 2006); Ira Berlin, *Many Thousands Gone: The First Two Centuries of Slavery in North America* (Cambridge: Harvard Univ. Press, 1998); Philip D. Morgan, *Slave Counterpoint: Black Culture in the Eighteenth-Century Chesapeake and Lowcountry* (Chapel Hill: Univ. of North Carolina Press, 1998); David Eltis, Philip Morgan, and David Richardson, "Agency and Diaspora in Atlantic History: Reassessing the African Contribution to Rice Cultivation in the Americas," *American Historical Review* 112, no. 5 (December 2007): 1329-1358.

9. See, for example, Joseph Miller, *Way of Death: Merchant Capitalism and the Angolan Slave Trade, 1730-1830* (Madison: Univ. of Wisconsin Press, 1988); Paul Lovejoy, *Transformations in Slavery: A History of Slavery in Africa*, 2nd ed. (Cambridge: Cambridge Univ. Press, 2000); Michael A. Gomez, *Exchanging Our Country Marks: The Transformation of African Identities in the Colonial and Antebellum South* (Chapel Hill: Univ. of North Carolina Press, 1998); Robin Law, "The Evolution of the Brazilian Community in Ouidah," *Slavery and Abolition* 22, no. 1 (April 2001): 22-41; John K. Thornton, *Africa and Africans in the Making of the Atlantic World, 1400-1800*, 2nd ed. (Cambridge: Cambridge Univ. Press, 1998); and David Eltis, *The Rise of African Slavery in the Americas* (Cambridge: Cambridge Univ. Press, 2000); James H. Sweet, *Recreating Africa: Culture, Kinship, and Religion in the African-Portuguese World, 1441-1770* (Chapel Hill: Univ. of North Carolina Press, 2003); James H. Sweet, "Mistaken Identities: Olaudah Equiano, Domingos Alvares, and the Methodological Challenges of Studying the African Diaspora," *American Historical Review* 114, no. 2 (April 2009): 279-306.

10. Claire Robertson and Marsha Robinson, "Re-Modeling Slavery as If Women Mattered," in *Women and Slavery: The Modern Atlantic*, vol. 2, ed. Gwyn Campbell, Suzanne Miers, and Joseph C. Miller, 253-283, quote on page 271 (Athens: Ohio Univ. Press, 2008).

11. Stephanie Smallwood, *Saltwater Slavery: A Middle Passage from Africa to American Diaspora* (Cambridge: Harvard Univ. Press, 2007), 196-200, quote on page 197.

12. Important exceptions include: James Sweet's work on sexuality in *Recreating Africa*; David Eltis's analysis of gender in shaping the slave trade in Africa and the Americas, *Rise of African Slavery in the Americas*; and the insightful analysis of Jennifer Morgan on enslaved women as producers and reproducers of slave culture, *Laboring Women: Reproduction and Gender in New World Slavery* (Philadelphia: Univ. of Pennsylvania Press, 2004).

13. For the role of *cabildos* in Afro-Cuban religious history, see, for example, David H. Brown, *Santeria Enthroned: Art, Ritual, and Innovation in an Afro-Cuban Religion* (Chicago: Univ. of Chicago Press, 2003), chapter 2; María Teresa Veléz, *Drumming for the Gods: The Life and Times of Felipe García Villamil, Santero, Palero, and Abakuá* (Philadelphia: Temple Univ. Press, 2000), 7-9; George Brandon, *Santeria From Africa to the New World: The Dead Sell Memories* (Bloomington: Indiana Univ. Press, 1993), 74-75. For the cabildos and rebellion, see, for example, Matt D. Childs, *The 1812 Aponte Rebellion in Cuba and the Struggle against Atlantic Slavery* (Chapel Hill: Univ. of North Carolina Press, 2006), chapters 3 and 4; Robert L. Paquette, *Sugar Is Made with Blood: The Conspiracy of La Escalera and the Conflict between Empires over Slavery in Cuba* (Middletown, Conn.: Wesleyan Univ. Press, 1988), 125. Philip Howard's *Changing History* comes closest to balancing an examination of how the *cabildos* functioned with their role in acts of resistance, but he focuses on explaining the latter.

14. Linda M. Heywood, "The Angolan-Afro-Brazilian Cultural Connections," *Slavery and Abolition* 20, no. 1 (April 1999): 10.

15. Elizabeth W. Kiddy, *Blacks of the Rosary: Memory and History in Minas Gerais, Brazil* (University Park: Pennsylvania State Univ. Press, 2005), 27-33; Heywood, "The Angolan-

Afro-Brazilian Cultural Connections," 19; Marina de Mello e Souza, *Reis negros no Brasil escravista: história da festa de coroação de rei congo* (Belo Horizonte: Editora da UFMG, 2002).

16. Giovanna Casagrande, "Confraternities and Lay Female Religiosity in Late Medieval and Renaissance Umbria," in *The Politics of Ritual Kinship: Confraternities and Social Order in Early Modern Italy,* ed. Nicholas Terpstra, 48–66 (Cambridge: Cambridge Univ. Press, 2000); Giovanna Casagrande, "Women in Confraternities between the Middle Ages and the Modern Age," *Confraternitas* 5, no. 2 (1994): 3–13.

17. Maureen Flynn, *Sacred Charity: Confraternities and Social Welfare in Spain, 1400–1700* (Ithaca: Cornell Univ. Press, 1989), 23.

18. Ibid., 34.

19. Ibid., 133.

20. Mariza de Carvalho Soares, *Devotos da cor: Identidade étnica, religiosidade e escravidão no Rio de Janeiro, século XVIII* (Rio de Janeiro: Civilização Brasileira, 2000); also see Heywood, "The Angolan-Afro-Brazilian Cultural Connections," 9–23; Elizabeth W. Kiddy, "Ethnic and Racial Identity in the Brotherhoods of the Rosary of Minas Gerais, 1700–1830," *Americas* 56, no. 2 (October 1999): 221–252.

21. Mariza de Carvalho Soares, "Can Women Guide Men: Gendering Politics among African Catholics in Brazil," in *Women and Slavery: The Modern Atlantic,* ed. Gwyn Campbell, Suzanne Miers, and Joseph C. Miller, 2:79–99 (Athens: Ohio Univ. Press, 2008).

22. Frederick P. Bowser, *The African Slave in Colonial Peru, 1524–1650* (Stanford: Stanford Univ. Press, 1974): 249–250, 339.

23. Nicole von Germeten, *Black Blood Brothers: Confraternities and Social Mobility for Afro-Mexicans,* foreword by Stephen W. Angell and Anthony B. Pinn (Gainesville: Univ. Press of Florida, 2006), see esp. chapter 2, 41–44. The best single-source for the central roles of honor, gender, race, and ancestry in colonial Latin America remains Ann Twinam, *Public Lives, Private Secrets: Gender, Honor, Sexuality, and Illegitimacy in Colonial Spanish America* (Stanford: Stanford Univ. Press, 1999).

24. Leslie B. Rout Jr., *The African Experience in Spanish America, 1502 to the Present Day* (Cambridge: Cambridge Univ. Press, 1976), 136; Jane Landers, *Black Society in Spanish Florida,* foreword by Peter H. Wood (Urbana: Univ. of Illinois Press, 1999), chapter 5; George Reid Andrews, *The Afro-Argentines of Buenos Aires, 1800–1900* (Madison: Univ. of Wisconsin Press, 1980), 142–151.

25. Ortiz, *Los cabildos y la fiesta afrocubanos del Día de Reyes,* 6; Montejo-Arrechea, *Sociedades de instrucción y recreo de pardos y morenos que existieron en Cuba colonial,* 14–16.

26. Landers, *Black Society in Spanish Florida,*109; López-Valdes, *Pardos y morenos,* 273–284.

27. Alejandro de la Fuente, with the collaboration of César García del Pino and Bernardo Iglesias Delgado, *Havana and the Atlantic in the Sixteenth Century* (Chapel Hill: Univ. of North Carolina Press, 2008), 161–170.

28. Morell de Santa Cruz, "El Obispo Morell de Santa Cruz oficializa los cabildos africanos donde nació la santería, convirtiéndolos en ermitas," Havana, December 6, 1755, in *Cuba: Economía y sociedad, del monopolio hacia la libertad comercial (1701–1763),* ed. Levi Marrero, 8:159 (Madrid: Editorial Playor, 1980).

29. Ibid.

30. Ibid., 8:159–160.

31. Ibid., 8:159.

32. "Diligencias sobre cuentos del cabildo de la nación Induri pos su capataz Nicolas

Veitia" (1800), Archivo Nacional de Cuba, Escribanía de Antonio D'aumy (hereafter ANC-ED), leg. 398, no. 23, fols. 1–5; ANC-EG, leg. 125, no. 3.

33. To date I have been unable to locate an original or a contemporary copy of the 1792 urban code. Some articles of the 1792 urban code as they relate to the *cabildos* have been reproduced in Ortiz, *Los cabildos y la fiesta afrocubanos del Día de Reyes,* 7–8; a discussion of article 39 of the 1792 urban code can be found in Barcia Zequeira, *Los Ilustres Apellidos,* 123. The 1792 urban code is often referred to in the archival documents that I used for this chapter.

34. Some of the cases produced in response to the 1792 urban code include, "José Xavier Mirabal y consortes contra Domingo Acosta y socios sobre pesos, trata del cabildo de Apapa" (1808–1830), ANC-ED, leg. 583, no. 5; "La nación mina contra Juana de Mesa" (1797), ANC-ED, leg. 673, no. 9; "La nación mina guagni contra Salvador Ternero sobre cuentas" (1794–1797), ANC-ED, leg. 893, no. 4; "La nación mina guagni contra Salvador Ternero sobre que de cuentas del producido del cabildo de la misma nación" (1794) ANC, fondo Escribanía Ortega (hereafter ANC-EO), leg. 65, no. 11; "La nación Caravali Umugini sobre división con la Osso y con la misma Umugini, y liquidación de cuentas con el capitán Pedro Nolasco Eligió" (1805–1806), ANC-EG, leg. 123, no. 15-A.

35. Antonio Bachiller y Morales, *Los Negros* (Barcelona: Gorgas y compañía, 1887), 114–115. Ortiz, *Los cabildos,* 4–6; Montejo-Arrechea, *Sociedades,* 12–13; Dechamps-Chapeaux, "Cabildos: Solo para esclavos," 51; Pedro Dechamps-Chapeaux, "Sociedades: La integración de pardos y morenos," *Cuba* 7, no. 71 (March 1968): 54; Howard, *Changing History,* 21–25.

36. Paul E. Lovejoy and David Richardson, "Trust, Pawnship, and Atlantic History: The Institutional Foundations of the Old Calabar Slave Trade," *American Historical Review* 104, no. 2 (April 1999): 347–349; also see the discussion in Randy J. Sparks, *The Two Princes of Calabar: An Eighteenth-Century Atlantic Odyssey* (Cambridge: Harvard Univ. Press, 2004), especially 59–60.

37. Paul E. Lovejoy, "Identifying Enslaved Africans in the African Diaspora," in *Identity in the Shadow of Slavery,* ed. Paul E. Lovejoy, 8 (London: Continuum, 2000); Howard, *Changing History,* 48, 53, 68–69, 109–110; López-Valdes, *Pardos y morenos,* 296–309. The classic treatment of Abakuá in Cuba remains Lydia Cabrera, *La Sociedad Secreta de Abakuá, narrada por viejos adeptos* (Havana: Ediciones, C. R., 1959). For recent interpretations stressing continuity and change from Ekpe to Abakuá, see Ivor L. Miller, *Voice of the Leopard: African Secret Societies and Cuba* (Jackson: Univ. Press of Mississippi, 2009); and Paul E. Lovejoy, "Transformation of Ekpe Masquerade in the African Diaspora," in *Carnival: "People's Art" and "Taking back the Streets,"* ed. Christopher Innes (forthcoming).

38. Peter Morton-Williams, "The Yoruba Ogboni Cult in Oyo," *Africa* 30 (1960): 362–374; J. A. Atanda, "The Yoruba Ogboni Cult: Did It Exist in Old Oyo?" *Journal of the Historical Society of Nigeria* 6, no. 4 (1973): 365–372; Robin Law, *The Oyo Empire, c. 1600–c. 1836: A West African Imperialism in the Era of the Atlantic Slave Trade* (Oxford: Clarendon Press, 1977), 61. For Yoruba imports into Cuba, see David Eltis, "The Diaspora of Yoruba Speakers, 1650–1865: Dimensions and Implications," in *The Yoruba Diaspora in the Atlantic World,* ed. Toyin Falola and Matt D. Childs, 17–39 (Bloomington: Indiana Univ. Press, 2004).

39. Toyin Falola and Adebayo Akanmu, *Culture, Politics, and Money Among the Yoruba* (New Brunswick: Transaction Publishers, 2000), 131–139, 153–154.

40. "Expediente relativo a la renovación de cargos de un cabildo de nación ante las autoridades en la ciudad de Matanzas," Archivo Nacional de Cuba, fondo Donativos y Remisio-

nes (hereafter ANC-DR), leg. 542, no. 29, fol. 1; some of the documentation for the Matanzas Karabali *cabildo* is published in "Constitución de un cabildo Carabali en 1814," *Archivos del folklore cubano* 1, no. 3 (1925): 281-283.

41. Archivo Nacional de Cuba, fondo Asuntos Políticos (hereafter ANC-AP), leg. 12, no. 9, fols. 45, 68v, 73.

42. Ibid., fols. 36v; ANC-AP, leg. 13, no. 1, fol. 101.

43. ANC-EG, leg. 125, no. 3, fol. 115-115v.

44. Pedro Alonso to unknown, Havana, October 10, 1759, Archivo Genral de Indias, Seville, Spain, fondo Audiencia de Santo Domingo (hereafter AGI-SD), leg. 1352; Fernando Ortiz, *Los negros curros* (1909; reprint, Havana: Editorial de Ciencias Sociales, 1986), 214.

45. ANC-AP, leg. 12, no. 9, fol. 30v.

46. ANC-AP, leg. 12, no. 27, fol. 12v.

47. John K. Thornton, "'I Am the Subject of the King of Congo': African Political Ideology and the Haitian Revolution," *Journal of World History* 4, no. 2 (fall 1993): 186-198.

48. "La nación lucumi contra Dn. Manuel Blanco y otros sobre propiedad del terreno en que se halla fundado el cavildo de nación" (1777-1781), Archivo Nacional de Cuba, fondo Escribanía de Cabello (hereafter ANC-EC), leg. 147, no. 1, fols. 41-42.

49. "Tomás Poveda, capataz de los cabildos Carabali Osso solicitando nombramiento de otra capataz" (1806), ANC-ED, leg. 610, no. 15.

50. "La nación Caravali Umugini sobre división con la Oso y con la misma Umugini, y liquidación de cuentas con el capitán Pedro Nolasco Eligio" (1805-1806), ANC-EG, leg. 123, no. 15A.

51. "Salvador Flores y demás individuos de la nación Carabali Ibo sobre que se suspenda capataz a José María Pimenta y que de cuentas" (1814), ANC-EG, leg. 123, no. 15; "Cabildo musolongo sobre nombramientos de Capataz" (1806), ANC-ED, leg. 548, no. 11; "La nación mina guagni contra Salvador Ternero sobre que de cuentas del producido del cabildo de la misma nación" (1794) ANC-EO, leg. 65, no. 11; "La nación mina contra Juana de Mesa" (1797), ANC-ED, leg. 673, no. 9; "La nación mina guagni contra Salvador Ternero sobre cuentas" (1794-1797), ANC-ED, leg. 893, no. 4.

52. Allan J. Kuethe, "The Status of the Free Pardo in the Disciplined Militia of New Granada," *Journal of Negro History* 56, no. 2 (April 1971): 109.

53. "R. C. sobre preemencias de oficiales y soldados milicianos," Buen Retiro, September 16, 1708, and "Reglamento para las milicias y infantería y caballería de la isla de Cuba," El Pardo, January 19, 1769, both in *Colección de documentos para la historia de la formación social de Hispanoamérica, 1493-1810*, ed. Richard Konetzke, vol. 3, tomo 1, pp. 80, 351-358 (Madrid: Consejo Superior de Investigaciones Científicas, 1962); Diego José Navarro, "Bando sobre prohibir el uso de armas y capas a negros y mulatos," Havana, May 4, 1779, in *Boletín del Archivo Nacional* 28, nos. 1-6 (January-December 1929): 103-104.

54. "José Xavier Mirabal y consortes contra Domingo Acosta y socios sobre pesos, trata del cabildo de Apapa" (1808-1830), ANC-ED, leg. 583, no. 5, fol. 24.

55. ANC-EO, leg. 65, no. 11, fol. 55.

56. ANC-EC, leg. 147, no. 1, fol. 41; also see Howard for the link between militia soldiers and *cabildo* activities (*Changing History*, 31-36).

57. Kimberly S. Hanger discovered that in New Orleans the town council often rejected petitions by blacks to hold dances, "but when the free black militia, represented by four officers, submitted its request in 1800" authorities approved it (*Bounded Lives, Bounded Places,*

Free Black Society in Colonial New Orleans, 1769–1803 [Durham: Duke Univ. Press, 1997], 132); also see Landers, *Atlantic Creoles in the Age of Revolutions,* chapter 4, for militia soldiers as leaders among the free people of color community in Havana.

58. "Expediente seguido por los de la nación Caravali Oquella sobre nombramiento de segundo y tercero capataces" (1804), Archivo Nacional de Cuba, fondo Escribanía de Varios (hereafter ANC-EV), leg. 211, no. 3114, fols. 9v–12.

59. José Antonio Diepa, "Capataz del cabildo nación Congo, sobre que se recojía los memoriales que promovió Cayetano García y socios para despojarlo del encargo de capataz del cabildo nación Congo Macamba" (1808–1809), ANC-ED, leg. 439, no. 16.

60. ANC-EO, leg, 6, no. 1, fol. 60v–61.

61. Kenneth F. Kiple, *Blacks in Colonial Cuba, 1774–1899* (Gainesville: Univ. Presses of Florida, 1976). See the summary tables in "Appendix: Cuba's Official Censuses, 1774–1899," 83–99.

62. Robert Francis Jameson, *Letters from the Havana during the Year 1820; Containing an Account of the Present State of the Island of Cuba and Observations on the Slave Trade* (London: John Miller, 1821), 39.

63. "R. C. al Gobernador de la Habana ordenándole haga observar el método y reglas que se expresan, en la exacción del derecho de alcabala de la venta de los negros esclavos coartados de aquella isla," Aranjuez, June 21, 1768, and "R. C. al Gobernador de la Habana previéndole que deben considerarse y según la misma regla que se dio para los esclavos enteros la de los coartados," San Ildefonso, September 27, 1769, both in *Colección de documentos para la historia de la formación social de Hispanoamérica, 1493–1810,* ed. Richard Konetzke, vol. 3, tomo 1, pp. 337–340, 360–361 (Madrid: Consejo Superior de Investigaciones Científicas, 1962). For an overview see, Manuel Lucena Salmoral, "El derecho de coartación del esclavo en la América Española," *Revista de Indias* 59, no. 216 (May–August 1999): 357–374; Alejandro de la Fuente, "Slaves and the Creation of Legal Rights in Cuba: *Coartación* and *Papel,*" *Hispanic American Historical Review* 87, no. 4 (November 2007): 659–692; Manuel Barcia, *Seeds of Insurrection: Domination and Resistance on Western Cuban Plantations, 1808–1848* (Baton Rouge: Louisiana State Univ. Press, 2008), 84–105, esp. 93–95.

64. Jameson, *Letters from the Havana during the Year 1820,* 44; Alexander von Humboldt, *Ensayo político sobre la isla de Cuba* (1826; reprint, with an introduction by Fernando Ortiz, Havana: Fundación Fernando Ortiz, 1998), 213; Fernando Ortiz, *Los negros esclavos* (1916; reprint, Havana: Editorial de Ciencias Sociales, 1975), 290; Paquette, *Sugar Is Made with Blood,* 63; Sherry Johnson, "'Honor Is Life': Military Reform and the Transformation of Cuban Society: 1753–1796" (Ph.D. diss., University of Florida, 1995), 120; Howard, *Changing History,* 11–12. The British *Anti-Slavery Reporter* noticed the difference between rural and urban access to freedom in Cuba: "Now, although the Spanish slave-law posses many humane features, and the rights of the slaves under it are guaranteed by a public opinion greatly in advance of any that ever prevailed in our own colonies, or that now exists in America, yet in the provinces it is by no means easy for the slaves employed on estates to assert their rights and claim their privileges owing to their being so remote from any local authority. Thus the humane provisions of the law are rendered almost inoperative" ("Cuban Slaves in England," *Anti-Slavery Reporter* 2, no. 10 [October 2, 1854]: 234).

65. Laird W. Bergad, Fe Iglesias García, and María del Carmen Barcia, *The Cuban Slave Market, 1790–1880* (Cambridge: Cambridge Univ. Press, 1995), 123.

66. Ibid., 132.

67. For accounts of the skilled labor performed by free people of color in Cuba, see Pedro

Deschamps-Chapeaux, *El negro en la economía habanera del siglo XIX* (Havana: Unión de Escritores y Artistas de Cuba, 1971); Rafael Duharte Jiménez, *El negro en la sociedad colonial* (Santiago: Editorial Oriente, 1988), 11–30, 91–115; Yoel Rodríguez Ochoa, "Situación socioeconómica de la población libre de color en Santiago de Cuba: 1844–1865" (Santiago, Cuba: Trabajo de Diploma en Licenciado, Universidad de Oriente, 1998); Paquette, *Sugar Is Made with Blood,* 39–40, 80, 106–107, 119; Franklin W. Knight, "Cuba," in *Neither Slave nor Free: The Freedman of African Descent in the Slave Societies of the New World,* ed. David W. Cohen and Jack P. Greene, 278–308, esp. 289–95 (Baltimore: Johns Hopkins Univ. Press, 1972); Franklin W. Knight, "The Free Colored Population in Cuba during the Nineteenth Century," in *Slavery without Sugar: Diversity in Caribbean Economy and Society Since the 17th Century,* ed. Verene A. Shepherd, 224–247, esp. 232–236 (Gainesville: Univ. Press of Florida, 2002).

68. For an analysis of wet-nursing by the enslaved and free women of African descent in Havana more broadly and the suggested link between wet-nursing and self-purchase, see Sarah L. Franklin, *Women and Slavery in Nineteenth-Century Colonial Cuba* (Rochester, N.Y.: Univ. of Rochester Press, forthcoming [2012]), chapter 5. Historian Camillia Cowling has shown for the late nineteenth century that working as a wet-nurse sometimes gave slave women the greatest boon a master could bestow—outright freedom, which was far superior to becoming *coartada.* Some masters promised freedom to ensure good treatment of their child, and others granted it in recognition of their nursing duties. Camillia Cowling, "Matrices of Opportunity: Women of Colour, Gender and the Ending of Slavery in Rio de Janeiro and Havana, 1870–1888" (Ph.D. diss., University of Nottingham, 2006), 171–173.

69. José Antonio de la Ossa to Juan de Aguilar, Havana, November 30, 1812, Archivo Nacional de Cuba, Havana, fondo Correspondencia de los Capitanes Generales (hereafter ANC-CCG), leg. 97, no. 4.

70. "R. C. para el remedio de los esclavos en el servicio de los esclavos negros," Aranjuez, April 29, 1752, in *Colección de documentos para la historia de la formación social de Hispanoamérica, 1493–1810,* ed. Richard Konetzke, vol. 3, tomo 1, pp. 260–261 (Madrid: Consejo Superior de Investigaciones Científicas, 1962).

71. Havana, January 31, 1809, Archivo de la Oficina del Historiador de la Ciudad, Havana, fondo Actas Capitulares (hereafter AOHCH-AC), leg. 76, fols. 56–57; AOHCH-AC, leg. 83, April 24, 1812, fol. 99v.

72. Leonardo Del Monte to Apodaca, Havana, June 15, 1812, Havana, Archivo General de Indias, Seville, Spain, fondo Papeles de Cuba (hereafter AGI-PC), leg. 1640.

73. ANC-ED. leg. 336, no. 1.

74. ANC-ED, leg. 439, no. 16.

75. See, for example, *Diario de la Habana,* February 3, 1812, p. 3; for an analysis of newspaper slave sales, see Antonio Núnez Jiménez, *Los esclavos negros* (Cuba: Fundación de la Naturaleza y el Hombre, 1998), 79–148.

76. ANC-EG, leg. 123, no. 15A, fols. 5–5v.

77. ANC-EO, leg. 65, no. 11, fols. 6–6v.

78. ANC-EC, leg. 64, no. 6, fol. 60.

79. ANC-ED, leg. 336, no. 1, fol. 38v.

80. "Expediente de cuentas que produce Tomás Betancourt de las cantidades que han entrado en su poder del cavildo Caravali Oquella" (1804), ANC-EO, leg. 3, no. 8, fol. 7v.

81. Ibid., fol. 6v; ANC-EO, leg. 6. no. 1, fol. 8v. For a discussion of the Spanish coffer, see Amy Bushnell, *The King's Coffer: Proprietors of the Spanish Florida Treasury, 1565–1702* (Gainesville: Univ. Presses of Florida, 1981), 1, 36, 45.

82. ANC-ED, leg. 398, no. 23, fol. 3.
83. ANC-ED, leg. 439, no. 16.
84. ANC-ED, leg. 439, no. 16.
85. ANC-EO, leg. 6, no. 1, fol. 33.
86. ANC-EO, leg. 6, no. 1, fol. 30v.

WORKS CITED

Archival Sources

CUBA

ARCHIVO NACIONAL DE CUBA, HAVANA

Asuntos Políticos
Correspondencia de los Capitanes Generales
Donativos y Remisiones
Escribanía de Cabello
Escribanía de Antonio D'aumy
Escribanía de Gobierno
Escribanía de Ortega
Escribanía de Valerio
Escribanía de Varios

ARCHIVO DE LA OFICINA DEL HISTORIADOR DE LA CIUDAD, HAVANA

Actas Capitulares

SPAIN

ARCHIVO GENERAL DE INDIAS, SEVILLE

Audiencia de Santo Domingo
Papeles de Cuba

Printed Primary Sources

Bachiller y Morales, Antonio. *Los Negros.* Barcelona: Gorgas y compañía, 1887.
"Constitución de un cabildo Carabali en 1814." *Archivos del folklore cubano* 1, no. 3 (1925): 281–283.
"Cuban Slaves in England." *Anti-Slavery Reporter* 2, no. 10 (October 2, 1854): 234.
Diario de la Habana (Havana, Cuba, 1812).
García Rodríguez, Gloria, ed. *La esclavitud desde la esclavitud: La visión de los siervos.* Mexico: Centro de investigación científica, 1996; 2nd edition, Havana: Editorial de Ciencias Sociales, 2003.
Humboldt, Alexander Von. *Ensayo político sobre la isla de Cuba.* 1826. Reprint, with an introduction by Fernando Ortiz. Havana: Fundación Fernando Ortiz, 1998.

Jameson, Robert Francis. *Letters from the Havana during the Year 1820; Containing an Account of the Present State of the Island of Cuba and Observations on the Slave Trade.* London: John Miller, 1821.

Morell de Santa Cruz. "El Obispo Morell de Santa Cruz oficializa los cabildos africanos donde nació la santería, convirtiéndolos en ermitas." Havana, December 6, 1755. In *Cuba: Economía y sociedad, del monopolio hacia la libertad comercial (1701–1763),* edited by Levi Marrero, 8:159–161. Madrid: Editorial Playor, 1980.

Navarro, Diego José. "Bando sobre prohibir el uso de armas y capas a negros y mulatos." Havana, May 4, 1779. In *Boletín del Archivo Nacional* 28, nos. 1–6 (January–December 1929): 103–104.

"R. C. al Gobernador de la Habana ordenándole haga observar el método y reglas que se expresan, en la exacción del derecho de alcabala de la venta de los negros esclavos coartados de aquella isla." Aranjuez, June 21, 1768. In *Colección de documentos para la historia de la formación social de Hispanoamérica, 1493–1810,* edited by Richard Konetzke, vol. 3, tomo 1, pages 337–340. Madrid: Consejo Superior de Investigaciones Científicas, 1962.

"R. C. al Gobernador de la Habana previéndole que deben considerarse y según la misma regla que se dio para los esclavos enteros la de los coartados." San Ildefonso, September 27, 1769. In *Colección de documentos para la historia de la formación social de Hispanoamérica, 1493–1810,* edited by Richard Konetzke, vol. 3, tomo 1, pages 337–340, 360–361. Madrid: Consejo Superior de Investigaciones Científicas, 1962.

"R. C. para el remedio de los esclavos en el servicio de los esclavos negros." Aranjuez, April 29, 1752. In *Colección de documentos para la historia de la formación social de Hispanoamérica,* 1493–1810, edited por Richard Konetzke, vol. 3, tomo 1, pages 260–261. Madrid: Consejo Superior de Investigaciones Científicas, 1962.

"R. C. sobre preeminencias de oficiales y soldados milicianos." Buen Retiro, September 16, 1708. In *Colección de documentos para la historia de la formación social de Hispanoamérica, 1493–1810,* edited by Richard Konetzke, vol. 3, tomo 1, page 80. Madrid: Consejo Superior de Investigaciones Científicas, 1962.

"Reglamento para las milicias y infantería y caballería de la isla de Cuba." El Pardo, January 19, 1769. In *Colección de documentos para la historia de la formación social de Hispanoamérica, 1493–1810,* edited by Richard Konetzke, vol. 3, tomo 1, pages 351–358. Madrid: Consejo Superior de Investigaciones Científicas, 1962.

Secondary Sources

Andrews, George Reid. *The Afro-Argentines of Buenos Aires, 1800–1900.* Madison: Univ. of Wisconsin Press, 1980.

Atanda, J. A. "The Yoruba Ogboni Cult: Did It Exist in Old Oyo?" *Journal of the Historical Society of Nigeria* 6, no. 4 (1973): 365–372.

Barcia, Manuel. *Seeds of Insurrection: Domination and Resistance on Western Cuban Plantations, 1808–1848*. Baton Rouge: Louisiana State Univ. Press, 2008.

Barcia Zequeira, María del Carmen. *La otra familia: Parientes, redes y descendencia de los esclavos en Cuba*. Havana: Fondo Editorial Casa de las Américas, 2003.

———. *Los Ilustres Apellidos: Negros en la Habana Colonial*. Havana: Ediciones Boloña, 2008

Bergad, Laird W., Fe Iglesias García, and María del Carmen Barcia. *The Cuban Slave Market, 1790–1880*. Cambridge: Cambridge Univ. Press, 1995.

Berlin, Ira. *Many Thousands Gone: The First Two Centuries of Slavery in North America*. Cambridge: Harvard Univ. Press, 1998.

Bowser, Frederick P. *The African Slave in Colonial Peru, 1524–1650*. Stanford: Stanford Univ. Press, 1974.

Brandon, George. *Santeria From Africa to the New World: The Dead Sell Memories*. Bloomington: Indiana Univ. Press, 1993.

Brown, David H. *Santeria Enthroned: Art, Ritual, and Innovation in an Afro-Cuban Religion*. Chicago: Univ. of Chicago Press, 2003.

Bushnell, Amy. *The King's Coffer: Proprietors of the Spanish Florida Treasury,1565–1702*. Gainesville: Univ. Presses of Florida, 1981.

Byrd, Alexander X. *Captives and Voyagers: Black Migrants Across the Eighteenth-Century British Atlantic World*. Baton Rouge: Louisiana State Univ. Press, 2008.

Cabrera, Lydia. *La Sociedad Secreta Abakuá, narrada por viejos adeptos*. Havana: Ediciones, C. R., 1959.

Casagrande, Giovanna. "Confraternities and Lay Female Religiosity in Late Medieval and Renaissance Umbria." In *The Politics of Ritual Kinship: Confraternities and Social Order in Early Modern Italy*, edited by Nicholas Terpstra, 48–66. Cambridge: Cambridge Univ. Press, 2000.

———. "Women in Confraternities between the Middle Ages and the Modern Age." *Confraternitas* 5, no. 2 (1994): 3–13.

Childs, Matt D. *The 1812 Aponte Rebellion in Cuba and the Struggle against Atlantic Slavery*. Chapel Hill: Univ. of North Carolina Press, 2006.

Cowling, Camillia. "Matrices of Opportunity: Women of Colour, Gender and the Ending of Slavery in Rio de Janeiro and Havana, 1870–1888." Ph.D. diss., University of Nottingham, 2006.

Deschamps Chapeaux, Pedro. "Cabildos: Solo para esclavos." *Cuba* 7, no. 69 (January 1968): 50–51.

———. *El negro en la economía habanera del siglo XIX*. Havana: Unión de Escritores y Artistas de Cuba, 1971.

———. "Sociedades: La integración de pardos y morenos." *Cuba* 7, no. 71 (March 1968): 54–55.
Duharte Jiménez, Rafael. *El negro en la sociedad colonial.* Santiago: Editorial Oriente, 1988.
Eltis, David. "The Diaspora of Yoruba Speakers, 1650–1865: Dimensions and Implications." In *The Yoruba Diaspora in the Atlantic World,* edited by Toyin Falola and Matt D. Childs, 17–39. Bloomington: Indiana Univ. Press, 2004.
———. *The Rise of African Slavery in the Americas.* Cambridge: Cambridge Univ. Press, 2000.
Eltis, David, Philip Morgan, and David Richardson. "Agency and Diaspora in Atlantic History: Reassessing the African Contribution to Rice Cultivation in the Americas." *American Historical Review* 112, no. 5 (December 2007): 1329–1358.
Falola, Toyin, and Adebayo Akanmu. *Culture, Politics, and Money Among the Yoruba.* New Brunswick: Transaction Publishers, 2000.
Flynn, Maureen. *Sacred Charity: Confraternities and Social Welfare in Spain, 1400–1700.* Ithaca: Cornell Univ. Press, 1989.
Franklin, Sarah L. *Women and Slavery in Nineteenth-Century Colonial Cuba.* Rochester, N.Y.: Univ. of Rochester Press, 2012.
Fuente, Alejandro de la. "Slaves and the Creation of Legal Rights in Cuba: *Coartación* and *Papel.*" *Hispanic American Historical Review* 87, no. 4 (November 2007): 659–692.
Fuente, Alejandro de la, with the collaboration of César García del Pino and Bernardo Iglesias Delgado. *Havana and the Atlantic in the Sixteenth Century.* Chapel Hill: Univ. of North Carolina Press, 2008.
Gómez, Michael A. *Exchanging Our Country Marks: The Transformation of African Identities in the Colonial and Antebellum South.* Chapel Hill: Univ. of North Carolina Press, 1998.
Hanger, Kimberly S. *Bounded Lives, Bounded Places: Free Black Society in Colonial New Orleans, 1769–1803.* Durham: Duke Univ. Press, 1997.
Heywood, Linda M. "The Angolan-Afro-Brazilian Cultural Connections." *Slavery and Abolition* 20, no. 1 (April 1999): 9–23.
Howard, Philip A. *Changing History: Afro-Cuban Cabildos and Societies of Color in the Nineteenth Century.* Baton Rouge: Louisiana State Univ. Press, 1998.
Johnson, Sherry. "'Honor Is Life': Military Reform and the Transformation of Cuban Society: 1753–1796." Ph.D. diss., University of Florida, 1995.
Kiddy, Elizabeth W. "Ethnic and Racial Identity in the Brotherhoods of the Rosary of Minas Gerais, 1700–1830." *Americas* 56, no. 2 (October 1999): 221–252.
———. *Blacks of the Rosary: Memory and History in Minas Gerais, Brazil.* University Park: Pennsylvania State Univ. Press, 2005.
Kiple, Kenneth F. *Blacks in Colonial Cuba, 1774–1899.* Gainesville: Univ. Presses of Florida, 1976.

Knight, Franklin W. "Cuba." In *Neither Slave nor Free: The Freedman of African Descent in the Slave Societies of the New World,* edited by David W. Cohen and Jack P. Greene, 278–308. Baltimore: Johns Hopkins Univ. Press, 1972.

———. "The Free Colored Population in Cuba during the Nineteenth Century." In *Slavery without Sugar: Diversity in Caribbean Economy and Society Since the 17th Century,* edited by Verene A. Shepherd, 224–247. Gainesville: Univ. Press of Florida, 2002.

Kuethe, Allan J. "The Status of the Free Pardo in the Disciplined Militia of New Granada." *Journal of Negro History* 56, no. 2 (April 1971): 105–117.

Landers, Jane G.. *Atlantic Creoles in the Age of Revolutions.* Cambridge: Harvard Univ. Press, 2010.

———. *Black Society in Spanish Florida.* Foreword by Peter H. Wood. Urbana: Univ. of Illinois Press, 1999.

Law, Robin. "The Evolution of the Brazilian Community in Ouidah." *Slavery and Abolition* 22, no. 1 (April 2001): 22–41.

———. *The Oyo Empire, c. 1600–c. 1836: A West African Imperialism in the Era of the Atlantic Slave Trade.* Oxford: Clarendon Press, 1977.

López Valdés, Rafael L. *Pardos y morenos esclavos y libres en Cuba y sus instituciones en el caribe Hispano.* San Juan: Centro de Estudios Avanzados de Puerto Rico y el Caribe, 2007.

Lovejoy, Paul E. "Identifying Enslaved Africans in the African Diaspora." In *Identity in the Shadow of Slavery,* edited by Paul E. Lovejoy, 1–29. London: Continuum, 2000.

———. *Transformations in Slavery: A History of Slavery in Africa,* 2nd ed. Cambridge: Cambridge Univ. Press, 2000.

———. "Transformation of Ekpe Masquerade in the African Diaspora." In *Carnival: "People's Art" and "Taking Back the Streets,"* edited by Christopher Innes (forthcoming).

Lovejoy, Paul E., and David Richardson. "Trust, Pawnship, and Atlantic History: The Institutional Foundations of the Old Calabar Slave Trade." *American Historical Review* 104, no. 2 (April 1999): 333–355.

Lucena Salmoral, Manuel. "El derecho de coartación del esclavo en la América Española." *Revista de Indias* 59, no. 216 (May–August 1999): 357–374.

Mello e Souza, Marina de. *Reis negros no Brasil escravista: história da festa de coroação de rei congo.* Belo Horizonte: Editora da UFMG, 2002.

Miller, Ivor L. *Voice of the Leopard: African Secret Societies and Cuba.* Jackson: Univ. Press of Mississippi, 2009.

Miller Joseph C. *Way of Death: Merchant Capitalism and the Angolan Slave Trade, 1730–1830.* Madison: Univ. of Wisconsin Press, 1988.

Mintz, Sidney W., and Richard Price. *The Birth of African-American Culture: An Anthropological Perspective.* 1976. Reprint, Boston: Beacon Press, 1992.

Moliner Castañeda, Israel. *Los Cabildos Afrocubanos en Matanzas.* Matanzas: Ediciones Matanzas, 2002.

Montejo-Arrechea, Carmen Victoria. *Sociedades de instrucción y recreo de pardos y morenos que existieron en Cuba colonial: 1878–1898*. Veracruz: Instituto Veracruzano de Cultura, 1993.

———. *Sociedades Negras en Cuba, 1878–1960*. Havana: Editorial de Ciencias Sociales, 2004.

Morgan, Jennifer. *Laboring Women: Reproduction and Gender in New World Slavery*. Philadelphia: Univ. of Pennsylvania Press, 2004.

Morgan, Philip D. *Slave Counterpoint: Black Culture in the Eighteenth-Century Chesapeake and Lowcountry*. Chapel Hill: Univ. of North Carolina Press, 1998.

Morton-Williams, Peter. "The Yoruba Ogboni Cult in Oyo." *Africa* 30 (1960): 362–374.

Núñez Jiménez, Antonio. *Los esclavos negros*. Cuba: Fundación de la Naturaleza y el Hombre, 1998.

Ortiz, Fernando. *Los cabildos y la fiesta afrocubanos del Día de Reyes*. 1921. Reprint, Havana: Editorial de Ciencias Sociales, 1992.

———. *Los negros curros*. 1909. Reprint, Havana: Editorial de Ciencias Sociales, 1986.

———. *Los negros esclavos*. 1916. Reprint, Havana: Editorial de Ciencias Sociales, 1975.

Paquette, Robert L. *Sugar Is Made with Blood: The Conspiracy of La Escalera and the Conflict between Empires over Slavery in Cuba*. Middletown, Conn.: Wesleyan Univ. Press, 1988.

Pichardo, Esteban. *Diccionario provincial de voces cubanas*. Matanzas: Imprenta de la Real Marina, 1836.

Price, Richard. "The Miracle of Creolization: A Retrospective." *New West Indian Guide* 75, nos. 1–2 (2001): 35–64.

———. "On the Miracle of Creolization." In *Afro-Atlantic Dialogues: Anthropology in Diaspora*, edited by Kevin A. Yelvington, 115–147. Santa Fe, N. Mex.: School of American Research Press, 2006.

Robertson, Claire, and Marsha Robinson. "Re-Modeling Slavery as If Women Mattered." In *Women and Slavery: The Modern Atlantic*, vol. 2, edited by Gwyn Campbell, Suzanne Miers, and Joseph C. Miller, 253–283. Athens: Ohio Univ. Press, 2008.

Rodríguez Ochoa, Yoel. "Situación socioeconómica de la población libre de color en Santiago de Cuba: 1844–1865." Santiago, Cuba: Trabajo de Diploma en Licenciado, Universidad de Oriente, 1998.

Rout, Leslie B., Jr. *The African Experience in Spanish America, 1502 to the Present Day*. Cambridge: Cambridge Univ. Press, 1976.

Rushing, Fannie Theresa. "Afro-Cuban Social Organization and Identity in a Colonial Slave Society, 1800–1888." *Colonial Latin American Historical Review* 11, no. 2 (spring 2002): 177–201.

Smallwood, Stephanie. *Saltwater Slavery: A Middle Passage from Africa to Ameri-*

can Diaspora. Cambridge: Harvard Univ. Press, 2007.

Soares, Mariza de Carvalho. "Can Women Guide Men: Gendering Politics among African Catholics in Brazil." In *Women and Slavery: The Modern Atlantic,* edited by Gwyn Campbell, Suzanne Miers and Joseph C. Miller, 2:79–99. Athens: Ohio Univ. Press, 2008.

———. *Devotos da cor: Identidade étnica, religiosidade e escravidão no Rio de Janeiro, século XVIII.* Rio de Janeiro: Civilização Brasileira, 2000.

Sparks, Randy J. *The Two Princes of Calabar: An Eighteenth-Century Atlantic Odyssey.* Cambridge: Harvard Univ. Press, 2004.

Sweet, James H. "Mistaken Identities: Olaudah Equiano, Domingos Alvares, and the Methodological Challenges of Studying the African Diaspora." *American Historical Review* 114, no. 2 (April 2009): 279–306.

———. *Recreating Africa: Culture, Kinship, and Religion in the African-Portuguese World, 1441–1770.* Chapel Hill: Univ. of North Carolina Press, 2003.

Thornton, John K. *Africa and Africans in the Making of the Atlantic World, 1400–1800,* 2nd ed. Cambridge: Cambridge Univ. Press, 1998.

———. "'I Am the Subject of the King of Congo': African Political Ideology and the Haitian Revolution." *Journal of World History* 4, no. 2 (fall 1993): 181–214.

Twinam, Ann. *Public Lives, Private Secrets: Gender, Honor, Sexuality, and Illegitimacy in Colonial Spanish America.* Stanford: Stanford Univ. Press, 1999.

Veléz, María Teresa. *Drumming for the Gods: The Life and Times of Felipe García Villamil, Santero, Palero, and Abakuá.* Philadelphia: Temple Univ. Press, 2000.

Von Germenten, Nicole. *Black Blood Brothers: Confraternities and Social Mobility for Afro-Mexicans.* Foreword by Stephen W. Angell and Anthony B. Pinn. Gainesville: Univ. Press of Florida, 2006.

Contributors

Ida Altman is Professor of History and Chair of the History Department at the University of Florida. She is the author of *Emigrants and Society: Extremadura and Spanish America in the Sixteenth Century* (Univ. of California Press, 1989) and *Transatlantic Ties in the Spanish Empire: Brihuega, Spain, and Puebla, Mexico, 1560–1620* (Stanford Univ. Press, 2000). Her most recent book is *The War for Mexico's West: Spaniards and Indians in New Galicia, 1524–1550* (Univ. of New Mexico Press, 2010). Currently she is studying interethnic relations and the formation of civil society in the early Spanish Caribbean.

Ras Michael Brown is Assistant Professor of Atlantic History and Africana Studies at Southern Illinois University Carbondale. He researches the dispersal of West-Central Africans and their spiritual cultures in the Americas. His book *African-Atlantic Cultures in the South Carolina Lowcountry* (Cambridge Univ. Press, 2012) examines perceptions of the natural world in the religious ideas and practices of African-descended communities in the Lowcountry from the colonial period into the twentieth century.

Hugh Glenn Cagle is Assistant Professor of History at the University of Utah. He specializes in the study of Brazil and the Portuguese empire, and in the history of early modern science. He has coauthored (with Michael Adas) the essay "Age of Settlement and Colonization, 1500–1900," which appeared in Ashgate's *Companion to Modern Imperial Histories* (2012). He is now revising a book manuscript titled "Dead Reckonings: Disease and the Study of Nature in Portuguese Asia and the Atlantic, 1450–1700."

Matt D. Childs is Associate Professor of History at the University of South Carolina. He specializes in Latin American, Caribbean, and Atlantic history, with a particular emphasis on the importance of understanding the historical legacies of slavery and racism in shaping the modern world. He is the author of *The 1812 Aponte Rebellion in Cuba and the Struggle against Atlantic Slavery* (Univ. of North Carolina Press, 2006) and coeditor (with Toyin Falola) of *The Yoruba Diaspora in the Atlantic World* (Indiana Univ. Press, 2005) and *The Changing Worlds of Atlantic Africa: Essays in Honor of Robin Law* (Carolina Academic Press, 2009).

Carla Gerona is Assistant Professor of History at the Georgia Institute of Technology. Her work focuses on early American, Atlantic, and Borderlands history. She is the author of *Night Journeys: The Power of Dreams in Transatlantic Quaker Culture* (Univ. of Virginia Press, 2004). She is currently working on "More than Six Flags: An Ethnohistory of an East Texas Place from the Caddos to the Texians," an interdisciplinary study of the multiethnic borderland around Nacogdoches before Texas's annexation to the United States.

Jane E. Mangan is Associate Professor of History and Chair of Latin American Studies at Davidson College. A specialist in colonial Andean history, she authored *Trading Roles: Gender, Ethnicity, and the Urban Economy in Colonial Potosí* (Duke Univ. Press, 2005) and edited José de Acosta's *Natural and Moral History of the Indies* (Duke Univ. Press, 2002). Her current project on families in Spain's first century of empire, "Transatlantic Obligations: Legal and Cultural Constructions of Family in Conquest-Era Spain and Peru," is under contract with Oxford University Press.

Sarah E. Owens is Associate Professor of Spanish at the College of Charleston. Her research focuses on the writings of religious women of early modern Spain and Latin America. She has published articles in journals including *Studia Mystica, Hispanic Journal, Colonial Latin American Historical Review,* and *Food and Foodways.* She is the editor and translator of Madre María Rosa's *Journey of Five Capuchin Nuns,* The Other Voice in Early Modern Europe Series (Iter and Centre for Reformation and Renaissance Studies, 2009). Her current research includes travel and healing in the early modern Iberian Atlantic world.

Allyson M. Poska is Professor of History at the University of Mary Washington. She specializes in women's history, colonial Latin American history, and the history of early modern Europe, especially early modern Spain. She is the author of three books: *Regulating the People: The Catholic Reformation in Seventeenth-Century Spain* (Brill, 1998), *Women and Gender in the Western Past* (coauthored, Houghton-Mifflin, 2006), and *Women and Authority in Early Modern Spain: The Peasants of Galicia* (Oxford Univ. Press, 2006). Since 1999, she has been the co-editor of a monograph series with Ashgate Press entitled "Women and Gender in the Early Modern World."

Nuria Salazar Simarro is a Researcher for the Coordinación Nacional de Monumentos Históricos at the Instituto Nacional de Antropología e Historia and Adjunct Instructor of Art History at the Universidad Iberoamericana, both in Mexico City. She is the author of more than thirty articles and book chapters in Mexico and abroad, with a focus on Mexican colonial nuns. She has two book publications: *La capilla del Santo Cristo de Burgos* (Instituto Nacional de Antropología e Historia, 1990) and *La vida común en los conventos de monjas de la ciudad de Puebla* (Gobierno del Estado de Puebla, 1990).

Lisa Vollendorf is Dean of the College of Humanities and the Arts at San José State University. She is the author of *The Lives of Women: A New History of Inquisitional Spain* (Vanderbilt Univ. Press, 2005) and *Reclaiming the Body: María de Zaya's Early Modern Feminism* (Univ. of North Carolina Press, 2001). She has edited three books: *Literatura y feminismo en España* (Anthropos, 2006); *Recovering Spain's Feminist Tradition* (MLA, 2001); and *Women, Religion, and the Atlantic World (1600–1800)* (coedited with Daniella Kostroun, Univ. of Toronto Press, 2009). Currently she is editing *Theorising the Ibero-American Atlantic* with Harald Braun.

Timothy D. Walker is Associate Professor of History at the University of Massachusetts, Dartmouth, and a visiting professor at the Universidade Aberta in Lisbon, Portugal. He is also the Associate Director of the UMass Dartmouth Center for Portuguese Studies and Culture, and an affiliated faculty member of the UMass Dartmouth Center of Indian Studies and the Program in Women's Studies. Walker is an affiliated Corresponding Researcher of the Centro de História de Além-Mar at the Universidade Nova de Lisboa. He is the author of *Doctors, Folk Medicine and the Inquisition: The Repression of Magical Healing in Portugal during the Enlightenment Era* (Brill, 2005).

Index

Abortion, 160–161, 178
Acosta, Domingo, 242
Africa. *See* West and Central Africa
African diaspora, 197–199, 232–235, 247. *See also* Black women; Iberian Atlantic; Slaves; *and specific colonies*
African retentions, 197–198
Agüero, Catalina de, 75n19
Aguilera, Francisco de, 82
Alba, Duke of, 77n37
Aldaña, Pedro de, 80n67
Aleman, Gabriel, 230
Aliaga, Gerónimo de (son), 94
Aliaga de Santomayor, Captain Gerónimo, 94
Almeida, Leonor de, 27
Altman, Ida, 2, 3, 6, 12n10, 23, 41, 57–71, 84, 97n10, 263
Alvarado, Francisco de, 69
Alvarado Cayatopa, Pedro, 94
Ampuero, Francisco de, 84
Ana de Cristo, Sor, 9–10
Anastácio, Vanda, 27
Anderson, Gary Clayton, 120
Andrade, Clemente, 242
Andrade, Paula de, 185
Angeles, Micaela de los, 131
Angulo, Antonio de, 72
Anpo, Catalina, 88
Anthimus, 142n32
Antonia (domestic servant), 184, 185–188
Apuntes para una biblioteca de autoras españolas, 6
Araújo, Alceu Maynard, 148–149
Arenal, Electa, 8
Armenteras, Rafaela, 246
Arocha, Francisco, 114–115
Arostegui, José, 246
Arriaga, Luis de, 60
Astorga, Benito de, 74n6

Astudillo, Gaspar de, 71
Atahualpa, 84
Audiencia (high court), 63, 65, 68, 70–73, 74n6
Aux, Luisa de, 69, 78n48
Avila, Isabel de, 72
Ayahibex, Catalina de, 176
Azevedo, Angela de, 26

Badillo, Sued, 78n49
Baeza, Teresa, 67
Bantu-Atlantic spiritual cultures, 196–197, 210–218
Baptista, Joana, 149–151, 166
Barcia, María del Carmen, 244
Bardecí, Lope, 68
Barr, Juliana, 51n38, 106, 108, 111
Barraga, Antonio José, 241
Barreto, Teresa, 243, 247
Barrionuevo, Francisco de, 68–69, 78n47
Barrionuevo, Pedro de, 69
Barrios y Jáuregi, Jacinto, 112–113
Bastidas, Rodrigo de, 79n56
Bauer, Ralph, 13n19, 142n15
Beatas, beaterio (lay religious), 8, 20, 30n9, 130
Becerra, Ana, 68
Becerra, Bachiller Juan, 78n41
Becerra, Juan, 78n41
Becerra, Licenciado Francisco, 68
Becerra, Licenciado Hernando, 78n41
Berbán, Juana María, 112
Berbán, María Antonia de, 116
Bergad, Laird, 244
Berlander, Jean Louis, 110
Bermúdez de Castro, Juan José, 144n44
Berrio, Luis de, 76n25
Bethencourt, Francisco, 153
Black women: in *cabildos de nación,* 230–131, 240–149; as cultural agents,

267

196; employment of, 245; as folk healers, 161–166, 175–177, 179; in Havana, 243–244, 243–246; and Mother Nganga, 196–197, 202–218; from West-Central Africa, 196–197, 200–218; wet-nursing by, 245, 255n68. *See also* Gender relations; Slaves

Blanco, Manuel, 242

Bobadilla, Francisco de, 60, 67, 75n11

Bosque, Dimas, 183

Botany. *See* Medicinal plants

Braga, Maria Luísa, 169n19

Brandes, Stanley, 49n22

Brayman Hackel, Heidi, 26–27

Brazil: *candomblé* in, 198, 200, 210–211, 217; convents in, 8–9; folk healers in, 148–149, 150, 151, 162, 175–176, 178; Nagô in, 201, 202; religious brotherhoods in, 236; slaves in, 175, 197; sugar production in, 175, 182; transplantation of Asian plants in, 181–182; West-Central African-inspired religion of, 196–197, 201, 210–212

Brotherhoods, Catholic, 222n42, 232, 235–240

Brown, Ras Michael, 6, 22, 23, 45, 130, 196–229, 263

Brujería (witchcraft), 198

Buenos Aires, 37, 39–40, 48n16, 48n18, 181, 237

Burns, Kathryn, 24, 79n55

Burton, Sophie, 123n30

Bushnell, Amy, 103

Caballero, Diego, 65

Cabildos de nación: and Catholic Church, 237–239; electoral process in, 230–231, 241, 243; finances of, 246–247; gender relations among members of, 215, 230–249; importance of, 216; leadership roles in, 240–248; location of *cabildo* houses, 238; militia soldiers as leaders of, 242–243; naming of, 231–232; origins and operations of, 235–240; and rebellion and resistance, 234–235; and Santería, 234–235; scholarship on, 234–235; slaves as members of, 240

Cáceres, Isabel de, 69

Caciques and *cacicas* (male and female native rulers), 62, 71, 75n17, 94, 78n47, 140, 176

Caddo Indians, 103, 106, 108–111, 116, 121

Cagle, Hugh Glenn, 2–3, 130, 166, 174–195, 263

Calderón, José Antonio, 114–115

Caminha, Alvaro de, 175, 179

Canary Islands, 57, 75n10, 77n31, 78n49, 105, 117, 121

Candomblé, 198, 200, 210–211, 217

Cañizares-Esguerra, Jorge, 3

Capuchins, 9, 20, 30n9, 128

Caridad Herrera, José, 241

Carlos III, King, 145n69

Carmelites, 8, 21, 26, 128

Carmo, Inês de, 162–164, 171n55

Carmona, Bartolomé, 98n19

Caro Baroja, J., 49n22

Carvajal, Francisco de, 90

Carvajal, María de, 90

Casa nganga, 213–215

Casañas de Jesús María, Fray Francisco, 109

Casta (race), 105

Castañeda, Antonia, 102

Castellanos, Rita, 246

Castellón, Tomás de, 69

Castillo, José, 247

Castro, Alvaro de, 71

Castro, Baltasar de, 79n51

Catalina de Jesús, Madre, 139

Catholic Church: and *cabildos de nación,* 237–239; and codes of femininity, 24, 26, 27; and conversion of Indians in East Texas, 114–115; in Hispaniola, 71; and indigenous women, 91; male experts in, referred to as "father," 212; missionaries of, 180–181, 185, 202, 205, 208, 209; Reformation of, in Spain, 236; religious brotherhoods and confraternities of, 222n42, 232, 235–240; and sending *mestizo* children to Spain, 78n45. *See also* Convents; Inquisition

Cazares, Alonso de, 71

Ceo, Violante do, 26

Chastity. *See* Sexuality

Chávez, Francisco, 110

Childbirth: maternal deaths from, 159; midwives for, 149–151, 156, 161, 178, 185, 245

Children: diseases of, 159; folk healing practices for, 150; mortality rate of, 159; wet-nurses for, 245, 255n68

Childs, Matt D., 6, 7, 22, 215, 230–262, 263

Chipman, Donald, 111
Chirinos, Andrés, 112–113, 116
Chumbo, Leonor, 94
Chuqui Tecla, Catalina, 94
Class hierarchies: in convents, 10, 128–129, 139–140; in Spain, 40–41, 44
Clothing: of free black women in Havana, 244; of indigenous women and girls, 87–88, 92, 95; of Spanish women, 70
Clusius, Carolus, 181, 191n34
Coartación (manumission by self-purchase), 244–245, 255n68
Cofradía (lay religious organization), 82
Colón, Bartolomé, 67
Colón, Diego, 59, 61, 67, 74n3, 75n12, 75n19, 77n37
Colón, Jerónimo, 70
Coloquios dos simples, e drogas e cousas medicinais da India (Orta), 181–182, 186, 188
Columbus, Christopher, 57, 60, 61, 67, 73, 75n11, 79n51
Conceptionists, 8, 128–41, 141n8, 141n12
Confraternities, 222n42, 232, 235–240
Convents: administration of, 132, 139; in Brazil, 8–9; class system of, 10, 128–129, 139–140; *curanderas* in, 135–136, 140, 155–156; diseases of women in, 137–139, 144nn49–51; dowry for entry into, 131, 132; expulsion of secular population from, 145n69; female population of, 132, 142n23; in France, 130; funding for, 79n56, 131, 132, 136, 143n39, 145n67; in Guatemala, 20; health care provided in, 133–141, 155–56, 176; in Hispaniola, 71, 73, 79nn55–56; indigenous women and girls in, 129, 140; in Italy, 130; laywomen in, 10, 129, 130–133, 143n38, 145n69; lifestyle of nuns within, 7–8, 128–129, 145n69; literacy of nuns within, 7; *mestiza* women and girls in, 79n55; in Mexico City, 20, 128–141, 141n12, 144n51; and mobility of religious women, 7–11, 20–21; multiethnic community in, 129–130, 139–140; in New Spain, 141n12; nurses in, 133–134, 140, 142n26; in Peru, 8, 20, 24, 30n9, 79n55, 93; physicians and surgeons for, 136–137, 140–141, 144nn44–47; in Portugal and Portuguese colonies, 9–10, 26; royal patronage of, 131–132, 139; servant class in, 10, 129, 132–133, 135–136, 139, 145n69; slaves in, 129; in Spain, 8, 21, 93; Teresa of Avila's impact on, 8; widows in, 131, 145n69; and writings by religious women, 6, 7, 8, 9, 19–20, 26–27
Conversos, 23, 25–26, 27, 78n49
Cook, James, 118
Corrales, María de, 95
Cortés, Hernando, 68
Costa, Antónia Nunes da, 152, 165
Costa, Cristovão da, 174–175, 177–178, 181, 185
Cowling, Camillia, 255n68
Creolization model, 198, 232–233
Criadas (servants or retainers), 60, 70, 72, 119
Criollas (Spanish women born in New World), 131, 139, 140, 142n15
Cruz, Juan de la, 116
Cruz, Miguel de la, 240
Cuba: *cabildos de nación* in, 230–249; Catholic brotherhoods in, 237–240; employment of freed black women in, 245; Lucumí in, 198, 201, 202; militia in, 242–243; population of Havana in, 243–244; rebellions, 234; *reglas de congo* in, 200, 212–217, 223n54; *reglas de ocha* in, 198, 200, 212; slaves in, 76n26, 234, 244–245, 254n64, 255n68; Spanish women in, 68, 71, 75n19; urban code (1792) in, 238, 252nn33–34; West-Central African-inspired religion of, 196–197, 200, 201, 212–217
Curanderas, curandeiras, 135–136, 140, 148–167
Cutter, Charles, 111–112

D'Alorna, Marquesa, 27
Daza, Pedro, 67
Deagan, Kathleen, 77n32
Death, in West-Central African spiritual cultures, 206–7
Degredados (exiled convict folk healers), 150, 152
Deos, João de, 162
Derbanne, François, 107
Derbanne, Jean Baptiste, 107–8
Díaz de Aux, Miguel, 69, 78n47, 78n48
Díaz de Corrales, Anton, 95
Diepa, Antonio, 243
Diseases, 137–139, 144n43, 144n46,

Diseases (*continued*)
144nn49–51, 158–160, 164, 165, 171n55, 176, 185, 186. *See also* Folk healers; Health care
Doctors. *See* Health care; Physicians and surgeons
Domestic violence, 114–115, 120
Domínguez, María Rosario, 240
Dominicans, 26, 71, 79n56
Durán, Juan Martín, 89
Durán, Rafael, 89
DuVal, Kathleen, 123n30

East Texas: Anglo cotton planters in, 104; Caddo Indians in, 103, 106, 108–111, 116, 121; Catholic Church's conversion of Indians in, 114–115; census (1795) of, 105–6; domestic violence in, 114–115, 120; founding of Nacogdoches in, 103; French in, 104, 107–8, 110–111; history of Spanish occupation of, 104–7; illicit sex in, 101, 112–119; indigenous people in, 106–110; intermarriage and interrelations in, 104–121; legal records from, 101, 111–121; *mestizos* and *métis* in, 104, 105; murder case in, 114–115; prostitution in, 114–115, 120; punishments for crimes in, 113–115; sexual relationships between indigenous women and Spaniards in, 106–7; slaves in, 106, 119; Spanish and French interrelationships in, 107–8; Spanish women in, 101–121; trade and contraband trade in, 101, 104, 105, 107, 109–113, 116–119
Echevarría, Juan, 230
Education and literacy: access to, 22; and books read by women, 22; in Iberia and the Americas, 18–29; of nuns, 7; and private and public reading, 22; scholarship on, 22–23, 28–29; Sor Juana Inés de la Cruz on women's right to, 8, 19; in Spain, 22; teaching of reading and writing as separate skills, 21–22; writings by religious women, 6, 7, 8, 9, 19–20, 26
Ekpe society, 238–239
Elliott, John H., 3, 18
Eltis, David, 233, 250n12
Encomenderos, encomienda (holders of land grants or indigenous labor) and martial status, 3, 61, 68, 75n19
England, 3, 4

Enlightenment, 154
Enríquez de Almanza, Viceroy Martín, 131
Enríquez de Rivera, Archbishop Payo, 132
Españolas, españoles (Spanish), 65–66, 105–6. *See also* Spanish women
Espinosa, Licenciado, 63–64

Familiares (lay collaborators of the Inquisition), 149, 155, 164, 167
Families. *See* Children; Marriage
Felipa de Estefanía, Madre, 138
Ferdinand, King, 3, 25, 59, 75n12, 77n37
Fernández, María, 60
Fernández-Armesto, Felipe, 78n49
Fernández de Oviedo, Gonzalo, 79n53, 176
Ferreira de Lacerda, Bernarda, 26
Fields, Sherry, 144n49
Figueroa, Licenciado, 64
Firth, Raymond, 155
Fisher, Andrew, 10
Flores, Juan, 87
Floyd, Troy S., 78n41
Flynn, Maureen, 236
Folk healers: abortions performed by, 161; Amerindian women as, 175–177; black women as, 161–166, 175–177, 179; in Brazil, 148–149, 150, 151; in convents, 135–136, 140; *curanderas* and *curandeiras* as, 135–136, 140, 148–167; *degredados* (exiled convict folk healers), 150, 152; demand for services of, in rural areas, 158–159; expectations of European clientele of, 151–152; gender ratio of, 152–154, 169n19; health problems treated by, 158–160, 164, 171n55; Inquisition trials of, 148–155, 157, 161–167, 169n22, 170n34, 178, 179; as midwives, 149–151, 156, 161, 178, 185; natural remedies of and cures by, 156, 158, 164, 165, 175–177; in Portugal, 149–156; positive function of, 154–155; power sources of, 156–157, 170n34; and protective magic, 155; as threat to the establishment, 156–157, 163, 166–167; in West-African spiritual cultures, 207–9, 215. *See also* Medicinal plants
Food, 58, 68, 132, 135, 142nn31–32, 158
France: Catholic brotherhoods and confraternities in, 236; convents in, 130; settlers from, in East Texas, 104, 107–8, 110–111
Francisca, Doña, 94–95
Franciscans, 9–10, 71, 106, 107, 141n8

Fuente, Alejandro de la, 237
Fuero rights (military privileges), 242–243

Gaitán, Father, 117
Galen, 137, 143–44n43
Gama, Antonio de la, 70
Games, Alison, 4
García, Beatriz, 72
García, Cayetano, 243
García, Francisco, 72
García, Inés, 80n67
García, Juan, 94–95
García, Marequita, 94–95
García, María, 72
García Jove, José Ignacio, 137, 144n47
Gavilan, Juan, 242
Gender frontier, 45
Gender history, 5–6, 22–23, 28–29. *See also* Gender relations; Women
Gender relations: and authority and objectivity, 178; in Bantu-Atlantic spiritual cultures, 196–197, 210–218; in *cabildos de nación*, 230–249; in Catholic brotherhoods and confraternities, 222n42, 235–240; Catholic codes of femininity, 24, 26, 27; and chastity of women, 40–41, 49n22, 174; and class hierarchies, 40–41, 44; Costa on, 174–175, 177–178; and economic activity, 38, 43–44; and female honor, 40–41, 45; and folk healers, 149, 152–154, 178–180; and indigenous women and girls, 45–46, 51n38; and legal system generally, 43; machismo and marianismo, 102; and power, 202–218; and professionalization of health care, 177–178; and Royal Pragmatic on Marriage (1776), 43; scholarship on, 42–43; in Spain, 40–41; in Spanish empire, 37–47; in West-Central African spiritual cultures, 202–10. *See also* Gender history; Women
Gerona, Carla, 2, 23, 41, 101–127, 264
Ginoves, Antonio, 88
Ginoves, Simón, 88–89
Glass, Anthony, 109, 110
Goa, India, 180–188
Gold mining, 57–58, 63, 65, 66, 67, 69, 73, 76–77nn28–29
Gomes, Maria, 152
Gómez, Antonio, 39
Gomez, Michael, 233
González, Joseph, 107–8

González, Pedro, 116
González, Victoria Margarita, 107–8
Gould, Eliga, 41
Govín, Cristóbal, 243, 247
Grácia, Maria, 164
Grande Terre, Jeanne de la, 107
Graubart, Karen, 12n11
Gregg, Josiah, 112
Griego, Pedro Tomas, 85
Guadiana, José María, 115–116
Guatiao (name exchange), 62
Guevara, María de, 25, 26, 27
Guilarte, Diego, 72
Gutierrez, Gonzalo (or Juan), 87
Guzmán, Gonzalo de, 75n19
Guzmán, Guiomar de, 71, 79–80n59

Hakims (Muslim physicians), 182, 185
Hanger, Kimberly S., 253n57
Haro, Andrés de, 78n49
Health care: and Ayurveda in India, 182, 183, 185; in convents, 133–141, 155–156, 176; funding for, in convents, 136, 143n39, 145n67; in Goa, India, 182–188; and humoral theory of Hippocrates and Galen, 137, 143–144n43, 144n57; medicinal uses of precious stones, 183, 191n36; medicines and medicinal plants for, 134–135, 144nn59–60, 148, 160, 161, 174–188; by midwives, 149–151, 156, 161, 178, 185, 245; by nurses, 133–134, 140, 142n26, 245; nutritious diet for the sick, 135; and pharmacists, 134–135; professionalization of, 177–178; salaries of medical personnel, 135, 136, 137, 144n44; treatments of diseases, 138–139, 144n43, 144n57, 164, 165; and women's knowledge of medicinal plants, 174–188. *See also* Diseases; Folk healers; Medicinal plants; Physicians and surgeons
Hernández, Blas, 66
Hernández, Francisco, 177, 179–180
Herrera, Francisco de, 75n19
Herrera, María de, 82
Heywood, Linda, 235
Hidalgo Bendaval, Cristóbal, 143n34
Hijos naturales (children born to unmarried parents), 93–94. *See also* Illegitimacy
Hinojosa, Juan de, 82
Hippocrates, 137, 143–144n43

Hispaniola: cacique group in, 62, 75n17; Catholicism in, 71; colonization projects in, 65; convents in, 71, 73, 79nn55–56; dangers to Spanish women in, 71–72; decline in indigenous population of, 62, 63, 65; departure of Spanish women and men from, 72–73; European settlements on, 57, 60; first *mestizo* born in, 78n47; housing in, 73; marriage of Spanish men and indigenous women in, 61–62; *mestizos* in, 68–69, 78n45, 78n47; number of women in, 62; Portuguese settlers in, 77n31; rebellion of Enriquillo on, 68; *repartimiento* of 1514 in, 62–63, 66, 71, 74n2; single Spanish men in, 67; slaves and slave raiding in, 68, 69, 77n32, 78n49; Spanish society in, 66–73; Spanish women in, 58–74; sugar production in, 64, 65, 77nn31–32; towns of, 62–64. *See also* Santo Domingo

Holler, Jacqueline, 20, 30n9
Honor code, 40–41, 45, 49n22
Hooper, Maria, 119
Howard, Philip, 238
Huayles Yupanqui, Inés, 84
Huayna Capac, 94

Iberian Atlantic: class system in generally, 10; colonization of, compared with English pattern, 3, 4; definition of, 3–5, 18–19; "entangled histories" of Iberia and, 4–5, 41–47; ethnic and racial variation within generally, 23, 28; interconnectivity of women in, 6–11, 24–25, 27–29, 41–43; stages of European expansion in, 57; trade between Spain and, 57–58, 70; West-Central African women in, 200–218. *See also* Black women; Convents; Folk healers; Gender relations; Health care; Indigenous women and girls; Spanish women

Iglesias, Fe, 244
Illegitimacy, 40, 41, 44, 46, 48–49n20, 85, 93, 94, 97n10, 103
Illnesses. *See* Diseases; Folk healers; Health care
Inca empire, 82, 84, 85–86, 94
India. *See* Goa, India
Indigenous women and girls: Christian instruction for, 71; clothing of, 87–88, 92, 95; in convents, 129, 140; dowry for, 86, 88–89; employment of, 87; gender norms for, 45–46, 51n38; and healing, 166, 175–177, 179–180; housing for, 92; and Inca empire, 84, 85–86; inheritance from, 82–83, 88, 89–97; legal suits involving, 24; money, property and other gifts from Spanish fathers of children of, 86–88, 98n19; as mothers in Peru, 82–97; removal of *mestizo* children from their mothers, 68–69, 78n45, 82–86, 90–94, 96; sexual relationships or marriage between Spanish men and, 3–4, 58–59, 61–62, 63, 75n11, 76nn20–21, 82–97, 84, 86; and Spanish women, 71, 73. *See also* Native Americans in East Texas

Inheritance practices, 40, 44, 46, 75n12, 75n19, 82–83, 89–97
Inquisition, 8, 24–28, 148–155, 157, 161–167, 169n22, 170n34, 178–180, 188
Isabel, Queen of Spain, 130
Islam, 23–24, 154, 165, 182, 185
Italy, 130, 235–236

Jacinta de São José, 8–9
Jackson, Jack, 118
Jameson, Robert, 244
Jaramillo, Diego de, 80n67
Jefferson, Thomas, 117
Jerónima de la Asunción, Sor, 9–10
Jesuits, 20, 107–8, 181, 182, 184
Jesús María Convent (Mexico City), 7–8, 128–141
Jiménez, Alfredo, 112
Josefa, 37–40, 41, 43, 47
Joseph, Harriet Denise, 111
Juana de Dolores, 142n26
Juana Inés de la Cruz, Sor, 8, 19–20, 23, 24, 27, 28, 132–133
Judaism, 23, 25–26. *See also* Conversos
Julius II, Pope, 130

Kaminsky, Amy Katz, 14n29
Kelly, Catherine E., 26–27
Kinship: in East Texas, 104–11, 118–121; and matriliny, 204–6; in West-Central Africa, 203–5. *See also* Marriage
Kostroun, Daniella, 18

La Vere, David, 110–111
Laguna, Andrés, 191n36
Landers, Jane, 237

Lando, Francisco Manuel de, 65–66
Las Casas, Bartolomé de, 79n51
Lavrin, Asunción, 7
Law. *See* Legal system
Law, Robin, 233
Leal, Antonio (son), 119
Leal, Antonio (trader), 101, 104, 110, 117–119, 121
Leal, Josefa, 119
Leal, Juan José, 119
Lebrón, Licenciado, 72
Legal system: Anglo-Americans' attitude toward Spanish legal system, 111–112; in East Texas, 101, 111–121; and illegitimacy, 103; and illicit sex in East Texas, 101, 112–119; and inheritance, 46, 75n12, 88, 89–97; and marriage, 3–4, 43, 59–61, 65, 74n2, 76n20, 76n23, 108; and murder case in East Texas, 114–115; punishments in East Texas under, 113–115; and removal of *mestizo* children to Spain, 85–86; and *Siete Partidas,* 2; and transatlantic gender analysis, 43
Léon, Alonso de, 110
Léon, Ignacio de, 110
León, Fray Luis de, 49n22
Léon, Manuel de, 110
Leonor of Cuzco, 82–83, 88
Lintot, Frances, 120
Literacy. *See* Education and literacy
Loomis, Noel L., 118
López de la Serna, Martín, 95
López Moroso, Francisco, 135
Louisiana, 105, 107, 110–111, 113, 123n30, 253n57
Lovejoy, Paul, 233, 238–239
Lucero, Cecelia, 80n67
Luisa de San Nicolás, Sor, 139
Lupiana, Pedro de, 87

Madres ngangas, 196, 213–216, 217
Madrinas, 215–216
Mães de santos (spiritual mothers), 196
Mágicos (magical offenders), 152–154
Malaver, Inés de, 67
Maldonado, Cristóbal, 90
Maldonado, Diego, 87
Manga Saya, 196, 200, 214–215
Mangan, Jane E., 1–17, 2, 23, 82–100, 264
Mannarelli, Emma, 84
Manrique, Isabel de, 70, 79n53

Manrique, María, 70
Manuel, Bernarda, 25–26, 27
Manzorro, Elvira, 68–69, 78n45
Manzorro, Rodrigo, 68, 78n41, 78n47
Marachai, Juan, 90
Marcaida, María de, 68
Marçal, João Baptista, 162
María de la Asunción, Madre, 138
María de la Visitación, Sor, 136, 143n38
María Gertrudis de San Lorenzo, Sor, 144n51
María Rosa, Madre, 9, 133
Maria Teresa (*mulata*), 166
María Teresa de San José, Sor, 142n26
Mariana de San Jerónimo, Sor, 139
Márquez, Ana, 73
Marriage: age at first marriage, 39, 40, 48n13, 48n18; of Caddo Indians, 108–9, 110, 116; domestic violence in, 114–115, 120; French and Indian intermarriage in East Texas, 110–111; incentives for, among Spanish settlers and recruitment of married couples, 3–4, 59–60, 64, 74n2; of indigenous women and Spanish men, 61–62, 63, 75n11, 76n20, 82–97; intermarriage and interrelations in East Texas, 104–121; legal discourse and royal decrees on, 3–4, 43, 59–61, 65, 74n2, 76n20, 76n23, 108; and métissage in Louisiana, 123n30; polygamy among Native Americans, 110; Royal Pragmatic on Marriage (1776), 43; Spanish and Indian intermarriage in East Texas, 110, 111, 114–115, 121; of Spanish women in Iberian Atlantic, 3–4, 58–74, 76n23; strategic marriages among wealthy, 69–70; of Wichita Indians, 109–110
Martha ("La Morenita"), Sor, 10
Martín, Diego, 80n67
Martín, Pedro, 72
Martinez, Francisco, 87
Martins, Francisco, 170n34
Martos y Navarette, Ángel, 113
Materia medica. See Medicinal plants
Matriliny, 204–6
Mayorga, Isabel de, 74n6
Mazzotti, José Antonio, 13n19, 142n15
Medicinal plants, 134, 148, 160, 161, 174–188
Medicine. *See* Health care; Physicians and surgeons
Medina, Antonio de, 86

Mendoza, Vélez de, 74
Meneses, Leonor de, 26
Mesa, Barbara de, 246, 247
Mestiza women and girls: in convents, 79n55, 93, 129, 131, 133, 142n26; in Hispaniola, 68–69, 78n45, 78n47; legal suits involving, 24; in Puerto Rico, 65; and Spanish women, 58–59, 74
Mestizos: acceptance of, as Spanish, 68–69, 84; in East Texas, 104, 105; first *mestizo* born in Hispaniola, 78n47; removal of *mestizo* children to Spain, 68–69, 78n45, 82–86, 90–94, 96; Spanish fathers' relationship with, 68–69, 84–86, 96. *See also Mestiza* women and girls
Métis and *métissage,* 105, 107, 123n30
Mexico: African population in Mexico City, 237; convents in, 20, 128–141, 141n12, 144n51; Cortés' conquest of, 68; health care in, 133–141, 143n42; illegitimacy rate in Guadalajara, 48–49n20; religious brotherhoods in, 237
Middle Passage, 3, 175, 197, 216, 234. *See also* Slaves
Midwives, 149–151, 156, 161, 178, 185, 245
Miller, Joseph, 233
Mining. *See* Gold mining; Silver mining
Mintz, Sidney, 232–233
Mira Caballos, Esteban, 78n47
Mita (forced labor draft), 4
Mogollón, Hernando, 79n51
Monardes, Nicolás, 177, 179
Monroy, Francisco de, 59
Montenegro, Juan, 91
Mora, Jacinto, 116
Mora, Juan de, 108
Morell de Santa Cruz, Bishop, 237–238
Moreno, Pedro, 79n51
Morgan, Jennifer, 250n12
Moriscos, 23–24, 75n13
Mother Nganga, 196–197, 202–218
Moya de Contreras, Archbishop Pedro, 131, 132
Mulatos/as, 129, 133, 166, 242
Munive, José Antonio, 110
Murder, 114–115
Muslims. *See* Islam
Músquiz, Lieutenant, 116
Mutual aid societies. *See Cabildos de nación*
Mwana, muana (child), 204, 216

Naborías (servants), 62, 63
Nacogdoches, Tex. *See* East Texas
Nagô, 201, 202
Nash, Gary, 104
Nasitir, Abraham P., 118
Native Americans in East Texas, 103, 106–111, 114–115, 116, 121
Natural histories and naturalists, 176–178, 181–182, 190n18
Nava, Alonso, 93
Nava, Catalina de, 93
Nava, María de, 93
New Mexico, 112
New Spain, 73, 80n67, 106, 141n12, 200. *See also* East Texas
Nganga, banganga (expert/s), 200, 202, 206–218
Nganga ngombo, 206–9
Nganga/prenda, 213–215
Nganga wisa (*nganga* of power), 210
Ngudi (mother), 200, 204–6, 209–213, 216–217, 222n37
Ngudi a nsimba (mother of twins), 204–5
Ngudi nganga, bangudi banganga (mother expert/s), 209–213, 217
Nkisi (consecrated objects), 207–8
Nolan, Philip, 101, 117–121
Nuestra Señora de Candelaria, 82
Nuñez, Mari, 66
Núñez de Guzmán, Pero, 75n19
Núñez de Haro y Peralta, Archbishop Alonso, 139
Nuns. *See* Convents
Nurses, 133–134, 140, 142n26, 245. *See also* Health care

Oconór, Hugo, 113
Ocuro, Alonso, 91
O'Hara, Matthew, 10
Oidores (judges), 63–64, 67, 68, 70, 72, 73
Olivares, Conde-Duque de, 26
Orta, Garcia de, 181–188, 191n34, 191n36
Ortíz, Baltazar, 90
Ortíz, Francisca, 90–93
Ortíz, Juana, 93
Ortíz, María, 90–93
Otte, Enrique, 76n28
Ovando, Nicolás de, 2–4, 59, 60, 62, 68, 71, 74nn2–3, 75nn10–12, 77n37

Owens, Sarah E., 1–17, 20, 22, 30n9, 128–147, 155, 176, 264

Pacheco, Angela, 114–115
Padilla, María, 113
Palla, Ana, 95–96
Paraíso Occidental (Sigüenza y Góngora), 131–132
Parda (woman of mixed race), 166
Paredes, Countess, 19, 20
Parteiras (midwives), 149–151, 156, 161, 178
Pastor, Francisco, 88
Pastor, Juan, 88
Pastor, Lucas, 88
Paul, Saint, 8
Paz, Pedro de, 71
Pearl trade, 57–58, 67, 68, 69, 73, 76n28
Pereira, Antónia, 157
Pereira, Duarte Pacheco, 177, 179
Peru: *cofradía* (lay religious organization) in, 82; convents in, 8, 20, 24, 30n9, 79n55, 93; housing in, 92; Inca empire in, 82, 84, 85–86, 94; indigenous women as mothers in, 82–97; religious brotherhoods in, 236–137
Pharmacists, 134–135. *See also* Health care
Philip II, King, 131–132, 236
Philip IV, King, 26
Physicians and surgeons: for convents, 136–137, 140–141, 144nn44–47; and folk healers, 156–157, 158, 162, 166–167, 177–178; in Goa, India, 182–185; and institutionalization of medical practice, 177–178; and medicinal plants, 174–175, 177–188; Muslim physicians (*hakims*), 182, 185. *See also* Health care
Pires, John, 163
Pitt-Rivers, Julian, 49n22
Pizarro, Francisco, 84
Polygamy, 110
Ponce de León, Juan, 70, 76–77n29, 79n51
Ponce de León, Leonor, 79n51
Popayán, Juan de, 89
Portillo, Manuel del, 240
Portugal: Catholic brotherhoods and confraternities in, 235; colonization by, compared with England, 3, 4; convents in, 9, 26; folk healers in, 149–167; folktales in, of enchanted Moorish women, 165; and Goa, India, 180–188; Inquisition in, 26, 148–155, 157, 161–167, 169n22, 170n34; Jews in, 25; links between Spain and, 25–26, 29; physicians and surgeons in, 149, 156–157, 158, 162; rural poor in, 158–159. *See also* Portuguese colonies; Portuguese women
Portuguese colonies: compared with English colonies, 3, 4; convents in, 9–10; cultural institutions in, 13n19; folk healers in, 148–149, 155–167, 175, 179–180; geographical range of, 25; Goa, India, as, 180–188; medicinal plants in, 180–188. *See also* Brazil; Iberian Atlantic
Portuguese women: in convents, 130; in Hispaniola, 77n31; in Puerto Rico, 66; Spanish language used by, 9, 26
Poska, Allyson M., 2, 6, 12n12, 21, 37–56, 103, 264
Poveda, Tomás, 242
Power: and assumption of male dominance, 203; definition of, 202–3; of folk healers, 156–157, 170n34; motherhood connected with, in West-Central African spiritual cultures, 203–5; in West-Central African spiritual cultures, 202–210
Powers, Karen, 84
Premo, Bianca, 24
Price, Richard, 232–233
Private sphere. *See* Public/private dichotomy
Prostitution, 41, 67, 114–115, 120
Public/private dichotomy, 22–23, 102–3, 104, 108, 120
Puerto Rico: beginning of Spanish occupation of, 76–77n29; census (1530) in, 65–66; dangers to Spanish women in, 71–72; departure of Spanish women and men from, 72–73; gold mining in, 66, 68, 69, 76–77nn28–29; illness and death of settlers in, 76n25; indigenous rebellion (1513) in, 71; indigenous workers in, 65; marriage of Spanish men and indigenous women in, 61; Portuguese settlers in, 66; San Juan in, 65–67; single Spanish men in, 67; slaves and slave raiding in, 65, 66, 69, 78n49; Spanish society in, 66–67, 69–70; Spanish women in, 65–74, 80n67; sugar production in, 69, 78n49; towns in, 65
Pulque, 135, 138, 139, 143n36, 144n59

Queba, Hernando de la, 94
Quiñones, Gertrudis, 119
Quiñones, Juana María (Leal), 119
Quiroz, Francisco de, 87–88
Quispe, Lázaro, 88

Ramirez, Francisco, 87
Ramirez Cavala, Pedro, 90, 93
Ramón, Diego, 107
Rape, 72, 84, 106, 114
Reconquista, 59, 165
Refugio de Jesús Santa María, María, 114–115, 120
Regla de ocha (Santería), 198, 212, 234
Reglas de congo, 200, 212–117, 223n54
Religious women. *See Beatas, beaterio* (lay religious); Convents; *and specific orders of nuns*
Repartimientos (grants of rights to indigenous labor), 59, 61–63, 66, 68, 69, 71, 74n2, 74n5
Richardson, David, 238–239
Rio, María de Jesús del, 116
Robertson, Claire, 234
Robinson, Marsha, 234
Rodríguez, Cristóbal, 75n11
Rodríguez, Lázaro, 243
Rodríguez-Sala, María Luisa, 143n41
Rojas, Juan de, 93
Romero-Díaz, Nieves, 25
Ruiz de Monjaraz, Marina, 80n67

Sabina, 176
Salamanca, Pedro de, 60
Salazar Simarro, Nuria, 2–3, 7, 22, 128–147, 143, 155, 176, 264–265
Salcedo, Juana de, 138
Salgado, Marcos José, 137, 144n46
Saludadores (healers), 152–157. *See also* Folk healers
Sánchez, Beatriz, 75n19
Sanchez, Miguel, 86
Sánchez Navarro, Manuela, 107
Sandoval, Governor, 107
Santa Clara nuns, 71, 79nn55–56
Santa Cruz, Alonso, 240
Santería (*regla de ocha*), 198, 212, 234
Santiago, María de, 90
Santo Domingo, 59, 61–64, 66–73, 77n37, 79nn55–56. *See also* Hispaniola

Santos, Gertrudis de los, 101, 104, 110, 116–121
Santos, José de los, 119
São Tomé, 200
Saracho, Juan de, 94–95
Sarmento, Clara, 13n21
Saucedo, Santiago, 115
Schlau, Stacey, 8
Sedeño, Antonio, 79n51
Serna, Ana de la, 95
Serna, Francisca de la, 95
Serón, Francisca Josefa, 135
Serpa, Isabel, 70
Serrano, Diego, 94
Servants: in convents, 10, 129, 132–133, 135–136, 139, 145n69; *criadas* as, 60, 70, 72, 119; in Goa, India, 183–186; *naborías* as, 62, 63; wages for, 87
Sexuality: and Catholic codes of femininity, 24, 26, 27; and chastity of women, 40–41, 49n22, 174; and illegitimacy, 40, 41, 44, 46, 48–49n20, 85, 93, 97n10, 103; and illicit sex in East Texas, 101, 112–119; and prostitution, 41, 67, 114–115, 120; of Spanish women, 67, 71, 101
Siete Partidas, 2
Sigüenza y Góngora, Carlos de, 131–132
Silva, Beatriz de, 130
Silver mining, 4
Sisa, Quispe, 84
Slaves: in Brazil, 175, 197; in Buenos Aires, 40; as *cabildo* members, 240; in Caribbean and Latin America generally, 6, 11; in convents, 129; in Cuba, 76n26, 234, 244–245, 254n64, 255n68; in East Texas, 106, 119; folk healing by, 175–177; in Hispaniola, 69, 77n32; Indian slaves, 68, 69, 78n49; Manga Saya as, 214–215; marriage of, 106; and Middle Passage, 3, 175, 197, 216, 234; in Puerto Rico, 65, 66, 69; scholarship on slavery and slave trade, 3, 232–234; self-purchase for freedom of, 244–245, 255n68; sexual relationships between masters and, 120; slave raiding in Hispaniola and Puerto Rico, 68, 69, 78n49; and Spanish women, 59, 71, 73; statistics on, 200–202; urban slaves, 244, 254n64; from West-Central Africa, 200–202
Smallwood, Stephanie, 234

Soares, Mariza de Carvalho, 236
Someruelos, Marques de, 230, 231
Spain: apprenticeships in, 85; Catholic brotherhoods and confraternities in, 235–236; Catholic Reformation in, 236; Chamin, Galicia in, 37–38, 40, 47*n*1; class hierarchies in, 40–41, 44; colonization by, compared with England, 3, 4; and colonization of Patagonia, 38, 39; convents in, 8, 21, 93, 130; Conversos in, 25–26; economic activity of women in, 38; "entangled histories" of Iberian Atlantic and, 4–5, 41–47; female reading literacy in, 22; gender norms in, 40–41; honor code in, 40–41, 49*n*22; illegitimacy in, 97*n*10; Inquisition in, 8, 24, 25, 27; Josefa's migration to Iberian Atlantic from, 37–40, 41, 43, 47; La Coruña in, 38, 39, 48*nn*17–18; links between Portugal and, 25–26, 29; medical board in, 137; *mestizo* children sent to, 68–69, 78*n*45, 82–86, 90–94, 96; Moriscos in, 23–24; Reconquista in, 59; sex ratio in, 38, 48*n*17; women as heads of households in, 38, 46. *See also* Iberian Atlantic; Inquisition; Spanish women; *and specific colonies*
Spanish women: on Columbus's second voyage, 60; dangers to, in Iberian Atlantic, 71–72; departure of, from Hispaniola and Puerto Rico, 72–73, 80*n*67; as early settlers in Hispaniola, 60; in East Texas, 101–121; elites among, 1; and formation of Spanish society, 66–73; in Hispaniola and Puerto Rico, 58–74; and indigenous women, 71, 73; marriage of, and settlement in Iberian Atlantic, 3–4, 58–73, 76*n*23; and *mestizas*, 58–59, 74; mobility of, as colonists of Caribbean with their husbands, 6–7, 10–11, 21; as prostitutes, 67; public versus privates lives of, 22–23, 102–3, 104, 108, 120; punishment of, by Bartolomé Colón, 67; rape of, 72; religious life of, 71; return of, to Spain from Iberian Atlantic, 72–73; sexuality of, 67, 71, 101; single women in Hispaniola, 62; and slaves, 59, 71, 73; stereotyping of, 102–3; as widows, 62, 71, 72, 73, 75*n*19, 78*n*48
Spiritual cultures of West Africans: continuity and change in gender roles in, 210–218; and location of West-Central African women in Iberian-Atlantic, 197, 200–202; and Mother Nganga, 196–197, 202–218; power and gender in, 202–210
St. Denis, Louis Juchereau, 107
St. Denis, Marie des Neges de, 107
Stoler, Ann, 1
Suárez, Catalina, 68
Suárez, Juan, 68
Suárez Pacheco, Diego, 67–68
Sugar production, 64, 65, 69, 77*nn*31–32, 78*n*49, 175, 182
Surgeons. *See* Physicians and surgeons
Sweet, James, 233, 250*n*12

Taino community, 58, 77*n*32, 176
Taquena, Catalina de, 93
Taquima, Isabel, 91
Tata (father), 200, 204, 210–214, 216–217
Terán, General, 106
Teresa of Avila, Saint, 8, 21, 27, 28, 144*n*50
Ternero, Salvador, 242
Texas. *See* East Texas
Theuderic, King, 142*n*32
Thornton, John, 233
Tisil, Melchora de la, 136
Tocta, Luisa, 98*n*19
Tocto, Isabel, 90–93
Tocto Coca, Isabel, 91
Tocto Ollo, Ana, 91
Toledo, María de, 67, 75*n*19, 77*n*37
Torres, Alonso de, 76*n*25
Torres, Esteban, 242
Torres de Moreno, Juan, 137, 141, 144*n*45
Twinam, Ann, 102–3, 108
Twinning, 204–5

Urrutia, Joseph, 106–7
Ursula del Sacramento, Madre, 139

Vaidyas (Hindu specialists in Ayurveda), 182, 183, 185
Vallejo, Father, 107–8
Varela, Consuelo, 75*n*12
Vargas, Luis de, 95
Vázquez, Lucas, 78*n*41
Vázquez de Ayllón, Lucas, 68
Vecinos, vecinas (citizens), 60, 63, 64, 68–72, 76*n*26, 77*nn*30–31, 78*n*49, 79*n*56, 87, 115

Vega, Garcilaso de la, El Inca, 84–85
Velázquez, Diego de, 9
Velazquez, Ana, 88–89
Veneciano, Alejandro, 85
Veneciano, Mateo, 85
Vidaguren, Pedro de, 73
Vieira, Antonio, 19, 182
Villalobos, Aldonza de, 70
Villalobos, Marcelo, 70
Villareal, Luis, 82
Villarte, Mateo, 230–231
Villasante, Antonio, 176, 179
Villasante, Blas de, 69, 78*n*49
Vitório, Felipe Rodrigues, 164
Vives, Juan Luis, 49*n*22
Voigt, Lisa, 25
Vollendorf, Lisa, 2, 6, 9, 18–36, 265
Von Germeten, Nicole, 237

Walker, Timothy D., 6, 23, 130, 136, 148–173, 178, 203, 265
Warnings to the Kings and Advice on Restoring Spain (Guevara), 25
Weber, Alison, 22–23
West and Central Africa, 196–197, 200–218, 231, 238–239, 241, 248

Wet-nursing, 245, 255*n*68
Wichita Indians, 109–110
Wilkinson, James, 117
Women: abortions by, 161, 178; and Catholic codes of femininity, 24, 26, 27; Costa on desirable qualities and vices of, 174, 177; employment of, 38, 44, 87, 245; as heads of households, 39, 46, 48*n*18; interconnectivity of, in Iberian Atlantic, 6–11, 24–25, 27–29, 41–43; and pregnancy and childbirth, 159; as subject, 5–6; writings by, 6, 7, 8, 9, 19–21, 26–27. *See also* Black women; Convents; Education and literacy; Gender relations; Indigenous women and girls; *Mestiza* women and girls; Sexuality; Spanish women; *and specific women*

Yanaguar, Isabel, 86
Y'Barbo, Antonio Gil, 106, 113–115
Yoruba, 201, 202, 211, 234, 239

Zuazo, Licenciado, 63–64
Zumárraga, Bishop Juan de, 130

www.ingramcontent.com/pod-product-compliance
Lightning Source LLC
Chambersburg PA
CBHW071017240426
43661CB00073B/2368